Japan

Also by Milton Walter Meyer

A History of the Far East
Asia: A Concise History
A Diplomatic History of the Philippine Republic
China: An Introductory History [two editions]
Southeast Asia: A Brief History [two editions]
India-Pakistan and the Border Lands
South Asia: A Short History of the Subcontinent

Japan

A Concise History

Fourth Edition

Milton W. Meyer

ROWMAN & LITTLEFIELD PUBLISHERS, INC.
Lanham • Boulder • New York • Toronto • Plymouth, UK

ROWMAN & LITTLEFIELD PUBLISHERS, INC.

Published in the United States of America
by Rowman & Littlefield Publishers, Inc.
A wholly owned subsidiary of The Rowman & Littlefield Publishing Group, Inc.
4501 Forbes Boulevard, Suite 200, Lanham, Maryland 20706
www.rowmanlittlefield.com

Estover Road, Plymouth PL6 7PY, United Kingdom

British Library Cataloguing in Publication Information Available

Library of Congress Cataloging-in-Publication Data

Meyer, Milton Walter.
  Japan : a concise history / Milton W. Meyer. — 4th ed.
      p. cm.
  Includes bibliographical references and index.
  ISBN 978-0-7425-4117-7 (cloth : alk. paper) — ISBN 978-0-7425-5793-2 (electronic)
  1. Japan—History. I. Title.
  DS835.M4 2009
  952—dc22

                                                                          2009004290

Printed in the United States of America

♾™ The paper used in this publication meets the minimum requirements of
American National Standard for Information Sciences—Permanence of Paper
for Printed Library Materials, ANSI/NISO Z39.48-1992.

In memory of
Sir George B. Sansom

Contents

Illustrations

Preface

The purpose of this book is to provide an introduction to the history of Japan. Approximately half of the material deals with pre-Meiji Japan, the period before 1868. The other half narrates domestic and relevant foreign events since that epochal date, a watershed in Japan's history that may be considered the transition from traditional to modern Japan. In the text, Japanese surnames, as is the usual practice, precede the personal ones.

I am indebted to many for help in the formulation of this volume. Sir George B. Sansom, through his lectures at Columbia University and lucid books, early opened vistas on fundamental aspects of Japanese life and culture. Further doctoral studies at Stanford University and travels to Japan broadened horizons, while my students at California State University, Los Angeles, in Japanese and related Asian history classes over three-and-a-half decades helped to focus the presentation and organization of the oral and written material.

Milton W. Meyer

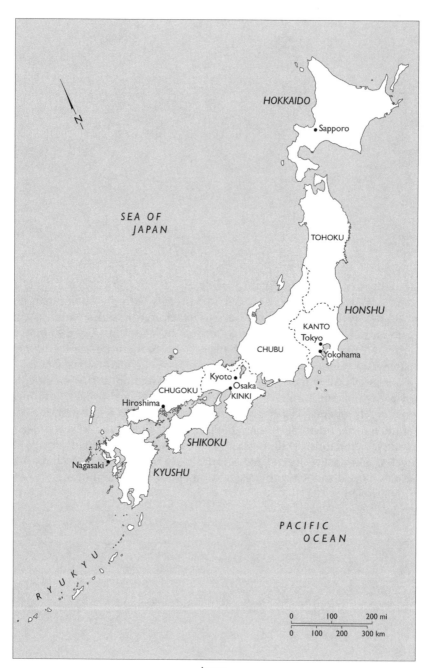

Japan

Introducing Japan

The emergence of Japan as a political and economic world power has been one of the success stories of modern history. Though small in geographic area, the archipelago is the tenth most populous country; its 128 million inhabitants crowd themselves into an area the size of the state of Montana. Its natural resources are almost nonexistent, yet today it ranks only second after the much larger United States as the most affluent and economically productive nation in the world. Drawing on a century of modernization as historical precedent, despite the catastrophe of World War II, the Japanese have developed over the decades an expert base for technological know-how.

The amazing record is of recent vintage. Although now involved in, and helping shape, international political and economic issues, Japan was traditionally more self-contained and semi-isolated in its islands off the Asian mainland. In the course of the premodern centuries, never a world power or even a regional one, Japan pursued its own historical path on the periphery of a great Chinese civilization. The Japanese borrowed cultural ideas from China, adapting some and rejecting others. This selective and filtered reception was repeated after the mid-1850s, when the West helped to open Japan to modern ways. It was again evidenced a century later during the American post–World War II occupation.

Despite accretions from East and West, the Japanese maintained an inner persistent core of traditional values. Agriculture was the primary occupation; land was the chief source of wealth. Group loyalties predominated; the individual was subordinated to considerations of the family, village, region, and country. At the center of the national Japanese family was the imperial line, one of the oldest continuous political traditions in history,

1

and one that provided an ideological and centralized focus for the people. Left to its own initiative in the process of historical development, rarely experiencing disastrous invasions at home, and only fitfully engaging in campaigns abroad, Japan set its own course over the centuries. Internally, it experienced a plethora of civil wars but never any major revolutions that resulted in drastic and sudden change. In an ongoing process, events chronologically superimposed themselves one after the other. Changes, whether induced domestically or externally, tended to fuse over time into a cumulatively linear historical pattern.

And so the continuity of recognizable indigenous features, made possible through geographic protection of the people in their close-knit offshore islands, coexisted with selectively imported elements. Hence contradictory stereotypes of Japan have persisted. Traditional arts, food, architecture, and modes of behavior appear alongside fast-paced manifestations of modern lifestyles. Japan was a repository for traditional and foreign ideas, of both the East and the West. Within the Eastern world, Japan maintained its unique associative historical process; in the Western perspective, it was the most modern of Asian countries.

THE GEOGRAPHIC SETTING

Japan consists of some 4,000 islands forming an extended arc off the coast of northeast Asia. Only a handful of islands are of sufficient size to sustain human activity. The 1,200-mile-long archipelago, if superimposed on the same latitudes in the Western Hemisphere, would stretch from Montreal to Tallahassee, Florida. The country lies chiefly in the temperate zone. It receives good rainfall, has fairly fertile soil, and is geographically located near mainland China and Korea to make acculturation all the easier. Japan is similar to the Middle Atlantic states of New York, New Jersey, Pennsylvania, Maryland, and Virginia in terms of topography, climate, and productivity. Less than 145,000 square miles in area, the country could be fitted into the United States twenty times over. Japan is smaller than France or prewar Germany, but it is larger than Italy or Great Britain. Geographical and historical comparisons with Great Britain seem natural. Both are insular nations, lying off great continental landmasses; both fashioned a great maritime and naval base of power. Both have been traditionally free from foreign armed invasions. Both are monarchies; both have developed distinct cultures that have been exposed, nonetheless, to neighboring mainland cultural influences.

Within the Japanese archipelago proper, there are only four sizable ones, the so-called home islands. The northernmost is Hokkaido (the Northern Sea Circuit, an old administrative designation), also known as Ezo, Matsumae, or Oshima. It lies in the latitude of the New England states and is cold and underpopulated; it has remained outside the mainstream of Japanese history. Honshu, the main island, is the largest and the most populated. Honshu contains huge cities and the chief agricultural areas, and it has provided the stage for important events in Japanese national life. To its south, across the beautiful Inland Sea, lie the two islands of Shikoku, traditionally known as the Four Provinces, and Kyushu, the Nine Provinces. Kyushu, in the latitude of the state of Georgia but with a subtropical climate, has played an important role in Japanese cultural history as the nearest and the most receptive of the four chief islands to early Chinese and Western influences. Stringing in an arc south of Kyushu toward Taiwan are the Ryukyu islands. For administrative purposes, Japan is divided into forty-five prefectures (ken) or provinces, an arrangement dating in present form to the late nineteenth century. All of Hokkaido counts as one prefecture (and is additionally the only district, *do*) as is the Ryukyu chain. The capital city of Tokyo with over twelve million, the largest in the country, is both a separate prefecture and a unique metropolis. Kyoto and Osaka are special urban prefectures. The Honshu island prefectures traditionally have been grouped into five regions, north to south: Tohoku, Chubu, Kanto, Kinki, and Chugoku.

Overall, Japan's climate is not given to extremes. Its fluctuations are determined in part by its closeness to the Asian mainland. Winter winds from the continent bring cold dry air; sometimes they pick up precipitation from the Japan Sea and drop rain or snow on the central mountain range, the spine of Honshu, including the Japanese Alps. These divide the populous, more temperate Inner Zone fronting the Pacific from the harsher, less developed Outer Zone paralleling the Japan Sea. Summer winds from the southwest China seas bring warm and heavy rains, as well as late summer or early autumn hurricanes, known in Asia as typhoons (from a transliteration of the Chinese *da feng*, meaning "big wind"). The climate is additionally conditioned by two gulf streams. The moderating Japan Current, known also as the Black Current or Kuroshio, brings a warm ocean stream northward from the tropics along the Pacific coast. This same stream circles off Alaska and down the North American west coast. The Oyashio, or Okhotsk stream, which is a cold current from the north, sweeps southward in the Japan Sea from Siberia.

Japanese topography is marked by extensive mountain areas. Almost all of the country is hilly or mountainous, with several distinct lesser ranges and many high peaks. There are more than five hundred volcanoes, of which sixty have been active in historic times. The most famous of these is Mt. Fuji, more than 12,000 feet high, a popular icon in Japanese art. On a rare clear day, it can be seen from Tokyo. It last erupted in 1707. Two-mile-high coastal mountain ranges coexist with nearby ocean depths that plummet five miles into the Pacific Ocean off the eastern Honshu coast into the great Tuscarora Deep. These great elevation differentials within such short distances produce additional stress on the earth's crust and its shifting tectonic plates; earthquakes are common in Japan. Up to 1,500 shocks a year are recorded. In September 1923, abetted by extensive fires, the most disastrous Japanese earthquake in modern times devastated the Tokyo-Yokohama area. Children born that year are familiarly known as the earthquake babies.

Less than a fifth of Japan's landmass is level. But it is an important fifth, because it produces most of the food. The chief Japanese plains lie along the axial east-central Honshu coast. The largest and the most famous of these plains is the 5,000-square-mile Kanto (eastern provinces) plain, where Tokyo is situated. This area has been a main source of national economic, military, and political power. To the southwest is the 600-square-mile Nobi plain, where Nagoya, one of Japan's main cities and an industrial center, is located. The third important plain is the Kansai, the traditional historic center with the five "home provinces." It is 500 square miles in area situated at the eastern end of the Inland Sea. Here Japan's first capital cities of Nara and Kyoto, as well as the modern commercial urban centers of Osaka and Kobe, are located. These three plains, and lesser ones, supporting great cities, provide most of the available but shrinking farmland. The further expansion of cultivable land, already encroaching upon hillsides in neat terraces, is restricted. Reclamation schemes, swallowing up some of the country's smaller inland bays or extending the coastline, add some agricultural acreage.

Tokyo: Haneda domestic airport in foreground, near city center

Tokyo: Narita international airport, in suburbs

Limitations in the extent of arable land are matched by deficits in natural resources. Japan has sufficient copper for industrial purposes, but it is handicapped by meager coal deposits and negligible oil and iron reserves. Japan's annual oil output is equaled in the United States every six hours, and Japan's known iron reserves would last only three months there. Probably its most important natural resource is water. Plentiful rainfall makes a lush countryside possible. Forests range from tropical stands in Kyushu to cold coniferous growth in Hokkaido. Forest products are harvested, vegetation abounds, and wood provides a main ingredient of the country's homes and buildings. Agriculture is based on wet or irrigated farming. Rice, the main crop, is grown in most parts of the country. The short rivers of Japan, unlike the mighty ones of mainland Asia, require no large-scale works or flood control projects. Streams are rushing and short (the longest is less than 300 miles), but they provide much hydroelectric power. With no broad, meandering rivers in the land, a riverine tradition is not prominent in Japanese literature, which has no counterparts to the Swanee, the quiet flowing Don, or the "sweet Thames." Counterbalancing this lack of rivers, however, is the accessibility of protected coastal sea transportation. Prominent among the clustered islands are sheltered bays, straits, the Inland Sea, and the lack of open ocean gaps between islands (as in the

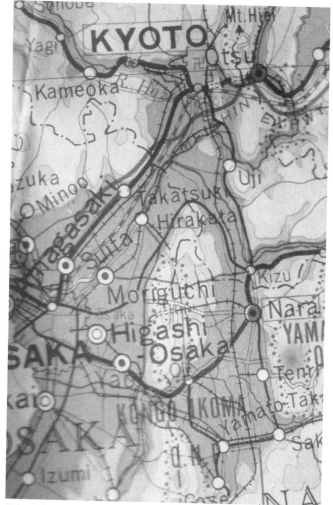

Triangular center of Kansai plain with three historic cities: Osaka, Nara, and Kyoto

Hawaiian chain). Japan's 17,000 miles of coastline (the United States has under 13,000 miles) provide many good harbors for maritime and fishing industries, so essential to the country's livelihood.

THE EFFECTS OF GEOGRAPHY

These diverse geographic factors have helped to shape Japanese historic life. Because of its insular nature, Japan developed in relative political isolation and homogeneity, for it lay 100 miles across the strait from Korea and five times that distance over open seas from China. Never occupied and never having experienced a successful invasion before 1945 (the Mongols were twice driven back in the thirteenth century), the Japanese, in spite of cultural borrowing, developed in their psychology a nationalistic, patriotic, "we-are-different" spirit. In their island country (Shimaguni), they fashioned a unique way of life.

In economic life, geography affected human activity in basic ways. The country was beautiful, but the rugged terrain caused many hardships. Poverty hid behind an agreeable topographical mask, for crops could not grow on mountains and rains leached the soil. Yet, while water took away, it also gave. Rain and climate favored rice production, paramount in Japanese and most other Asian diets. A nutritious cereal, double-cropped up to the Tokyo latitude, it gave the highest yield of any grain for the area cultivated, chiefly on small farms averaging two-and-a-half acres in size. Surrounded by water, Japan also pursued coastal and deep-sea fishing. In lieu of relatively scarce dairy and meat products, fish provided high-protein food sources. Rangeland for grazing cattle has been limited; meat is more of a luxury item than a staple. Noodle dishes made from rice or wheat grown in northern climes are popular, as is the ubiquitous soybean curd. The simple Japanese

Japanese aesthetics: Rice stalks neatly stacked

Osaka: Short-order chef

meal consists of rice, fish, and vegetables. More elaborate spreads involve complementary dishes, but whatever is served, much attention is devoted to the color, arrangement, and eye appeal of food items. Tea (*cha*), particularly the green variety, is the staple drink; beer (*biru*) and rice wine (*sake*) are also popular.

In its historic domestic agrarian economy, land was the traditional source of wealth. Ruling classes lived off land revenues collected in the form of rents or taxes. The numerous civil wars prior to the modernization of the country reflected in no small way attempts to control productive rice lands in contiguous or scattered tracts. Large Buddhist monasteries and extended ruling families built up their estates while attempting to keep them off the government's tax rolls. Because of the geographical limitations imposed on the extent of arable acreage, intensive, rather than extensive, agricultural patterns were practiced. Many men and women, in seasonal bursts of planting and harvesting, cultivated small parcels of land. A vast expenditure of muscle power particularly went into the cultivation of rice, which was traditionally planted and harvested by hand. Because of the high ratio of people to productive land, population problems and food supplies became acute considerations in modern times. After having remained comparatively static for some time prior to the mid-nineteenth century, in the course of the past century and a half, Japan's population skyrocketed from 30 million in the 1850s to over four times that number in the 1990s. It has then leveled off and the country is experiencing a phenomenally aging population.

Besides political and economic ramifications, geographic factors also have had social and cultural effects. The length of the island chain helped to account for early and differing racial strains in the Japanese people, whose forebears immigrated into the country from a variety of neighboring overseas areas, including Sakhalin Island (Karafuto) off Siberia in the north, Korea and China to the west, and Taiwan to the south. But from whatever direction they came, by the early centuries of the Christian era, the Japanese were melded into a distinct homogeneous racial entity. They constitute 99 percent of the total population. Racial minorities are rare; the aboriginal Ainu in Hokkaido are few in number. The Korean community of over half a million, transported from the homeland when Japan was overlord, is the most visible. Among the Japanese themselves, there exists an outcast group, the *eta*, or *burakumin* (people from special villages), dating from medieval times, ostracized from their fellow nationals by virtue of distastefully considered work or low social status. The Japanese in the modern age, because of their location as the closest of Asian peoples to the United States, played the reverse role as interpreters of Occidental culture and its ways to East Asians. In the mid-1850s, the United States through Matthew Perry began to open the country, which in turn helped later to end Korean isolation and to participate in the modernization process in China.

Yet Japan continued to retain many of its traditions; its semi-isolation contributed to a degree of cultural conservatism. Foreign pressures did not brush aside all old ways; these were retained alongside newer ways. Japan could simultaneously accommodate various religious and secular ideologies such as animism, Shintoism, Buddhism, Confucianism, and Christianity. Major historical phases in the theater arts were superimposed on each other: the thirteenth-century Buddhist-inspired No dramas, the later Kabuki and puppet plays (*bunraku*) and the modern Western dramatic forms. All of these expressions can be enjoyed today in Tokyo theaters. Partial isolation made the Japanese cognizant of their cultural borrowings. It is not certain if they fully understood the content of foreign ideas borrowed, but they were at least aware of the variations in the imported ideas from indigenous practice. Concepts that came by sea rather than by land routes were the more easily identified, contained, and debated. Imported ideas, such as Buddhism, the Chinese script, and the centralized Chinese political and administrative patterns also left their noticeable marks, but the Japanese retained much that was uniquely theirs.

This uniqueness was reflected in the persistence of simple prehistoric religious beliefs and attitudes that undergirded later and more sophisticated ideologies: the ongoing historical continuity of one imperial line, the associated political and military long-lived family hierarchies, and the close-knit consciousness of a unique, self-directed, and autonomous national identity. The Japanese fashioned their own domestic architectural forms and furnishings, such as the *tatami* (straw floor mats), the *shoji* (sliding paper wall panels), the airy home structures, the *tokonoma* (alcove) for art objects, the *hibachi* (charcoal heating braziers), and the wooden and iron bathtubs. If the Japanese borrowed, they also exported and traded abroad. Their maritime trade as early as the fourteenth and fifteenth centuries penetrated east and south Asian coastal waters, where they preceded the Western presence.

Despite human pressures on the geographic landscape, scenery infused a love of beauty among the Japanese, who early developed a sense of aesthetics with regard to nature. They took pleasure in reflecting on selected beauties of the countryside. They dedicated poems relating to inspirational settings, enjoyed outdoor picnics in scenic spots, and held annual cherry blossom viewing parties in the springtime. Many localities enjoyed their own particular attractions, but a national park system (*kokuritsu-koen*), inaugurated in 1934, counted twenty-seven in number on the fiftieth anniversary of the system. Additionally, there are fifty-four lesser "semi" national parks (*kokutei-koen*). Three national sites (*Nihon-sankei*) are particularly venerated: Matsushima, a collection of 250 small pine-studded islands in a bay off Sendai in northeast Honshu; Amanohashidate (Bridge of Heaven), another pine-dotted sandbar on Miyazu Bay on the Japan Sea coast; and Miyajima (or Itsukishima), a shrine near Hiroshima with its lone *torii* (gate) rising out of the waters of the Inland Sea. The Japanese attitude toward nature was more one of awe or appreciation than of fear. Mountains were the homes of benevolent gods and saints rather than of evil spirits. Monasteries were built on high peaks. Traditional structures blended into the landscape whether constructed on high ground or low. Readily available, wood was the most common material; little stone and almost no brick were used, partly to circumvent earthquake damage.

A final comment on the effects of geography on Japanese society and culture would indicate the dominance in Japanese life of the coastal areas, in a line ranging eastward from northwestern Kyushu up along the Inland Sea to Honshu with its plains and on to the Tokyo area. This geographical axis was the country's richest historical vein, the home of the greatest cultural achievements, the most productive area in commerce, industry, and agriculture, the site of the best climate, the most densely populated, and most advanced infrastructure, including the route of the high-speed "bullet train" (*shinkansen*). The story of Japanese history is centered here.

HISTORICAL PERIODS AND RECORDS

The Japanese call their country Nippon or Nihon. These words are derived from the Chinese characters *ri-ben* that loosely translate as "The Land of the Rising Sun." A variation of this Chinese-derived term also crept into Western use. Marco Polo, who served in China under Mongol rulers in the thirteenth century, heard this appellation for a country that lay across the sea, a land that the Venetian never visited. In a subsequent translation of his memoirs in Europe, the transcriber approximated the translation as Chipango or Zipango. In time, these designations became latinized as Japan. From the Chinese original, both Japanese and Westerners adapted their respective related nomenclatures for the country.

Japanese history may be divided into six overall convenient political eras (*jidai*). These eras are named after geographic centers of political power or after families who indirectly wielded the decision-making process in the name of the imperial line. First, early indigenous culture was shaped from prehistoric times to about 400 CE. Then, secondly, for approximately three centuries, continental influences, mainly Chinese, filtered into ancient Japan, which voluntarily sought out and selectively welcomed them. Third, from about 700 to 1200, a synthesis of foreign and native ideas and institutions took place, resulting in the first major definable political eras of history, with centralized capitals located first at Nara and then at what is now Kyoto.

Fourth, in the ensuing four centuries, 1200 to 1600, Japan experienced what has been termed a period of military feudalism, characterized by the growth of militant groups, political factions, and civil wars. Fifth, by the turn of the seventeenth century, chiefly through the efforts of three successive outstanding military leaders, Japan was politically reunified for two-and-a-half centuries under the Tokugawa shogunate. Lastly, in the mid-1850s, with the advent of Perry and other men and forces from the Western world, Japan entered its modern phase. The cliché "Japan between East and West" has sometimes been used to describe Japan's modern century.

The Japanese themselves have written extensively of their history over the centuries. Though Japan was mentioned in Chinese annals as early as the first century CE, the first Japanese to order an official history was Japan's first great statesman, Prince Shotoku Taishi (d. 621). This work has been lost, but within a century two official general histories, derived from the Chinese both in language and in execution, were compiled. The first one, the earliest native history still extant, the *Kojiki* (*Record of Ancient Matters*), was compiled in 712, although it drew on earlier editions, some dating to 628. It consists mainly of legendary tales preserved by bards attached to the leading families of early Japan. Within eight years, in 720, another compilation, the *Nihon Shoki* or *Nihongi* (*History of Japan*), was drawn up. This constituted the first volume of what became the so-called Six National Histories that brought the story down to 887. Augmenting these early official general works were *fudoki* (local histories) of various provinces, composed by order of the central government. Only one of these, compiled in

733, has survived intact. Others are extant only in part; one is an abstract contained in another work. In addition to the official tradition of compiling general or local chronicles, early native or Shinto ritualistic texts were written.

In these eighth-to-tenth-century works that constituted the first period of historical literature, there was a conscious imitation of the millennium-old principles of Chinese historiography. The writing of historical annals—as it developed in China and as it was borrowed by Japan—consisted of four parts. First came the records of the imperial family; second, the genealogical tables and lists of officials and the bureaucracy; third, the essays and commentaries, such as those relating to Confucian ceremonies, religion, economic development, and literature; and last, the biographies of prominent officials and military figures, as well as résumés of foreign relations. This framework, which emphasized emperors, courts, and officialdom, was adopted by the Japanese, but without the full range of lives and treatises that were found in a standard Chinese history. Probably this was due in part initially to the lack of biographies and monographic material. In their adaptations, Japanese historians also were faced with another problem of history. Traditional Chinese histories were dynastic in nature (China was ruled by some two dozen dynasties or families between the eighteenth century BCE and the twentieth century CE, each with their own histories). But because Japan held the theory of having only one unbroken imperial dynasty dating back to 660 BCE, historians usually chose for their texts the more convenient time span of a single regnal period or an arbitrarily designated group of successive reigns grouped into eras.

In the course of the second period of Japanese historiography, roughly from the eleventh to the fourteenth centuries, a vernacular tradition in writing arose, one that used Japanese phonetics based on similar-sounding Chinese ideographs. In this period, family histories, known as *kagami* (mirrors) or *monogatari* (narratives), abounded. These works, of which half-a-dozen are most prominent, related the numerous civil wars and the fortunes of the military factions in these ongoing campaigns. Some of the works embodied causal principles in order to justify certain actions or to advance the biases of the protagonists involved. A Buddhist historical tradition also became evident in these centuries. One of the most outstanding works in the genre was *Gukanshu* (*Fool's Miscellany*), 1224?, composed by the priest Fujiwara Jien. This might be considered as the first Japanese attempt to survey and to interpret Japanese history within the Buddhistic context. Because political anarchy prevailed in these centuries, cloisters became refuges of learning and of writing, as had the contemporaneous Christian monasteries in medieval Europe.

In the sixteenth century, with the reunification of Japan in the Tokugawa period and with the restoration of law and order after decades of intermittent civil war, the strong central authority again officially encouraged works in the Chinese language that stressed obligations to superiors and obedience to rulers along Chinese models. One branch of the official Tokugawa family at Mito began an exhaustive general history of Japan in 1657 to cover events from Japanese origins to 1393. Stressing the paramount role of the imperial family, the initial 100 volumes (with 146 more to go) was completed in 1709. A subsequent edition of seventeen volumes covered the years 660 BCE to 1412 CE. Other individual historians, with or without official Tokugawa patronage, also drew up multivolume projects. The growth of printing encouraged the writing of history, and the rise of modern libraries, including that of the imperial family, helped to preserve records.

After the reopening of Japan in the mid-nineteenth century, historical scholarship borrowed techniques from the West. The Japanese erected national libraries, founded universities, established professorships, started scholarly journals, and promoted research institutes. In 1869, the government called for another edition of Japanese history. Eight years later, a Bureau of Historical Compilation was founded. Within another decade, this agency was incorporated into the newly created Imperial University of Tokyo, which became the country's leading center for historical studies. The first modern efforts, official and otherwise, continued to stress political events, though with the advent of the twentieth century, cultural, social, and economic topics also were introduced. Pre–World War II studies reflected not only a diversity of approaches but also the growth of monographic literature, reference works, and emphasis on primary source materials. With the rebirth of militarism in the 1930s and with the Pacific War, historical writing was diverted into directed channels. In the postwar period the varieties of Japanese historical scholarship sprouted anew. Comprehensive compendiums in the language were produced. The *Illustrated Compendium of Japanese Cultural History* covered fourteen volumes; the *Dictionary of Japanese History* reached twenty volumes; and the *Encyclopedia of World History* ran to twenty-five volumes. The output was noticeably smaller in scope in foreign languages, including English. Revisionist histories sanitized Japan's role in World War II and downplayed its military actions, which infuriated occupied Asian neighbors.

PROBLEMS OF UNDERSTANDING

Though the Japanese produced voluminous works relating to their own history, less study in this area was accomplished by Western authors. Before World War II, only a handful of specialized texts on Japan were written by Occidentals. A few Englishmen, resident in Japan, though nonprofessionals in the historical discipline, made the first attempts. James Murdoch authored a three-volume *History of Japan* (1903–1926), and his compatriot Sir George Sansom published in 1931 the first edition of the classic *Japan: A Short Cultural History*. American scholarship was even more restricted in scope. The first serious work was by William E. Griffis, a science teacher in Japan, who wrote *The Mikado's Empire* (1876), in popular use prior to World War I. Later American historians, some concentrating on diplomatic affairs with relation to the United States, worked mainly in Western sources. Few scholars knew Japanese; prior to 1941, in the United States probably only a dozen universities taught subjects relating to Japan.

The Pacific War stimulated the study of Japanese language and history by government agencies. The ranks of professionally trained American historians of Japan swelled with additions of postwar students. University centers at Harvard, Yale, Columbia, and Stanford, among others, and in Michigan, Washington, California, and Hawaii promoted Japanese studies. Specialized monographs were published; library holdings relating to Japan zoomed ninefold from 90,000 volumes in 1940 to more than 800,000 in 1958. The need to study Japan had suddenly become imperative. The country's early modernization, its rise to world power, World War II, and the American occupation provided immediate impetus, while Japan's contemporary importance in Asian and world affairs, particularly in economic matters, merited continued close study, analysis, and understanding. In Tokyo, the national Diet Library (Parliament) has a plethora of printed matter on foreign affairs dating back to sixteenth century missionaries. University libraries augment this core collection.

The short period of U.S. relations with Japan, only a century and a half, contributed to difficulties in mutual understanding. American interpretations and images of Japan varied in this period, swinging between extremes of depicting Japanese either as passive imitators or as land-grabbing barbarians. During the first decades of Japanese-American contact, in that period between the advent of Perry in 1853 and the Russo-Japanese War of 1904–1905, there was general American approval and approbation of Japan by those individuals who showed any interest in the country. Since the Japanese had adapted to Western ways, at least on the surface, they had culturally resembled Westerners, and hence were more understandable and likable, the simplistic argument ran.

On political grounds, Japan was not yet to be feared, for there was little conflict with U.S. interests in Asia. On aesthetic grounds, Japan and the Japanese were considered quaint, exotic, and slightly ludicrous. Gilbert and Sullivan's *The Mikado*, composed in 1885, enjoyed great vogue with its stereotypical Japanese theatrical characters. Puccini's opera, *Madame Butterfly*, adapted from a play that in turn was based on a novel, portrayed a classic story of love cutting across racial lines. Western writers living in Japan also contributed to exotic images. Born of Irish-Greek parents, Lafcadio Hearn went to live in Japan in 1890. There he became a Buddhist, lived in a Japanese house, and took a Japanese name and a Japanese wife. He wrote widely read books of stylistic excellence, including *Japan: An Attempt at Interpretation*, which portrayed traditional and modernized aspects of Japanese life.

With the establishment of Japan as an Asian power of considerable importance after the Russo-Japanese War, relations with the United States took a turn for the worse. Japanese territorial expansion in Asia particularly affected U.S. treaty rights in China, as well as the security of the Philippines, acquired by the United States from Spain in 1898. Rivalry also developed in naval and commercial matters. American immigration exclusion laws acerbated Japanese sensitivity. Friendship turned into enmity, which finally erupted in the Pacific War.

Yet after the maelstrom of war and the resulting occupation, a defeated Japan was again characterized familiarly as a bastion of democracy and an ally against communism. In the early postwar decades in the United States, a craze for things Japanese developed. Japanese architectural landscapes blossomed in American gardens; department store bargain basements promoted, among other items, shoji screens and electric hibachis; the study of what was taken to be instant Zen Buddhism flourished. Americans borrowed many outward forms from Japan, as the Japanese themselves had

Tokyo: Near the financial district, a corner of the Imperial palace, allegedly the world's most valuable real estate property

Emperor Hirohito and Empress Nagano, Los Angeles, 1975

done for centuries from both East and West, but American appreciation and understanding of the complex Japanese substance and content proved more difficult to absorb.

Real estate is so valuable in downtown Tokyo that the imperial palace property is anecdotally estimated to be worth as much as the entire state of California, eighth richest economy in the world.

Japan: Administrative Divisions

Islands	Regions	Prefectures (ken)	Prefectural Capitals
Hokkaido	Hokkaido	Hokkaido (also *do*)	Sapporo
Honshu	Tohoku	Aomori	Aomori City
		Akita	Akita City
		Iwate	Morioki
		Miyagi	Sendai
		Yamagata	Yamagata City
		Fukishima	Fukushima City
	Chubu	Niigata	Niigata City
		Toyama	Toyama City
		Ishikawa	Kanazawa
		Fukui	Fukui City
		Shizuoka	Shizuoka City
		Yamanashi	Kofu
		Nagano	Nagano City
		Aichi	Nagoya
		Gifu	Gifu City
	Kanto	Tokyo (also *do*)	Tokyo
		Ibaraki	Mito
		Tochigi	Utsunomiya
		Gumma	Maebashi
		Saitama	Urawa
		Kanagawa	Yokohama
		Chiba	Chiba City
	Kinki	Shiga	Otsu
		Nara	Nara
		Wakayama	Wakayama City
		Mie	Tsu
		Hyogo	Kobe
		(Kyoto and Osaka are *fu*)	
	Chugoku	Okayama	Okayama City
		Hiroshima	Hiroshima City
		Yamaguchi	Yamaguchi City
		Tottori	Tottori City
		Shimane	Matsue
Shikoku	Shikoku	Ehime	Matsuyama
		Kagawa	Takamatsu
		Tokushima	Tokushima City
		Kochi	Kochi City
Kyushu	Kyushu	Fukuoka	Fukuoka
		Oita	Oita
		Miyazaki	Miyazaki
		Saga	Saga
		Nagasaki	Nagasaki
		Kumamoto	Kumamoto
		Kagoshima	Kagoshima
Ryukyu	Ryukyu	Okinawa	Naha

I

TRADITIONAL JAPAN

PREHISTORY TO 1185

Traditional Japan developed from both indigenous and imported roots. The Japanese in prehistoric and recorded eras evolved certain peculiar characteristics. A divine imperial family reigned but did not rule, for the political direction was provided by other families who functioned behind the imperial facade. Pronounced hierarchical patterns characterized society; the economy was overwhelmingly agrarian. Embryonic art and architectural forms were crystallized in early abstractions. Native Shinto was formulated; imported Buddhism added theological and cultural dimensions to life. The Chinese script was adopted, and ancient literary models were molded by proto-historians borrowing Chinese concepts. By grafting compatible alien ideas onto native beliefs, the early Japanese achieved a higher degree of cultural sophistication.

1

Ancient Japan

(to ca. 400 CE)

Sources of early Japanese history consist of both unwritten and written records. Archaeology has uncovered a variety of artifacts, tombs, seashell mounds, physical remains, and human skeletal forms scattered all over the country. Chinese dynastic histories, with information dating to the first century CE, corroborate some of these archaeological finds; these foreign Asian annals help to fill some of the physical gaps. In subsequent centuries, Japanese began to compose their own histories, but their works tended to confuse facts with myths, and emperors with gods. Yet these works do contain germs of historical accuracy, for they chronicle in allegorical form the foundations of the ancient Japanese state. In subsequent times, more and more detailed information relating to early Japan came to light, but knowledge remained conjectural about Japan prior to the fifth century CE, when Chinese writing was adopted by the Japanese, who possessed no native script. Despite projections back to antiquity, recorded Japanese history, bolstered by the tradition of one long continuous imperial dynasty, is comparatively recent, as major civilizations go. The Roman empire was disintegrating as the Japanese commenced patterns of recognizable historical development. And over the previous two millennia neighboring China had long since evolved major definable cultural traits.

ARCHAEOLOGICAL PERIODS

Little is known of the racial origins of the Japanese. The oldest present inhabitants are the Ainu (Human) once spread throughout Japan, but now restricted chiefly to government reservations in Hokkaido, where some 15,000 of them reside. The Ainu are related to the earliest culture, and they are proto-Caucasians, possibly from a group that split off from the white race in ancient times. They are relatively hairy, fair-skinned people and sometimes have blue eyes. They contributed little of note to Japanese culture except possibly some physical characteristics, including the relative hairiness of Japanese men as compared to other East Asian types. Later immigration waves from northern and southern Asian regions either absorbed them or pushed them farther north. Earlier and more prominent, the northern Asian strain helped to fashion Japanese life. Artifacts related to those uncovered in Mongolia, Korea, and Manchuria have been found in early Japan. Similarities in language have enhanced cultural connections between the Japanese and northeastern Asians, for the Japanese language is one of the Altaic group, which includes Korean. Because Japan is nearest to the Asian mainland at points opposite Korea, the geographical propinquity lends support to the theory that ancient cultural and racial invasions emanated from that direction.

A lesser southern strain came later, probably up from south and east China and southeast Asia. Physical anthropology reveals that many Japanese, smaller in stature and darker in complexion than northeast Asians, resemble Malayans, who live closer to the equator. Cultural anthropology discloses some similarities in language, in the propagation of the wet rice culture so pronounced in tropical Asia, in the architectural trait of highly slanted house roofs and eaves, in a diet that includes raw fish, and in the existence of a matriarchy in early times (still noticeable in certain parts of Myanmar—formerly Burma—and the large island of Sumatra in Indonesia). Though of mixed origins, these diverse and ancient Japanese racial elements blended together, so that by historic times, around 400 CE, the Japanese had become a racially homogeneous people, unified by common language and culture.

Archaeological records note several successive cultures in prehistoric Japan. These records consist entirely of artifacts, for none of the ancient evidence includes written symbols or primitive hieroglyphics. In 1949, Paleolithic, or Old Stone Age (100,000 to 30,000 years ago), finds were unearthed in at least three different strata at Iwajuku in the Kanto plain, but few conclusions have yet been drawn from the extant evidence. Possibly the first Paleolithic culture waves entered the islands as early as 200,000 years ago by Asian land bridges formed with the ebb and flow of the ice during the glacial age, disconnected around 11000 BCE. Stone implements uncovered from excavations are roughly flaked; some of the larger specimens resemble chopper instruments found elsewhere in Asia. A later culture wave produced similar tools but smaller in size. No skeletal evidence, however, has as yet come to light, but recent finds since 1949 indicate that man existed in Japan prior to the inception of pottery cultures, the earliest of which archaeological evidence places in northwest Kyushu to about 10000 BCE.

The first major Japanese culture dates to the Mesolithic, or Middle Stone Age; dates of its inception vary widely (between 14000 and 300 BCE), but it lasted until around 300 BCE. Its people, in immigration waves from the continent, drove the earlier inhabitants, the *emishi*, further north. The *emishi* may or may not have been identified with the Ainu. Proceeding through at least five stages of increasingly sophisticated pottery specimens, the era is termed Jomon, from a Japanese word meaning "cord pattern," because most of the pottery (*yori-ito bunka*) discovered from this extended time period had such a pattern impressed on external surfaces. Early types of pottery were simple, in bulbous shape, apparently to be inserted partway into the ground. Over the centuries, the specimens became more ornamental and florid in design. Several hundred Jomon sites have been uncovered throughout Japan as well as in the Ryukyu islands. Most of the remains, however, have been unearthed in eastern and northern Japan, where the culture persisted the longest. Artifacts include shell mounds, stone weapons, pottery in over seventy shapes and forms, and *dogu*, or clay figures, representing simplified abstractions of men and animals, which have been found near the shell mounds. Excavated clay female figurines, with exaggerated physical features, might have had some relation to the practice of sorcery or fertility rites. Stone implements and pottery were used for ceremonial purposes or for cooking.

The Jomon were not a settled agricultural people but were nomads who hunted, gathered roots and nuts, and ate fresh and saltwater shellfish, the remains of which were left scattered about near home sites. Weaving was unknown, clothes were often furs. These early people lived in primitive semi-sunken rectangular or round houses of thatch and bark that was stretched over wood frames. Floors were dug into the ground about two feet. Usually the floors were earthen, but sometimes they were stone paved. A central hearth provided heat and cooking. Implements included shell combs, jade, daggers, and various household items that suggested the existence of trade with Okinawa. Living in collective fashion in small settlements, the people appeared to have been egalitarian in social behavior. In religion, the Jomon were animists who worshiped natural objects more out of reverence than of fear. Important natural sites became centers of religious worship. The deceased were interred coffinless into the ground without tombs; their arms and legs were bent into a fetal position; sometimes a stone layer weighted down the chest.

The next culture phase has been called the Yayoi, derived from a Tokyo suburb where a more advanced type of pottery was first discovered in 1884. Lasting from approximately 300 BCE to 300 CE, Yayoi culture (Yayoi bunka) spread over Japan from its origins in Kyushu, extending north and displacing the Jomon. Historians debate the origins of the Yayoi. Some claim they inherited the Jomon culture and fashioned from continental influences a more sophisticated one. Others maintain that the Yayoi constituted new waves of mainland immigrants coming at the time the Great Wall was constructed in north China that deflected border tribes to either the east or the west (third century BCE).

The Yayoi, a Neolithic, or New Stone Age, people who extended into the metal age, practiced rice cultivation in paddy fields to augment hunting and fishing. The use of irrigated rice fields (began possibly around 8000 BCE in the Yangtze River delta in China), opening up new lands, created a degree of wealth that gave rise to a need for community leadership. Settlements (*kuni*) grew in size that now contained a hundred or more families tightly knit into social and economic units. Political organization appeared to distinguish between leaders and led, rulers and ruled. Some continued to live in pit dwellings; others resided in raised-floor houses, elevated above the ground by wooden poles, and with thatched roofs. Excavations at Toro in Shizuoka Prefecture have been particularly rich in yielding artifacts relating to Yayoi village and rural life. Yayoi pottery, over three periods of development, in simple and neat lines, more delicate and advanced in technique than that of the Jomon, is found in more than three-dozen types and was created by the potter's wheel. Some of the jars have scenes incised on the surfaces. Stylistically, the pottery types divide into eastern and western patterns, meeting on the shores of the Inland Sea.

In the later stages of their culture, the Yayoi cast simultaneously iron and bronze implements, including mirrors, swords, spears, and so-called bells. From the former material were fashioned utilitarian items, from the latter came ornamental and ceremonial ones. Most interesting of the artifacts were the *dotaku*, or bronze bells, from four to five feet in height, quite thin, with no clappers (as were the Chinese contemporaneous prototypes). Many of them have geometric designs or depict scenes from life. Not found everywhere in Japan, the bells are concentrated in the Kinki (Kansai) plain of central Honshu. But unlike their Chinese-inspired musical models, these bells appear to have been utilized more as ceremonial or ritual objects of worship. Bronze weapons, but few bells, are found in north Kyushu sites; the central Kanto area lacks either bells or weapons. Yayoi burial sites were more ostentatious than those of their predecessors, for the dead were now interred in stone or earthenware jars, with low mounds erected over them, in cemetery sites somewhat removed from the inhabited villages.

Sometimes considered as the last phase of the Yayoi, the tumulus period, or tomb culture (*kofun*), ca. 300–600 CE, was superimposed on, and extended by, the existing inhabitants with new waves of immigrants coming from Korea. Like the previous cultures, it spread from Kyushu northward.

These newcomers were a militant and aristocratic people, whose invading warriors rode horses, wore helmets and armor, and used iron swords. The new advances in continental military techniques that were transferred to Japan induced a more centralized concentration of power in the Kansai area, the heart of the culture. Settlements continued to grow in size; inhabitants now all lived in heavily thatched houses raised off the ground, much like present-day Japanese farmhouses.

The tumuli, or period name, derives from remains of high artificial-earth mounds containing tombs or stone burial chambers, similar to those erected in ancient Korea and in northeast Asia. These tomb areas, the burial sites of early Japanese priest-kings, are found mostly in the ancient capital district of Nara and Kyoto in the Kansai plain. Some of the earth tombs above ground are quite large. One mausoleum (misasagi) that honors the sixteenth emperor, Nintoku (303–399 CE), in the Osaka area, ranges 1,700 feet in length and over 100 feet in height and is surrounded by moats. Some tumuli are round in shape, some are square, and others resemble a keyhole in three tiers. Entombed items include various insignia of rank, such as jewelry, mirrors, and swords—similar in nature to Korean ornaments and weapons. Outlining the tomb precincts are *haniwa*, or hollow clay figures. Placed in circles that mark the site as sacred, they consist

Imperial tumulus, Osaka

of pottery cylinders surmounted by figures of varying size, but usually two to three feet in height, of red-painted men and women, animals, warriors, and domiciles. The origin of *haniwa* is unknown; one theory posits that sculptural representations of humans replaced live burials or original domestic items. Whatever the source, these artifacts provide important historical information of the time, including costumes. The figures reveal men wearing outfits with narrow clinging sleeves and loose baggy trousers. Warriors display arms, including helmets and swords. Women utilized a short skirt over a full dress. These garments reflect a practical bent in an active life, unlike the present-day kimono.

CHINESE AND JAPANESE ANNALS

Early Chinese historical annals complement these ancient Japanese archaeological finds of successive cultures. Chinese historians viewed Japan, as they did all other surrounding areas, simply in a politically and culturally subordinate and inferior position to China, Chinese interests, and Chinese prestige. They called Japan the land of Wa, a derogatory term in China meaning dwarf. As narrated by a mid-fifth century, ca. 445 CE, official annual, *The History of the Later Han Dynasty*, the first recorded contact between China and Japan took place in 57 CE, when a Japanese envoy came from the Wa state of Nu, possibly in Kyushu, to the Chinese capital of the great Han dynasty, which, in its second half of existence (the later or eastern han, 23–220 CE), was located at Luoyang in north-central China. The Japanese ambassador received a gold seal from the Chinese emperor; such a gold seal was found in 1784 in north Kyushu. The seal seems to read, "King of Nu of Wa (Vassal of Han)."

Another Chinese dynastic account, *The History of the Wei Kingdom* (220–265), compiled around 300 CE, incorporated a fairly authentic account of Japanese life as it was evolving from Yayoi to tomb culture. The history recorded the existence in Japan of a hundred states, or, more properly, tribes, thirty of whom had relations with China. The political units varied in size, and they were headed by kings or queens, of whom the most remarkable was a Queen Himiko (or Pimiko), an archaic Japanese term meaning "Sun Daughter." The Chinese annals pictured a law-abiding but liquor-loving society that followed the arts of agriculture, spinning, weaving, and fishing. It described very marked social differences among the Japanese, and, as indicated by *haniwa* dating from the period, it confirmed tattooing and body-marking practices in Japan. Later Chinese histories, compiled after the fifth century, portrayed the growing unification of Japan under the imperial clan, a story by then also being chronicled by the Japanese themselves.

The two main Japanese sources of ancient history, the compilation of the *Kojiki* and the *Nihon Shoki* of the early eighth century, are often inaccurate and contradictory. Their creation myths relate the story of the Sun Goddess, advance the concept of the divinity of the emperor, and posit the uniqueness of the Japanese race, beliefs held by them until recently. (Not until New Year's Day of 1946, in the early months of the American occupation, did an imperial rescript disclaim the doctrine of imperial divinity.) The two works reshaped Japanese mythology and history to enhance the prestige of the ruling family clan in the Kansai plain. They created through their reconstructed genealogical studies a contrived picture of antiquity and centralized rule to bolster the imperial claims to legitimacy and primacy of governance. Yet in these allegorical studies of gods, goddesses, and heavenly events, the mythology paralleled possibly historical figures and events. The later and more contemporaneous sections of the histories became more credible than the earlier portions.

The creation stories were naive and crude and were concerned mainly with the procreation of a multitude of deities and of the islands of Japan. Among the first of the heavenly host were the brother and sister, Izanagi and Izanami, who between them produced some fourteen islands of Japan and three dozen deities, the last of which was the Fire God. Consumed by the birth of this final offspring, Izanami died. She descended to the nether world, where Izanagi visited her, only to be driven away because of the putrefied state of her body. Cleansing himself, Izanagi, by discarding his clothes and washing away various parts of his body, created another group of Japanese islands and gods. Included this time around were the Sun Goddess (Amaterasu), the Moon God, and Susa-no-o, who, as an adversarial force, embodied the enemies of the imperial family. In turn, Amaterasu and Susa-no-o produced more progeny, but animosity developed in the course of the relationship, after which Susa-no-o was banished to Izumo on the north coast of west Honshu. Archaeology does not show the Izumo area to be a major center of early Japanese culture, but the great shrine there is the oldest and second most important one in Japan.

The two Japanese chronicles continue to relate that Ninigi, a grandson of the Sun Goddess, descended from heaven to Kyushu. More myths center about his activities on that island, which, as noted, was a major cultural region and chief point of contact with the continent. Ninigi brought with him the three imperial regalia (*sanshu no jingi*), all of which were plentiful in the tomb culture. These were a bronze mirror (*yata no kagami*) to represent the sun; a curved jewel (*magatama*), the moon; and an iron sword (*murakumo no tsurugi*), a lightning flash. In turn, Ninigi's great-grandson, Jimmu (Divine Warrior), migrated up from southeast Kyushu via the Inland Sea to the eastern shore and settled near the present-day Osaka in the Yamato (Great Peace) area in the Kansai plain. After campaigns lasting three years to subdue the resisting inhabitants, he ascended the throne as Jimmu Tenno (a Chinese political term connoting a "heavenly emperor") on February 11, 660 BCE at Kashiwara, the first capital of Japan and founding date of the imperial family, observed as a holiday into recent years.

Such an arbitrary ancient date is naturally suspect. The year was arrived at much later in the early seventh century CE by Japanese rulers, who were then adopting Chinese time concepts by counting back 1260 years, which was a major cycle (and multiple of the basic sixty-year reckoning) of historical time according to the Chinese. The month and date, again borrowing from the Chinese calendrical calculations, possibly was the commencement of the lunar new year. The reigns of the Yamato rulers after 660 BCE to 400 CE proceeded on an uneven course. The subsequent fifteen successor priest-kings after the founder (Jimmu Tenno ruled for 78 years, 660–582 BCE) collectively ruled over an improbable millennium. Two of these monarchs were credited with reigns of a century. Whatever its claim to legitimacy, the imperial clan and the Yamato state emerged as the strongest political entity in Japan by historic times (400 CE).

The story of Jimmu Tenno's conquest eastward follows the archaeological record, but the actual parallel historic migration was probably a thousand years later than that recorded in legend. It probably occurred sometime in the first half of the fourth century CE. The state of Yamato, because of its central location and rich agricultural resources, grew in size and power during the next two centuries, until its rulers could claim suzerainty over 121 political units in Japan alone. These rulers, probably members of a solar cult (strains of which recur throughout these early Japanese histories), set up their chief shrine to the Sun Goddess at Ise, on the east coast of central Honshu facing the rising sun. This became the most important shrine in Japan. Members of the imperial family regularly visited Ise into the twentieth century, to report important events, including accessions to the throne, to their grand ancestor of the sun line.

Expanding outward from their base, the early Yamato rulers won control over their neighbors. They governed over lands north to the Kanto plain and south to Kyushu and for a time across the strait into Korea. Political ties with Korea were close. In the fourth century CE, Japanese rulers sent military expeditions to the peninsula, beset with civil strife, where the Japanese established themselves in the state of Mimana on the southern Korean coast until 562 CE. One early major invasion from Kyushu was credited to the empress-regent Jingo, whose son, the Emperor Ojin, was later deified as Hachiman, the Shinto god of war. Japanese also interfered in intra-Korean affairs, for that peninsula was divided at the time into three warring states of Paekche, Silla, and Koguryo. In the fifth century, through Korea, Japan sustained regular ties with Chinese in the "Southern Courts" centered in the Yangzi delta after the fall of the Later

Han in 220 CE, when that country experienced endemic warfare for more than three centuries afterwards.

Accompanying military and diplomatic contacts were close cultural ties with neighboring Korea. Some scholars with Chinese learning from Korea were dispatched to Yamato (by then Chinese colonies and culture had been present in Korea for some five centuries). As early as 284 CE, the Japanese requested, and received, from Paekche, the service of the scholar Wani, who allegedly introduced the Chinese script into the country. These Koreans, and other unrecorded Chinese immigrants, were literate, highly skilled, and in great demand in early Japan. They were given noble rank and honored. One-third of the entries listed in a seventh-century "Who's Who" of Japan were descendants of Koreans or Chinese. The scholars, tutoring Japanese in the Chinese language, the medium of expression for religious and secular ideas, installed at Yamato in official capacities, kept records in Chinese; the two earliest Japanese histories drew on these studies. With these first cultural impulses from the mainland, Japan commenced its historic life.

CHRONOLOGY

BCE

200,000–30,000	First possible Paleolithic cultural waves
ca. 14,000 to ca. 300	Jomon culture
660, February 11	Traditional date for founding of Yamato state by Jimmu Tenno
ca. 300 to 300 CE	Yayoi culture

CE

57	First recorded Japanese contact with China
284	Scholar Wani in Japan from Paekche
ca. 300–600	Tomb (Kofun) culture
ca. 300	Chinese dynastic record, *History of the Wei Kingdom*, relates Japanese events
ca. 400	Yamato state emerges; historic Japan commences
ca. 445	Chinese dynastic annals, *History of the Later Han Dynasty*, narrates information on early Japan

JAPANESE SOVEREIGNS AND REIGNS
(FEMALE RULERS ARE IN ITALICS)

1. Jimmu Tenno, 660–582 BCE
2. Suizei, 581–549
3. Annei, 548–511

   4. Itoku, 510–476
   5. Kosho, 475–393
   6. Koan, 392–291
   7. Korei, 290–215
   8. Kogen, 214–158
   9. Kaika, 157–98
  10. Sujin, 97 BCE–30 CE
  11. Suinin, 29–70 CE
  12. Keiko, 71–130
  13. Seimu, 131–191
  14. Chuai, 192–200
      Jingo Kogo, 209–269, regent for son
  15. Ojin, 270–310, deified as Hachiman, God of War
  16. Nintoku, 313–399

2

Yamato Japan

(ca. 400–700)

By the advent of the fifth century, a clear historical focus centers on the imperial family. Its location on the Yamato plain was propitious for economic and security reasons. The region, though small in area, was agriculturally productive, with easy access to the Inland Sea. The core of the early indigenous state was fashioned in this favored spot. Because the cradle of Japanese civilization was Yamato, the place name itself came to connote, in particular, any uniquely Japanese phenomenon (such as Yamato-e, paintings or representations of native scenes) or in general a Japan portrayed in a romantic, idealistic, or nostalgic fashion (as the numerous Yamato-named restaurants).

The emperors, a grandiose designation for a ruler of circumscribed power and area, initially exercised authority indirectly through the clans in a form of vassalage. With the gradual rise of clans other than the imperial one to greater real power, the Yamato monarchs were relegated to secondary political influence. They lost authority, though they were kept on the throne and maintained their claim to divine status. They reigned but did not rule. This form of monarchy was an aspect of Japanese political history that persisted into the twentieth century. Never in history was the imperial family overthrown and replaced, despite occasional dissatisfaction. Rather, political struggles centered on great families who endeavored to control the imperial line and by so doing sought to direct the destinies of Japan. The system from early times of rulers who were theoretically absolute and divine but subject to political figures behind the scenes with actual power constituted a basic Japanese political phenomenon.

SOCIETY

Yamato society, by the end of the tomb era, had become hierarchical, hereditary, and closed. It revolved around a loose federation of extended families or clans, called *uji*. The uji were a later, smaller, and more refined unit than had been the hundred tribes mentioned in early Chinese chronicles. They consisted of members who claimed descent from a common god and who worshiped this deity (*ujigami*) under a patriarchal chief (*uji no kami*). As first among equals, the imperial uji traced its descent from the Sun Goddess. As high priests, they served also as sacred symbols. The interlocking of religious and secular duties derived from ancient days; the archaic Japanese term for government (matsurigoto) means the practice of ritual ceremonies. The royally affiliated uji were Omi. Other aristocratic clans claimed ancestry from lesser gods who later joined the sun line or who were descendants of earth gods who had submitted to Jimmu; these were the Muraji. As leaders of each faction, the posts of Great Omi and Great Muraji assumed importance in the Yamato court. Some clans received titles (*kanabe*) from the emperor; recipients of the highest orders served at court and its environs.

Some uji were grouped according to occupations, and these concerned themselves with primary functions in military, literary, or religious matters. Among the more prominent were the Mononobe, or Armorers, and the Nakatomi, or Court Ritualists. The court represented appointees from the various clans, and its personnel (*kuge*) were responsible for ongoing matters of state. They were supported by incomes from large-scale irrigation projects in rice lands that were steadily extended in area under royal control. Big log warehouses were constructed in the capital area by 500 to store the grain tribute from surrounding provincial tributaries as well as to serve as storage space for cultural artifacts brought over from the mainland.

As clan structures became more complex, subsidiary attendants, termed *be* or *tomo*, were attached to the uji. In reality labor forces, these were also hereditary groups, organized like the clans under their own chiefs. They provided necessary economic and agricultural support services. Most grew rice that fed not only themselves but their overlords; other groups specialized in certain forms of livelihood such as fishing, weaving, or ceramic making. Skilled foreigners were grouped into this category, because through adoption by Japanese families they could be assimilated into the existing social structure.

Lowest on the social and economic scale were the commoners and slaves (*yatsuko*), the latter few in number (perhaps 5 percent of the population) and of minor economic importance. Within the larger groupings, the immediate family was the basic unit. In it, generally the eldest male presided over family matters. Monogamy usually prevailed, but those who could afford concubines or secondary wives kept them within an indefinite social framework. All children, whether from the legal spouse or others, were considered legitimate. Even in the imperial family there was great irregularity, and the heirs were not necessarily the firstborn sons of reigning empresses.

Yamato religion was early Shinto. Nameless at first, this primitive religion received a Chinese appellation, loosely translated as "the way of the gods" to differentiate it from Buddhism and from Chinese Confucian beliefs that had entered Japan. Shinto was brought to Japan by those early Japanese who had emigrated to the islands from other regions of Asia. In time, Shinto became indelibly regarded as the Japanese national religion. In its broadest sense it was an attitude, a feeling, an aesthetic involvement toward things Japanese. Early polytheistic Shinto embraced cults of diverse origins: animism, fertility rites, ancestor worship, nature reverence, and the complex of heroes, gods, and goddesses, among whom the Sun Goddess was paramount. Despite the existence of many cults and shrines, of which at least 3,000 existed by the eighth century, all cults acknowledged the divinity of the emperor. Shinto worshipers believed in *kami*, a superior thing or person. In animistic fashion, anything and anyone could be kami, including beautiful sites, great trees, unusually shaped stones, and deceased warriors. An expression of the most intimate Japanese sentiments, Shinto possessed no founder, no inspired sacred book, no teachers, no saints, and no martyrs.

A Shinto shrine (*jinja*) usually was a simple affair. Constructed of wood, it consisted of a single room, sometimes partitioned, raised from the ground, with steps at the side or in front. At each end side were freestanding pillars of wood extending from the ground to the projecting roof. Rarely containing imagery or icons, it enshrined symbolic articles such as mirrors or swords representing kami. A *torii* stood outside, as did a water basin to cleanse the mouth and the hands of worshipers. Acts of worship were simple. They involved clapping of the hands, bowing toward the sacred objects, and proffering modest offerings of food, drink, cloth, or money. Ceremonial dances were performed, and shrine festivals were usually gay. Shinto possessed neither moral code nor philosophy; it had no sense of sin or guilt. Rather, emphasis was placed on cleanliness, a feature adumbrated in the creation myths. Ritual impurity could be caused by a number of events or conditions, including physical dirtiness, sexual intercourse, menstruation, childbirth, wounds, or death. The main point was to wash away these impurities. Elementary and primitive Shinto, essentially a cheerful and sunny religion, remained part of Japanese culture until modern times.

SINIFICATION, THE FIRST PHASE: ASUKA OR SUIKO PERIOD (552–645)

To this indigenous, primitive heritage of Yamato, the Japanese added an element of sinification, or Chinese influence (sini- and sino- are prefixes that indicate things relating to China or the Chinese). Long in contact with Chinese culture, the Japanese first borrowed from their neighbor slowly and unconsciously. Not until the mid-sixth century did some of the Japanese elite become aware of the advantages of the great continental culture and of the desirability of learning more about it. The result was a sudden acceleration around 550 in the rate of importation of Chinese concepts in religion, politics, economics, and language, initiating a period of voluntary cultural borrowing that persisted for about three centuries.

During this time, China exerted great power, for this was the era of the Sui dynasty (589–618), which reunited the empire after more than three centuries of political division, and its successor, the Tang (618–907), the greatest of all China's two-dozen dynasties and the largest empire in the world at the time. Through its great prestige and strength, China attracted not only the Japanese but also other Asian peoples and states into its recognizable world. For their part, Japanese ruling classes experimented with Chinese ideas. By the sixth century, they had acquired a higher degree of culture but recognized the desirability of importing certain concepts to strengthen the centralized government to manage more efficiently the loose clan system. Nothing was forced on them from the mainland. The Chinese (in contrast with the later Mongols) were never interested in the physical conquest of Japan. In their semi-isolation, the Japanese were free to adapt Chinese importations as they desired.

Buddhism (*Bukkyo*) was the first major conscious borrowing from China. Its adoption in Japan, to the point of becoming the state religion for a time, was a remarkable story. The faith conducted neither holy wars nor proselytizing campaigns. The religion came to Japan from China and Korea, but it had originated in India a millennium earlier. Its historical founder, whose traditional dates are 567–487 BCE, had several names, the personal ones of Gautama or Siddhartha, as well as the appellations of Sakyamuni (Sage of the Sakya Tribe) and the Buddha (Enlightened One). Born the son and heir of a king ruling over part of present-day south-central Nepal, Gautama was brought up in luxury, received a good education, married and fathered a son. A sensitive man, however, he brooded continually over the mysteries of human life and the problems of suffering, sickness, calamities, and death. He renounced his riches and royal succession to find answers to these problems.

After subjecting himself to various experiences to find the truth, Gautama finally reached enlightenment after long meditation under a fig tree. He concluded that life consisted of four truths. These truths posited that life equaled suffering, that suffering was caused by desire, that to rid oneself of suffering one had then to eliminate desire, and that desire was eradicated through the practice of the eightfold path. The eightfold path in turn, he declared, consisted of right views, resolve, speech, conduct, livelihood, effort, mindfulness, and concentration. For further guidance, he also gave his disciples ten commandments, similar in nature to those of the Old Testament. He stated that through these precepts each individual had to find the path to salvation, which he termed *nirvana,* or the annihilation of self. The Buddha never claimed to be divine himself, and he set up no gods or religious pantheon. For half a century he preached his gospel to rich and poor, high and low, including his son and mother. Admitting women to the faith, he founded an order of nuns.

After his death, his disciples propagated the faith that in time gave rise to differing interpretations. To help preserve doctrinal unity, councils were periodically called in India, but by the fourth council, around 100, two basic branches of Buddhism had developed. The earlier and purer form was termed Hinayana, or the Lesser Vehicle (*Shojo Bukkyo*), because it rejected all later accretions. It is known also as Theravada, its main and only surviving sect. Drawing from the Buddha's sayings and doctrine, Hinayana emphasized self-salvation. Though monastic orders grew in this branch, emphasis was placed on the layman's activity to gain merit through the performance of ritual acts. In time, however, the concept of salvation by faith in the historical Buddha arose; obeisance to him would procure redemption. Hinayana became widespread in Sri Lanka and the Southeast Asian countries of Myanmar (formerly Burma), Thailand, Cambodia, and Laos. Monks here wear saffron colored robes, since tradition holds that when the Buddha received enlightenment, his skin turned golden.

The later, amended Buddhistic thought was called Mahayana, or the Greater Vehicle (*Daijo Bukkyo*). First formulated in north India, it spread into China, Korea, and then on to Japan. This branch advanced fundamental differences from Hinayana doctrines. Over the centuries, nebulously and anonymously, Mahayana developed the concept of salvation by faith in a plethora of buddhas, including the historical one, who was venerated as only one of several enlightened deities. In this exalted buddha rank (*nyorai*) came to be included Amida, the Buddha of the Western World or of Paradise; Dainichi (or Rushana), the Universal Buddha; and Yakushi, the Buddha of Medicine and of Healing.

Mahayana adherents also revered compassionate bodhisattvas (*bosatsu*), or beings of wisdom, who postponed their own salvation, though qualified for it, until they could save others. The main bodhisattvas who were revered in Japan (as they had been earlier, along with the buddhas, in China), included Kannon, the goddess of mercy and the handmaiden of Amida, and Miroku, now a bodhisattva in heaven but who will come to earth as a buddha at the end of the world in most troublesome times (*mappo*) to save humanity. A host of popular gods and holy men also were embraced in the wide-ranging theological field of Mahayana adherents. Moreover, to substitute for a "nothingness" nirvana, Mahayana advanced the reality of an afterlife. The idea of a western paradise arose, as did a hierarchy of heavens and hells to reward believers or to punish unbelievers. In simpler and more understandable theology expressed in vivid artistic forms, Mahayana took hold in East Asian countries.

Differing in basic respects, both major streams of Buddhism, nonetheless, adopted the canonical categories of the Tripitaka (Three Baskets): that for conduct, which were rules for monks and nuns; that for discourses, which consisted of the Buddha's sayings or sutras; and that for supplementary doctrines, which were works of Buddhist psychology and metaphysics. The Tripitaka, in its three divisions, was elastic as to content and scope, not only between Hinayana and Mahayana, but among the various Mahayana sects themselves. A specific, orthodox canon in the Tripitaka was never crystallized, and national and regional variations remained distinct. A recent compilation of the Mahayana texts as utilized by the various Japanese Buddhist sects required several dozen volumes. Both variants subscribe to the Three Treasures of Buddhism: the Buddha himself, his teachings, and the monkhood (*sangha*).

Although in theological variance, Buddhist sects all conformed to strict canons of artistic representation in sculpture and in painting. Also originating in India over the centuries, representations of holy figures with their distinguishing features, especially of the buddhas and the bodhisattvas, are portrayed in standard iconography of paintings or sculptures. The physical features might vary from country to country, but the basic imagery projects orthodoxy, symbolism dating from early Hindu ideas and incorporated into later Buddhism. In Hinayana countries, the viewer might correctly identify the image contemplated as the historical Buddha, because only he is venerated. In Mahayana representations, including those in Japan, with their varied personalities but outwardly similar artistic attributions, the saint is more difficult to define.

Originating in India and transmitted by China and Korea, the new alien faith appealed to the Japanese for several reasons. It filled a religious vacuum, for Shinto had no moral teachings. Through the concept of reincarnation, Buddhism buttressed not only ancestor worship but the continuity of Japanese national life. It compromised with Shinto for it admitted Shinto gods as buddhas or bodhisattvas in what has been called Dual Shinto (*Ryobu Shinto*). The Sun Goddess, progenitress of the sun line, was equated with Dainichi, the Universal Buddha. Moreover, the adoption of Buddhism was meshed with Japanese domestic and foreign politics.

According to the traditional account as contained in the Nihon Shoki, in 552 (538 is a suggested alternative year), Paekche, an ally of Japan (and known there as Kudara) and probably the Korean state most subject of the three to Chinese culture, sent a Buddhist image and scriptures to the Yamato court. The message stated that Buddhism had come from China and that great prestige lay behind it. It urged the Japanese to adopt Buddhism as the true religion. At the same time it implied that the Korean ally could use Yamato help in its military campaigns then progressing against neighboring Silla. This traditional date of the introduction of Buddhism inaugurated the so-called Akusa epoch, after a capital site location in the Yamato plain, or the Suiko era after a reigning empress (593–628), whose famous name is bestowed on the whole period.

The uji in Yamato split over the issues of aiding Paekche and of adopting Buddhism. The military and religious clans, the latter dominated by the Nakatomi, who were Shinto ritualists, opposed continental and religious involvements. Advancing a contrary position was a rising clan, the Soga, who wanted to enhance its position at court. Though the emperor sent no material aid to the Korean supplicants, he permitted the Soga to worship the image in private, at least until an epidemic broke out. Blamed for the pestilence, the image was thrown into a moat, and the Soga family temple was razed. Nothing much is then heard about the story until 584, when another member of the clan, Soga no Umako, received two images from Korea. He erected a second temple to enshrine them, and a Korean priest living in Japan at the time ordained three girls as nuns. After another plague, the images were again thrown into a moat, and the nuns defrocked. But the disease continued to spread, and the emperor, a nephew of Umako, agreed to allow the Soga to follow Buddhism. The nuns' robes were restored, and more Korean priests arrived. At court the Soga grew in influence. In 587, it overthrew the rival Mononobe and reached its height under Shotoku Taishi, an outstanding individual, a son of the emperor Yomei, who might be called Japan's first statesman. He lived from 574 to 622.

He acted as regent (*sessho*) for his aunt the empress Suiko from 593 to 622. In his high position as Great Omi, head of the royally affiliated uji, Shotoku also was a scholar and a devout Buddhist who composed three commentaries on Buddhist texts, still preserved today. He promoted the new faith, as well as a centralized government focused on the imperial clan in 603 with the inauguration of the "twelve caps" ranking system in the bureaucracy. The following year, he expanded ideas of centralization in the so-called Seventeen Article Constitution (*Jushichijo no Kempo*), more a set of guiding principles than of high binding laws. This document, ascribed to Shotoku, was probably a later work dedicated to him a generation or more after his death. At any rate, the declaration represented his ideas, based on the Chinese Confucian ethical system (*jukyo*) that sought political unity and obedience to authority, which he was eagerly seeking to promote in Japan.

The document consisted of a set of injunctions to the somewhat independently minded uji to adopt Buddhism and to support the empress. The articles emphasized the highly centralized Chinese governmental structure as it existed in Sui dynastic politics, which were based on Confucian virtues of sincerity, love, goodness, form and ritual, and the validity of Buddhism as a peaceful, unifying religious force. The theme was set in the first article, which advanced a plea for unity in words taken directly from the Analects of Confucius: "Harmony is to be valued, and an avoidance of wanton opposition to be honored." In this statement of principles, the prince endeavored to unite the loosely federated uji, subject to Soga guidance, under imperial rule.

In Japan, Shotoku and his Soga colleagues constructed some of the earliest Buddhist temples and monastic compounds (*garan*) with certain common features. Although few of the originals exist today, they or their reconstructed versions are priceless works of architecture. The most ancient of these, commenced in 593, was the Shitennoji (Four Heavenly Kings Temple; the suffix *ji* denotes a temple) in Naniwa, part of present-day Osaka. It was bombed in the course of World War II but subsequently restored to its original outlines. The main buildings are arranged in a north-south axial plan.

Osaka: Reconstructed Shitennoji temple, oldest in Japan, with traditional features: colonnade, main gate, pagoda, and kondo (statue hall)

Nara: Horyuji temple, oldest extant wooden structure in the world

Another contemporaneous temple, also begun late in the sixth century, was the Hokoji or Asukadera (dera also connotes a temple), now gone, farther inland. The most famous of Shotoku's structures is the Horyuji (Temple of the Original Vow) complex built in 607 at his residence in the Nara area. It was destroyed by fire in 670 but rebuilt around 700. Inspired by Chinese models, the temple is a Buddhist architectural gem along formal classical lines. The grounds are surrounded by a rectangular covered colonnade (*horo* or *kairo*) with a prominent middle gate (*chumon*) guarded on each side by likenesses of protecting deities. Inside the compound are located, on an east-west axis, a five-storied pagoda (*gojunoto*) and the golden hall (*kondo*), much reconstructed but probably the oldest wooden building in the world, which houses the principal paintings and imagery. Outside to the rear of the compound are the lecture hall (*kodo*) and subsidiary buildings.

These temples contained early sculptural representations (*butsuzo*) of Buddhist gods. The Horyuji is rich in statuary. In its buildings are contained a bronze Yakushi Buddha (607) and a bronze Shaka trinity (623) with the historical Buddha flanked by two bodhisattvas, attributed to the famous Tori Busshi, grandson of a Chinese immigrant. It also houses a larger-than-life standing statue of the Kudara (Paekche) Kannon. The nearby nunnery, Chuguji, contains a charming seated contemplative Miroku. Another Miroku (or Kannon?) is at the Koryuji in Kyoto, which is identical to Korean models of the time. The affinity between Korean and Japanese

Nara: Kannon, Bodhisattva Goddess of Mercy
allegedly sent by Paekche state in Korea to
Soga clan (British Museum)

Buddhistic sculpture at this time was so close that the issue of provenance
of the figures is sometimes a matter of scholarly debate.

The Imperial Household Collection has a colored portrait on paper that
is purportedly of Shotoku Taishi and his two sons (or a son and a brother),
but few paintings of the Asuka period exist. The sides of the Tamamushi
shrine, also in the Horyuji, execute scenes from a *jataka* tale, one of the earlier lives and manifestations of the Buddha as a bodhisattva before coming
to earth, done in 567, in a mixture of lacquer and oil. The temple also pre-
serves fragments of textiles from the times, and the Chuguji has a tapestry
showing Prince Shotoku in paradise.

Shotoku and his colleagues borrowed other Chinese ideas. The Chinese
calendar was adopted at the turn of the seventh century (and so the 660
BCE dating of Jimmu Tenno's founding of Yamato). Official Chinese hierarchical patterns were grafted onto the imperial family and the court
bureaucracy, both of which were graded and ranked. To get word of the
latest developments on the continent, with the consent of his empress aunt,
Shotoku dispatched three embassies to Sui China; that of 607 comprised
more than 600 members. On the basis of equality, he addressed his communications from the ruler of the Rising Sun to that of the Setting Sun.

Accustomed to subservience from foreign monarchs, the Chinese emperor was not amused. After Shotoku (between 630 and 838), thirteen more official missions were sent to China. The cost, size, and perils of these missions were great. Generally they consisted of several ships carrying from five to several hundred men. To avoid capture by hostile Koreans, they usually sailed directly across the 500 miles of open sea to ports on the central Chinese coast. The missions were successful in bringing to Japan the latest Chinese cultural and technological advances. Students and Buddhist monks mingled with official Yamato emissaries and spread Chinese ideas and customs on their return to Japan.

SINIFICATION, THE SECOND PHASE: HAKUHO (645–710)

After the death of Shotoku Taishi, the Soga line with two successors maintained political strength, but their high-handed actions (including designs on the throne) generated opposition from other clans. One of the Nakatomi uji, together with a prince later to become the Emperor Tenchi, in 645 seized power and reorganized the government. In recognition for services rendered, the emperor rewarded the Nakatomi with the new surname of Fujiwara, which has survived into contemporary Japan as the appellation of one of the oldest, most continuous aristocratic families in the world. After the accession of these new parties to power, the Fujiwara retained Buddhism, which was a change of attitude, because the Nakatomi had previously been the guardians of the Shinto faith.

This development was a tribute to the groundwork that Shotoku had laid, for in the second overall attempt at sinification through the Taika (Great Change) reforms of 645–650, the Fujiwara and the emperor-to-be preserved Buddhism and further strengthened centralized imperial rule. In time reckoning, the Japanese were now adopting the year period, or reign names (*nengo*), of the Chinese (a practice there dating back to 140 BCE), wherein the rulers characterized all or part of their reigns by descriptive terms. Great Change, the first of these in Japanese context, was most apt. These Taika reforms presaged the so-called overall Hakuho period, after the reign name of a prominent monarch of the time, the Emperor Temmu (673–685). (The Chinese, from whom the concept of reign names was borrowed, never extrapolated them into designating periods before or after the appropriate ruler as the Japanese did.)

With ideas borrowed whole from China, the Taika reforms sought to transform Yamato economically and politically. They posited long-range and ambitious goals, which, had they been fully realized, would have had far-reaching impact. A central bureaucracy was outlined, to include a Department of Worship (*Jingikan*), which concerned itself with all non-Buddhist ceremonies. This took precedence over a Department of State (*Daijokan*), effecting secular duties, with a chancellor, various ministers, and eight ministries. Under the central government, fifty-eight provinces (*kuni*), districts or counties (*gun*), and townships of about fifty household (*ri*) administrations were organized. In the world of education, to train officials, the reforms established a state university (*daigaku*) and provincial ones (*kokugaku*). Despite these training academies that presumed office by merit, hereditary accession to high places continued to be widely practiced.

Private ownership of land was abolished. All land was nationalized in the name of the emperor, who redistributed it on the basis of households in an equal-field system (*handen*), wherein each able-bodied adult, as in China, received equal allotments of land to till. To implement this policy, periodic censuses were required. Three main types of taxes were imposed on individuals in the households: a grain tax in kind, usually rice, about 3 percent of the crop produced; a tax on products other than cereals, such as textiles and handicrafts, if these were made; and a labor or corvée tax, which might involve compulsory military duties or public works projects of sixty days for the state, but which might be commuted by payment of other taxes. Peasant communities were blocked into groups of five families each, and these groups were held mutually responsible for the implementation of official directives. A farmer's burdens were onerous in themselves, but additional state duties provided unrequited hardships.

Toward the end of the period, in 702, the Taiho (Great Treasure) Code was promulgated. Drawing on two earlier legal formulations, it elaborated a criminal code (*ritsu*), defined the specific bureaucratic ranks and duties for the officials (*ryo*), and outlined the general laws of political conduct for the people. A council of state was created to advise the emperor, with a prime minister and ministers of the left and right. Then came eight ministries and in turn scores of lesser offices and bureaus. Servicing the structure was a bureaucracy that was eventually divided into twenty-six ranks, each subdivided again into senior and junior classes, with the latter again into upper and lower grades. Offices proliferated; Chinese bureaucratic models mired down on Japanese shores.

The effects of such wide-ranging policies, which included the implied destruction of the uji and the reorganization of land patterns, could have been drastic. Actually, as so often occurred in Japanese practice, only nominal changes took place. New forms were merely imposed on existing patterns, otherwise the procedures would have been too bloody and too revolutionary. In the restructuring of wealth and political power, the uji, earlier dependent on historical claims to preeminence, now enjoyed the full sanction, in their ranks, of the imperial system as a civil nobility. They brought into the ensuing aristocratic age their lineages and their sophisticated ways. In the provinces, the local elite simply received new titles, and the same persons carried on in new paper titles. As holder of crown land, the cultivator was to pay the taxes directly to the state in order to eliminate the creation of a class of tax-exempt and privileged landowners. But in time, tax-exempt estates grew with impunity as a weakened central government was unable to effect its Taika tax policies. The reforms, never fully implemented, gradually broke down because the Japanese could not totally absorb the Chinese ideas. Even in Tang China, as in other Chinese dynasties, this highly centralized economic and political system itself had operated on an effective basis only irregularly and only under strong emperors and strong regimes. It was too much to expect that such grandiose experiments, which were difficult enough to effect in China, would work more efficiently in Japan.

As ambitious political and economic structures were imported and grafted onto the Japanese systems, Buddhism grew in imperial favor. Although previous rulers and aristocrats individually had espoused the faith, it was elevated to court status under the Emperor Temmu and his successors. With official aegis, the religion grew in imperial favor and dispositions. Few physical remains, however, date from the Hakuho period. The east pagoda of the Yakushiji (Temple of the Healing Buddha) near Nara, with its three sets of double-tiered eaves (*tahoto*), provides an insight not only into Japanese architectural styles of the time but into those of Tang China, where original prototypes have long since disappeared because of civil turmoil and the attrition of time.

In the same temple compound is now kept a bronze trinity of Yakushi and two bodhisattvas. The incomparable Horyuji, with its storehouse of Buddhist treasures, includes a Miroku in meditation (645) and the Lady Tachibana's shrine, with painted panels and a small sculpted Amida trinity inside. The walls of the kondo were decorated with frescoes of Mahayana Buddhist scenes, including Amida trinities in Tang style, but in 1949 fire and smoke destroyed many of these priceless wall paintings. Yet from what was left behind from this remarkably creative period in both religious and secular spheres, much can be learned about the advancing sophistication of the Japanese.

CHRONOLOGY

552 (or 538?)	Traditional date for introduction of Buddhism into Japan from Paekche
522–645	Asuka or Suiko period
562	Japanese withdrawal from Mimana state in Korea
574–622	Shotoku Taishi
589–618	Sui dynasty in China
593	Construction of Shitennoji and Hokoji (Asukadera)
593–622	Shotoku as regent for aunt Empress Suiko

593–628   Empress Suiko reign
604   Traditional date for Seventeen Article Constitution
607   First building of Horyuji; burns down 670
607, 608, 614   Shotoku Taishi's three embassies to Sui China
618–907   Tang dynasty in China
630–838   Thirteen Japanese official missions to Tang China
645–650   Taika reforms
645–710   Hakuho epoch
673–685   Reign of Emperor Temmu
ca. 700   Horyuji rebuilt
702   Taiho code

JAPANESE SOVEREIGNS AND REIGNS
(PROMINENT YEAR PERIODS APPENDED)

17. Richu, 400–405
18. Hansho, 406–410
19. Ingyo, 411–453
20. Anko, 453–456
21. Yuryaku, 456–479
22. Seinei, 480–484
23. Kenso, 485–487
24. Ninken, 488–498
25. Buretsu, 498–506
26. Keitai, 507–531
27. Ankan, 531–536
28. Senkwa, 536–539
29. Kimmei, 540–571
30. Bidatsu, 572–585
31. Yomei, 585–587
32. Sujun, 588–592
33. *Suiko*, 593–628
34. Jomei, 629–641
35. *Kokyoku*, 642–644; abdicates
36. Kotoku, 645–654; "Taika," 645–650
37. *Saimei*, 655–660 (the earlier Kokyoku)
38. Tenchi, 661–670
39. Kobun, 671–672, civil war, throne usurped by
40. Temmu, 673–685; "Hakuho," 673–685
41. Jito, 686–696; abdicates
42. Mommu, 697–706; "Taiho," 701–703
43. *Gemmyo*, 707–714; abdicates

A JAPANESE MAHAYANA BUDDHIST
(DAIJO BUKKYO) PANTHEON

Buddhas (Nyorai—manifestations of the historical Buddha):

Amida: Buddha of the Western Paradise
Dainichi (or Rushana): Universal Buddha; illuminates the universe with truth.
Shaka: Historical Buddha
Yakushi: Buddha of Medicine

Bodhisattvas (Bosatsu), main ones revered:

Fugen: sits on elephant; helps women especially to attain enlightenment.
Jizo: guards children on road to netherworld as well as adults through six transient stages on the way to enlightenment; has shaved head, holds staff in one hand, gemstone in the other.
Kannon or Sho-Kannon, with thirty-three manifestations, a rare and greatly worshiped goddess.
Miroku or Maitrreya bodhisattva in heaven, to come down as Buddha in world's final stages.
Monju: God of Wisdom, edited Buddhist scriptures; rides a lion.
Nikko and Gakko: former with sun in crown; latter with moon.

Other figures:

Arhats (Rakan), holy men, hermits, disciples of the Buddha
Ashura: three faced and six armed; protects Buddhist realm.
Bonten (Brahma): creator, wears a Chinese garment over armor; gentle but decisive; affiliated with Taishakuten (Indra), with same garments, seated on elephant.
Fudo Myoo: Deity of Fire; incarnation or attendant of Dainichi
Nio (Deva): two guards at temple gates, to keep out evil spirits with fierce countenances; facing gate, on left stands Gongo with mouth open (Ah, first Sanskrit syllable) and on right Rikishi with mouth closed (Hum, last Sanskrit syllable).
Shitenno (Four guardian kings): north, Tamonten; south, Zochoten; east, Jikokuten; west, Komokuten
Seven Deities of Good Luck (Shichi Fukufin), popular folk heroes affiliated with the faith:
    Benten: Goddess of the Arts and Wisdom; only female in group; plays the biwa.

Bishamon: God of War and Defense; holds magical spear, wards off evil, holds small pagoda.

Daikoku: God of Wealth and Harvest; right hand with gavel to bring luck, carries bales or sacks of rice to indicate wealth.

Ebisu: God of Fishing and Commerce; right hand has fishing rod, left hand a big red fish; happy face, big smile.

Fukurokuji and affiliated Jurojin: Gods of Wealth and Longevity; old man with elongated bald head, carries rolled scroll containing secrets of richness and long life.

Hotei: God of Happiness and Prosperity; fan in hand, potbellied, carrying treasure sack on back; a jolly countenance.

Asia: Spread of Buddhism

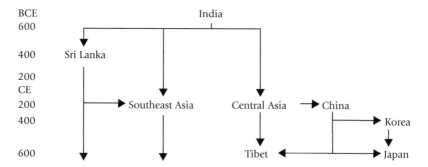

3

Nara Japan

(710–794)

The Japanese continued to borrow basic Chinese concepts such as city planning. They settled down in their first long-term fixed capital at Nara, or Heijo (City of Peace), as it was then called, on the fertile Yamato plain, where a centralized capital was laid out to house the imperial family. Previously, monarchs had resided on their personal estates scattered about in the Yamato area; the political capital moved according to the location of the new ruler's residence, the last one, in 694, at Fujiwara kyo. Perhaps the chief reason for this continual movement was the concept of ritual impurity caused by sickness and death of the predecessors, which precluded their heirs from remaining in the same residence. Primitive architectural styles of palaces and homes facilitated the many moves. But in 710, after extended planning and taking the cue from the centralized Chinese capitals, Nara became the site of a permanent Japanese governing town. It provided a headquarters and focus for both the country's government and the Buddhist religion. Nara was chosen in part because Buddhist temples already existed there and in part because of its propitious natural geographical setting as interpreted by geomancers. The powerful Fujiwara, led by Fujiwara no Fuhito (659–720), who shared imperial power through family connections, abetted the move.

Nara was designed on the model of the Tang Chinese capital of Changan (modern Xian), which was a great-walled metropolis measuring some five by six miles and embracing about two million inhabitants, the largest city in the world. The new Japanese capital, similarly shaped in a rectangular pattern but considerably smaller, measured two and two-thirds miles by three. It was laid out at the northern end of the Yamato plain. The palace was located in the northern section of the city, which lacked walls. The western half was never developed. The city in time withered away when the capital was relocated in Kyoto, and the Nara of today developed from a medieval town that later grew up around the old Buddhist monasteries and Shinto shrines at the edge of the eastern hills (temples are Buddhist, shrines are Shinto). In the eighth century, Nara was Japan's only urban center. Commercial centers, like those in China, had not developed in Japan. The main focus of Japanese life continued to be principally religious and political and was concentrated at the capital, a city of some 200,000 in a country with an estimated population of six million.

POLITICS AND SOCIETY

Nara politics revolved around the sovereign and court life. In theory the concept persisted of a strong monarch, designated as tenno, as in Jimmu Tenno. But the emperors, having already lost effective rule, were actually quite weak. They were subject to manipulation at court by powerful families. Inter-clan rivalries swirled around the throne. Although the Fujiwara held primacy, their position was countered by ambitions of other clans, notably the Tachibana. The monarchs remained weak, now additionally sapped, through the practice of royal abdication that arose in the eighth century. The rulers, because of either devout religious calling or strong pressure from outside sources, became cloistered in Buddhist monasteries or took up other duties. Removed from the political scene, the ex-monarchs confined themselves to religious rituals or other innocuous works, though a few of them in later times tried vainly to reassert their imperial influence and rule.

The *kuge*, or court nobility, concerned itself with much ritual and ceremony. Orchestral music and dances were partly imported from China. Gagaku, the imperial musical dance tradition, though it died out on the continent after the Tang, persisted in Japan into contemporary times. It became one of the oldest authenticated music and dance traditions in the world. Its dances (*bugaku*) utilized brilliant costumes and fanciful masks, while the orchestral accompaniment (*kangen*) drew on string, wind, and percussion instruments, including a pair of huge hanging drums representing the sun and the moon. The Japanese borrowed other concepts as well. Chinese-derived administrative codes continued to formalize an elaborate bureaucracy that was based on birth and family connections, rather than meritocracy as in its homeland. These codes followed Tang models to a great extent, but were modified to allow for conditions in Japan.

The Taiho Code of 702 provided the base for a revised version in the Yoro Code of 718, which embraced both penal laws (*ritsu*) and administrative practices (*ryo*) as in the Yamato state. The latter code, which was not effectively promulgated until four decades later, confirmed the Japanese concept of the emperor's divinity. This interpretation departed from the Chinese, who had always held that the monarch as a temporary adjudicator of the will of heaven held office by virtue and good behavior through a mandate of heaven to rule effectively and please the gods. To help administer central political affairs, the Yoro Code confirmed a Department of Religion. This was again unique to Japan, for there was no counterpart to this organ in China. Drawing again upon earlier offices, the code also continued to provide for a Department of Government that consisted of a supreme council of state, a chancellor, ministers of left and of right as high administrative officers, councillors, and eight ministries. Six of these ministries were based on time-honored Chinese prototypes: rites, civil office, treasury, punishments, war, and home affairs. The Japanese added another two, the imperial household and its treasury. The Chinese-inspired legal and administrative measures that promoted the concept of a centralized political order were termed the *ritsuryo* state, because they combined penal laws (*ritsu*) and administrative practice (*ryo*).

The local government structure confirmed the three tiers of provinces, districts, and town or village units. Officially approved highways radiated out from the capital to connect outlying areas. The emperor appointed provincial governors. As men of high rank, who included princes, the governors received as income some two dozen acres of land for their rank and about five additional acres for their office. Some officials grew rich on these economic emoluments derived from their estates or manors (*shoen*). Many spent their time in the capital and delegated their administrative duties to subordinates, who were the district officials. District magistrates also were imperial appointees, usually ranking members of local clans. They collected the taxes, and they also amassed fortunes. District appointments were often made for life, but the office in time became hereditary, a pronounced tendency in Japanese political affairs.

Commoners, at the bottom of the political and social structure, either were held in bondage (*semmin*) or enjoyed free status (*ryomin*). In the former category were serfs and slaves; the latter group consisted chiefly of farmers, who had been the beneficiaries of land redistribution policies during the Taika. Now a free man received about one-half an acre of land, while a woman received two-thirds as much. An entire family probably averaged holdings of two to three acres in size. They paid the land or grain tax amounting to about 5 percent of total yields in kind.

In this departure from the earlier equal field system, land was now distributed on the basis of rice production, with adjusted scales for sex, age, and the status of each member of the household. The Taika reforms had provided for the reallotment of land every few years to keep it in the hands of the free farmers. This policy proved difficult to implement, and large landholdings were accumulated, particularly by aristocrats and monastic orders. Theoretically all lands were taxable, but increasingly, the nobility and the monasteries, through court connections, received fiscal immunity. With the growth of these nontaxable estates, the conditions for those peasants who had to bear the burden of taxation worsened. Life became harder for them, and some escaped to frontier areas, became vagrants or socially displaced people (*ronin*), or put themselves under the protection of higher and more powerful persons. Because of the additional difficulty in implementing the labor tax, the conscription of peasants was abolished. A military corps of soldiers was now formed from sons of local officials and clans to provide palace guards, but these contributed more show than valor.

Realizing the problem of effective taxation, the Nara government decreed a policy of replacing state control by privatization as early as 743, when private ownership of rice land was made legally possible. The government also embarked on a program of expanding and of reclaiming arable land areas, which for incentive purposes were made nontaxable for a number of years. But because the reclamation projects required capital outlays, most schemes were undertaken by monasteries or the nobility, which had the means and which was already exempt from taxes. The newly acquired lands remained free from taxation. The common people continued to assume increased tax burdens, and agrarian poverty was widespread. The central government lost interest in the estates that provided no income, a phenomenon that helped to lay a basis for the later economic and political decentralization of feudal Japan. In commerce, barter continued to be the chief method of exchange, but as early as 708 copper coins (*wado kaiho*) were minted, although they were more restricted in use to court circles than to general circulation.

RELIGION

While time-sanctioned economic and political patterns atrophied in the later Nara period, Mahayana Buddhism grew. Six Nara sects (*Nan to-rokshu*) flourished, of which a few emerged as the more prominent at the time. Their philosophies, partially influenced by self-oriented Hinayana, arose in India, were fashioned in China, and transmitted directly or indirectly via Korea to Japan. Difficult to understand, the main philosophical features of Nara Buddhism were concerned with the problems of negation and of the illusion of the material world, with the attainment of enlightenment through the mental powers (because the only reality was man's own consciousness), and with the doctrine of the harmonious whole that emphasized a cosmological harmony under the Universal Buddha. Buddhism in the Nara period tended to be aristocratic, elitist, and exclusive, for the peasant in the field lacked both the time to appreciate and the comprehension to understand the complex religions.

First in point of time of arrival, the Sanron (Three Treatises) sect had been earlier introduced in 625 by a Korean monk. Its idealistic philosophy stressed the unreality of material phenomena. A second, the Jojitsu, with a similar doctrine, soon merged with the senior group. Another, the Kusha, also dealt with the metaphysical. Its origin is unclear and it might not have existed as a separate corporate entity. The Ritsu, emphasizing ritual and ordination practices, was founded by the blind Chinese monk Jianchen (Ganjin), 688-763. After five unsuccessful attempts to reach Japan, he finally located in Nara at the Toshodaiji (Temple Brought from the Tang) in 759. His sculptural likeness at the site is the oldest surviving representation of a historic person in Japan. The temple buildings themselves are pure copies of Tang architecture, most of which have long since disappeared on the main land. The main building, the *kondo*, is particularly striking. It is typically raised on a solid platform, with a wide front veranda and pillars set into the floor to support the heavy, drooping gabled and hipped roof; intricate intermeshing brackets fan out from the top of the columns. The Hosso sect, the leading one of the time, had been introduced into Japan around 650, and its main temple came to be the Horyuji. Like the others, it tended to stress the unreality of the physical world and the reality of consciousness.

Nara: Toshodaiji temple Kondo, built by blind monk Ganjin, in traditional Chinese Tang Dynasty architecture

Another major sect, the Kegon (Flower Wreath sutra), was introduced by another Chinese monk. In the art of this sect, the Universal Buddha of the harmonious whole, equated with the Japanese Sun Goddess, is portrayed on a lotus throne of a thousand petals, each of which is a universe containing millions of worlds. The best example of such a Buddha image is in the Todaiji (Great Eastern Temple) in Nara itself. In 735, following a pestilence, as a devout Buddhist, the Emperor Shomu, a grandson of Fujiwara no Fuhito and who ruled from 724 until his abdication in 749, ordered the construction of the image and its encasing temple. It took fourteen years to complete the bronze figure, which is fifty-three feet high, sits on a lotus throne sixty-eight feet in diameter, and is surrounded by lesser figures. Vast amounts of material went into its construction: one million pounds of copper, 17,000 pounds of tin and lead, 2,000 pounds of mercury, and 500 pounds of gold gilding (gold was fortuitously discovered in 749). Bronze segments for the image of ten feet by twelve and a half feet thick were cast. The huge Buddha figure was housed in the Great Hall, 284 by 166 feet and 152 feet high.

Destroyed in subsequent civil strife, the present hall was rebuilt in the sixteenth century at one-third the original size, but it remains the largest wooden building in the world. In 752, at the dedication of the image and the hall, an international assembly gathered that included two Indian monks, a Brahman (an Indian of the highest caste), a Cambodian monk, and a Chinese scholar, who was the president of the University of Nara. The Emperor Shomu gave the temple tax-free lands, and he promulgated Buddhism as the state cult by ordering branch monasteries and nunneries to be constructed throughout all the provinces (*kokubunji*). In a practice dating to Shotoku Taishi, he attempted to use the faith in an ideological and institutional manner to strengthen and continue to centralize the political state. After his abdication late in life, he retired to the cloisters.

The Emperor Shomu's widow gave to the monastery a log cabin warehouse, the Shosoin. It contained many of the personal belongings of the imperial family, including some nine thousand items, still extant. Some items apparently had traveled long distances, traversing the Silk Road in Central Asia. These artistic artifacts included Byzantine marble, Roman-inspired glass and pottery, and Persian articles. The emperor's daughter, the Empress Shotoku, who ruled from 764 to 770 in the second of two reigns (earlier as the Empress Koken, 749–758, directly after her father), was also a devout Buddhist. She fell in love with a Buddhist monk, Dokyo, a master of the Hosso sect, whom she promoted to be chief minister. Dokyo wanted to be emperor, but he was ousted from office by the powerful Fujiwara family after the death of the empress. So important were the Emperor Shomu and his family to the development of Buddhism that the Nara period is alternately designated as Tempyo, after one of his year periods. After 770, the influence of Buddhism at court waned slightly. Subsequent to the unfortunate experience of mixing religion with politics and gender, Japan had no more women rulers of any consequence after the Empress Shotoku, who is important in Japanese Buddhism for another reason. She had a million Buddhist charms printed, each to be contained in a small wooden pagoda (*hyakumanto*), many of which remain today as the earliest examples of woodblock printing in the world. The art had developed earlier in China (the first specimens have been lost).

Thanks to the copying of Chinese models, not only in religious ideas but also in visible architectural forms, the Japanese preserved for history a better understanding of the contemporaneous Tang, and Chinese, culture. Nara abounded with temples and monasteries. Some of the temples were privately sponsored by families; others were official. The imperial court under the Emperor Shomu made the Todaiji the national temple of Japan. Protective attributes were bestowed on the structure; they were believed capable of warding off evil and disasters. Complementing buildings from the times, later reproductions faithful to the period were fashioned. Temple complexes that reflect the flavor of the Nara era include the Kofukuji, the Saidaiji (Great Western Temple), and some minor structures in the Horyuji complex. These include the octagonal Yumedono (Hall of Dreams), erected at the site of Prince Shotoku's private chapel, and the nearby Dempodo, originally Lady Tachibana's residence.

Few paintings exist from the Nara period but beautiful statuary filled the halls. The chief works in the earlier decades of the Nara period were executed in bronze. In later years the dry lacquer medium was preferred. The statue would be shaped, either on a solid wooden core or over a hollowed center replaced by a wooden skeleton. In this manner were sculpted the Eight Guardian Devas (734), now in the Nara museum, of which the most famous is the Ashura, who before his conversion was a Hindu delamon king. Clay statues were also shaped. Guilds continued to shape pottery forms and glazed Sue ware, inspired by Chinese or Korean models, fired at high temperatures in kilns built into hillsides. Also introduced from Tang China was the three colored (*sancai*) ware, in one to all three colors, predominantly yellow, green, and white. Nobility also copied clothing from the mainland, which consisted of a shirt worn over pants that narrowed at the knees. Cloth was made from linen, hemp and silk, always richly embroidered. The Shosoin contains objects of the Nara period with either religious or secular motifs.

Although Buddhism took hold of the arts and crafts, it did not supplant completely the native Shinto, which affected the daily lives of the common folk. Both faiths operated at differing levels of religion and philosophy. Moreover, even at the sophisticated level, the imported religion could simply be grafted on to indigenous belief, in the ongoing process of theological fusion. In Dual Shinto, as in the Yamato era, Shinto deities continued to be equated with Buddhist gods; each group reinforced the other in the religious hierarchy. As the leading family, the Fujiwara built both Buddhist and Shinto temples; the latter family shrine in Nara is the Kasuga. Unaffected by the complex theology and ramifications of the alien faith, the commoners continued in their simple acts of belief performed before local shrines and kami. Because Shinto transcended formal religious worship as a state of mind or reverence for things indigenous, it would have been difficult to eliminate or to replace.

LITERATURE AND LANGUAGE

Centers of learning continued at the Nara university and in provincial schools. Literature flourished within a sophisticated cultured Nara court. The *Kojiki* and *Nihon Shoki* were compiled in this period. The former history was written partly in the difficult Chinese script and partly in Chinese characters used phonetically to represent Japanese syllables of similar pronunciation. The latter work was written in pure Chinese, and it was quite detailed and involved. It not only incorporated the mythology relating to the evolution of the Sun Line but also included some metaphysical explanations for the creation of the world according to popular Chinese intellectual thought and philosophy of the day. This outlook emphasized harmonious relations among heaven, earth, and man. Such harmony, it taught, was to be sought in convenient groupings of a duality—the Chinese yang (the positive, male, bright element) and the yin (the negative, female, and dark element). This school of thought affected later Japanese historical writing. The *Nihon Shoki* commenced with a story of genesis in which heaven and earth had not been separated and the yang and the yin not yet divided. The universe was a chaotic mass, likened in a simile to an egg of indefinite proportions. Through time, the purer and clearer part of the egg became drawn out and formed heaven, while the yolk was transformed into the earth.

In addition to histories, collections of poetry were edited at Nara. Compiled in 751, an anthology, *Kaifuso* (*Fond Recollections of Poetry*), with a preface, contained 120 poems written in Chinese. This collection included works composed over a previous seventy-five-year period. Among its authors were emperors. Some poems sounded quite stilted, for they resembled copybook exercises of Chinese literary forms. Other poems, reflecting Japanese attitudes, reached a keen level of native expression. Another poetry compilation, the *Manyoshu* (*Collection of Ten Thousand Leaves*), of 760, contained 4,516 poems composed over the previous century. The work borrowed from Chinese characters that were utilized in a phonetic sense in most cases. Though some of the poems are long (*choka*), the majority of them are *tanka* or *waka*, short poems consisting of five lines with thirty-one Japanese syllables in a 5-7-5-7-7 pattern. Some tanka have impressionistic themes, such as the emptiness of human life or the beauties of nature. Others deal with a wide-ranging variety of topics such as loyalty to the sovereign, reverence for national deities, the weariness of frontier life, and clandestine affairs.

The basis for written Nara literature was Chinese characters, which had been introduced into Japan perhaps as early as the mid-third century. Because of the great prestige of Chinese learning and the lack of any native Japanese script, the imported forms were utilized by Japanese scholars. Inherent in this cultural borrowing were basic problems. Oral Chinese, which is monosyllabic, is quite different from the Japanese, which is polysyllabic and uses different sounds and pronunciations. Written Chinese hardly reflects the Japanese style of phonetics. One Chinese character stands for one sound in Chinese, but because there are more than 40,000 Chinese characters and only several hundred sounds or vocables, many characters are pronounced in the same sound (homophones) but in different tones. On the other hand, agglutinative Japanese words, like polysyllabic English, require several Chinese characters used in a phonetic sense to spell out every separate syllable to approximate the single Japanese word. Although some Chinese characters were adopted for their similarity to Japanese sounds, other characters were utilized for their ideas. *Kanji* are formal Chinese characters used for their meaning, and *kana* (of which there are two versions) are Chinese characters utilized for their approximate sounds. The Japanese grappled with these linguistic issues. The Manyoshu used the phonetic approach to Chinese characters to introduce Japanese words and expressions, but because there was no standardization of forms at this time, one Japanese sound could be expressed by a number of similarly spoken Chinese characters.

THE END OF NARA

After having settled in Nara for seven and a half decades, the court moved again. The Emperor Kammu (who ruled 781–806), championed by the Fujiwara, wanted to rule effectively and to free himself from the insubordination of the great monasteries, whose growth his royal predecessors had encouraged. In 784, he transferred his court to Nagaoka, thirty miles northwest of Nara, where, during a five-month period, with 300,000 men working day and night, a palace and royal center were erected. To defray the costs of this expensive undertaking, the peasantry was heavily taxed. Their suffering increased, and available clothing and food proved inadequate. Within a decade, the emperor undertook a second move. Bad omens had plagued Nagaoka, epidemics were frequent, and the heir to the throne, who had been exiled after palace intrigues, had died and his vengeful spirit had to be placated. In 794, the transfer was made to Heian (Peace and Tranquility). There the imperial capital remained, in later times known as Kyoto, until 1868, when it was relocated to Tokyo.

The Nara epoch saw the peak and the beginning of the decline in borrowing from the Chinese. Now geographically encompassing all of Kyushu and Honshu with effective control as far north as present Sendai, the central government zealously promoted Buddhist religion and art, which existed in concrete, recognizable, and vivid forms. The transplantation of the more complex, detailed, and less vivid Chinese political and economic concepts proved more difficult. Those Chinese ideas that could be pragmatically adopted or those that were similar or understandable to Japanese concepts persisted, such as the notions of hierarchy, titles, and court rituals. Those ideas that proved impractical or unassimilable died out, such as the concept of a strong state based on extended and well-structured economic, political, and administrative forms.

While the Japanese borrowed wholesale, they also insisted on retaining their own traditions. Bureaucracy was maintained through hereditary aristocracy and not through the Chinese Confucian system of education, examination, and meritocracy. The Japanese continued to emphasize the divinity of the emperor. They never accepted the Chinese idea of the mandate of heaven, which implied the right to revolt. As propounded in China by Confucian scholars, the mandate could be used against evil emperors, who, because of their immorality and injustice, became unfit for their office, which required, in theory, virtuous men to perform virtuous functions amenable to the gods. The Japanese retained their emperors and only changed their ruling families behind the throne. Despite heavy doses of sinification, Nara traveled its own cultural path.

CHRONOLOGY

708	First minting of copper coins
710–784	Nara, or Tempyo, period
712	Kojiki compiled
718	Yoro code
720	Nihongi or Nihon Shoki compiled
724–749	Rule of the Emperor Shomu
743	Private ownership of rice lands permitted
751	Kaifuso compiled
752	Dedication of Todaiji temple
760	Manyoshu compiled

764–770   Reign of the Empress Shotoku (earlier ruled as the Empress Koken)

781–806   Reign of the Emperor Kammu; moves to Nagaoka, then Heian (Kyoto)

JAPANESE SOVEREIGNS AND REIGNS

44. *Gensho*, 715–723; "Yoro," 717–723
45. Shomu, 724–749, "Tempyo," 729–749; abdicates
46. *Koken*, 749–758; abdicates
47. Junnin, 758–763; deposed and murdered by
48. *Shotoku* (the earlier Koken), 764–770
49. Konin, 770–780
50. Kammu, 781–806

4

Heian Japan

(794–1185)

The city of Heian took shape in new surroundings. Its geographic location was propitious, at the northern end of the Yamato plain, nestled on three sides by ranges of hills. It enjoyed convenient access to the Inland Sea by river. Roads radiated out from the capital in all directions; the most famous road came to be the Tokaido (Eastern Sea Circuit), popularized in later literature and woodblock prints. Like Nara, the new capital was laid out on the Chinese model but on a larger scale than the previous one; it roughly measured three miles by three and one-third miles. No walls were erected, but a moat surrounded the city. Broad avenues intersected the area into squares; the imperial residence, with fourteen gates, was located in the northern sector facing south. Most structures in the city were of wood.

During the first four centuries of imperial rule here, classical Japan reached its height, principally through regents of the notable Fujiwara family. So powerful was the family during part of the time that the subperiods of its history include a Fujiwara era. According to one classification, the first century of Heian Japan is known as the Konin or the Jogan (794–894), after extended year-periods of two emperors; the latter sub-era is designated as the Fujiwara (895–1185). Some historians subdivide the overall period into three parts: early Heian (794–967), mid-Heian or Fujiwara (967–1068), and late Heian (1068–1185). However subdivided, historiographically by around 1000 CE, the aristocratic central Heian government was changing into a state where provincial and local political entities were assuming greater importance.

POLITICS AND ECONOMICS

Although the Emperor Kammu tried to reexert imperial rule through the *ritsuryo* system of detailed centralized penal and administrative codes from earlier times, the royal position at Heian continued to remain secondary. Great families exerted indirect control over the monarchs. The first three sons to succeed the emperor on the throne were more interested in learning than in ruling. As the most influential of the families, the Fujiwara diligently promoted their own cause. They capitalized on their past affiliations or blood relationships with emperors. They cornered a monopoly on the interpretation and performances of the intricate court ceremonies. They arranged marriages between their daughters and imperial heirs. The practice of emperors withdrawing to monasteries (*insei*, cloistered government) began under Fujiwara pressure. Of the thirty-three emperors who reigned during the Heian period, nineteen abdicated (five in the ninth century), one was deposed, and thirteen ruled to death. Occasionally, because of the early age of imperial retirement, there were two ex-emperors living at the same time as the titular emperor.

Court life was concerned with much form and elaborate ritual. Like a miniature Versailles, the court officials (*kuge*) assembled daily. Social behavior and costumes were regulated to the minutest point. Solemn edicts fixed the color of official robes, the length of swords, and the nature of salutations. Women could wear no more than six skirts. The emperor and his ministers paid greatest attention to these rites and were left with little time to devote to pressing political and economic questions, a state of affairs that was encouraged by the Fujiwara.

In 858, Yoshifusa, a sixth-generation Fujiwara, assigned himself as regent (*sessho*) for a nine-year-old grandson whom he placed on the throne. This was the first time that a minor had been put on the throne and the first time that anyone outside of the imperial line had acted as regent. The Fujiwara went a step further in 884 when Mototsune assumed the post of regent (*kampaku*) for adult emperors. The tide was temporarily checked by the Emperor Daigo, in whose reign (897–930) the regency was suspended. The Fujiwara rebounded to reach their height under Michinaga (966–1027), who as their titular head (995–1027) married four daughters to emperors, and placed two nephews and three grandsons on the throne. His son Yorimichi (992–1074) acted as regent for another fifty years, and so for eight decades two Fujiwara in effect ruled Japan.

Respecting hereditary authority, the Fujiwara never usurped the throne, which enjoyed a theoretical yet special religious aura. By the thirteenth century, the family had so proliferated that its branches were known by inherited titles or by streets on which its palaces were located. Until the nineteenth century, regents were traditionally chosen from its five main branches (*gosekke*). Despite the appropriation of honorific titles by the Fujiwara, the family declined in political power after the Heian. Their eclipse came with the rise of other families and with the weakening of the powers of the central government, where the Fujiwara had concentrated their efforts.

Because of the changing nature of the Japanese political scene, the Heian period experienced modifications in the operations of the central government. The Chinese-styled offices established by Shotoku Taishi and his successors continued in form but they lost effective power. Such offices as the ministers of the right and of the left, the prime minister, and the councilors continued into the nineteenth century, but they became hereditary and lost political significance. A pragmatic realignment of political duties had become necessary because of the growth of important military families, the overall rise in population pressing upon available natural resources, and the accumulation of wealth and prestige outside of the capital.

By the early ninth century, three organs emerged to simplify and streamline the central government. In 790, an audit office (*kageyushi*) was established to check accounts of local retiring bureaucrats. In time, this office branched out to regulate tax matters, whatever was left of them, between the central administration and the provinces. In 810, to regulate court procedures, a bureau of archivists (*kuravdo-dokoro*) was created to draft decrees and arrange interviews with the emperor. About a decade later, to ensure law and order, police commissioners (*kebi ishicho*) were instituted. Police commissioners replaced the palace guards and the draft conscripts. From their original base in the capital, they issued laws.

The tax-land structure continued to weaken during the Heian. As tax exemption increased for the estates that had been forming from the Nara period, the central government received less revenue. More and heavier taxes fell upon fewer peasants. Akin to arrangements that developed in the Middle Ages in Europe, the taxable peasants commended their lands to a tax-free lord or monastery for self-protection. Through this process of commendation they received fiscal immunity. Similarly, in the reverse process of benefice, the peasant received certain rights or benefits for the protection guaranteed to him. The arrangements did not necessarily involve a change in landownership. These mutual rights of the holders in regard to land were known as *shiki*. Often several tiers of relationships were involved. A protector (*honke*) at court would provide the ultimate guarantee of safety and legality. He would bestow immunities upon the main proprietor (*ryo shu* or *ryoke*) of the land, who, in turn, often an absentee resident also at the capital, would depend on a class of managers (*shokan*) to administer the estate and provide the focus of management and of civic protection. Under these managers, the peasant workers or owners (*shomin*) tilled the soil.

The tax-exempt private holdings (*shoen*) of manor and field dated from Nara times. The central government tried to arrest the trend. In 902, it forbade false claims to tax-free status, and in 1069, the emperor decreed that all shoen without charters attesting to fiscal immunity would be abolished. However, the decrees were of little effect because the chief offenders included the high-ranking court officials themselves. Tax-free holdings of nobles and monasteries remained extensive. In 850, the Todaiji controlled some 30,000 acres of rice lands, or 1 percent of all cultivated land in Japan at the time.

These divisive trends in Japan led to the growth of feudalism, an elastic term capable of varying definitions in varying contexts. Feudalism historically denoted economic, political, and social relationships resulting from rights and privileges as based on land arrangements, the nature of which were described previously. In a broader political sense, feudalism implied a breakdown of central authority and the growth of small, divided, autonomous units. By the latter half of the Heian, both specific and general definitions could be applied to the Japanese situation. An economic base for feudalism was shaped through the presence of several phenomena. The continued growth of tax-free estates created economically independent units. Provincial landowners furthered their own interests by increasing their own holdings. Estate managers, representing absentee court or monastic landowners, administered lands and they passed on to the proprietors a share of their income. Court members, themselves in exile or voluntarily seeking to enhance their position, built up their fortunes in the provinces. From this fluid situation, new economic and social forces emerged in the peripheral rural areas of the country.

The latter half of the Heian also experienced the growth of military institutions in Japan. In the vacuum left by the decline of central authority in the provinces, local chieftains raised havoc on their own. Mounted and armed soldiers (*bushi*) roamed the countryside to prey on travelers and farmers. Pirates operated on the Inland Sea and along coastal areas. The Ainu proved troublesome, and the Emperor Kammu levied thousands of troops from various parts of the kingdom to suppress them. He gave command of the troops to the first significant military leader in Japanese history, Sakanoue Tamuramaro, who received the title of Sei-i-tai-shogun (abbreviated as *shogun*), or the Great Barbarian Subduing General. The Ainu were defeated, but the temporary military commission became permanent, to evolve in later centuries as the power behind the throne.

Clerical wars added to military confusion. Strong and militant Buddhist temples, maintaining their own guards of unruly armed monks (*akuso*) for self-protection, fought against each other, against the nobles, and against the court. Clans that were rival to the Fujiwara, which gradually faded to the background in the national scene by the end of the Heian period, began to contest for power behind the throne. Outside the capital, the Taira (or Heike) and the Minamoto (Genji), both distantly related to the imperial house, clashed with each other in the latter half of the twelfth century. In the course of what amounted to a thirty-year war, the two clans fought it out for military supremacy, as the politically and culturally oriented Fujiwara at the capital receded in influence. The fortunes of war varied. In the Hogen War of 1156 and the Heiji War three years later (both year periods), the Taira twice vanquished the Minamoto. Over the next two decades, principally under Kiyomori, the clan leader, the Taira concentrated on affairs at the capital and appropriated Fujiwara court policies as the provinces were neglected. In the east, at their political center of Kamakura, the Minamoto, under Yoritomo and his younger brother Yoshitsune, regrouped. In another round of engagements known as the Gempei War (1180–1185), they emerged victorious and commenced a new political, military, and feudal period in Japanese history known as the Kamakura, during which they relocated near present-day Tokyo the focus of power while keeping the monarchy on hold in Heian.

BUDDHISM

Buddhism grew amidst political and economic confusion. Continuing the process begun in pre-Nara times, the religion absorbed native cults. It conditioned Heian art, literature, politics, language, and culture. As Buddhism became a more popular religion, it spread from the capital into the provinces with the establishment of more monasteries, particularly in Kyushu and in the Kanto plain. It introduced innovations in Japanese society, such as the practice of cremation to replace the custom of mound burial. Buddhism somewhat softened life, at least in the first centuries of the period. Banishment rather than execution was the recourse of justice, though the banished parties often suffered violent deaths in exile. The faith proscribed meat eating, but in Japan the vegetarian Buddhists allowed the eating of fish, a major dietary staple.

Buddhism affected Japan in basic ways, and Japan in turn affected Buddhism. Shinto continued to absorb buddhas and bodhisattvas, and the strands of the two religions were not separated until the nineteenth century. Buddhist egalitarianism was changed to fit Japanese hierarchical patterns in tiers of monastic organizations and in doctrines that emphasized several stages of enlightenment. There was a general relaxation of beliefs marked by a trend away from the Hinayana-inspired Nara Buddhist sects, in which each believer was to achieve his own salvation, toward the more popular Mahayana forms, which advanced the doctrine of salvation by faith through which the believer could let the saints lead one to salvation. More sects were founded, and in this era of institutional expansion and easing of doctrinal rigidity, two esoteric (secret) schools particularly dominated Heian Buddhism.

One was the Tendai sect, founded by the monk Saicho (767–822), known posthumously as Dengyo Daishi (Great Teacher). A few years before the court moved to Heian, he had established a little temple, the Enryakuji, at Mt. Hiei to the northeast of the town. This was an auspicious location because that direction traditionally was considered as a source of danger and evil. The monastery gained the favor of the Emperor Kammu, who may have relocated his new capital near Heian partly because of the monastery. Unlike the independent Nara Buddhist sects, the Tendai remained subservient to the court. In 804–805, Saicho was sent to China by the court to study the latest Buddhist doctrines. Upon his return he established at his temple the new school that borrowed heavily from the Chinese Buddhist Tiantai sect (transliterated in Japanese as Tendai).

Known also as the Lotus School (Hokkeshu), the doctrine emphasized that sutra as the supreme expression of the Buddha's doctrine, one that promulgated the bodhisattva ideal and glorified Amida, the Buddha of the Pure Land or the Western Paradise. It declared that one could achieve salvation through moral perfection, which was attained through meditation, virtue, good work, and scripture reading. Deriding the Nara scriptures as derivative and secondary, Saicho championed the Lotus Sutra as the one that purportedly contained the Buddha's own words. A strict moralist, organizer, and disciplinarian, he established three classes of monks at his monastery. The first rank, as the treasures of the nation and the most exemplary ones, remained at Mt. Hiei. The second and the third ranks went out to the court and into the countryside to lecture and to preach. His monastery spawned later famous founders of other sects and grew to a complex of 3,000 buildings by the late sixteenth century, when many of them were destroyed in civil wars.

The second chief Heian Buddhist school was the Shingon (True Word), derived from another Chinese Buddhist sect, the Chenyen. Its founder was Kukai (774–835). An extraordinary genius, he was a poet, artist, calligrapher, philosopher, and prodigious writer. Many miracles were attributed to him. A light shone at his birth; he could order rain and he could stop it; he was credited with the introduction of tea and kana into Japan. Posthumously known as Kobo Daishi (another Great Teacher), he was probably Japan's most beloved and best-known Buddhist saint. He came from a great aristocratic family who had opposed the move from Nara and so was disgraced. Kukai decided to become a Buddhist monk, though he read widely in other doctrines. At the age of seventeen he composed a book on the tenets of Confucianism, Buddhism, and the Chinese philosophic school of Daoism. In it he proclaimed the supremacy of Buddhism that incorporated, he declared, ideas of the other two schools. In 804, he sailed to China in the same mission as Saicho but on a different ship. Kukai studied at the Tang capital of Changan for two years and returned to Japan in 806. The Emperor Kammu's son favored him, and he was well received by the court. A decade later, he built his monastery on Mount Koya near Osaka, some distance from Heian. However, Kukai spent most of his time at the capital, and after the death of Saicho, who was first a friend and then a rival, he became the abbot of the temple that commanded the main entrance to the capital.

The doctrine of the True Word maintained the unity of Dainichi, the Universal Buddha, the idea that the whole universe was his manifestation and that all action centered in him. But the path to salvation, Kukai claimed, was through the True Word, or the final ultimate secrets that the master of the sect would impart orally just before his death to the one outstanding disciple. Full of mysteries, formulas, incantations, and oral transmissions, the doctrine emphasized the importance of speech as one of the three mysteries, the others being those of the body and of the mind. The mysteries of the body included ways of holding the hands and postures of meditation (Sanskrit mudra). The mysteries of the mind referred to the methods of perceiving truths. The mysteries of speech included the true words and secret formulas. These truths of esoteric Buddhism were absolute and independent of place and of time. Only the thoroughly initiated could aspire to understand them. Some of this doctrine was written out, and Kukai himself composed the Ten Stages of Religious Consciousness, which ranged from animal life through Shingon (he placed Tendai eighth on the list). The True Word doctrine was expressed in great artistic and aesthetic works. Vivid paintings with inscription-filled halos and many-armed gods (Sanskrit, mandala, a circle) indicated the schematic arrangements of its philosophic ideas and propelled the meditating viewer hopefully toward enlightenment.

Some doctrinal amalgamation between the two main Heian sects of Tendai and Shingon was effected. The monk Ennin (Jikaku Daishi) of the Tendai monastery of Enryakuji, who traveled in Tang China between 838 and 847, left behind a detailed and absorbing diary of these years. He combined esoteric with exoteric (popular) Buddhism, to release the secret doctrines to all. Also of the Enryakuji, Genshin (942–1017), in his work *The Essentials of Salvation* (*Ojoyoshu*), portrayed the horrors of hell and the beauties of paradise. Forerunners of later popular sects that stressed salvation by faith, these monks propagated the new doctrine stressing divine love and compassion. They claimed that buddhas and bodhisattvas could help one achieve salvation simply by invoking their names, especially that of Amida (*nembutsu*) or those of sutras and holy works, particularly the Lotus Sutra that worshiped Amida (*daimoku*). This more popular approach fit in with the politically fluid times in subsequent centuries.

As the Nara region had been, the Kyoto area soon became dotted with temples, including the large compound of the Toji (Great Eastern Temple) with the highest pagoda in Japan, as the main Shingon temple. Other Shingon complexes located themselves in more remote hilly areas, away from the distractions of court and city life. By their distance from the political center, with its ever-increasing involvement in factional and civil strife, they managed to preserve their physical grounds and theological independence. A few buildings remain from the Heian period. These include the golden hall and the miniature pagoda of the Muroji, a Shingon temple located some forty miles from Kyoto in a beautiful sylvan setting, and the Jingoji and Kozanji, also in wooded areas but nearer the capital. Religious sculpture continued to be fashioned in bronze, clay, and dry lacquer, but wood grew in favor in later decades. The humanitarian Buddhism gave impetus to representation of the gentle Amida, but the fierce Fudo, a protector of the Buddhist realm, was also portrayed.

CULTURE

While Buddhism flourished and expanded, the Shinto cult, though relegated to the background, also prospered. Shrines were erected throughout the country; a list at the beginning of the tenth century enumerated more than 2,800 of them, both local and official. The Ise imperial shrine remained the focal point of worship, but there were innumerable private and village places of worship. At least half a dozen different types of shrine architecture flourished in Heian times.

At the Heian court, an aristocratic refined sense (*miyabi*) in the cultural world was expressed. Beautiful natural or man-made phenomena evoked a feeling of sensitivity (*aware*), later to be tinged with sadness as many of the things observed tended to be fleeting or transitory, as a leaf caught fluttering downward in the wind. In architecture, palace structures, eschewing now the more ornate Chinese style, utilized unpainted wood; tiled roofs were replaced by simple thatched ones in many buildings. The so-called Fujiwara style of construction provided for light, airy pavilions connected by covered passageways, surrounded by subdued landscapes and quiet ponds. Most representative of this type was a Fujiwara temple erected at Uji south of Kyoto: The eleventh century Phoenix Hall (Hoodo) of the Byodoin, with an Amida carved by a famous sculptor, Jocho, associated with Michinaga and his son at the height of the Fujiwara power.

In painting, in addition to Buddhist art, secular themes expressed themselves in Yamato-e, or representations of Yamato in court scenes or selections from novels that were illustrated on scrolls, among other media. These illustrated narrative scrolls (*e-makimono*) came into vogue. One such

Uji: Statue of Amida, Buddha of Light, in Byodin (Phoenix Hall)

scroll, the work of several court painters in the 1120s, depicts episodes from *The Tale of Genji,* Japan's first lengthy novel (described shortly). Another, the Toba scroll, is a satire on court life and portrays humans as animals playfully cavorting. In the homes of nobility, sliding doors (*fusuma*) and folding screens (*byobu*) were decorated with Yamato-e-style paintings. The aristocratic culture immersed itself in such art forms and sought a new sophistication in ceremonies, food habits, and dress. Native tastes were reasserted in arts and letters, and cultural missions to China, of which the last had returned in 838, were officially terminated in 894.

Heian crafts were of varied nature. Lacquer and mother-of-pearl were used for decorative media on sutra boxes to hold Buddhist literary works, chests, tables, and other items of furniture. Pottery and stoneware continued to be made. Based on a Korean style, and dating to the Kofun and Nara eras, blue-gray Sue was high-fired and sometimes splashed with a darker glaze from ash that formed in drops on the ceramic while being fired. But with the Chinese contact lessening, no new strides were recorded. Metal works included bronze mirrors. Although few textiles have been preserved from this time, literary accounts descried the elaborate court habits of men and women, both of whom utilized much silk.

In Heian literature, the Japanese continued to adapt Chinese characters for their own use. Pure Chinese (*kanji*) was used for Buddhist and official literature, with kana as the phonetic variations of Chinese developed for use in general secular literature. Two forms of kana were formulated. Katakana, a pronunciation aid syllabary of some fifty sounds in which part of a Chinese character was adopted for a Japanese sound. Hiragana utilized a whole Chinese character abbreviated for the sound. These three forms of writing came into use into the twentieth century: kanji for ideas, kana as phonetics, or a confusing combination of the two. In 905, a book of poetry, the *Kokinshu* (*Ancient and Modern Collection*) was compiled on imperial order by a Chinese scholar and chief of the court library. Almost all of its 1,100 poems are the short, thirty-one-syllable tanka. It contains a preface, the Tosa diary (*Tosa nikki*), an early form of Japanese prose, written by an author who narrated a trip home to Heian from Tosa in Shikoku, where he had been a governor. An early feminine diary, *The Gossamer Years* (*Kagero Nikki*), chronicled on a daily basis various events and romances spread out over a two-decade period (954–974). Other diaries (*nikki*) were composed, as were prose tales (*monogatari*), real or fictional. Family chronicles, including those of the Fujiwara, were composed. Glorifying that family were the *Eiga Monogatari* (*Tale of Splendor*) of the late eleventh century, and the *Okagami* (*Great Mirror*) of the early twelfth century.

In the tenth century several novels were written. One was the *Bamboo Gathering Stories* (*Taketori Monogatari*), which told of a three-inch maiden found in a bamboo tree, her development into a beautiful woman, and her subsequent love affairs. Another, *Tales of Ise* (*Ise Monogatari*), revolved around the love affairs of young court nobles. The latter theme again was taken up by Sei Shonagon, a woman of remarkable talent and wit at court, in her *Pillow Book* (*Makura no Soshi*), composed about 1002. If lacking in great depth, it was filled with impressionistic accounts, delicate nuances, and moments of comedy as they related to aristocratic court life.

In a class by itself was Lady Murasaki Shikibu's *Genji Monogatari* (*The Tale of Genji*). Probably written during the first years of the eleventh century, it was the great masterpiece of early Japanese literature. It was a historical novel of complexity, magnitude, and broad scope, dealing mainly with the life and loves of Prince Genji, the son of an emperor by a concubine, who was the composite of all commendable manly characteristics. Underneath, however, lay the themes of subtle pathos, the transience of life, and the impermanence of human relationships. *The Tale of Genii*, as well as most other literary works of the Heian, though sensitive to beauty and to life, portrayed but one aspect of Japanese affairs, that of the luxurious and shallow ways of nobility. More virile and realistic life and leadership were emerging from areas beyond the effete capital.

Aristocratic Japan of the period focused on official affairs. Continuing to borrow concepts from China but shaping them to native needs, at Heian the Japanese evolved a system of government that met their requirements. The phenomenon of indirect rule by families through an emperor claiming divine status persisted, although the governmental structure became more complex, with the custom of royal abdications and the cloistering of the former monarchs. After the first centuries of political centralization, divisive factors became noticeable in the land. As the central authority atrophied, trends toward growing economic, military, and political decentralization resulted in the greater importance of provincial areas. Yet this very decentralization helped to round out Japan's geographical borders. And in spite of factors favoring regionalism, general cultural advances were made. Buddhism became more popular, architectural styles reflected refined states, art flourished, and indigenous literature enjoyed a golden age. Japanese life pursued several paths.

CHRONOLOGY

767–822	Saicho and Tendai sect
774–835	Kukai and Shingon sect
784	Move to Nagaoka
790	Audit office established
794	Heian founded
794–894	Jogan or Konin period
802–812	Campaigns against Ainu by shogun
804–805	Saicho in China
804–806	Kukai in China
810	Bureau of archivists founded
816	Kukai founds Koyasan monastery
ca. 820	Police commissioners inaugurated
838	Last official mission returns from China
838–847	Ennin in China
858	Fujiwara Yoshifusa becomes regent for minor emperor
884	Fujiwara Mototsune becomes regent for adult emperor
894	China missions terminated
895–1185	Fujiwara period
905	*Kokinshu* compiled
942–1017	Genshin
966–1027	Fujiwara height under Michinaga (from 995)
992–1074	Fujiwara Yorimichi
ca. 1000	Writings of Sei Shonagon and Lady Muraski
1156	Hogen War; Taira victorious

1159   Heiji War; Taira again victorious
1180–1185   Gempei War; Minamoto victor

JAPANESE SOVEREIGNS AND REIGNS

50. Kammu, 781–806; carryover from Nara via Nagaoka
51. Heizei, 806–809; abdicates
52. Saga, 809–823; "Konin," 810–823; abdicates
53. Junna, 823–833; abdicates
54. Nimmyo, 833–850
55. Montoku, 850–858
56. Seiwa, 858–876; "Jogan," abdicates
57. Yozei, 877–884; abdicates
58. Koko, 884–887
59. Uda, 887–897; abdicates
60. Daigo, 897–930
61. Suzaku, 930–946; abdicates
62. Murakami, 946–967
63. Reizei, 967–969; abdicates
64. Enyu, 969–984; abdicates
65. Kazan, 984–986; abdicates
66. Ichijo, 986–1011
67. Sanjo, 1011–1016; abdicates
68. Go-Ichijo, 1016–1036
69. Go-Suzaku, 1036–1045
70. Go-Reizei, 1045–1068
71. Go-Sanjo, 1068–1072; abdicates; cloistered emperor, 1072–1073
72. Shirakawa, 1072–1086; abdicates; cloistered emperor, 1086–1129
73. Horikawa, 1086–1107
74. Toba, 1107–1123; abdicates; other retired emperor, 1123–1129; cloistered emperor, 1129–1156
75. Sutoku, 1123–1141; abdicates; other retired emperor 1141–1158
76. Konoye, 1141–1155
77. Go-Shirakawa, 1155–1158; abdicates; cloistered emperor 1158–1192 (into Kamakura period)
78. Nijo, 1158–1165
79. Rokujo, 1165–1168; abdicates; retired emperor, 1168–1176
80. Takakura, 1168–1180; abdicates; retired emperor, 1180–1181
81. Antoku, 1180–1183; deposed
82. Go-Toba, 1183–1198; into Kamakura period; abdicates

II

FEUDAL JAPAN

(1185–1868)

In feudal Japan (an alternative designation is medieval Japan), patterns of political, economic, and social life rearranged themselves. Particularly important was the role of the military in central and local leadership. Civilian families, such as the Fujiwara, lost ground to military families, who, however, continued to exercise indirect authority through the imperial line at Kyoto. Mounted warriors and their foot retainers grew in social stature. After vanquishing the Taira opposition, the Minamoto at first managed to retain political control over most of Japan. In the latter decades of their epoch, and particularly in the ensuing shogunal rule of the Ashikaga, the country fell apart politically. Yet commercial activity at home, and with China, improved. Buddhism reached its popular apex. After Japan experienced its political low point in administrative fragmentation, in the latter half of the sixteenth century three strong-willed men managed to reunite the country.

The Tokugawa, who emerged on top in this successive country-welding process, ruled the land with an iron hand. Because of prior periods of extended civil war, the Tokugawa tried to freeze society at home and forbade contacts with foreigners in the land or those abroad for two-and-a-half centuries. They hoped to preserve political stability. Yet try as they might, the shogunal rulers could not prevent changes as the decades progressed. By the mid-nineteenth century, when the West was knocking on Japan's doors most persistently, the domestic situation favored the opening up and the modernizing of Japan. This led to the Tokugawa downfall by 1868 and the "restoration" of power to the new young emperor, who, with his advisers, embarked Japan on a new course of action.

5

Kamakura Japan

(1185–1333)

YORITOMO'S LEGACY

In 1185, after overcoming the Taira family and the opposing court factions, Yoritomo of the Minamoto family devised a form of government grafted on to the atrophying ritsu state. This government persisted well into the nineteenth century with only minor modifications. Yoritomo located his political center at Kamakura, a pleasant seaside town outside Tokyo, which had been his base of power. For the first time in Japanese history, the de facto or effective capital was located in the provinces, apart from the court, emperor, and regents. But Yoritomo retained much of the traditional political and administrative structure of the central government that he had inherited. He kept the imperial house at Kyoto, and he continued to issue decrees in the name of the reigning monarch, from whom he and his successors derived authority. Yoritomo did not eliminate the Fujiwara, who continued as regents at Kyoto, nor did he circumscribe the estates or ritualistic duties of the court families, over whose political affairs he kept close control. He maintained the provincial and local administrators in civil functions dating to Nara times. In 1192, Yoritomo received from the cloistered emperor, who had endorsed his cause, the title of shogun or generalissimo. For the first time in its three-hundred-year history, he transformed the shogunate from a simple military organ into an effective military agency of indirect rule.

Onto the existing countrywide administrative system, Yoritomo added his own family governing structure, a pattern that was followed throughout the country by his military retainers. Japan became a patchwork of decentralized units that were controlled only through a combination of strong shogunal rule and loyal vassal allegiance (*gokenin*) to it. This system of government presumed some elements of a feudal system, wherein those hereditary military groups pledged personal allegiance and loyalty to the lord and received their lands as fiefs from him. Yoritomo did not technically endow his retainers with the estates as had been the case in European feudalism, because his warriors, as the owners or managers of the estates, continued to derive their titles to the property from Kyoto rather than from Kamakura. However, the distinction was negligible, because the shogun rewarded or redistributed estates as he saw fit, even if he did not assign the titles.

Yoritomo attempted to systematize land distribution by appointing to each estate stewards (*jito*), or overseers, responsible directly to him. Earlier, the Taira had to a limited extent utilized the steward system, but Yoritomo sought to perpetuate it throughout the whole country. Previously the estate managers had been appointees of the owners; now they became the self-supporting personal retainers of Yoritomo. Stewards were supported by *shiki*, or their share of the estate produce. They maintained peace and order on their property, and they performed the various functions of the local government. They also collected taxes even if the estates previously had been exempted from taxes, for Yoritomo did away with the tax-free shoen. Unlike the extensive lands of Europe, those in Japan generally consisted of small, scattered, irrigated rice fields. In this sense, these lands resembled the agrarian holdings of the earlier uji, yet they were also different because the communities on the estates were grouped less by blood or common ancestry than by the bonds of shiki, feudal rights, and privileges. Taxes were largely paid in rice or other produce, but copper cash, some imported from China, was circulated in the political centers of Kamakura and Kyoto. The steward emerged as an important figure in late twelfth-century provincial society, and the position, like most others, became hereditary. Yoritomo designated himself the Steward General. In time, some of the later lesser gentry and samurai or retainers came from the ranks of the stewards.

In 1185, to give some cohesiveness to the decentralized steward pattern, Yoritomo appointed one retainer in each province to a managerial rank that came to be known as protector or constable (*shugo*). These persons were in essence military governors who were responsible for maintaining peace and order in their provinces and for commanding the local retainers in wartime. The system again was not new, but Yoritomo endeavored to make it lasting and uniform. The post of military governor also became hereditary, and the holder sometimes doubled up as the civil governor of the province. Yoritomo became the Constable General. There were some irregularities and regional variations in the pattern, but the system worked fairly well, and it persisted after Yoritomo's death. The *daimyo*, or great lords, so important in the late feudal period and in the Tokugawa era, evolved from the constable ranks.

The title of shogun gave Yoritomo control of all military forces of the land. The administration to which he gave form was known as the shogunate or *bakufu* (tent government, a concept borrowed from the Chinese). At Kamakura he created three central boards: an administrative board (*mandokoro*) to act as a central policymaking body, a board of retainers (*samurai-dokoro*) to regulate the affairs of his followers, and a board of inquiry (*monchujo*) that served as an appellate court of final jurisdiction in the administration of customary family law. His courts developed careful and exact judicial procedures, and the judges appeared ready to implement an evenhanded justice, at least as it was defined by the military of the time. Through consensus, all boards arrived at unanimous decisions, a process that gave impetus to a Japanese predilection for collective responsibility and for collective decision making.

As a result of the newly imposed Minamoto family system on traditional political norms, complex groupings of administrative rights arose during the Kamakura period. Many of Yoritomo's retainers acted in several official capacities. As a more extreme example, one Yoritomo retainer in southern Kyushu, in the Kagoshima area that later came under the famous Satsuma family, was the steward of an estate and the constable over three provinces. But he was not the civil governor, and under the old Taika code still on the books, he was responsible to that officer. Because he had the effective military authority, he could keep all civil officials off his estate. He also enjoyed court rank, and he had obligations to the emperor and to Kyoto. Yet as vassal of Yoritomo, he could not present himself at court without the permission of the bakufu. The multiple loyalties imposed by court, Taika, and feudal laws were not easily reconciled, but the feudal obligations in the early Kamakura period proved the most overriding.

This emerging dominance of the military over the civilian authority had continuing significance in Japanese national life. Japan turned its back upon the Chinese example of the supremacy of the educated civilian bureaucrat in political affairs. In the Japanese tradition of a ruling, hereditary, and landed aristocracy that stressed military strength, Japan was more nearly like western Europe of the time than like China. Perhaps this was one reason why the Japanese adjusted more readily to Western stimuli in the nineteenth and twentieth centuries than did China, and why the military could have dominated Japan into World War II. In theory, the military organization continued to rest on a drafted peasant army and an elite corps of capital guards, but in fact the provinces and estates through local defense groups carried on decentralized but effective military institutions.

As a descendant of the ancient mounted warrior of the tumuli period and the aristocratic armored knight, the retainers of Yoritomo re-emerged in the twelfth century as a men of military prowess. Armed with bows and arrows, the mounted warrior wore armor consisting of small strips of steel held together by leather thongs. He fostered ideals of bravery and of loyalty, and the extrafamily ties that existed between him and his lord ranked higher than family bonds (quite unlike in China, where the family remained the strongest social unit). By the late twelfth century, his tactics included suicide through a process of disembowelment (*seppuku*), more popularly known as *harakiri* (belly slitting), probably arising from a fear, if captured, of torture and beheading by the enemy.

THE HOJO REGENCY

After Yoritomo died in 1199, his family did not hold power for very long. His line constituted essentially a one man's rule. Yoritomo himself contributed to the premature decline of his family, because he was very jealous of his close relations, including especially the position and military success of his sibling Yoshitsune, with whom he refused to deal. He did away with an uncle, and he had another brother put to death. When Yoritomo died, the only remaining close family members were two immature sons. In 1205, actual power in the form of a hereditary regency passed to the hands of the Hojo, a family ironically related to the Taira and from whose ranks came Yoritomo's widow, the strong-willed and redoubtable Lady Masa. The Hojo, from Izu province, proved to be astute advisers, and Lady Masa's father became regent for the young sons of Yoritomo, who in turn became shoguns. Both sons met with early and untimely deaths, and as the Minamoto faded out, three successive generations of the Hojo family helped to consolidate strong Kamakura rule.

After 1252, the Hojo, who chose not to accede as shogun but in effect continued as the real power in the bakufu in the role of regents (*shikken*), set up imperial princes as shoguns. During the remainder of the Kamakura period a confusing pattern of political power persisted. In Kyoto, an emperor resided, but he had long since lost his power to others behind the throne. All these royal factions in the capital were controlled from Kamakura by a titular shogun, who, however, had been supplanted in power by a Hojo regent. Japan in the thirteenth century experienced the height of indirect rule.

The court was weak and divided, but in 1221, one cloistered emperor, Go-Toba (Toba II), tried to reassert his power. He had strengthened his own military forces from the imperial estates over the years, and in the uncertain times that prevailed between the end of the Minamoto family and the consolidation of the Hojo, a showdown occurred between the troops of Go-Toba and those of the shogunal regent (the Shokyo War, from the year reign, or the Jokyu Incident). The Kamakura army quickly put down the rebellion, and the monarch was sent into exile. A more amenable brother was installed in the position of retired emperor, although he had never been enthroned. Shogunal deputies were stationed in Kyoto to tighten control, and the court was more closely watched than ever before. The Hojo confiscated royal and court lands and redistributed them to their followers. But they continued to show the traditional respect for the imperial position as the source of all legitimate, orthodox power.

For some decades afterward, the bakufu through the Hojo regents ruled Japan efficiently and ably. In 1232, the central administrative board drew up a written code, based on the preceding half century of Minamoto experience, to regularize the conduct of the warrior classes. Based on customary family law, this Joei code or formulary (*Joei shiki moku*), named after the year period, crystallized and epitomized military relationships. Not meant for the people, the code consisted in essence of a set of judges' rules. Unanimity continued to be the rule for arriving at decisions. Written in difficult Chinese, it included a solemn oath to be taken by the shogun and all his advisers, who were to be fair and uniform in meting out justice.

The code consisted of fifty-one sections. The first few articles dealt with the proper maintenance of Shinto and Buddhist sites and the observance of religious rituals. Some nine or ten articles then outlined the duties of stewards and constables. Several articles related to the tenure of fiefs and rights of succession. Property was to remain in the possessor's name, which meant the practical retention of land by military men since they occupied most of it. Rights were granted to women, who had begun managing estates while their husbands were away at war. Women could adopt heirs, hold fiefs, and even obtain divorces. Some articles outlined contractual relations; others regulated personal relationships. Punishments were prescribed for breaches of the peace. The code reflected actual conditions of feudalism and was grounded in practical experience. Unlike earlier imperial codes, this was not a Chinese importation but rather a pragmatic response to existing situations.

In the countryside, peasant life continued much the same. Little was written about the farmers or their unglamorous lives. The lowest classes were tillers of the land and workers in corporations and guilds. Some peasants had minimal property rights, but there was no real improvement in their status. The distinction between the farmer and the foot soldier was not very clear in this period, for often the two were identical. In time of peace the farmer was a cultivator; in time of war he became a soldier. The line between commoner and foot warrior, as differentiated from the mounted warrior, blurred. But the lower classes, because of the economic and military necessities of the time, were incorporated into a leavening society to a greater degree than they had been previously. For the first time, their life and activities were portrayed in some picture scrolls of the period.

RELIGION AND CULTURE

The Kamakura era was marked by striking developments in Japanese religion. Originally the faith had been the property of aristocrats in the capital and of the great monasteries. In the course of time, however, Buddhism spread to the provinces, and it began to penetrate the lower social strata. Buddhism was becoming a popular religion, and it was taking on distinctively Japanese forms. The leaders of the new sects were chiefly of humble origin, and they wrote in simple Japanese. More Buddhist schools were founded and more of their doctrines became intelligible to the common man. Both the masses and the military responded to the new versions. Some converts looked for escape from the endemic warfare of the age; others sought easier paths to salvation. For some, Buddhism filled a void; for others, it offered a consolation of, or a discipline for, the spirit.

One central feature of some of the new schools that appealed to the ordinary Japanese was the concept of salvation by faith in a buddha or a bodhisattva. This belief had found earlier expression, but not until the Kamakura did it give rise to distinct schools in this period of warfare, pessimism, and the possible advent of the millennium or *mappo*. In 1175, Honen (1133–1212), a monk from Mt. Hiei, founded the Jodo (Pure Land) sect, which emphasized faith and salvation in the pure land, the western paradise, of the Buddha Amida. A derivative of a similar Chinese Buddhist school called Qingdu, it maintained that salvation would be achieved simply by a repetitious invocation or *nembutsu* of Amida's name, Namu Amida Butsu. The faith was simple; it involved no temples, no priesthood, and no ritual. The simplicity elicited violent reaction from the older more traditional sects. Honen was sent into temporary exile by the court, an act that marked an unusual instance of persecution and intolerance in the otherwise accommodating annals of Japanese Buddhism.

One of Honen's followers, Shinran (1173–1262), carried the idea further in his Jodo Shinshu (True Pure Land) sect, sometimes designated simply as the True (Shin) sect. Discarding the idea of a repetitious cycle of Amida's name, he maintained that only one wholehearted and sincere invocation of Amida was sufficient to ensure salvation in the western paradise. Elaborating on the element of simplicity, he discarded any monastic church organization and most of the Buddhist scriptures or sutras. He preached the faith to the masses through evangelical messages. He permitted his priests to marry, to lead normal lives, and to mix with believers in congregational groupings. His disciples were to live as members of lower ranks of society and to be teachers rather than monks. Egalitarian at first, Jodo Shinshu grew in popularity but later developed strict hierarchical patterns. Later centered in Kyoto in the Eastern and Western Honganji, it attracted more adherents than any other Buddhist sect in the country. In time, offshoots split off from the Pure Land sects, including that of the Jishu (Timely) sect, founded by the monk Ippen (1238–1289). A singing and dancing priest who traveled widely, he popularized the Amida cult among the lower classes.

A third major school of the popular faith movement took the name of its founder, Nichiren (1222–1282), a descendant of humble fishermen from the Kanto area. He found the way to salvation in the Lotus sutra, rather than in Amida, and he taught his followers to chant the formula, Hail to the Sutra of the Lotus of the Wonderful Law (Namu Myoho Renge Kyo). Accordingly, this sect also became known as the Lotus (Hokkeshu) sect. Nichiren, a dominating personality, was aggressive, passionate, and highly intolerant of other Buddhist schools. His teachings were quite nationalistic in tone; he had never traveled abroad, unlike most earlier founders of sects. He argued that Japan was the center of the Buddhist faith and that his doctrine was the one true one. He damned his religious rivals. He predicted national calamities, and the Mongol invasions of Kyushu in his later years seemed to bear out his pessimistic and dire predictions. Buddhist concepts in feudal Japan as advanced by Honen, Shinran, and Nichiren, which stressed salvation by faith, a paradise, and a highly monotheistic concept of one Buddha or of

Kyoto: Nigashi Honganji, Jodo Shishu sect

one teaching, plus the use of vernacular in scriptures, paralleled in certain aspects the development at that time of Christianity in Europe.

The other dimension to the religious revival was the rise of Zen, the meditation school. Originating in India and termed *dhyana* in Sanskrit, it was transmitted to China, where it was known as Chan. Dhyana was adopted into Japanese phonetics in two characters pronounced *zenna*, a term later abbreviated to *zen*. Its tenets had been known previously in Japan, but again it was not until the Kamakura that it gained status as a separate school. It existed in two main branches. In 1191, Eisei (1141–1215) brought the Rinzai variation of Zen back from China, and in 1227, his disciple Dogen (1200–1252) introduced the Soto, also from the mainland. Eisei established his headquarters at Kamakura, where in later times one of the chief Zen temples, the Enkakuji, was constructed. Eisei also brought back tea from China. Known for some time in Japan, tea did not become popular until it was praised by the monk for its therapeutic values, later becoming the national drink of the country. Dogen, a more rugged individualist, located on the isolated west coast of Honshu. Both Zen variants adopted the posture of *zazen*, or sitting in meditation, which the Soto emphasized, and *koan*, an intellectual riddle (How do you clap with one hand?) on which the Rinzai focused. Eschewing dogma, Zen declared that enlightenment came through sudden inner experience. Its anti-scholasticism, simplicity, austerity, discipline, and close relationship between master and disciple appealed particularly to the military. In Kamakura, the seat of the bakufu, other Zen temples arose, including the Kenjochi and the Engakuji (distinct from the Enkakuji).

The Buddhist fervor reflected itself in Buddhist art. There was a great spurt of temple building. Monasteries throughout Japan became repositories of art and learning much as Christian monasteries had been in medieval Europe. The huge fifty-two-foot bronze Great Buddha (another Daibutsu, like the one in the Todaiji in Nara), representing Amida at Kamakura, was one of the more grandiose efforts at monumental art. Constructed in the mid-thirteenth century, it was originally placed in a temple, which was later demolished by storms; it remains an imposing freestanding outdoor religious monument. Multistoried architecture patterned after the Chinese Song dynasty (960–1279) models was reflected in pagodas and towering main temple gates. Although few extant examples remain from the age, there are the Shariden, a small scriptural depository in the Enkakuji at Kamakura; the Sanjusangendo (Hall of the Thirty-three Bays) with its thousand identical many-armed images of Amida in Kyoto; and the Tahoto shrine, near Otsu, a unique architectural blend of an Indian rounded stupa built into a tiered pagoda. Sculptural realism was depicted in statues of sect founders or prominent monks; these were mainly fashioned in wood. The noted sculptor Unkei and his son Tankei carved the two guardians (*nio*) that grace both sides of the main south gate to the Todaiji in Nara.

Many of the larger temples were decorated with picture scrolls illustrating their histories, their leaders, and their religious ideas. The Hungry Ghosts scrolls represent one of the more typical styles that illustrate vividly the tortures of the damned in the various Buddhist hells. These picture scrolls (*nise-e*, likenesses) also depicted secular life, and they provide us with data on feudal life and times. Historical themes and personages are portrayed, as in the portrait of Yoritomo in the Jingoji. Tea drinking became the fashion among Zen adherents as an aid in meditative vigils. The custom gave rise to the ceramic industry, which turned out beautiful but simple cups and pots to contain the hot liquid. At Seto, near Nagoya, an artisan who had visited Song China introduced a style that gave rise to the well-known Seto ware (Seto mono). Religious urges also promoted carving and lacquer making, and artistic items were offered as gifts to the buddhas. In the meantime, military campaigns fostered the art of master swordsmiths, and swords with their names inscribed exist today.

The Kamakura age made no outstanding contributions to literature. At court, anthologies of poetry continued to be compiled, of which the most prominent, a collection of short poems, was the *Shin Kokinshu* (*The New Ancient and Modern Collection*), completed in 1205. Travel diaries were composed, as were court miscellanies and records. A retired Shinto priest wrote the *Hojoki* (*Tales of My Hut*) that recalled court intrigues and the military turmoil of his times. Other realistic military tales appeared. These war stories (*gunki monogatari*) recounted chiefly the struggles between the Taira and Minamoto. One of the more important of these literary endeavors is the *Heike Monogatari* (*Tale of the House of Taira*). A true Japanese epic, it not only related feats of arms but also dealt with the theme of the evanescence of glory. Even military men felt the transience of power and life, which was symbolized, among other metaphors, by the falling petal blossom tossed about in the wind. Emotional and sentimental, the poetical prose was chanted to the accompaniment of a lute (*biwa*), and it became the source of many popular ballads. Two shorter volumes also dealt with episodes in the inter-clan struggle: the *Hogen Monogatari* (*Tale of the Hogen War*), of 1156, and the *Heiji Monogatari* (*Tale of the Heiji War*), of 1159–1160. In the mid-thirteenth century, the entire narrative was reconstructed as the *Gempei Seisuki* (*Rise and Fall of the Minamoto and Taira*). Legal documents from the time also survive.

KAMAKURA DECLINE

Although the Kamakura system of Yoritomo and the Hojo regents weathered the challenges of change for a century or so, in its latter decades it encountered serious difficulties. Internal circumstances helped to weaken the ruling line, whose drive and vigor dissipated in ensuing generations.

Succession quarrels at court plagued the shogunate, for through the last will and testament of an early monarch, the imperial title, often contested, after 1246 was to alternate (but not necessarily in sequence) between the descendants of two heirs, from whom derived the senior and the junior lines. While the shogunate endeavored to remain neutral, it could not help becoming embroiled in these court squabbles. Factional discord became acute, and the rapid turnover of occupants of the throne resulted at one time in five living ex-emperors in Kyoto.

Moreover, warriors' initial emphasis on simplicity and economy vanished with their exposure to court and town luxuries. With the passage of time, their loyalty, which had at first been given unstintingly to Yoritomo, wore thin to his figurehead successors. The warriors gave only lip service to military codes and ethics, and many found it easy to switch allegiances. Rewards and spoils for their service in the forms of offices and estates dried up. Retainers fell into debt; the financial situation became so desperate for the warriors that in 1297, the Kamakura government issued a general cancellation or postponement of the debts and mortgages (*tokusei*) of its followers. After four or five generations of Minamoto and Hojo rule, confidence in the government had broken down.

An external factor, the Mongol invasions (*genko*) helped to hasten the end of Kamakura rule. The Mongols, under Kublai Khan, who had overthrown the Song dynasty in north China, established a new ruling house in Peking. Consolidating his rule, at home as well as expanding into the weak border areas of China, as early as 1266, Kublai sent envoys to demand tribute from Japan. The Hojo regent refused to comply. After sending several more unsuccessful missions, the Mongol ruler resorted to force. In November 1274 he launched from southern Korea a force of some 900 ships with 25,000 Koreans and Mongols to land at Hakata Bay (Fukuoka) in northern Kyushu. The Kamakura government dispatched forces to counteract the invasion, but the brunt of the fighting fell upon its retainers in the area. The first encounter (the Bun'ei war) turned out to be only a one-night stand, for in the face of foul weather and heavy winds, the invaders re-embarked and retired to the mainland.

After this initial defeat, Kublai sent more messengers to demand submission, but the Hojo regent twice executed the Mongol's envoys. Busy with the subjugation of south China, Kublai did not return his forces until midsummer of 1281 (the Koan war). Numbering now about 150,000 Chinese, Mongols, and Koreans, the expeditions, in some 4,000 ships, proceeded from both Chinese and Korean ports to rendezvous in Kyushu, where the bulk of the troops landed again at Hakata. In the interim years, the Japanese had erected a wall around the bay, and the enemy forces were restricted to a narrow beachhead. For fifty-three days, the Mongols were held at bay, until a hurricane struck. A large number of the vessels were destroyed and many of the troops were stranded. Probably only half of the invading forces managed to return to the mainland.

The Japanese maintained the Kyushu defenses for another twenty years, but the Mongols did not return. Not until 1945, at the end of World War II, did foreigners again penetrate Japan, this time a peaceful occupation by American troops. Japanese valor, geography, and climate factors helped to defeat the Mongols. The Japanese themselves usually ascribed their successes to their insularity and uniqueness as a divinely protected land (*shinkoku*), buttressed by the notion that the hurricane, called *kamikaze* (divine wind) destroyed the enemy. The invasions were vividly and impressionistically recorded in the so-called Mongol Scroll, which, composed by an artist who had witnessed the events or who had drawn on eyewitness accounts, depicted fighting scenes. The many claims for rewards and spoils by the Kamakura retainers who had helped repel the invaders went unheeded and contributed further to disenchantment with the shogunal regents.

The final blow that overthrew the Kamakura came from Kyoto. At court, the junior and senior lines had become involved in another of many succession disputes, and the shogunate interfered in the contest. This interference was resented by the reigning emperor, Go-Daigo (Daigo II), who wanted to keep the succession in this branch, the junior line, of the family. He was one of the few ambitious monarchs in Japanese history. In 1321, he ended the time-honored custom of cloistered emperors wielding power behind the throne. Four years later, at the instigation of a Zen master, he dispatched the first official embassy since the Tang to Mongol China, no longer a threat in its waning decades. Most audaciously, he desired independence from Kamakura as well, and rallied some of the court and military to his cause.

In 1331, when the shogunate attempted to force his premature retirement, the emperor went into open rebellion (the Genko War, after the year period). At first, he enjoyed considerable success, but Kamakura forces captured him and exiled him to a remote island. Revolts by imperial partisans continued, and in 1333 Go-Daigo escaped and continued the fighting. The Kamakura general, Ashikaga Takauji, sent to capture him, proved a turncoat. He switched loyalties, pledged allegiance to the emperor, and seized Kyoto for the monarch. Events moved quickly, and in the ensuing military turmoil, Kamakura was captured and burned by antishogunal forces. That same year, the Hojo regency came to an end. Japan entered the Ashikaga era, a new politically and militarily confusing period that constituted another two-and-a-half centuries of feudalism.

The Kamakura period chronicled the height of indirect rule with the existence of emperors, cloistered and retired emperors, regents, shoguns, and shogunal regents. The unwieldy chain of command could operate effectively only when exercised by strong men in top posts. This proved to be the case during Minamoto Yoritomo's effective shogunate and the early Hojo regency, although the system broke down in later decades with lesser men and the attrition of time. With the growing decentralization of power in the central organs of government came the increasing importance of regional forces, such as the constables, stewards, and warriors. Political and economic power spread countrywide, as did culture. Buddhism experienced its height in conversions, formed its most popular sects, and brought continued realistic and artistic expressions of its faith. Yet despite the rapid spread of the pacifistic religion, militarism was pronounced. Retainers, warriors, and lords provided the backdrop to the militant life. With the growing insecurity, and often left to fend for themselves and for their estates, they assumed more duties and powers of necessity in their respective domains, which were scattered throughout Japan. Japanese history became more complex and multifaceted.

CHRONOLOGY

960–1279	Song dynasty in China
1133–1212	Honen, founder of Jodo sect
1141–1215	Eisei, founder of Rinzai sect of Zen
1173–1262	Shinran, founder of Jodo Shinshu sect
1192	Yoritomo appointed as shogun
1200–1253	Hogen, founder of Soto sect of Zen
1205	Hojo family as regents; *Shin Kokinshu* compiled
1221	Go-Toba rebellion (the Shokyu War, or Jokyu Incident)
1222–1282	Nichiren, founder of Lotus sect
1232	Joei code
1239–1289	Monk Ippen and Jishu (Timely) sect
1246	Inauguration of senior and junior imperial lines
1274, 1281	Mongol invasions
1279–1368	Mongol dynasty in China
1297	Shogunate cancels or postpones debts or mortgage payments of followers
1331–1333	Rebellions of Go-Daigo (Genko war)
1333	Kamakura period ends

JAPANESE SOVEREIGNS AND REIGNS

82. Go-Toba, 1183–1198; from Heian period; abdicates; cloistered emperor, 1198–1211
83. Tsuchimikado, 1198–1210; abdicates
84. Juntoku, 1210–1221; abdicates
85. Chukyo, 1221 (70 days); deposed (known also as Kanenari)
86. Go-Horikawa, 1221–1232; cloistered emperor, 1232–1234; Go Takakura, 1221–1223, cloistered emperor but never on throne
87. Shijo, 1232–1242

88. Go-Saga, 1232–1242; abdicates; initiates senior and junior lines; retired emperor, 1246–1272
89. Go-Fukakusa, senior line, 1246–1259, abdicates; retired emperor, 1288–1301
90. Kameyama, junior line, 1259–1274; abdicates; retired emperor, 1274–1287
91. Go-Uda, junior line, 1274–1287; abdicates; retired emperor, 1301–1308
92. Fushimi, senior line, 1288–1298; abdicates
93. Go-Fushimi, senior line, 1298–1301; abdicates
94. Go-Nijo, junior line, 1301–1308
95. Hanazono, senior line, 1308–1318; abdicates
96. Go-Daigo, junior line, 1318–1339; into Ashikaga period

KAMAKURA APPOINTED SHOGUNS

1. Minamoto Yoritomo, 1192–1198
2. Minamoto Yori-iye, 1199–1202; abdicates
3. Minamoto Sanetomo, 1203–1218
4. Fujiwara no Yoritsune, 1219–1243; abdicates
5. Fujiwara no Yoritsugu, 1244–1251; abdicates
6. Prince Munetaka, 1252–1265; abdicates
7. Prince Koreyasu, 1266–1288; abdicates
8. Prince Hisa-akira, 1289–1307; abdicates
9. Prince Morikuni, 1308–1333

HOJO REGENTS (SHIKKEN)

1. Tokimasa, 1203–1205; abdicates
2. Yoshitoki, 1205–1224; abdicates
3. Yasutoki, 1224–1242
4. Tsunetoki, 1242–1246
5. Tokoyori, 1246–1256
6. Nagatoki, 1256–1264
7. Masamura, 1264–1268
8. Tokimune, 1268–1284
9. Sadatoki, 1284–1301
10. Morotaki, 1301–1311, followed by four regents in five years
11. Takatoki, 1316–1326

6

Ashikaga Japan

(1333–1603)

Aided by his new Ashikaga ally, the victorious monarch, Go-Daigo, planned to reestablish imperial control over Japan. In the three years 1333–1336 (the Kemmu Restoration, *Kemmu no chuko*), he busied himself at Kyoto with reviving civilian government and appointing nobles to high offices. But the court had neither the troops nor the resources to govern the country. Ashikaga Takauji, after eliminating his chief military rivals, again proved opportunistic and seized Kyoto in 1336. He supported a member of the senior branch of royalty to the throne, and Go-Daigo, of the junior faction, fled with some of his supporters south to Yoshino, located in the mountains near Nara, where he established his capital. Japan had now two rival courts (Nambuko-cho) at two capitals, the southern court (Nancho) and the northern court (Hokucho), a political phenomenon that lasted for half a century.

In 1338, Takauji appointed himself shogun, a position that his family retained in Kyoto until 1573. But his shogunate differed from that of Yoritomo. Where the Minamoto and the early Hojo had maintained effective control over all of Japan's many feudal families, and the retainers owed them loyalty, at least in the initial half of their regime, the Ashikaga never exercised effective control over the warrior class as a whole but only over their few supporters. They kept the Kamakura government structure, but it soon became inoperative except in the Kyoto area. Provincial figures (especially the military governors and the stewards, in charge of tax receipts) emerged as powerful competitors for central political power.

STRIFE

Military chaos and political decentralization followed the accession of Takauji as shogun. A half century of general strife ensued; succession disputes divided the northern and southern courts. Many noble families changed allegiance at will. The whole land was in a state of commotion and strife. It was an age of turncoats and opportunism as many quickly amassed great fortunes and lands and just as quickly lost them. New lords suddenly emerged; defeats shortly after plunged them once again into oblivion. One family, the Yamana, who in 1390 managed to gain control over eleven provinces, a domain equivalent to one-sixth of the land area of Japan, was subsequently defeated by the Ashikaga and reduced to governing two provinces. From Kyoto, the Ashikaga ruled these few areas, which they controlled effectively. They established their headquarters in the Muromachi section from 1392 to 1573 (the Ashikaga period in this shorter time frame is alternatively designated as Muromachi). In the capital they maintained their power and controlled the imperial court more effectively than had the Hojo, but political disintegration continued in the countryside. There was little or no obedience to central authority; loyalty, if it existed, was extended only to the immediate lord.

In 1392, the third Ashikaga shogun, Yoshimitsu, persuaded the southern court to return to Kyoto, and he pledged that the throne would again alternate between the two branches. The court returned, but the shogun did not live up to his promise. Go-Daigo's junior line never occupied the throne again and eventually disappeared, though some Japanese historians have claimed it as the legitimate one. The later Ashikaga-sponsored emperors were weak and impoverished for lack of imperial funds. One monarch was reduced to selling specimens of his calligraphy on the streets of the capital. Another remained unburied for six weeks.

Factional strife continued, and the first half of the Ashikaga period experienced a variety of domestic disturbances. Some fighting was predicated on political grounds. Shoguns allied with or pitted themselves against provincial and feudal lords, especially the shugo, the regional military figures left over from the Kamakura. Lords, backed by their retainers, took on each other. Because no dominating feudal family emerged until the mid-sixteenth century, autonomous feudal entities ruled their own vassals according to their own laws. Economic unrest, following periods of heavy taxation and famine, also contributed to violence. Beginning to dimly realize their importance, peasants rose in revolt and attacked moneylenders, pawnshops, and warehouses. Agrarian protest movements on a large scale resulted, although they lacked leadership and sustaining programs. The peasants usually demanded acts of grace and moratoriums or cancellations of debts. They burned legal documents. These outbursts indicated some class antagonism to the military or civilian overlords. There were also Buddhist uprisings. Large temples and monasteries with their own military forces acted in an independent manner and sometimes established autonomous political administrations. Members of the Jodo Shinshu instigated rioting elsewhere. Because of their religious fanaticism, they became known as the Ikke (Single-minded) sect.

A low political point was reached during the Onin War (1467–1477), designated after the year period of the emperor, when succession disputes between two factions claiming the throne became especially acute. Fighting became endemic in the streets of the capital itself, and, in the course of the decade, Kyoto was nearly destroyed. Many of the court and monks fled to the provinces, a process that inadvertently helped to spread culture to outlying areas as well. But so destructive physically was this decade that some Japanese historians have maintained that Japanese history really began only after this period. The Onin War triggered another century of warfare, known appropriately to indigenous historians as *sengoku jidai*, a hundred years of warring states, a period of rapid social and political change in which those below overthrew those above (*gekokujo*). Smaller, more tightly knit domains, better adapted for survival in turbulent times, were established by warring states' barons (*sengoku daimyo*), the local military leaders.

The process of reunification was slow and tortuous, for in the post-Onin age of strife, the shogunate became even more enfeebled, and local lords acquired greater powers. Later evolving into the daimyo, these lords were despots or petty kings. Each had his strict house laws to govern relations with retainers. The captains of the growing daimyo armies were still mounted, but their position had changed from one of importance in Kamakura to subordination to great lords in Ashikaga times. In the fourteenth and fifteenth centuries, the foot soldiers became very important. They gradually displaced the individual knight as the basic military unit. Lines between warriors and commoners were blurred considerably. The distinction between high- and low-born commoners also disappeared, though the latter were replaced by the *eta*, or outcasts. The eta came from diverse origins, but the majority probably became outcasts from the nature of their occupations, such as tanning and butchery, which violated vegetarian Buddhist precepts against the taking of animal life.

Landownership, as well as society, underwent great change. Estates were reshaped during the Ashikaga period. Former private estates, the shoen, over the centuries were assimilated into the daimiates. Court estates shrank in size, and the nobility became particularly impoverished after the Onin War. New, smaller estates replaced the eroding larger and older shoen. They grew in importance as regional economic and political units, while villagers assumed more prominence in local administration as the basic units of rural organization. Enjoying considerable local autonomy, the individual or contiguous villages generally were located near shrines, convenient trans-portation facilities, or sources of water. Their inhabitants paid their taxes to the ruling lord, and they performed labor services for him. The old mana-gerial class on the late Heian and Kamakura estates became amalgamated more into the peasant than into the aristocratic ranks, but they retained importance as village headmen. In these times of political elasticity and growing land scarcity, a form of primogeniture developed to replace the practice of division of property. To maintain land and position in family hands, fathers passed on titles to one successor, not necessarily the eldest son, but the strongest and the most able natural or adopted heir.

COMMERCE

Domestic trade flourished despite military strife. A money economy com-plemented barter trade. Although as early as the eighth and ninth centuries the government had promoted a money economy, the effort proved pre-mature and failed. The government mint disappeared, but with the resur-gence of trade in feudal times, rather than minting new coins, the Ashikaga imported Chinese copper cash. The growth of a money economy coincided with the development of towns and of urban centers. As in later medieval Europe, commercial centers of varying types emerged in the Ashikaga period. There were port towns, such as Sakai, the port for Osaka, which achieved commercial prominence and independent municipal status. There were castle towns like Osaka and Edo (early Tokyo) built around important daimyo capitals. There were temple towns developing near important Bud-dhist monasteries or Shinto shrines (as contemporary Nara). A merchant class rose, probably from enterprising lower echelons of society. Guilds, known as *za*, dating from the twelfth century, also became important in the Ashikaga era. The trading societies, receiving protection from lords or religious orders, found new commercial solidarity among themselves. The widespread political chaos helped to unite them in a common cause within their growing urban centers. They began to develop along the lines of the medieval European city-states, but they did not become a powerful mer-cantile community as did the German cities. When Japan was closed to the outside world in the seventeenth century, urban society thereafter became stratified along rigid occupational lines.

Overseas trade, mainly with China, also received impetus. It had begun to assume significant proportions in the late twelfth century. At first, Koreans were the intermediaries in this trade, but slowly the Japanese themselves appropriated the trade channels. By the fourteenth and fifteenth centuries, they began to dominate the Chinese shipping and commercial lanes. Trade was both legal and illegal, private and official. Japanese pirates, known as *wako,* preyed on Chinese and Japanese vessels and became a serious menace. In spite of the insecurity of sea routes, the Chinese trade proved lucrative for those who participated in it. In 1404, the shogun Yoshimitsu revived official missions to China. In this resumption of formal contacts, he agreed to recognize Chinese suzerainty and to be invested as the "King of Japan" by the emperor of the Ming dynasty (1368–1644), which had replaced the Mongol in China. For this submissive act, he earned the condemnation of later Japanese historians. According to the terms of the treaty, the Japanese were to send every decade a mission of two ships to China. But instead of one mission Yoshimitsu dispatched six embassies in as many years. In 1411, his son terminated the agreement, but trade was resumed in 1432 and lasted until 1549. In these 117 years, eleven official embassies, consisting of up to nine vessels each, sailed to China.

In this international trade, Japan imported tropical products, manufactured goods, and luxury items such as silks, porcelain, books, works of art, and copper cash. Japan exported sulphur, lumber, gold, pearls, mercury, mother-of-pearl, swords, screens, and painted folding fans, an invention of theirs. The curved swords of medieval Japan were in great demand throughout East Asia. One trade mission to China in 1483 alone brought with it 37,000 swords. Not only did the shogun and the court participate in the trade, but also the feudal families, especially those in Kyushu, and Buddhist monasteries, particularly the Zen orders. Proceeds from this China trade helped Zen monks to build monasteries, including that of the Tenryuji in western Kyoto.

CULTURE

Cultural inspiration drew from both civilian and military sources; cross-infusions from court and warrior interests melded into artistic ends. The shoguns particularly were the patrons of the arts and Buddhism. To bring order into the burgeoning Zen monastic ranks, Yoshimitsu designated five principal temples of the Rinzai sect in Kamakura: Kenchoji, Enkakuji, Jufukuji, Jochiji, and Jomyoji (*Kamakura gozan*). In Kyoto he listed another five: Tenryuji, Shokokuji, Kenninji, Tofukuji, and Manjuji (*Kyoto gozan*). Zen grew in importance and favor during the Ashikaga period, partly because of its participation in the China trade. Paradoxically, in spite of its antischolastic foundations, its monasteries became centers of learning and art. Zen monks, among the first to learn of creative culture trends in China, reintroduced the use of pure Chinese in texts and literary works.

They also led in the development of, though they did not create, Japan's first great dramatic form, the *noh* (ability) drama. Drawing on secular backgrounds, noh was given religious impetus. Derived in part from *sarugaku* (mimes or monkey music), a tradition originating in India, and in part from *dengaku* (Japanese harvest songs), noh consisted of symbolic dances and poetic recitations chanted by actors and by an accompanying chorus. The epics of noh have remained one of the great dramatic legacies of the Japanese. The drama unfolded on a bare stage with a chief actor (*shite*) and subordinate characters wearing masks. Entering from off stage to the left through a curtain, the players shuffled along a passageway to the main proscenium, jutting out into the area where the audience was. A few musicians sat in the back facing front, and on the right side was a chanting chorus of a handful of men who kept the narrative moving; these men faced the actors on stage. Intermittently moving amidst the action were helpers dressed in black (meant to be invisible), who changed costumes and performed minor functions. All acting roles were played by men, who wore masks to impersonate characters, both male and female, for which they were physically unsuited. Although the action was slow, and the painted scenery on the back wall minimal, the costumes were gorgeous. A play usually ran for six hours and traditionally was divided into five parts. Each successive act related to gods, a warrior, a woman, a mad person, and a concluding festive piece. To provide comic relief, *kyogen* (crazy words) were interspersed between the noh acts; these were realistic satires on society of the times.

Zen culture, through a blend of native tradition and imported ideas, developed other arts. Imported from China, these arts included landscape gardening, flower arrangements, and the tea ceremony. Based on the theory that universal truths and beauty could be appreciated through the expression of the intimate, the small, and the simple, landscapes and rock gardens became miniature replicas of nature as a whole. In this art, as well as in other forms, a spirit of suggestiveness in the object, coupled with a feeling in the observer that could not be directly uttered (*yugen*) was to be caught in indirect, intuitive, inarticulated responses. An early name in garden architecture was that of the Zen priest Muso Soseki (1275–1351), who, among other works, created the beautiful and justly famous moss garden of the Saihoji in Kyoto. Both dry garden (*karesansui* or *sekitei*) and the pond version (*nihon-teien*) existed; in the former, sand or white pebbles represented water; in the latter, the water, with bridges, rocks, and trees, was sometimes shaped in the form of a Chinese character. A famous representation of the dry garden type is the rock and sand version at the Ryoanji (or Ryuanji) in Kyoto, by an unknown architect and of uncertain date.

Bonsai (potted dwarf trees on plates), *bonkei* (miniature landscapes on trays), and *bonseki* (dry representations, as rocks and sand, on trays) became other expressions of the cultivation of the little. Flower arrangements, initially associated with the placing of floral offerings before Buddhist deities, in themselves became a fine art, and no Japanese *tokonoma* or alcove was complete without its *ikebana* (floral arrangement). In a beautiful but simple environment, the tea ceremony (*chanoyu*) also became an aesthetic spiritual ritual: often it took place in a simple, detached modest structure in a garden setting. This was one expression of sabi (or *wabi*), the Japanese sense of subdued, refined taste.

The shoguns might have been weak in military power, but they provided a focus for cultural leadership, and their courts at Kyoto became cultural centers. Of the fifteen Ashikaga shoguns, Yoshimitsu was probably the most active in this regard. Not only did he promote trade with China, but he also sponsored the arts in the capital, which under his shogunate experienced an outburst of cultural energy. In 1397, upon his retirement to Buddhist orders, he built as his residence the Kinkakuji (Golden Pavilion) in the northern hills of the Kitayama district (which bestows its name to his age). The beautiful structure unfortunately was burned down by an arsonist in 1950 and only imperfectly restored. Similarly, the eighth shogun, Yoshimasa, upon his retirement in 1473, built the Gingakuji (Silver Pavilion), in the Higashiyama area (Eastern Hills), also designated as that cultural epoch. Although the structure never assumed a silver face, it retained the designated name. These two buildings constituted the most outstanding examples of architecture in the Ashikaga period. Graceful and pleasing, the structures continued to utilize the light architectural forms of aristocratic Japan.

With Zen in the ascendancy, sculptural representations of its priests and deities were effected. Realistic noh masks were carved for male players, particularly for those playing women's roles or supernatural beings. Yoshimitsu patronized noh drama and encouraged its development through the actors Kanami (1333–1384) and his son Zeami (1363–1443). His successor, Yoshimasa, also surrounded himself with talented cultural men, whose ranks included the "three amis" of noh: Noami (1397–1471), his son Geami (1431–1485), and his grandson Soami (d. 1525).

There was renewed interest in Shinto as well. Overshadowed by Buddhism with its institutional sects, the fortunes of the indigenous faith persisted. It continued to compromise with Buddhism in its dual form; its shrines at Ise and Izumo maintained and promoted the ancient cult and deities; national gods were credited in part for the defeat of the Mongols. The misfortunes of the royal family drove conservatives to study, preserve, and protect the imperial lineage in troublesome times. One writer, Kitabatake Chikafusa (1293–1354), authored a history of Japan to advance the legitimacy of the southern Yoshino junior line.

Harking back to Song art concepts, Ashikaga painters sought to convey the essence of nature in a few bold ink brushstrokes, termed the *sumi-e* style. In these paintings the painters eliminated minor details, and they placed man and his works in small, insignificant stature so that they blended with or were subordinate to the natural setting. Josetsu, active around 1400, of whose work only one extant copy exists, painted in this style. Among the greater artists in this manner were his disciple Shobun (fl. 1414–1465) and the latter's disciple Sesshu (1420–1506). Sesshu probably was the greatest of Japanese painters in this tradition.

Other schools and styles flourished. The Kano school, commencing with Masanobu (1434–1530) and his son Motonobu (1476–1559), transformed landscape painting into an art monopolized by a hereditary school of painters, who as professionals worked on commissions from their patrons, the shogun. The school's adherents worked on a grandiose scale, covering screen panels of silk or paper with bright decorative compositions in the Chinese style. Kano endured as the paramount school of painters until the nineteenth century. The Tosa school, another hereditary line of scroll painters, was founded by Yukihiro (ca. 1400s) and lifted to greater heights by Mitsonobu (1438–1525). These painters took for subjects sacred and secular historical topics in the Yamato-e tradition. The imperial court patronized this school.

Military epics and court miscellanies continued to be composed in prose. Describing wars and campaigns from 1318 to 1368 is a work with the incongruously worded title of *Taiheiki* (*Chronicle of Great Peace*). A court poet, Yoshida Kenko (1238–1350), who later became a Buddhist monk, in the mid-fourteenth century composed *Tsurezure gusa* (*Essays in Idleness*), a miscellany of stories and personal observations. In poetry, the *renga*, or chain poem, appeared, in which the traditional thirty-one-syllable *tanka* was split, alternating three- and two-line units of 5-7-5 and 7-7 syllables, respectively. The chain poem, a verbal scroll to match the picture scroll, proved popular, and it became a game of literary art and wit to interplay the three- and two-line verses in rapid succession.

REUNIFICATION

Against the backdrop of political disunity and cultural growth in the sixteenth century, the gradual reunification of Japan proceeded. In the process of attrition, provincial leaders in some instances gradually amassed greater territory under their jurisdiction with the help of their sizable professional armies. As weaker and smaller entities disappeared, the geographic coalescence into larger units resulted in a countrywide reunification effected by a succession of three contemporaneous ruthless names: Oda Nobunaga (1534–1582), Toyotomi Hideyoshi (1536–1598), and Tokugawa Ieyasu (1542–1616). So prominent were they that the Japanese have usually designated them only by their given names. The latter two started their careers as lieutenants of Nobunaga, but each in succession as subsequent top military leader came to bring more of Japan under his sway. Yet their tactics were disparate. Their differing personalities were reflected in popular epigrams.

Of Nobunaga it was said, "If the cuckoo doesn't sing, I'll kill him"; of Hideyoshi, "If the cuckoo doesn't sing, I'll make him"; and of Ieyasu, "If the cuckoo doesn't sing, I'll wait until he does."

Nobunaga, the first of the trio, was the son of a relatively obscure lord in a province bordering Nagoya. A courageous and able general, he built his fortunes on his father's estates and branched out to conquer neighboring lords. Attracting the attention of the reigning emperor, who was seeking the support of a military man, he was invited by imperial commission to restore order in Kyoto. He accomplished that task, but he did not become shogun himself. Rather, he dominated the figurehead Ashikaga, who was titular possessor of that office until 1573, after which the shogunate remained vacant for some thirty years. Controlling the capital or heartland of Japan, Nobunaga from this strategic location enhanced his power. From his position as only one of many feudal lords, he rose to prominence through his abilities and the maximum use of opportunities.

Nobunaga located his headquarters near Kyoto at Azuchi, a castle town on Lake Biwa. After disposing of his immediate enemies, he directed his efforts against the Buddhists, who posed serious political and military threats. On these grounds, rather than on any religious antipathy, he used military force and divide-and-rule tactics to eliminate their strongholds. In 1571, he subdued the Enryakuji temple of the tendentious Tendai sect on Mt. Hiei, where he laid waste to the 3,000 buildings and slaughtered most of the 20,000 monks. In a ten-year campaign, Nobunaga conquered the rebellious Ikko sect in northwest Honshu, and he leveled their stronghold in Osaka. Buddhism never again regained a strong temporal position in Japan. Nobunaga could be cruel toward his secular and religious foes. He massacred thousands, burned captives alive, and killed noncombatants. Through forceful measures, he was master of half of Japan by the time he was assassinated in 1582.

Four of Nobunaga's leading vassals appointed themselves as regents for Nobunaga's successor, his infant grandson. The regency was a failure, and Hideyoshi, who had been pacifying west Honshu, seized power. Hideyoshi's own story had a rags-to-riches theme. Born of humble origins, he was a foot soldier, who, through sheer ability and the breakdown of class lines of the time, rose in ranks. Lacking even a surname, he adopted three of them in succession until he finally settled on Toyotomi (Abundant Provider). With his power base at Osaka, Hideyoshi came to terms with Tokugawa Ieyasu, who ruled the Kanto area. He conquered northern Honsu, Shikoku, and Kyushu in huge campaigns that involved up to 250,000 troops. Like his predecessor, Hideyoshi declined to become shogun, but he assumed the old title of *kampaku*, previously held only by the Fujiwara. Faced with realities, this family simply adopted him in order to maintain tradition. Although he located his capital in Osaka, he built a palace near Kyoto called Momoyama (Peach Hill).

Osada: Hideyoshi's Momoyama castle

Quite ostentatious, his palaces and castles were huge, ornamental, and flowery. He restored prestige to the imperial office and rebuilt the royal palaces. At Kyoto he erected a Daibutsu, or Great Buddha, statue, larger than those at Nara and at Kamakura, but it was destroyed in an earthquake of 1596. Artists turned out flowery gold screens, beautiful textiles, elaborate noh costumes, lacquerware, and several types of decorative or utilitarian ceramics, such as Karatsu, Raku, Shino, Oribe, Bizen, Iga, and Shigaraki. There were main pottery centers in Kyushu, which received fresh artistic impulses from neighboring Korea and continental China. The Tosa school continued as did the Kano in painting. The latter particularly flourished under Motonobu's grandson, Eitoku (1534–1590). Hasegawa Tohaku (1539–1610) founded another school.

Hideyoshi's domestic policies reflected his background. He ruled through the feudal structure of vassalage. Akin to Yoritomo's system, it centralized authority in practice, but the general permitted the daimyo in theory to enjoy local autonomy. Possibly because Hideyoshi retained the daimyo system and imposed his will through the lords, he was able to reunify Japan more quickly than otherwise would have been the case. Reminiscent of the Taika reform, he conducted an exhaustive land survey of all Japan and had the population registers kept up to date. In 1588, through a "sword hunt" edict, Hideyoshi disarmed all nonsamurai, and he tried to prevent those of common birth, as he had been, from rising in society. Through other decrees he endeavored to fix class distinctions, freeze occupations, and forbid changes in residence. He minted gold, silver, and copper coins, and he augmented military settlements with financial rewards to his former enemies. Although he stripped the nobility of power, he was generous to the court. In his latter years, a strain of megalomania became pronounced, and Hideyoshi turned to extreme measures. After the birth of his son, Hideyori, he killed his nephew, other children, and wives. As Yoritomo had done, he practically eliminated his family. Not stopping there, he proposed grandiose yet desperate schemes in foreign policy.

Desiring to subjugate China, Hideyoshi hoped to achieve this goal by an invasion of Korea. His foreign policy probably was motivated partially by a desire to divert attention from internal problems and to keep his numerous military followers occupied. China was an attractive magnet, and Hideyoshi in his grand, deluded dreams wanted it. He equated the subjugation of the Ming empire of some 65 million people to that of a domestic campaign. In 1590, he informed the Korean ambassadors of his plans of conquest. Two years later, he established advanced headquarters at Kyushu, and he gathered some 150,000 troops for the invasion. Though Hideyoshi himself never landed in Korea, his force of nine armies invaded south Korea. They proceeded north to capture Seoul and Pyongyang in the west and to reach the Tumen River in the extreme northeast frontier. His troops slaughtered thousands of Chinese and Koreans and sent their ears and noses back to Japan, where they were buried in the famous ear mound at Kyoto.

The campaigns, however, bogged down. The winters were severe, and the Korean navy played havoc with supporting Japanese sea-lanes. Included in the Korean maritime arsenal were the bizarre tortoise boats that confounded the enemy. These strange-looking vessels had strong roofs, resembling turtle shells, covered with iron plates and spikes, which covered the whole ship. Long and narrow, the iron ships were heavily timbered to withstand the shock of collisions. They had rams at either end and a battery of oars that could be manipulated in either forward or reverse directions with equal speed. Faced by a stalemate on land and sagging sea support, the Japanese negotiated with the envoys of the Ming, who had dispatched troops to Korea to help stop the Japanese. The long talks proved fruitless. The Ming rejected Japanese demands. Instead, they sent an embassy to Japan to claim investiture of the emperor, a practice that Chinese monarchs traditionally considered their sovereign prerogative in confirming rulers of neighboring lands. The infuriated Hideyoshi redeclared war, and new invasions proceeded in 1597. But the next year, after a brief illness, Hideyoshi died, and the Korean adventure collapsed. The men returned home, bringing with them Korean printers and potters, who were to enrich Japanese cultural life.

Hideyoshi's ambitions knew no bounds. He wanted to incorporate into a Japanese empire the Philippines, Indochina, and Siam. He desired a base near the mouth of the Yangtze River in central coastal China from which to direct his overseas conquests. He had two maps of the world, which in his times meant East Asia. One was on a folding screen in his palace, and another was on a fan, which, while in use, literally fanned his ambitions. Despite his foreign failures, Hideyoshi secured for himself a high place in Japanese history, ranking as possibly the greatest premodern popular figure. Many books and plays were written about him, and the corpus of popular literature on his exploits remained voluminous. His personality was domineering, but his domestic and foreign policies were based on his personal power, and some policies did not survive after his lifetime.

The five regents appointed to administer affairs of state for Hideyoshi's young son cooperated no better than had the four for Nobunaga's heir. Tokugawa Ieyasu, a stay-at-home person who bided his time in the Kanto plain, arose to the top in the ensuing free-for-all after Hideyoshi's death. In the struggle for power, Ieyasu won out in 1600 in the battle of Sekigahara, a town controlling a vital pass near Lake Biwa. Three years later, he assumed the title of shogun, and the country embarked upon the Tokugawa period, the last of the traditional Japanese political eras (*Tokugawa jidai*).

WESTERN INTRUSION

Concurrent with domestic controls came the outlawing of foreign trade, foreign contacts, foreign ideas, and the foreign religion of Christianity. By the time the doors slammed shut to outsiders in the early Tokugawa period, the Japanese had been exposed not only to the rich Chinese markets but also to the first European traders and missionaries. The Portuguese were the first Westerners to land in Japan. The traditional story relates that in 1542 Portuguese sailors voyaging along the south China coast were blown far off course to the shores of Tanegashima, a small island off the southern coast of Kyushu. They brought with them firearms, which they instructed the local inhabitants how to use. These came to be called *tanegashima*, after the island. More Portuguese ships appeared (they had already been in Chinese waters for some three decades), and the southern feudal lords took readily to the idea of trade with foreigners as well as to the utility of firearms. (Chinese was the language of communication.)

Commercial contacts with southern Japan were soon followed by missionary endeavors. The Jesuit Francis Xavier, who had been preaching in Asian Portuguese colonies, was persuaded in Goa by one Anjiro, a Japanese youth carried there on a Portuguese ship, to go to Japan to convert the people. In company with a brother missionary, Xavier landed at Kagoshima in southern Kyushu in mid-summer of 1549. He remained in the country for two years, preaching in western Japan and in Kyoto. The missionary was much taken with what he saw as sterling qualities—discipline and courage—of the inhabitants. Other Jesuits arrived to carry on the cause that included not only proselytizing but also the establishment of a printing house to spread the gospel.

In spite of linguistic problems, the Japanese at first received the clerics well, and Nobunaga himself bestowed favors on them. Converts were made from the ranks of both commoners and daimyo. The order established a home base at Nagasaki, where the local lord had been converted. By the early 1580s, the Jesuits claimed 150,000 souls, principally in southern Japan. The Japanese lords in contact with them were impressed not only with the firearms brought by the secular counterparts of the priests but also with the cultural aspects of Christianity. Some, for political reasons, saw in the new faith a counterpoise to Buddhism. Others professed to see resemblances to Buddhism in doctrine and in country of origin, for Catholicism had come to Japan via India. There were probably many sincere converts, as well as those who joined the church from political or economic motives.

In defiance of imperial and papal rulings, the Spanish followed the Portuguese into Japan. In 1581, when Portugal and Spain were united under Philip II, the monarch confirmed to his Portuguese subjects the exclusive right to trade in Japan. Four years later, the Pope conferred upon the Jesuits the sole right to enter Japan as missionaries. Although Hideyoshi at this time was involved in campaigns of domestic conquest, he sent an embassy to Manila to demand recognition of Japan as suzerain power. In reply, the Spanish governor sent two missions to Japan that included four Franciscan friars disguised as ambassadors. More Jesuits and missionaries of other orders arrived, and they were permitted to land on the understanding that they would not preach Christianity. They accepted this prohibition but violated it by preaching not only in the countryside but also in the cities of Nagasaki, Kyoto, and Osaka.

After Hideyoshi had completed the subjugation of western Japan, he issued a decree in 1587 ordering all Christian missionaries to leave Japan. Engrossed in other matters, for a decade he made little effort to enforce the decree. But he became increasingly suspicious of the political implications of Christianity. The idle boasting of a Spanish pilot to the effect that missionaries were preparing the way for a political conquest quickened his fears. He was irritated by sectarian feuds among the various Catholic orders, and his authority had been defied by open preaching. In 1597, he ordered the first major wave of executions of Christians. Six Franciscans, three Japanese Jesuits, and seventeen Japanese laymen were crucified at Nagasaki.

Other Westerners arrived. The Dutch followed the Portuguese and the Spanish, but they limited themselves to trade alone. In 1600, the first Dutch ship reached Japan. It was one of a fleet of five vessels that sailed across the Pacific by way of the Straits of Magellan, and when blown from its course in the central Pacific it sought refuge in Kyushu. The captain of the vessel, Will Adams, was of English origin. Because of his wit and maritime ability, he was employed by Ieyasu as adviser in matters of commerce and navigation. Other Dutch ships arrived, and a Dutch factory, or warehouse-residence-office complex, was constructed at Hirado, an island near Nagasaki. By the time Ieyasu had assumed the shogunate, Westerners had a toehold in Japan. Their activities and peculiarities gave rise to pictorial representation known as *namban* art, portraying the Western cultural "barbarians" who had arrived from the south. But they were not to keep their precarious position in Japan for long, for in the process of Tokugawa control and the self-imposed policy of isolation for the country, Ieyasu's successors put an abrupt end to their activities in Japan.

In a new era, the Tokugawa restored order to the country. They reversed the trend toward political and economic disintegration that had accelerated during the Ashikaga period, which had caused the loss of effective central control and the persistence of widespread and chronic strife in many forms. In these previously chaotic times, social and economic lines had been rearranged. Estates changed hands, landholdings grew or shrank, lords won and lost power, villages assumed importance as semi-autonomous administrative units, cities sprang up, and guilds formed. Commerce and trade registered gains at home and abroad.

Cultural vitality was maintained. The Japanese practiced popular arts, appreciated impressionistic-type paintings, developed early dramatic forms, wrote poetry, and erected architectural gems. But Buddhism had seen its heyday, and it was checked as a potent political force. Oda Nobunaga dealt the blow, and his two military successors continued the policies of eliminating the divisive forces in the land. Because of their cumulative campaigns, Japan once again achieved political reunification by the advent of the seventeenth century.

CHRONOLOGY

1275–1351	Landscape architect Muso Soseki
1283–1350	Poet Yoshida Kenko
1293–1354	Historian Kitabataki Chikafusa
1333–1384	Noh actor Kanami
1336–1392	Northern and southern courts (Nambokucho)
1338–1573	Ashikaga shogunate
1363–1443	Noh actor Zeami
1368–1394	Yoshimitsu as shogun (d. 1408); Kinkakuji
1368–1644	Ming dynasty in China
1392–1573	Muromachi subperiod of Ashikaga

1397–1471	Noh actor Noami
ca. 1400	Painter Josetsu flourished
1404–1549	Intermittent missions to China
1414–1465	Painter Shobun flourished
1420–1506	Painter Sesshu
143 1–1485	Noh actor Geami
1434–1530	Painter Kano Masanobu, founder of Kano school
1438–1525	Painter Tosa Mitsonobu
1443–1472	Yoshimasa as shogun (d. 1490); Ginkakuji
1467–1477	Onin War; initiates century of fighting (Sen goku jidai)
1476–1559	Painter Kano Motonobu
1525	Noh actor Soami dies
1534–1582	Oda Nobunaga
1536–1598	Toyotomi Hideyoshi
1539–1590	Painter Hasegwa Tohaaku
1542	Portuguese arrive; firearms introduced
1542–1616	Tokugawa Ieyasu
1543–1590	Painter Tosa Eitoku
1549–1551	Jesuit Francis Xavier in Japan
1568	Nobunaga as de facto shogun
1571	Nobunaga destroys Enryakuji on Mt. Hiei
1573	Shogun title vacated
1573–1615	Momoyama cultural subperiod
1582	Hideyoshi succeeds to Nobunaga's power
1587	Hideyoshi decree expelling missionaries
1588	Hideyoshi's sword hunt decree
1592, 1597–98	Hideyoshi's Korean campaigns
1597	Hideyoshi authorizes first wave of Christian executions
1598	Ieyasu succeeds to Hideyoshi's power
1600	First Dutch ships arrive with English captain, Will Adams
	Pivotal battle of Sekigahara
1603	Ieyasu appointed shogun

JAPANESE SOVEREIGNS AND REIGNS

96. Go-Daigo, junior line; carryover from Kamakura, 1318–1339
97. Go-Murakami, 1339–1367
98. Chokei, 1368–1383; abdicates
99. Go-Kameyama, 1383–1392; abdicates
100. Go-Komatsu, 1392–1412; court reunited under northern faction; abdicates
101. Shoku, 1412–1427

102. Go-Hanazone, 1428–1463; abdicates
103. Go-Tsuchimakao, 1464–1499
104. Go-Kashiwabara, 1500–1525
105. Go-Nara, 1526–1556
106. Ogimachi, 1557–1585; abdicates
107. Go-Yozei, 1586–1610, into Tokugawa era; abdicates

ASHIKAGA SHOGUNS

1. Takauji, 1335–1357; abdicates
2. Yoshiaki, 1358–1367; abdicates
3. Yoshimitsu, 1368–1393; abdicates
4. Yoshimochi, 1394–1422; abdicates
5. Yoshikazu, 1423–1427
6. Yoshinori, 1428–1441
7. Yoshikatsu, 1442
8. Yoshimasa, 1443–1472; abdicates
9. Yoshihisa, 1473–1489
10. Yoshitane, 1490–1493; abdicates
11. Yoshizumi, 1494–1507; abdicates
12. Yoshitane (reinstated), 1508–1520; abdicates
13. Yoshiharu, 1521–1545; abdicates
14. Yoshiteru, 1546–1564; murdered
15. Yoshihide, 1565–1567
16. Yoshiaki, 1568–1573; deposed

7

Tokugawa Japan

(1603–1868)

Stability

Tokugawa Ieyasu and his immediate successors were faced with the fundamental choice of resisting or accepting change. Recalling the previous periods of political disunity and of the terrible civil wars, they chose as their foremost policies those of political stability and national isolation. They resisted change, tried to control and freeze society in a number of ways, and suppressed many of the creative tendencies in the land. In these goals they were successful, for Japan was to enjoy two-and-a-half centuries of social tranquility and domestic seclusion. But these ends were achieved only at great costs, for the shoguns retained anachronistic forms of government and administration at a time when Western countries in these same centuries were breaking their binding medieval shackles and were forging ahead in domestic programs and foreign explorations. Some of the later shogunal advisers endeavored to introduce policies of limited modernization, but their short-term attempts to come to grips with changing times proved abortive.

SOCIETY

As Nobunaga and Hideyoshi had ruled from bases near their own sources of power, so did Ieyasu as shogun rule from his new military stronghold at Edo (present-day Tokyo) on the fertile Kanto plain. Just as the Minamoto and the Hojo regents had also previously ruled at Kamakura some distance from Kyoto, so did the Tokugawa establish themselves in familiar territory away from the imperial capital. From their great fortress complex, the fifteen Tokugawa shoguns governed Japan. Protected by wide moats, great embankments, and stone walls, the shogunal fortress was arranged in a series of concentric structures with an overall diameter of more than two miles. The inner circles of the great fort now constitute the imperial palace in the center of Tokyo, where the emperor and court, having remained in Kyoto for almost eleven centuries, moved in 1868.

Augmenting this impressive physical symbol of shogunal rule was the centralized administration at Edo, composed of a variety of positions and organs to serve the shogun. At the top of the political structure was a prime minister (*tairo*), a post sometimes left vacant by the shogun. A council of state of half a dozen elders (*roju*) advised the Tokugawa on weighty political matters, while a similar number of junior elders (*wakadoshiyori*) managed the affairs of the petty vassals. A large bureaucracy implemented the civil administration, and a corps of secret police (*metsuke*) spread out from Edo throughout the countryside to ferret out subversives and malcontents.

Located three hundred miles from Kyoto, the Tokugawa nonetheless kept rigid controls over the emperor and the court, which, as sources of potential trouble, were isolated from the daimyo. All previous shoguns had accepted the concept of the divinity of the emperor as the sole source of political authority, and the Tokugawa continued this tradition. In theory, shogunal powers derived from the emperor, and Edo rulers effected measures through the Kyoto imperial channels. But they stationed representatives at

Kyoto: Nijo Palace of Kamakura Shogan's representative to court

the capital in Nijo palace to keep a watchful eye on royal affairs. All visitors, prior to making appointments at the court or with the emperor, had to clear with these deputies. Although emperors were the sources of theoretical political power, in reality they continued to be weak. The practice of abdication returned, and of the fifteen sovereigns (including the last empress, Meisho) during the Tokugawa shogunate, ten left office before death.

The Tokugawa also imposed controls over the daimyo, or feudal lords, who were grouped into three categories. First and highest were *shimpan*, collateral families of the shogunal line itself. Outside of Edo, the major branches were centered in three strategic areas in central Honshu: at Mito, east of Edo; at Nagoya, near the geographical center of the Tokugawa lands; and at Wakayama, south of Osaka in the west. Then there were the so-called *fudai* (inside) lords, who had been allies of, or were friendly to, Ieyasu prior to the fateful battle of Sekigahara of 1600. They were given some liberties and a degree of autonomy in local affairs. Finally, there were the *tozama* (outside) lords, who had been enemies of the Tokugawa before Sekigahara, and who always remained a potential source of trouble. Located mainly in western areas, they resented their subordinate position; in the 1860s, some of them proved instrumental in the downfall of the shogun.

Through the principle of *sankin kotai* (alternate attendance), all daimyo were required to spend some time at Edo. Most spent every other year there, and they left their families behind as hostages in Edo when they returned to their *han*, or fiefs. Others spent only part of a year in residence. Reminiscent of a similar policy of Louis XIV in France, this double residence proved costly to the lords (a deliberate consideration on the part of the shogun to keep the lords in financial hardship); the practice usually claimed about a quarter of annual daimyo income. Rank and status heightened obligations, and, as a more extreme example, one rich lord maintained, besides his home quarters in northwest Honshu, four costly residences at Edo staffed by 10,000 retainers. The trains of these lords and their followers to and from the shogunal capital represented an economic boon to the country. Roads were extended and improved. Towns sprang up in locations where merchants, hostelries, and service professions benefited directly from these endless processions on the shogunal roads. Edo itself reached a population of more than a million before the end of the era.

All daimyo also were ranked according to the assessed value of their rice land production, the major economic factor in Japanese life. To attain rank as daimyo, the landlord had to record an annual minimal assessed yield of 10,000 *koku* (about 50,000 bushels) of rice on his land. In the early seventeenth century, Japan produced an estimated annual 24.5 million koku from daimyo fiefs of 10,000 koku or more. Of this total, the Tokugawa possessed over a third, or 8.5 million koku. They controlled as fiefs most of the fertile rice lands of central Honshu, as well as that island's most important cities of Nagoya, Kyoto, and Osaka (in addition to Edo). Some 150 fudai lords held about 6 million koku. The remaining 120 tozama lords, and others with holdings in miscellaneous categories, reaped 10 million koku. The most extensive daimyo holdings, which were tozama, exceeded 1 million koku, although the average lord had 100,000 koku. The size of the lands and the number of daimiates varied in the course of the Tokugawa period as families became extinct or as fiefs were amalgamated or divided by the shogun. Because of this economic factor, one based on assessed rice land yields, stringent social and military hierarchical arrangements, rights, and privileges arose.

Not only were the lords ranked, but all society was divided into occupational groups, who were intended to remain hereditary. Drawing on precedent from both Hideyoshi, to whom the Tokugawa owed much, and from hierarchical Confucian doctrines that once again became important during this period, the Tokugawa froze Japan's population into four classes. The highest class, numbering some 10 percent of the population, were military administrators drawn from the daimyo and their samurai (now a generic term loosely applied to the military class as a whole). As members of the hereditary aristocracy, the samurai were permitted two swords, a long one for warfare and a short one for harakiri. Second in rank were the peasants, the primary producers, probably constituting about 85 percent of the populace. Rated high in theory but in reality treated with disdain, the peasant in the Tokugawa structure, as in earlier Japanese times and in traditional Chinese society, lived poorly. Attention was paid to agriculture but not to the agriculturist, who bore the brunt of taxes and agrarian rents. The third and fourth social ranks consisted of the artisans and the merchants, respectively, who, as secondary or tertiary producers, according to Confucian thought, bordered on economic parasitism. Despite their real intellectual and cultural status, merchants were placed last because theoretically they were an unproductive class. There was to be no change in class for any individual, and distinctive dress, habits, and symbols were prescribed for each class.

A multitude of codes governed Tokugawa life. In Japanese history, each political era (*jidai*) or shogunal dynasty had its own codes, and in this respect, the Tokugawa were no exception. Ieyasu started the codification process, and his successors elaborated it. There were several basic types of decrees. One group of laws governed royal affairs. Consisting mainly of moral maxims, they enjoined the court to study diligently, to observe proper protocol, to follow regulations on dress and etiquette, and to behave discreetly. Other laws were directed at the feudal nobility. Also embracing moral and educational tenets, these stipulated that the daimyo and their military followers, in the absence of any campaigns to fight, were to redirect their efforts to intellectual pursuits, to the study of literature, and to the practice of frugality.

Public laws, posted on notice boards to be read to the illiterate populace, also were predicated on ethical bases, which were important foundations for Japanese legal and administrative life. Finally, overall and comprehensive codes, such as the Hundred Regulations of 1742, applied to all. These covered criminal and civil behavior, procedures to follow in filing suit, and sentences to be imposed. Decapitation was decreed for adultery; banishment to peripheral areas, such as Hokkaido, was imposed; and confession by torture through four progressively more horrible stages was permitted. The continuing rain of edicts sought to stabilize the populace. Augmenting the social measures were others that closed Japan to foreign influences.

ISOLATION

Westerners, initially welcomed by Hideyoshi and Ieyasu, were subjected to increasingly restrictive measures in the early decades of the seventeenth century. By the inception of the Tokugawa shogunate, a Dutch factory, as noted previously, had been constructed at Hirado. In 1641, the Dutch were forced to move to Deshima, a small artificial island in Nagasaki harbor. The English came last to Japan and left the earliest. They maintained an unsuccessful factory at Hirado from 1612 until 1623, when they abandoned it to concentrate their commercial efforts in India and Southeast Asia. The French had no trading interests in Japan.

Ieyasu initially reversed the stern policy of his predecessor vis-à-vis Christianity, and he befriended even the Spanish missionaries in order to maintain trade ties. But the nonproselytizing Protestant Dutch and English traders persuaded the shogun that it was not necessary to tolerate Christianity to retain economic contacts. About 1613, pursuing his goal of political stability, Ieyasu reverted to Hideyoshi's policy of persecuting Christians. In 1617, his successor, Hidetada, executed European and native Christians. Over the next few years, the persecutions mounted in earnest, and all missionaries were killed or were forced to flee Japan. Thousands of Japanese Christians were faced with martyrdom unless they renounced their faith. A common practice of the time to ferret out Christians was to order those suspected of the religion to tread upon a cross or some other sacred symbol or icon, and to execute those who refused.

The persecutions of Christians came to a dramatic climax in 1637–1638, when the peasantry of Shimabara near Nagasaki, in a daimiate early associated with Christianity, in desperation rebelled against economic, agrarian, and religious oppression. With leadership provided by some dissatisfied *ronin*, or masterless samurai, 30,000 peasants in an old fortress held out for almost three months against the assault of 100,000 shogunal troops supported by Dutch naval power. The Christian rebels eventually were exterminated. After this catastrophe, Christianity, which had grown to an estimated half-a-million converts, ceased to exist as an organized, formal religion in Japan. The intertwined political, economic, and religious character of the uprising alarmed the bakufu, and the rebellion gave impetus to formulating an exclusion policy.

Tied to the proscription of Christianity was the cessation of most foreign trade contacts. In the Tokugawa zeal for maintaining the status quo, the doors were closed to most commercial contacts, and, at this time, foreigners were in no position to retaliate. Although the English left Japan voluntarily, the Spanish were expelled in 1624, and the Portuguese were ejected in 1638, because of suspected complicity in the Shimabara rebellion. When a Portuguese mission returned a few years later in an effort to reopen trade links, its envoys were summarily executed. Only the Dutch trading post at Deshima, established in 1641, was permitted to operate, but the merchants of the Dutch East India Company were kept in virtual year-round imprisonment. Under close supervision, Chinese merchants also were permitted to visit and to trade at the port. Some foreign contacts were additionally maintained with China by individual daimyo who controlled the Tsushima Islands in the Korean straits and the Ryukyus to the south. The Tokugawa shoguns did not cut off all contact with foreign countries, but their policy of limited, controlled trade contributed to the later downfall of the bakufu, because modern foreign ideas continued to seep into Japan through Deshima.

Aliens were not allowed to enter the country, and in 1637, the Japanese were forbidden to leave it. Those abroad were not permitted to return, because the Tokugawa feared that they might return with subversive ideas. Another decree prohibited the construction of large ships that might be used in overseas trade. As a result, the indigenous merchant marine was restricted to small vessels engaged in limited coastal commerce among the home islands. The overseas expansion of Japanese trade and commerce came to an abrupt end. Many Japanese abroad were permanently cast adrift from their homeland, to be absorbed by the native populations of the cities of Southeast Asia. The dynamic quality of Japanese international relations, noticeable during the Ashikaga era, was thwarted, and the country closed at a time when Europeans were beginning to expand. Had the process of Japanese overseas expansion been permitted to continue, in the concurrent absence of similar drives in China, Southeast Asia, or India, it is intriguing to speculate just where and how the Japanese would have encountered and reacted to Western forces of expansion in Asia.

The West left little immediate and appreciable impact during Japan's "Christian century." Christian theological ideas were difficult to comprehend, and the social doctrine of individuality conflicted with vassal-lord relationships. There were political reasons for leaders to fear the faith, for the shogunate could reasonably project a possible alliance among the daimyo converted to Christianity, who then would also enjoy special relations with Western powers. Some religious opposition to Christianity existed in the central government, but this opposition was based mainly on political grounds and was not basically different from Nobunaga's bloody suppression of Buddhist orders. Not viewing their policies for the eradication of Christianity as peculiar or unique, the leaders of a reunified Japan treated the alien faith as a domestic issue. But in spite of the suppression of their religion, Westerners bequeathed some secular legacies to Japan. Firearms began to play an important part in Japanese military campaigns. Castle construction on a grand scale with massive stone walls and moats received impetus. The Portuguese contributed a few words to the Japanese vocabulary. Some new plants, such as tobacco and potatoes, were introduced. The more fundamental Western secular effects were not immediately discernible, because modern political and economic ideas were to enter Japan in later years through the Dutch base at Deshima.

EFFECTS OF ISOLATION

In its aim of securing national political stability, the isolationist policy of the Tokugawa proved successful. For two centuries or more, no major revolution, strife, serious disturbances, or grave incidents threatened their rule. Japan slumbered fitfully on in its ocean-protected, semi-isolated co-coon. The peace of the land was broken only by occasional and sporadic eruptions of man or nature such as fires in Edo, earthquakes, rice riots by impoverished country or city dwellers, and, in 1707, the last eruption of Mt. Fuji. Nothing occurred on a national scale to threaten the existing Tokugawa structure.

A good example of the carefully imposed political stability of the time was reflected in the true story of the forty-seven ronin that illustrated the potential stresses that could arise between samurai obligations to the ruling shogun and to their own lord. In 1700, a lesser feudal lord of Ako, insulted by a higher lord within the shogun's palace, drew his sword and wounded his antagonist. Because the act of drawing a sword within the palace was an offense that carried a death sentence, the Edo authorities ordered the lesser lord to commit harakiri and appropriated his domains. His loyal feudal retainers (*Ako-gishi*) lost their samurai status and became dispossessed men.

Forty-seven of these ronin vowed to avenge themselves upon the daimyo who had caused their master's disgrace. To quiet the suspicions of the police, who were anticipating such an act of revenge, they bided their time. Their leader assumed a life of debauchery to cast off suspicion. Finally, one winter's night, two years later, they reassembled at Edo and took vengeance by beheading their lord's old enemy and several of his retainers at his abode. By taking justice into their own hands, they had defied shogunal authority, but they became heroes through their self-sacrificial act of loyalty to their lord. Caught in crosscurrents, the bakufu debated the case for over a year, when finally it permitted the ronin to commit harakiri. Today, the simple graves of the forty-seven ronin lie side by side in a Tokyo temple compound that has become a national shrine.

The centuries of stability, seclusion, and conformity left their mark on the Japanese. The adventurous, spirited people of earlier centuries were transformed by the nineteenth century into a regimented nation. On all issues they looked to their leaders for guidance, and without dissent they obeyed authority. Patterns of social intercourse were firmly set. Society became structured and rigid, but the crowded Japanese managed to live together on their small islands in peace and with few outward signs of friction. Yet the feudal outlook and structure were preserved long after they had become outdated. On the other hand, in part because of the attitudes formed in the Tokugawa period, Japan accepted Western norms more easily than any country in Asia. After being opened by the Western powers, it forged ahead of its continental neighbors. Paradoxically, the Tokugawa legacy proved to be both a boon and a bane.

Tokyo: Forty-seven ronin graves

CHRONOLOGY

1609–1641	Dutch at Hirado
1612–1623	English at Hirado
1613	Ieyasu commences persecutions of Christians
1617	Ieyasu's successor, Hidetada, continues persecutions of Christians
1624	Spanish expelled
1637	Japanese forbidden to leave the country
1637–1638	Shimabara Christian rebellion
1638	Portuguese expelled
1641	Dutch move to Deshima
1700–1702	Incident of the forty-seven ronin
1707	Mt. Fuji's last eruption
1742	Hundred Regulations

JAPANESE SOVEREIGNS AND REIGNS

107. Go-Yozei (carryover from Ashikaga), 1586–1610; abdicates
108. Gomizune-e, 1611–1629; abdicates
109. Meisho, 1629–1643; abdicates
110. Go-Komyo, 1643–1653
111. Go-Sai-in, 1654–1662; abdicates
112. Reigen, 1663–1686; abdicates
113. Higashiyama, 1687–1709; abdicates, "Genroku"
114. Nakamikado, 1709–1735; abdicates
115. Sakuramichi, 1735–1746; abdicates
116. Momozono, 1747–1761
117. Go-Sakuramachi, 1762–1770; abdicates
118. Go-Momozono, 1770–1778
119. Kokaku, 1779–1816; abdicates
120. Ninko, 1817–1845
121. Komei, 1846–1867

TOKUGAWA SHOGUNS

1. Ieyasu, 1603–1604; abdicates
2. Hidetada, 1605–1622; abdicates
3. Iemitsu, 1623–1650
4. Ietsuma, 1651–1679
5. Tsunayoshi, 1680–1708

6. Ienobu, 1709–1711
7. Ietsugu, 1712–1715
8. Yoshimune, 1716–1744; abdicates
9. Ieshige, 1745–1759; abdicates
10. Ieharu, 1760–1786
11. Ienari, 1787–1836; abdicates
12. Iehoshi, 1837–1853
13. Iesada, 1853–1857
14. Ieshige, 1858–1866
15. Yoshinobu (Keiku), 1867; abdicates

8

Tokugawa Japan

Change

Try as they did, the Tokugawa shoguns could not completely freeze social and economic patterns over a period of 250 years. Signs of change and of growth were too pronounced to be ignored. Unlike European countries that sloughed off medieval concepts, Japan merely grafted new elements onto the old traditions. Japan advanced to another and unique stage in its evolution of feudalism, that of modernization based on timeworn concepts. Surface stability was maintained, but economic, social, and intellectual currents were stirring underneath. By the time the West arrived to help open Japan's doors in the mid-nineteenth century, the Japanese themselves were more than ready for a change.

SOCIAL AND ECONOMIC TRENDS

One aspect of change was the growth of cities and towns. This trend toward urbanization continued during the Tokugawa regime, which itself contributed to the phenomenon. Warriors followed their lords to castles, samurai concentrated in or near the chief cities in each of the han, and the processions of the daimyo trains to and from Edo favored trade. By the mid-eighteenth century, Kyoto and Osaka each had half-a-million inhabitants, and Edo itself a million. About twenty other cities had populations ranging from 50,000 to 100,000. In the first half of the period, Japan's population doubled from 15 to 30 million.

The growth of urban life was accompanied by an increase both in numbers and in influence of the merchant class. The merchants might have been relegated to a low rank in society, but they possessed the money and great economic power. Their funds opened up new areas to cultivation; the loans to the military, who needed money rather than grain to pay for their many expenses in both town and country, made them creditors of daimyo and samurai. While in theory the military-administrative group was the highest social class, distinctions were breaking down because of relations and marriages with lower echelons. Sons of merchants were adopted by military families, and sometimes the reverse was true. The cities were hubs of mercantile activity. Banking facilities flourished in cities; grain markets, particularly those in Osaka and in Edo, dealt in volume transactions and speculated in futures. Within the more efficient and larger daimyo and shogunal holdings, trade barriers were eliminated, and commerce flowed more freely along domestic routes than in earlier eras. The shogun's territory was the most suitable for commercial activity, because it contained the largest cities with the greatest wealth, offered the most protection, and had proportionately fewer military men and contingents to support than had the daimyo on their less extensive holdings.

In towns, guilds broke down into smaller and more individually run units, though merchant associations continued to fix credit rates, stabilize prices, and control distribution patterns of particular products. Family wholesale and retail commercial firms grew in importance. One of the largest private enterprises in the world today, the Mitsui, began in the early Tokugawa years. In 1620, the family was operating a sake (rice wine) brewery in the strategic area near the national Ise Shinto shrine. By judicious investment and expansion, it soon branched out to deal in rice transactions, pawnshop operations, and haberdashery outlets. In 1691, the family became the banker for both court and shogun, and through succeeding years, it continued to grow and flourish.

While merchants luxuriated, the military became impoverished. Participation in the good but expensive life of the cities caused the daimyo and the samurai to fall into debt. The daimyo received their chief income from the land taxes, which constituted a certain percentage of the produce of the peasant, though in the latter years of the Tokugawa up to 20 percent of the tax was paid in money. From these proceeds of rice or its equivalent, the daimyo in turn supported through fixed stipends the samurai, whose living costs were rising. Sometimes the lords defaulted or retrenched on their payments to their retainers, who in turn tried to squeeze more out of the farmers. Peasants were forced to occasional rebellion or flight, and strains developed in the economic arrangements of the military pyramid.

The agrarian economy also was in a state of flux. As long as the villages paid their taxes, they maintained their semi-autonomy. But villagers remained overtaxed, for the feudal mentality of the Tokugawa continued to emphasize the necessity of agrarian taxation and neglected potential sources of revenue from urban sectors. Yet through reclamation and irrigation projects, the acreage of arable land increased. New plant types augmented diets, and commercial fertilizers added to yields. In addition to subsistence farming of the necessary grain produce, commercial or cash crops, such as cotton, sesame, sugarcane, and tobacco, were cultivated. Village industries expanded with such enterprises as silk production, textile weaving, cotton spinning, and sake brewing. Entrepreneurial skills developed in the country, and by the end of the Tokugawa era in every village there was at least one wealthy farming family that had more land than the others as well as profitable auxiliary handicraft industries. But other villagers became poorer, went into debt, or became dispossessed. They drifted to the cities, where they formed the base for an unskilled or semi-skilled urban labor force. Through shifting patterns, encouraged by the growth of tenancy, the rise of a wage-laboring class, and a variety of crops that required special intensified skills, large extended families and large landholdings tended to break down over the centuries into smaller agrarian groupings.

The seventeenth century registered the greatest agricultural, population, and urban growth in any period of Japanese history to that time. This growth and expansion peaked in the Genroku era (1688–1704), named after the year period of the reigning monarch, Emperor Higashiyama. In the latter decades of his reign, however, commercial growth slackened somewhat. This was due in part to governmental retrenchment policies that insisted on the primacy of an agrarian base for revenues rather than on more comprehensive well-balanced financing from other taxable sources. Monopolistic practices by merchant associations restricted fuller trade, and the purchasing power of the shoguns and the daimyo, who constituted the major buyers and consumers of the time, did not develop appreciably. Yet in the eighteenth century, there were increased agricultural production and commercialization. Overall continued economic growth was possible despite restrictions, in part because the lower classes, excluded from political activity, could pursue economic ends fairly single-mindedly.

In the process of readjustment to realities, by the end of the Tokugawa, all major classes had become dissatisfied with their status. The peasants remained overtaxed, and although they produced most of the country's wealth, they shared only minimally in its increase. Despite their economic importance, the city merchants and artisans lacked commensurate political and social standing. The military administrators had prestige—and increasing debts. These changes in Japanese society had repercussions in the development of Japanese political life.

CULTURE

Whereas the court in aristocratic Japan and the Zen monks in Ashikaga times had dominated the cultural life of their respective epochs, the *chonin* (townsmen) in the great cities of Edo, Osaka, and Kyoto dominated the new Tokugawa culture. The cities became centers of art and culture. Despite the sumptuary laws of the shoguns regulating the spending of money, city folk enjoyed a degree of social freedom and of flamboyant fashions. Amusement quarters flourished, and the geisha (a person of the arts) or professional female entertainers provided a new kind of social relationship for Japanese men. Since polite mixed society did not exist, the Japanese male turned to those avenues of entertainment and to the houses of prostitution for romance and for social intercourse, which were almost nonexistent in prearranged marriages and formalized family life. The rise in this form of popular entertainment indicated the decline in the status of women in Japan from its relative eminence in the classical and early feudal periods.

Reflecting more prosperous and ostentatious times, Tokugawa architecture also became more complex and more gaudy than it had been in earlier periods. Gone were Zen simplicity and deep religious spirit in art. The magnificent palaces and public buildings, such as the Nikko shrines, which were the mausoleums for Ieyasu and his grandson, were elaborately constructed. More simple and traditional construction, resembling the earlier Fujiwara style, however, continued in the Katsura Detached Palace,

Nikko: Tokugawa Ieyasu's mausoleum

Nikko shrine, three monkeys: "hear no evil, see no evil, speak no evil"

an imperial villa near Kyoto. On the campus of the International Christian University at Mitaka, a suburb of Tokyo, is the Kusa-no-ya (Grass House), a prototype of a Tokugawa teahouse.

Sculpture was second-rate and lacked any spiritual impulse present in Buddhism. Only minor results were recorded in the plastic arts that produced such miniature products as the *netsuke*, small ivory carvings used in the fastenings of tobacco pouches and pillboxes. Ceramic art reached a new height at Arita, an area in Kyushu with its port of Imari. Other prominent ceramic names included those of Kakeimon, Nabeshima, and Kutani. Lacquer and textile production continued. *Mingei* (folk art) took its place alongside the aristocratic. In the graphic and pictorial arts, gorgeous decorative screens and panels depicted brightly colored scenes. The Kano school continued with Eitoku's grandson, Kano Tannyu (1602–1674) and his brother Naonobu (1607–1650). Other contemporary artists included Honnami Koetsu (1588–1637), Tawaraya Sotatsu (1576–1643), Ogata Korin (1658–1716), and Maruyama Okyo (1733–1795). The adherents of the Nanga (Southern) school, who wanted to return to the techniques of the Chinese style, flourished in the Kyoto area. Their ranks included amateur painters who pursued the art for pleasure rather than for money.

Ukiyo-e, pictures recording fleeting impressions of the contemporaneous secular life, the "floating world," became prominent. Ukiyo-e became particularly associated with woodblock prints, perhaps the type of Japanese art best known to the West. At first the woodblock prints had been illustrations in printed works, but soon they evolved into independent works of art. The prints were considered quite vulgar in Tokugawa times, and they did not achieve artistic distinction until later decades. Quite complex in process, the production of a woodblock print involved not only the artist but also a publisher to sponsor the print, an anonymous but expert woodcutter to cut the scenes (each color or shading required a separate cutting), and a printer who produced the final result by careful superimposition of the various cuts onto the same print.

One of the earliest artists (they are usually known by their given names) in the medium is Hishikawa Moronobu (1618–1694). He was followed by Suzuki Harunobu (1725–1770), Toni Kiyonaga (1752–1815), and Kitagawa Utamaro (1753–1806), who portryed sophisticated sensuous ladies. Toshusai Sharaku (active for only a brief span of some ten months in 1794–1795), who may have been a noh actor, sketched fierce representations, bordering almost on caricature, of kabuki types. The most familiar of the artists to the Westerner, however, were Katsushika Hokusai (1760–1849), who produced a series of thirty-six views of Mt. Fuji (*Fugaku Sanjurokkei*), and Ando Hiroshige (1797–1858), whose work includes two sets of the fifty-three stations on the Tokaido road (*Tokaido Gojusantsugi*).

In literature, there were new developments in the Japanese drama. The classical puppet theater emerged. It was called variously *joruri* after its texts, *bunraku* after the stage-manipulated puppets, and *gidayu* after the personal name of one of the earliest playwrights (Takemoto Gidayu, 1651–1714) to compose in this medium. These puppet tales were recited to the accompaniment first by a *biwa* (lute) and then by the *samisen*, a three-stringed plucked instrument resembling the banjo. Puppet drama developed at Osaka, where today the Bunrakuza is the outstanding theater.

The chief name in the development of puppet texts was Chikamatsu Monzemon (1653–1724), known by his family name. His librettos drew their inspiration basically from two sources: historical drama and contemporaneous domestic themes. One of his most popular plays was *The Battles of Koxinga*, which dealt with the daring exploits of a pirate of Japanese-Chinese descent who ravaged the Chinese coast during the Ming era. The play's initial Osaka run lasted seventeen consecutive months. At first the puppets were small in dimension, but in time they were enlarged to two-thirds the actual size of human beings. Three men on stage were required to manipulate each figure; all three were dressed in black, as in the noh drama, to denote anonymity. The leader (*omozukai*) manipulated the puppet's right arm, hand, and head. The second (*ashizukai*) controlled the legs, and the third (*hidarizukai*) maneuvered the left arm and hand.

A second dramatic form to emerge at this time was *kabuki*. Its development dated from the early seventeenth century in Kyoto, where a renegade Shinto priestess led a troupe of dancers and actors in salacious dances. Because of the low moral tone of kabuki, the authorities soon banned women from the stage, and the drama was limited to performances by male actors, as early Shakespearean drama had been. Those assuming female impersonations were designated as *onnogata* (or *oyama*); some actors in these roles garnered national acclaim. The kabuki texts borrowed from a variety of sources, such as puppet themes and librettos, the noh drama, and secular tales. Like noh, the kabuki often used an onstage chorus to chant the narrative portions to instrumental accompaniment. Stage settings were quite realistic and elaborate; often visually striking tableaux (*mie*) were struck. A revolving stage added to the sense of drama, and a runway from the stage into the pit gave the audience a sense of participation in the play. The kabuki tradition was kept alive through hereditary lines of great actors. The Kabukiza theater in Tokyo presents the finest interpretations of the art.

Poetry experienced the further refinement of the earlier five-line, thirty-one-syllable tanka through the regna or chain poem to the *haiku*, which reduced the poems even further to the first three lines of the seventeen syllables arrayed in a 5-7-5 syllabic pattern. This concise poetic form pleased bourgeois society, which amused itself by composing in the medium. Haiku appeal lay in its stress on sharp wit through brevity and on mental dexterity. Probably the greatest composer of haiku, who also composed chain poems, was Batsuo Basho (1644–1694), a former samurai and haiku master at Edo.

Finally the growth of printing stimulated the development of literature. Literacy was necessary for city life and commerce, and new stimuli for printing came from the Korean printers brought back by Hideyoshi's armies and from the Jesuits, who had operated a press to print Christian tracts. The Japanese knew about movable type, but they did not use it. Instead, printers employed the woodblock medium, which permitted the inclusion of illustrative material. Many very popular booklets were printed in *kana*. Among these booklets were collections of moral maxims, short tracts on miscellaneous topics, historical writings, guidebooks, and sundry anecdotes.

The novel as a literary form was influenced by the new urban society. One of the more prominent novelists of early Tokugawa times was Ihara Saikaku (1642–1693), an Osaka townsman, who presented amusing and colorful portrayals of city types. His first important work was *An Amorous Man*, which sold so well that he followed it with sequels such as *An Amorous Woman* and *Five Amorous Women*. Many novels were pornographic but were popular in spite of Tokugawa censorship. Other stories reflected Japanese traditions. One dominant theme in Tokugawa novels was the clash in an individual between *gin* (duty) and *ninjo* (passion). A typical theme might be the futile love of a rich young man for a geisha, an attachment that ran contrary to his family duty and social obligations. Neither love nor duty won out, and the solution in the impasse was for the two parties to commit suicide, which was

viewed as a romantic, reasonable, and respectable escape from an unresolv-
able situation in Japan at the time.

INTELLECTUAL TRENDS

Cultural changes in Tokugawa Japan were matched by intellectual ferment.
The latter was derived from two contributing streams. Foreign works advocating modernization seeped into Japan chiefly through the Dutch at
Deshima, while internal intellectual studies promoted the restoration of
power to the emperor. In the early years of the exclusion policy, the European powers were in no position to protest its disadvantages to them. But
changes that were occurring in Europe during the Tokugawa regime placed
Europe and the United States in a position to challenge Japan. Fundamental growth in the West included increases in wealth and in population in
disproportionate relation to Japan; improved military and naval technology, which through the clipper ships and steamships made easier Western
contact with the Far East; and, particularly, the rise of Russia and America
on the world scene. In the late eighteenth and early nineteenth centuries,
Japan received warning signals of the expansion of Western interests in Asia
and their own home islands. The Japanese noted more foreign shipping
along their coasts, and they came into contact with more missions trying to
enter the country. Through the Dutch at Deshima, they also were cognizant
of British territorial encroachments in India and of the Western exaction of
special rights from a weak Manchu-ruled China.

The Dutch were the main source of foreign ideas. The manager of the
company went to Edo yearly to make his report, while the shoguns kept
continual check on the Dutch through local daimyo on Kyushu. Neighboring lords assigned samurai to learn Dutch, and these men in time became
valuable interpreters, although sometimes they fell under suspicion by their
countrymen because of the association with Westerners. By 1720, Edo, safe
in its isolation, removed the long-standing bans on the study of Western
subjects and on the importation of European books, excepting those relating to Christianity. A small but intellectually vigorous native group of
students of the European sciences arose. Some social topics, technology,
and medicine were studied, but pursuit of philosophy or the humanities
was frowned upon. A text on anatomy was translated into Japanese, and a
Dutch-Japanese dictionary was compiled in the pursuit of Dutch learning
(*Rangaku*).

By the middle of the nineteenth century, Japanese scholars were well
versed in some Western sciences such as gunnery, smelting, shipbuilding,
cartography, and medicine. These scholars built model steam engines, and
they erected brick furnaces. Although few in number, they became a valu-

able nucleus of scholars who would later seize the initiative in conducting scientific work on a much grander scale when the opportunity presented itself. Cognizant of the superiority of Western technology, some Japanese concluded that modernization was necessary. They helped to lay the groundwork for change before the Westerners in strength arrived in Japan.

Among the few thoughtful Japanese who pondered on the desirability of importing Western ideas to strengthen the country were some samurai. In their ranks was Honda Toshiaki (1744–1821), a gifted man, who was a samurai from a tozama fief in a west Honshu province somewhat removed from direct Edo influence. He learned the Dutch language, studied mathematics and astronomy, and opened a school. He wrote on a variety of subjects, including shipping, foreign affairs, and the conservation of natural resources. In 1798, he composed a volume entitled *A Secret Plan of Government* in which he proposed state control of industry, commerce, shipping, and colonization. He was among the first Japanese to realize that the closed economy of Japan, with its modest resources, was incapable of supporting an expanding higher standard of living in a capitalist society without the benefit of growing trade. In defiance of official Tokugawa edicts, he argued for a merchant marine capable of overseas traffic, and he advocated establishment of commercial relations with Russia. To enhance national power, he stated that Japan needed gunpowder, metals, ships, and colonies. He was even disposed to accept the validity of Christianity in the process of modernization.

Another representative of the military class who thought along similar lines was Sato Nobuhiro (1769–1850), a native of northern Japan. He had definite views on the necessary correlation of colonies attached to a strong homeland. He declared that the country's leaders could not sit idly by but that they should seize lands around the Japanese perimeter, including Korea, Manchuria, and eastern Siberia. Such conquests, he argued, would entail reorganization of the country. To this end he advocated a unified national army command, a strong national government, the end of feudalism, and a strong economic base. In his *Maritime History of Nations*, he argued that the greatness of nations lay in commerce and the navy. An imaginative man, ahead of his time, Sato foretold Japan's future remarkably accurately, but his works were suppressed by the Tokugawa authorities, who still hewed to the isolationist policy.

Complementing this small but rising group of Japanese who wished to transform Japan into a strong, modern power in world affairs were Japanese intellectuals who were dissatisfied with the bases of existing governmental structures. They criticized the Tokugawa shoguns guardedly, for the secret police were omnipresent. They aimed their barbs indirectly through a comparison of Japan with strong European powers. These thinkers did not coalesce into any political movement because of government repression and censorship. Criticism remained in a theorizing vein. Nevertheless, one result of this intellectual activity was the denial of the legitimacy of Tokugawa rule and support for the emperor to play the central role in national life. Two areas of speculation contributed to this end: Confucianism and Japanese historical studies.

As Buddhism went into a precipitous decline during the era, the Tokugawa, as had Shotoku Taishi and his successors centuries before, advocated Confucianism as the official doctrine in the hope that it would contribute to stability by its emphasis on proper relationships between rulers and subjects, its sense of loyalty to the duly constituted political authorities, and its stress on harmony. The shoguns sponsored a school of Confucianism at Edo, and samurai were enjoined to participate in its studies. Fujiwara Seika (1561–1619) left the Buddhist fold and initiated the school. His disciple, Hayashi Razan (1583–1657), was adviser to Ieyasu. His descendants founded at Edo the official Confucian university, and in 1670, it finalized a history based on Chinese forms, *The Comprehensive Mirror of Our Country.* Other histories were compiled by schools and individuals, such as Arai Hakuseki (1657–1725), a shogunal official.

The orthodox philosophy, borrowed from China, was known as neo-Confucianism because of metaphysical accretions from Buddhist and Taoist thought. As crystallized in the Song dynasty by the Chinese philosopher Zhuxi (1130–1200), the school recognized a moral law or order in the universe, to which man was to adapt himself. Known in Japan as Shushi, the school pleased the Tokugawa because the core of the thought emphasized loyalty. It set great store on the importance of learning, but it insisted on orthodoxy. Other variants of neo-Confucianism arose in both China and Japan, including that known in Japan as Oyomei, derived from the Chinese philosopher Wang Yangming (1472–1529) of the Ming dynasty. Wang's teaching was opposed to that of Zhuxi because it held that self-knowledge was the highest type of learning, and it emphasized intuition and introspection as means to acquiring knowledge. Because this approach could encourage independence of thought and of action, the Tokugawa shoguns discouraged it.

The Tokugawa, like earlier Japanese advocates of Confucianism, also omitted or ignored other fundamental aspects of the Chinese ethical system, such as the concepts of the mandate of heaven and of the right to revolt. According to both Confucian and neo-Confucian theory as it developed in traditional Chinese thought, the emperor of China ruled by virtue. When the emperor was virtuous, good times followed; if his evil acts brought misfortune, as in an accumulation of national disasters, he could be overthrown. Because there were no shoguns in China, blame fell directly on the monarch and not on any usurping authority. But within the existent structure of Japanese politics, critics leveled their charges against the actual rulers of Japan, who were the shoguns, not the emperors. Arguing abstractly rather than pointedly, Japanese students of Confucianism inferred that within the Japanese system the shoguns had been military usurpers who ruled not by virtue but by arms and conquest. The implication was that shoguns could be overthrown because the emperor was the legitimate ruler and should rule in fact.

The necessity of restoring power to the emperor was a theme simultaneously advanced by those samurai and ronin who were reinterpreting their national history. Lacking formal functions, they took the lead in turning idle time into domestic historical studies. The military ranks were swelled by certain Shinto scholars, including Motoori Norinaga (1730–1801), who resurrected the early *Kojiki* and *Nihon Shoki* as bases for imperial power. From their own national history, these writers sought the origins of dissatisfaction with the contemporaneous regime. They re-created the Sun Goddess myth that emphasized the divinity and the central role of the imperial family. They idealized the semi-historical and historical periods through the tenth century prior to shogunal rule. They glorified the Heian era, which they interpreted as the high point in Japanese art, culture, and politics. During these centuries, they projected back the notion of a peaceful, prosperous country ruled by just monarchs. Subsequent eras, they continued, were degenerate, because imperial power had been usurped by the military, who had neither the virtue nor the legitimacy to rule.

Again, to avoid direct criticism, the historians did not include the Tokugawa period in their studies but rather provided the inference that their works were tracts for the times. Because of strong government controls, no revolutionary movement, no party organization, and no national leadership emerged to correlate and coordinate the ideology that was subversive to the bakufu. Nevertheless, these concepts were to culminate in the downfall of the shogunate and the restoration in 1868 of the emperor to the central position in Japanese politics and life.

CHRONOLOGY

1558–1637	Artist Honnami Koetsu
1561–1619	Scholar Fujiwara Seika
1576–1643	Artist Tawaraya Sotatsu
1583–1657	Scholar Hayashi Razan
1602–1674	Artist Kano Tanyu
1607–1650	Artist Kano Naonobu
1618–1694	Woodblock artist Hishikawa Moronobu
1642–1693	Novelist Ihara Saikaku
1644–1694	Bunraku playwright Takemoto Gidayu

1653–1724	Bunraku playwright Chikamatsu Monzaemon
1657–1725	Scholar Arai Hakuseki
1658–1716	Artist Ogata Korin
1687–1704	Genroku period, during reign of Emperor Higashiyama
1720	Ban on most Western studies removed
1725–1770	Woodblock artist Suzuki Harunobu
1730–1801	Scholar Motoori Norinaga
1733–1796	Artist Maruyama Okyo
1744–1821	Honda Toshiaki, advocate of Westernization
1752–1815	Woodblock artist Toni Kiyonaga
1753–1806	Woodblock artist Kitagawa Utamaro
1760–1849	Woodblock artist Katsushika Hokusai
1769–1850	Sato Nobuhiro, advocate of Westernization
1794–1795	Woodblock artist Toshusai Sharaku flourishes
1797–1858	Woodblock artist Ando Hiroshige

9

Tokugawa Japan

Western Intrusion

By the mid-nineteenth century, Japan faced two crises. Internally, there was discontent among all major classes in Japanese society in addition to a growing ideology that saw a need for Japan's modernization and for strong imperial power. Externally, the second crisis resulted from the gradual but forceful expansion of the West backed by great economic and military strength. The interacting crises were brought to a head by the United States in the guise of Commodore Matthew C. Perry when he arrived in Japan in mid-1853. Yet he represented only the culmination of Western efforts to open Japan. The Russians, expanding eastward into Siberia through the centuries, had early probed Sakhalin Island (Karafuto) and the Kuriles (Chishima retto). One Russian expedition landed in a Japanese jail. Russia halted further activity between 1813 and 1852, when the czar dispatched an admiral on a mission to Japan to seek its friendship against the British and the Americans. This Russian mission arrived in Nagasaki as Perry steamed into Tokyo Bay in 1853. During the first half of the nineteenth century, the British embarked on fitful trips to or near Japan, but they made no effort to open the country.

END OF ISOLATION

A decade after the British had taken the initiative in opening China with the first Western treaty in 1842, the United States concluded the first treaty between Japan and a Western power. There were several reasons for strong American interest in Japan. By the early 1850s, the United States had expanded its borders to the Pacific. California had been admitted to the

Union, and the northwest coast was being opened. Now a Pacific power, the United States had the west coast as a base for further expansion into the huge ocean, and the great circle route via the Alaska coast was the shortest way to Asia. Moreover, Japan could be reached before China, and even those Americans who dreamed of a great China trade and of vast Chinese markets saw the necessity of Japan as a way station.

By this time, the American whaling trade in the north Pacific had become highly important; up to 200 whaling ships plied those seas each year. Some of the ships were wrecked by storms on Japanese coasts, where sailors were summarily executed or imprisoned in accordance with the prevailing laws and policy of seclusion. Japan was thought to be rich in coal deposits, and Americans emphasized the need for coaling stations there to meet the requirements of the new steamships. In addition, there was great naval interest in the Pacific, and interest reflected in the naval rank of some of the official American personnel and missions to Japan and to other Pacific countries. Finally, a policy of realpolitik dictated the necessity of freezing European powers out of Japan by getting there first; this power position interested not only the navy but some high civilian officials in Washington as well.

At least two dozen times before Perry, American ships had come to Japan. In 1791, efforts by two merchant vessels to initiate fur trade failed. Six years later, an American ship under Dutch charter entered Nagasaki. In 1815, Captain David Porter, a hero of the War of 1812, sought to convince President James Madison of the necessity of introducing the Japanese to the modern world. Edmund Roberts, the first American diplomat to Eastern countries, conveyed a letter from President Andrew Jackson to the Japanese emperor, but the envoy died in Macao in 1836 prior to his arrival in Japan. That same year, an American businessman in Canton organized an embassy to repatriate seven Japanese sailors, who had been stranded abroad, but none was permitted to land. Caleb Cushing, who in 1844 had concluded the first U.S. treaty with China on the heels of the British, was authorized to deal with Japan, but he had left China prior to the arrival of his instructions. In 1846, two U.S. Navy vessels sailed into Edo Bay, but they were repulsed by Japanese authorities when the American commander refused to face a showdown. Three years later, another naval official, using opposite tactics, at Nagasaki forced the Japanese to surrender fifteen American sailors who had been in chains for months in Japan. In 1851, the commander of the American squadron in Asian waters was ordered to visit Japan, but he was recalled from his command after Perry took his place.

At the age of sixty, Perry was a distinguished naval officer. He was among the most articulate of the navy's policymakers in advocating a strong expansionist stand. Applying the concept of manifest destiny to overseas areas, he was interested in securing naval bases in the Pacific and in establishing a large number of American settlements there. Before departing, Perry read all available books about Japan, which numbered about forty. In them, estimates of Japan's area ranged from 9,000 square miles to 266,000 square miles (it was some 140,000 square miles). Population density was said to be from 184 to 4,000 per square mile (it was about 210), and the total population was reported at between 15 million and 50 million (it was approximately 30 million). Edo alone was thought to have a population of 10 million.

Perry's expedition departed from the East Coast, and, taking a traditional clipper ship route to China, sailed around Africa and across the Indian Ocean to the Chinese coast. At Canton, Perry picked up an American missionary fluent in Chinese to be the official interpreter, but, as it later transpired, negotiations with the Japanese were to be conducted mainly in Dutch. With his four ships, including the first two steamships ever seen in Japan, the commodore, bypassing Nagasaki, sailed directly into Edo Bay on July 8, 1853. His arrival did not take the Japanese by surprise, for the Dutch had warned the shogun that the Americans were coming up from the south via the Ryukyus, where the fleet had spent some time. But the appearance of the squadron precipitated more immediate crises in Japan, although Perry was unaware of Japanese domestic problems or the nature of the dual government then existing in Japan. He insisted on dealing only with top-ranking officials of the shogunate (he mistook the shogun for the emperor), and to them he presented President Millard Fillmore's letter requesting peace and friendship, free trade, good treatment of shipwrecked whalers, and provisioning of coal for vessels. Displaying great firmness, Perry promised to return within a year with a larger force to implement the requests and sailed away after a sojourn of nine days.

The shogunate was thrown into confusion. It was in a particularly vulnerable position, because the shogun was ill (he died before Perry returned), and the shogunal advisers were divided in council. They recognized that if they acceded to the requests, other nations would certainly make similar demands, as they had in China. On the other hand, if they did not grant the requests, the Americans might resort to the use of force to gain compliance. Force was implied in Perry's tactics; it had been overtly used by Westerners in obtaining their first Chinese treaties between 1842 and 1844.

After Perry had departed, to help resolve the dilemma, the shogunate embarked on several unusual steps. It lifted all restrictions on shipbuilding in order to permit the Tokugawa themselves and the daimyo to construct naval vessels and steamships. It also took the unprecedented step of requesting the opinions of the lords on the appropriate course of action to take with respect to the foreign stipulations. Going further, it consulted with the emperor on the issue. For the first time in six-and-a-half centuries of shogunal rule, the bakufu had requested imperial advice on an important problem of state. Though the shogunate probably had political motives in sharing responsibility for any decision that might be taken, the precedent for consulting other parties had been set. And while the bakufu had expected a uniform reaction, it received mixed replies, although the majority of the lords opted for continued isolation. The ensuing—and confusing—period of Japanese political crosscurrents over the next decade-and-a-half is known as the *bakumatsu* (end of the bakufu).

The dilemma remained unresolved when Perry returned in February 1854, earlier than planned, to forestall British and Russian advances. Under the threat of the eight-ship fleet (including now three steam-powered vessels), the Tokugawa had no choice but to conclude a treaty with the Americans. After several weeks of negotiations that involved exchanges of gifts and official receptions, the treaty was signed on March 31, 1854. Sometimes termed the Treaty of Kanagawa, after the small port town south of Tokyo and now part of that megalopolis, it contained several basic provisions. It called for peace between the two countries; for the opening for supplies of the relatively inaccessible ports of Shimoda in central Honshu, south of Edo on the Izu peninsula, and Hakodate in Hokkaido; for good treatment of shipwrecked sailors, for limited trade; for consular residence at Shimoda; and for the most-favored-nation clause (which meant in effect that a privilege extended by Japan to any one country, or the most favored one, would be extended to all).

Perry did not worry about details. He wanted to sign a treaty, any treaty, before European ships took advantage of the foothold gained by American ships to secure concessions for themselves. The treaty was rushed to the United States, where the Senate promptly and unanimously consented to ratification by the president. The Japanese emperor also approved it, and the necessary exchange of ratifications subsequently took place in Japan. What both Perry and the Japanese feared did happen, for the fleets of seventeen nations followed the Americans into Edo Bay. British and Russian treaties shortly followed that of the Americans; within two years, additional treaties were concluded between the Japanese and other European powers.

Perry's success was in part due to its timing, to the domestic crises in the country, to Japanese awareness of Chinese diplomatic and territorial defeats, and to the commodore's own tactics of firmness, determination, and show of strength. Perry's mission made a great impact on Japan, but it was paid little attention at home. The American press and President Franklin Pierce almost ignored it. The Congress took issue with the outrageously extravagant cost of printing the several volumed official report on the mission. New York City presented Perry with a silver-plated serving set, and Boston merchants honored him with a medal. Perry at the time was better known in Japan than in his homeland. His significance then was lost on his countrymen, not to be realized until a later day. As Mr. Dooley (the humorist Finley Peter Dunne) at the time expressed it, "Whin we rapped on the dure, we didn't go in, they come out."

WESTERN RIGHTS AND JAPANESE REACTIONS

In accordance with provisions of the Kanagawa treaty, Townsend Harris was sent as the first consul general, in August 1856, to reside at Shimoda. Harris, a New York City merchant with some previous experience in Asia, possessed an excellent mind and a fine character, and was an abstemious bachelor. He had fallen on hard days and welcomed the assignment. He arrived in Japan alone, unknown, and unwelcomed. Shimoda was a remote town with a poor harbor. The Japanese, who only grudgingly had accepted American treaty terms, hoped to quarantine and to isolate the American representative. They almost succeeded in their aims. Harris was forced to live in a cockroach-infested temple, and vendors at the markets sold him their worst food. Harris was held incommunicado from his own country—he wrote in his diary that he had not received a letter from home in over ten months. He received no instructions from the Department of State for one-and-a-half years.

But Harris was a patient man. As the Japanese witnessed encroaching European interests in China in the late 1850s, he advanced the timely argument that were the shogun to deal first with Americans, he would receive a second, more favorable and more comprehensive treaty as a model for more enduring arrangements. In 1857, Harris concluded a convention with the shogunate that permitted the right of residence at the two open ports of Shimoda and Hakodate, the provisioning of supplies at Nagasaki, and extraterritoriality (extrality for short), in criminal cases. This was the juridical right in foreign countries for aliens to be tried according to their own country's laws and by their own authorities, because the newcomers thought those of the host country to be too barbarous for use by civilized nations.

Harris then traveled to Edo to conclude a full-scale commercial treaty. Now wielding great authority, he proceeded there with a retinue of 350. No gunboats accompanied him. He performed no obeisance, and he was the first Westerner received in audience by the shogun. Despite the lack of show of force, a new comprehensive treaty was signed on July 29, 1858, on an American ship docked in Edo Bay. The terms of the treaty were wide-ranging. They provided for diplomatic representation in the capitals of both powers. They opened to trade four new ports—Nagasaki, Kanagawa, Niigata, and Hyogo (Kobe). The treaty permitted the right of residence at Osaka and at Edo, and it broadened extrality to include civil cases. No opium was permitted into Japan. (Its importation into China had been the immediate and ostensible cause of the Anglo-Chinese War of 1839–1842, dubbed the Opium War.) Religious freedom was granted to foreigners, customs duties were regulated on exports and imports, and the usual most-favored-nation clause was included. After July 1872, upon one year's prior notice, revision of terms was possible. The treaty also provided for American mediation on international issues, if requested, between Japan and other powers, for the purchase of weapons and ships in the United States, and for hiring American technical assistants. Within three months, the British, French, Russians, and Dutch also concluded similar treaties.

The bakufu seemed satisfied with and agreed to the terms, but this time a more independently minded emperor refused to consent to the ratification of either the 1857 or 1858 American treaties. But Americans took both as valid, as did other powers. Accepted by European nations as the model, the 1858 Harris treaty, in spite of imperial disfavor (a technical point that was to surface later in the problems between the court and shogunate) remained the fundamental document in Japanese foreign relations until the turn of the century. It was a great personal and official victory for Harris, for suasion had succeeded as much as the earlier policy of implied force. This time, ratifications were exchanged in 1860 in Washington. A Japanese diplomatic mission of seventy, representing those factions that had accepted the treaty, proceeded to the United States across the Pacific via San Francisco. At the nation's capital, the Japanese became the object of great curiosity and the recipients of lavish entertainment. Elevated to ministerial rank, Harris remained in Japan until 1862, despite failing health, to preserve American gains.

The bafuku continued to be squeezed between conflicting pressures, and the differing reactions to the shogunal request for information as to how to handle Perry revealed the varying attitudes on this issue among the Japanese. Many remained unreconciled to the presence of the increasing number of foreigners in the land, and they continued to press for an exclusion policy. Despite the consolidation of initial treaties with the West, rejection of the West was advanced by some thinkers. An adherent to this school of thought was Aizawa Seishisai, a Mito samurai, who in 1825 had advanced his creed in the New Proposals. His work had been occasioned by the appearance of foreign shipping in Japanese waters and the detention of crewmen from a British whaler in the Mito feudal domains. The opening portion of Aizawa's tract presented the concept of *kokutai*, the essence of Japanese nationalism. Welding together imported and native concepts of Shintoism, Confucianism, and *bushido* (code of the warrior), the author identified the Sun Goddess with heaven, ascribed to her the moral law and political order among men, and related the Confucian virtues of loyalty and of filial piety to Shinto worship. Kokutai had simultaneous religious, ethical, and political overtones. Emphasizing the uniqueness of Japan, kokutai had little place for the accommodation of foreign ideas. Aizawa argued that alien contacts were useless for Japanese development.

Another school of thought in regard to Westernization advocated instead the opening of Japan gradually from within, through a process of self-strengthening and blending of Western science and Eastern ethics. Akin to ideas earlier advanced by Honda Toshiaki and Sato Nobuhiro, Sakuma Shozan (1811–1864), a samurai from a central Honshu province, submitted an eight-point program to his daimyo as the basis for shogunal policy: fortify strategic coastal points, construct armaments, expand the merchant marine, develop efficient maritime trade, build Western-type warships, introduce a modern school system, establish an open but firm system of rewards and punishments, and inaugurate a merit system in selecting government officials.

Following this tradition was Sakuma's disciple, Yoshida Shoin (or Torajiro, 1830–1859), who had been adopted into the samurai class in Choshu in western Honshu. In disobedience of the exclusion edicts, he tried to stow away on one of Perry's ships but was apprehended. Yoshida advocated selective borrowing from the West, the abolition of feudalism, the emancipation of the peasants, and the building of a modern army. He had no concrete program of action to promote his goals, but he conceived instead a spectacular act of bravery to dramatize his ideas. He attempted to assassinate one of the shogun's representatives in Kyoto, and for this act, which failed, he was executed at Edo. Nonetheless, Yoshida's self-discipline and bravery transformed him into a heroic figure for later generations.

A few Japanese advocated complete Westernization. In this group was Fukuzawa Yukichi (1834–1901), a pioneer of modernization. Born in Kyushu in a lower samurai rank, he early learned Dutch and English. He traveled to the United States in the 1860 diplomatic mission. Seven years later, he returned on a second trip, and also traveled in Europe. As Japan eventually opened its doors to Western ideas in the latter half of the nineteenth century, Fukuzawa was in the vanguard. He promoted the ideas of utilitarianism and of liberalism, founded a newspaper, and established the prestigious Keio University. His accommodating approach won out in the early decades of modernization, but the advocates of self-strengthening and of kokotai were first to have their say.

THE FINAL DECADE OF TOKUGAWA RULE

In the decade following the 1858 treaty settlement, the economic effects, some of them adverse, of Westernization were immediately registered in Japan. The volume of exports and of imports through foreign channels grew appreciably because of the low tariff rates imposed on Japan by the unequal treaties (unequal because Japan did not receive similar concessions for the most part abroad). The inequities had an unsettling effect on the domestic economy. Fuel products, such as kerosene, were imported in large quantities. Cotton yarn could be imported more cheaply than silk or cotton that could be spun in Japan. Because Japanese domestic industry was still in the handicraft stage, its products could not compete with cheap imports in mass volume, a result of the industrial revolution. A consequent depression of handicraft industries occurred both in the cities and in the countryside. The process of economic dislocation in the late Tokugawa period resulted in many revolts by peasants. With their fixed incomes, the military, already in economic straits, suffered further reverses with the influx of goods and with rising prices.

The political situation was also getting more complex. The years after 1858 witnessed a struggle between factions supporting the emperor and those backing the hard-pressed shogun. Subsequent to the conclusion of Western treaties, the influence of the shogunate lessened. The influence of the emperor, the court, and certain tozama grew, particularly the four clans of Tosa in Shikoku, Hizen and Satsuma in Kyushu, and Choshu in southern Honshu. Supporting the imperial institution, these daimyo attacked the joint enemies—bakufu and foreigners. The action of the shogun in signing the Harris treaties without the consent of the monarch provided ammunition against the Tokugawa. The court informed the shogun, who had already promised the foreigners to implement terms of the treaties, that they would not be accepted and that all aliens should, on the contrary, be expelled. Japan teetered on the brink of civil war, and the lives of foreigners were endangered. Samurai and other ultra-patriots attacked them and tried to discredit the shogunate with the slogan "Revere the emperor and expel the barbarians." With so much bitter opposition, it was surprising that only a few Westerners were killed in this unsettled decade. Three Russian naval officers were murdered, the Dutch interpreter for the U.S. legation was cut down, and a British diplomat, C. L. Richardson, was killed near Yokohama when he did not dismount as the high-ranking, anti-Western lord of Satsuma passed by him.

Harris believed that the shogun was doing his best to preserve order, but the English reacted strongly to the Richardson incident. They demanded an apology and an indemnity. Getting no satisfaction, in August 1863, their fleet bombarded Kagoshima, the capital of the Satsuma fief. This proved to be a turning point in the antiforeign campaign, for the Satsuma, after a face-saving formula of claiming to have driven away the foreign fleet, had been so impressed with British naval power that they became friends of the English. The clan became the leading advocate of a modern navy, patterned after the British model, in Japan over the next half century, and its members filled top-ranking naval positions.

Modern Yokohama harbor, approximate site of Perry's landings and treaty

Meanwhile, the court and the Choshu clan had been acting independently. On his own authority, in 1862, the emperor canceled the institution of alternate attendance. He fixed June 25, 1863, as the date for closing the country. When that day arrived, despite the shogun's objections to the royal ultimatum, Choshu began shelling foreign ships from their capital of Shimonoseki, which guarded the narrow but strategic strait between Honshu and Kyushu, the shipping lane to China from the Inland Sea out to the Yellow Sea. Foreign ships, including an American merchant vessel, were damaged.

In a rare instance of overt use of military action at this time anywhere in the Far East, the United States retaliated by dispatching a warship to punish the recalcitrant lord. In the resultant fray, five Americans were killed and six wounded. The Congress applauded the brave act and directed the Treasury to compensate the crew for meritorious service. The French also sent two ships to punish Choshu, who continued to be obstreperous, and, in contravention of treaty terms, closed the strait for a year. Finally, in September 1864, an allied expedition of seventeen ships (nine British, four Dutch, three French, and one American), defeated the daimyo, from whom a $3 million indemnity was demanded. Eventually the United States realized about $800,000 of this sum, but an act of Congress in 1883 returned the proceeds to the Japanese, who used some of the money to construct the Yokohama harbor breakwater in Tokyo Bay.

Like Satsuma, Choshu learned its lesson by force. It dropped its opposition to the foreigners and instead concentrated its efforts against the shogun. Choshu leaders became paramount in the development of Japan's modern army, as Satsuma had been with the navy. The emperor also capitulated to Western force. His consent to the 1857 and 1858 treaties was obtained in late 1865, after a show of naval strength off Osaka by a cooperative undertaking of nine foreign ships (five British, three French, and one Dutch). At that engagement, the American charge d'affaires, lacking a ship of his own country, hitched a ride with the British.

With foreign issues settled and the Western powers placated, the tozama daimyo concentrated on the shogun's downfall. The times were conducive to change. In September 1866, the shogun died, and in the following February the emperor was also gathered to his ancestors. Another shogun and a young emperor ascended to their respective positions. In the new atmosphere, the tozama in 1867 sent an ultimatum to the Tokugawa demanding that he surrender his shogunal powers. Already predisposed to do this, the shogun renounced his political rights, and he declared his intention to retire. On January 3, 1868, the court issued a rescript announcing the restoration of power to the emperor (*Meiji Ishin*). The monarch, through the advisers, then asked the ex-shogun to surrender his lands. This demand, which undercut the economic strength of the former bakufu, was refused. Not until May, after some months of fighting, did the Tokugawa relinquish their territories. Treated well in defeat, the former shogun was given princely rank, and the family turned their fortunes to business enterprises.

As the central figure in the restoration period, the fifteen-year-old emperor, Mutsuhito, assumed the reign name of Meiji (Enlightened One). Through his tozama advisers, he chose to follow a policy of modernization that was enunciated in general terms through two proclamations. In April 1868, the Charter Oath (*Gokajo no Goseimon*), drawn up by a few young advisers in the name of the emperor, in five short articles pledged the establishment of deliberative assemblies and the decision of all matters by public discussion; declared that all classes, high and low, were to unite in vigorously effecting affairs of state; permitted the common people, no less than the civil and military officials, to pursue their individual callings; sought to break away from the evil customs of the past; and stated the desire to seek knowledge throughout the world to strengthen the foundations of imperial rule. A more extended document, the so-called constitution of June 1868, supported similar ends. To symbolize the new era, the capital moved from Kyoto to Edo, renamed Tokyo (Eastern Capital), where the Meiji emperor ruled until his death in 1912 in the imperial palace (*kokyo*), appropriated from the Tokugawa.

Another political period began in Japan. Many new ideas and forces were in evidence, but old ways persisted. As it had done before, Japan was to borrow and to utilize foreign ideas to an appreciable extent, this time on the road toward modernization and international status. But this borrowing was only part of the story of the rise to power, for native institutions were not wholly discarded in the process. The Japanese, as in earlier times, were once again to strike their own balance between imported and indigenous features.

CHRONOLOGY

1811–1864	Sakuma Shozan
1825	Aizawa Seishisai's New Proposals
1834–1901	Fukuzawa Yukichi
1853	Perry first in Japan
1854	Perry, or Kanagawa, treaty; British and Russian treaties follow
1856–1862	Townsend Harris in Japan
1857–1858	Harris treaties, concluded with shogun, without imperial ratification
1860	Exchange of ratification in Washington of 1858 treaty
1863	Satsuma subdued
1864	Choshu subdued
1867	End of shogunate
1868	Meiji restoration; capital to Tokyo; Charter Oath (April); and June constitution

III

MODERN JAPAN

1868–1945

With the Meiji restoration in 1868, Japan started on its way to modernization, as well as political and economic world status. In the almost fifty years of Mutsuhitu's rule to 1912, the country laid the bases for domestic growth and foreign expansion. Then, over the next several decades, through World War I and the 1920s, Japan in imperial guise rose to even greater heights of international standing and home productivity by a combination of factors unique to the land and times. After Japan had built up one of the greatest empires in the world in bursts of activity and mostly through the use of force, the success story culminated in the tragic holocaust of World War II in Asia and the Pacific. Once again, after 1945, the country reverted to its pre-Perry territorial status, with energies confined realistically to its home islands. Within less than a century, the historical process of rise and decline had gone full cycle.

10

Meiji Japan

(1868–1912)

Politics

In the four-and-a-half decades that constituted the Meiji period, Japan modernized its political, economic, and social institutions and achieved status as a world power. During this period, national wealth increased, because both the agricultural and industrial sectors of the economy kept pace with the burgeoning population. Economic modernization, political stability, and the stimulus of foreign trade contributed to steady development. Policy was directed by oligarchic ruling groups, and Japanese society responded willingly to their direction. The lack of any appreciable policy differences or conflicts in outlook among the rulers themselves, or between the leaders and the led, in regard to national goals helped to smooth the process of modernization.

BACKGROUND

Meiji Japan can be conveniently divided into two periods. During the first two decades, from 1868 to about 1890, the leaders were concerned primarily with internal changes and laid the foundations for modernization on immediate pragmatic considerations. During this initial period, the formulation of long-range goals was of secondary importance. In political affairs, the leaders dealt with pressing matters of state, such as the achievement of stability, the consolidation of unified domestic rule, and the establishment of effective government organs. In economics, because of the great scope of programs involved, financing remained precarious in the years immediately following the restoration, though practical steps were taken to solve adverse budgetary conditions. Modern industries were instituted. The textile industry, already present with a historical base, was one of the first to show appreciable gains. Appearing on the industrial scene at the time were the *zaibatso* (cartels) that became a dominant characteristic of Japanese economic life. In cultural matters in the early Meiji years, many Japanese seemed to go overboard in adopting Western customs and ideas, and Western philosophies of education temporarily won prestige.

In the latter half of the Meiji period, from 1890 to 1912, Japan became a world economic and political power. Internal growth matched concurrent foreign expansion, for each activity sustained the other. Once immediate political considerations had been met, the government turned to the delayed long-term issue of constitutionalism, which it resolved at a leisurely pace and in a conservative manner. In economics, more lasting fiscal solvency resulted from retrenchment policies in the 1880s. Like the nineteenth-century economic pattern in England, Japan, after initially registering growth in the textile field, subsequently emphasized the foundations for heavy industry. The zaibatsu grew in economic and political importance, and they commenced overseas operations. In cultural affairs, the pendulum swung back to the revival of traditional ways, and the national system of education, after early experiments involving heavy doses of Western philosophies, was put on a more securely Japanese footing. Japan had now become an empire.

In a Cinderella-type story, within the Meiji period, Japan became a modern state. The young reformers, who in the early years of the restoration began to modernize Japan, saw their goals achieved within their lifetime. Their aim was reflected in the slogan "Enrich the nation and strengthen its arms." They desired to build up concurrently both military and industrial power to achieve equality with the West; they were additionally successful in effecting progress in economic, social, political, and cultural sectors. They displayed a readiness to experiment with new methods and to push boldly ahead, but they also adhered to traditional ideas and virtues. By 1912, as the first in Asia to do so, Japan had acquired all the requisites for a modern state. It possessed a strong national government, a constitution, a military based on universal conscription, a wide-ranging education program and a high literacy rate, a money economy, a growing industrial, commercial, and urbanized society, an adequate labor supply in city and country, and sufficient food production. Agricultural yields helped to increase the national wealth, and industry and modernization were sustained by growth in the rest of the economy. In their own way, the Japanese met the challenge of the times.

Yet it is debatable whether the success of Meiji Japan, which is held up as a model of early modernization for underdeveloped nations, has contemporary relevance for other countries desiring to pursue a similar overall end. Meiji Japan faced no ideological conflicts, as some modern states experience. It had fewer sources of foreign aid and hesitated to use those available for fear of strings attached. Change was evolutionary, and Japan did not rush toward modernization. Perceived foreign threats could be managed. Conditioned by historical background, particularly the centuries of regimented Tokugawa rule, the Japanese were prepared to accept leadership and direction from above. Features unique to Japan prevailed in the latter decades of the nineteenth century and the early years of the twentieth. Some of the factors contributing to Japan's modernization were not easily exportable nor were they necessarily applicable elsewhere.

Both the leaders of modernization and the Japanese people accepted common values, such as loyalty to the emperor and devotion to the nation. Although there were naturally some dissent and extremism during the Meiji years, the leaders and the populace focused on the imperial office as their sanction for modernization. The Emperor Meiji (and with him the practice arose of each emperor's having one reign period for the duration of rule rather than several possible subperiods) was the great symbol of Japan's modernization. Yet because of the sanctity of his person, little was known of him. Although he did embark on several national tours, in Tokyo he remained apart from the world. The throne continued divine and mystical in concept. Augmenting imperial seclusion and aloofness was the emperor's personality. Not wishing to dominate the government, he relied heavily on his advisers. He won their admiration with his accommodation, and because of agreements on ends and means between emperor and advisers, it was easier to maintain the exalted position of the throne. Modern Japanese nationalism, already possessing features dating back to early eras, required little stimulus from the West. National consciousness and emperor worship combined into a national creed in the form of state Shinto. Moreover, the presence of a historic strain of Confucian ethic, with its reliance on vital moral forces and on ethical guidance devolving from sage-kings, enhanced the imperial role in the modernization process.

REALIGNMENTS

In the decade following the restoration, all major classes of Japanese society were affected by the change. The daimyo were liquidated as a class. Their samurai, particularly those of the han of Satsuma, Choshu, and others of western Japan, in an effort to avoid further civil war, persuaded their own lords, already backing the imperial cause, to surrender their domains to the emperor (*hanseki hokan*). They complied, and the rest of the countrywide lords, taking the cue, followed in a similar vein. Typical of the "grassroots" samurai who persuaded their lords to relinquish their lands was Kido Koin

(1833–1877) of Choshu, a disciple of Yoshida Shoin. He had early realized the futility of his fellow clansmen's violent anti-foreign demonstrations when Choshu was so weak. He reorganized his clan's forces and led them against the shogunate in the ferment of 1867 and 1868. He engineered the coalition of forces that eventually overthrew the Tokugawa and abolished feudalism. Rather than precipitate domestic strife over the issue, Kido used his persuasive talents to convince the daimyo to surrender their fiefs as a patriotic gesture and moral obligation.

By 1869, within a year of the restoration, no feudal domains remained in Japan. All land had reverted in name to the emperor. Because of the tremendous nature of the change, for the two transitional years between 1869 and 1871 the daimyo were appointed as governors of their former estates, and they were permitted to retain one-tenth of former revenues as salaries. In 1871, the fiefs were entirely abolished, and the land was divided into new political divisions called prefectures—political and administrative structures that have lasted into contemporary times. This act terminated the status of daimyo as feudal lords, although the government eventually pensioned them off with lump-sum payments in the nature of government bonds, a form of payment that helped to ensure support of a viable new regime.

The old daimyo left the political scene, but many were incorporated into the new peerage (*kazoku*) that was created. The government bestowed upon them titles of nobility, divided into five ranks in accordance with the size of their previous domains. The last Tokugawa shogun received the rank of prince, and the former holders of the smallest states became barons. Some of the former daimyo, using their capital and bonds judiciously to build up commercial ventures, became part of the growing capitalist class in Japan. In some ways, they were better off in the new society. The government canceled or assumed most of their debts, the ex-lords had no more samurai to support, and their income was generally higher in their newer ventures than from the previously feudal estates.

The merchants welcomed the restoration. They had helped to finance it, because they desired political changes to ensure them the status commensurate with their economic growth and importance. Because the government had shouldered the previous debts that the military had owed the commercial class, the confidence of the zaibatsu and merchants in the new regime was generally ensured. However, the farmers, who constituted the largest group in the population, became worse off. The majority of them had not been tenants, because under the laws of the Tokugawa, the land could not be alienated. Within a few years after the restoration, about a third of the farmers became tenants through heavy debts and through the legalization of processes by which acquisitive landlords could acquire more land. The peasantry by and large became a dispossessed class.

The samurai, probably the most important social and active group involved in the restoration, were phased out of existence. Constituting with their families some 2 million, or 5 percent of Japan's population, they lost their feudal rights and privileges. The government divided the class into two echelons; the lower, by decree, were absorbed as commoners (*heimin*); the higher temporarily retained their status (*shizoku*). With the introduction of universal military training in 1872 and 1873, all lost their time-honored position as warrior-aristocrats. With the disappearance of the feudal lords and their fiefs, the dependent samurai also lost their traditional source of revenues. As in the case of the daimyo, over an eight-year period (1868–1876), the government paid the shizoku pensions in lieu of the former hereditary stipends. In 1876, the government commuted these pensions into relatively small lump-sum final payments. Now ordinary subjects, the ex-samurai were left to fend for themselves. Some managed well, for they used their payments to start successful business enterprises. Others were attracted to the officer corps of the new army or to the police forces.

Another blow to samurai privilege also came in 1876, when the government prohibited them from wearing the traditional two swords that had marked them as a separate class with special historic rights. For some samurai conservatives, these developments had been too drastic. They went into opposition against those of their own class or clansmen who were directing the changes. The most serious samurai revolt broke out in Satsuma itself. There, conservatives rallied around Saigo Takamori (1827–1877), one of the ex-samurai himself but one who felt that the new government was going too far and too fast in its reforms. Saigo opposed the universal conscription law, the capitalist interests in government, the official policy of not using ex-samurai in foreign wars, and what he termed an appeasement policy in the mid-1870s toward Koreans who had mistreated Japanese envoys in summary fashion. Disgusted with the trend of events, Saigo returned from Tokyo to Satsuma, where he built up his forces and rebelled in 1877. The new imperial conscript army with modern weapons roundly defeated his anachronistic samurai forces. Saigo's rebellion was significant as the last protest of a dying feudal system, for the great majority of the Japanese, including the ex-samurai, tacitly or openly concurred with the policies of realigning social classes. Although he died for a lost cause, Saigo became a hero revered by future generations of Japanese patriots.

With little effective dissent to hamper them, the leaders borrowed administrative techniques, centralized government control, adopted the Western calendar, provided for religious toleration, and modernized the law enforcement, financial, postal, and juridical systems. One early restoration leader who favored change directed by a ruling group was Okubo Toshimichi (1830–1878). Also of Satsuma and a boyhood friend of Saigo, he differed with his clansmen as to the nature and extent of internal reforms and of foreign policy goals. Okubo stressed the necessity of achieving internal stability, of systematizing progress, and of concentrating on domestic rather than on foreign affairs. He enlisted in his cause capable supporters from other fiefs, transcending clan loyalties. A chief engineer of Japan's modernization, Okubo served as minister of finance and minister of home affairs. He was a moderate who stood for the evolution of constitutional government. In 1878, he was assassinated by an assailant who claimed he was motivated by a desire to avenge the death of Saigo, for which Okubo, as home minister, had been responsible. Within one year, three early heroes of the restoration—Kido, Saigo, and Okubo—had died in their prime of life. Yet others came forth to formulate and to consolidate on a long-term basis the policies begun in early Meiji times.

NEW LEADERSHIP

One such emerging figure in Japan's second and newer line of political leadership was Ito Hirobumi (1841–1909). Of lowly Choshu samurai background, Ito rose through a hierarchical society to pinnacles of power. As a youth he had vigorous induction into bushido, the code of the warrior. From his teachers, among whom was Yoshida Shoin, he inherited strong traits of self-discipline and loyalty. He also was impressed with the necessity of acquiring Western knowledge. In 1863, he went to Europe on an English ship, and on his return he became, as Kido had earlier become, a leading Choshu advocate of coming to terms with the West. After the restoration, he rose to become an important member of the inner government oligarchy. His first appointment was in the new Bureau of Foreign Affairs, and he later moved on to become minister of finance and industry, and, finally, to the prime ministership. In 1870, a second mission to the West included a stay in the United States. During 1882–1884, Ito made a third trip to the West as the head of an imperial commission to study constitutions. He was particularly impressed by Bismarck's new Germany, which resembled Japan in some ways, and by the centralized concepts of Prussian statism.

Although he thought of himself as a moderate, middle-of-the-road statesman who supported neither despotism nor democracy, Ito was at times openly hostile toward parliamentary forms of government. In his quest for a constitution appropriate for Japan, he came into conflict with leaders of newly emerging political parties and movements that also demanded a voice in constitution making. His chief opponents arose in Tosa on Shikoku and Hizen in Kyushu, which, as former tozama clans, had helped to overthrow the shogunate but which, subsequent to the restoration, found themselves outpaced by the Satsuma-Choshu clique in gaining top government office and widespread political influence. The excluded clans founded political parties and complicated the Meiji political scene.

Meiji statesman Ito Hirobumi

Political parties were a novelty in nineteenth-century Japan; the word had to be coined in the Japanese language. A Western concept, parties had no place in traditional Japanese political thought of consensus, in which open criticism of duly constituted authorities and policies was not tolerated. Itagaki Taisuke (1837–1919) of Tosa was an early proponent of political parties. After the restoration, he served as a councillor or cabinet member in Tokyo, but, in 1874, he returned home to establish the first Japanese political cal party, which translated as the Public Society of Patriots (*Aikoku Koto*). The next year at a conference at Osaka, the party petitioned the government to establish a legislative assembly and a judiciary and to call a conference of prefectural governors to consider a future form of national government. Not quite democratic in nature, the party drew its strength mainly from Tosa samurai. It desired parliamentary participation to be limited to ex-samurai and to a small class of wealthy peasants. Despite its self-imposed restrictions, within a few years, the party outgrew its local origins to become established on a national basis. It showed some strength in forcing political concessions from the central government, because in 1878, the government called for elected prefectural assemblies.

In 1879, the franchise was extended to males who paid at least five yen or more in land taxes. Acting solely in an advisory capacity, the prefectural assemblies were nonetheless the first elected legislatures in the non-Western world. In 1880, similar assemblies were constituted in towns and in smaller units of local government. Giving with one hand and taking with the other, the government passed gag ordinances that year that required the stamp of official approval three days prior to holding any political meetings and the reporting of all names and addresses of groups and parties at such meetings.

Allying himself with Itagaki in the opposition to the government was Okuma Shigenobu (1838–1922) of Hizen. After the restoration was announced, he joined the foreign office in Tokyo and became a cabinet member. In March 1881, he presented the emperor with a memorial outlining steps toward achieving a parliamentary form of government. Okuma suggested a definite date for the opening of a parliament, thinking in terms of a year or two. The impact of Okuma's sudden political demands on his colleagues was dramatic, and Ito, a gradualist, particularly took issue. Four months later, in July, Okuma went on to challenge the government's economic policy, charging that insiders were profiting from the proposed sale of the assets of the Hokkaido Colonization Office, which in the previous decade had been given responsibility for the development of that island.

Crying scandal, he forced a showdown in the cabinet not only on the issue of the disposition of government-owned industries and lands but also on the personalities dictating policies. Ito and his faction won, and the liquidation of assets of the office to private interests proceeded as planned. Okuma was forced out of office, but by way of compromise, the throne promised a constitution by 1890. To advance their views in the matter, the opposition founded new and broader political parties. In 1881, Itagaki formed the Liberal Party (*Jiyuto*), and the next year Okuma organized the Constitutional Progressive Party (*Rikken Kaishinto*). The government responded by creating in 1882 the Constitutional Imperial Rule Party (*Rikken Teiseito*), which hewed to the official line.

THE MEIJI CONSTITUTION

Ito was commissioned by the emperor to draw up the promised constitution. He began work after his return in the early 1880s from the trip abroad to study constitutional governments. To eliminate the danger of pressure and conflicting views from the various political camps, all work was done in official privacy within the imperial household. A privy council (*sumitsu-in*) secretly worked with Ito and ratified the documents. Finally, on February 11, 1889, the anniversary date of the traditional founding of Yamato state, the emperor bestowed the constitution upon the people as a royal gift. The realization of representative government, the first east of the Suez Canal, had been drafted by an oligarchy, bestowed through imperial grace upon the people, and accepted obediently by them. The constitution, which had taken twenty-one years of deliberation and preparation, became official in a ten-minute speech by the emperor. The document lasted for fifty-eight years without amendments until a new version replaced it during the post–World War II occupation.

The Meiji constitution consisted of a preamble and seven chapters with seventy-six articles. At the apex of political power was the emperor, whose traditional position of divinity was affirmed. As fountainhead of sovereignty (*tenno*), sacred and inviolable, the direct descendant of the gods, the emperor enjoyed special powers. He could issue imperial ordinances, executive acts in the general interest, and emergency laws when parliament was not in session. Also conferred on him were parliamentary powers. He was the supreme commander of the military forces, he convoked and adjourned parliament, he declared war and concluded peace, he sanctioned all laws, and he controlled foreign affairs conducted by the cabinet. Government in his name was the source and wellspring of power. Attached to the emperor was the Imperial Household Ministry with its two important positions of lord keeper of the privy seal and minister of the imperial household. Imperial House Law, taking precedence over parliamentary law, governed such matters as succession and other royal affairs.

The parliament, or Diet as it was termed by the Japanese, was bicameral. The upper chamber, or the House of Peers (*Kizoku-in*), resembling the English House of Lords, embraced members of aristocratic standing. Its membership was divided into six categories: princes of the imperial blood; princes and marquises; representatives of counts, viscounts, and barons, who served seven-year terms; imperial appointees for life selected because of special service to the state; delegates from the Imperial Academy with seven-year terms; and representatives of the highest taxpayers. The lower body, or House of Representatives (*Shugi-in*), initially consisted of 300 members (raised to 381 in 1900 and to 466 in 1925), were elected by males over the age of twenty-five who paid an annual tax of fifteen yen or more. All statutes required majority votes of both houses, but they were subject to imperial veto. The Diet was convoked annually by the emperor. It had the right to introduce bills although it was not usually exercised, for most of these were presented instead by the government to initiate legislation. Parliamentary power over finances was constricted. It did not apply to fixed expenditures in the budget, and it was not permitted to legislate either expenditures of the imperial household or bureaucratic salaries.

Another constitutional organ was the privy council. Initially created to review and accept the constitution, it remained as the highest formally constituted advisory body in the land. Its membership of twenty-six was selected by the emperor on the advice of the prime minister. In turn, the prime minister was appointed by the emperor, on the advice principally of elder statesmen. On matters of state the prime minister had direct access to the throne. He presided over the cabinet (*neikaku*), where ministers (*daijin*), however, were responsible to the emperor rather than to the parliament. A limited bill of rights for all subjects was incorporated into the constitution, but its provisions could be changed by law. Despite its modern form, the Meiji document embraced some time-honored Japanese political concepts, all of which were at variance with Western jurisprudence. These concepts included the ideas that the ideal state was the patriarchal family headed by the emperor as father of the nation, that government by men prevailed above government by law, that group obligations took precedence over individual rights, and that man by nature was created unequal. Here was yet another example, in the political arena, of the persistence of traditional Japanese ideas continuing on into modern life.

EXTRACONSTITUTIONAL ORGANS

Omissions in the constitution proved to be as important as its provisions, if not more so. Although not stipulated in the document, several extraconstitutional groups and organs developed and gained power and influence in national life over the years. The bureaucracy, one such collective group, assumed importance. It had started on an experimental basis; the emperor appointed to it military and civilian personnel. Cliques, particularly from Satsuma and from Choshu, filled the ranks of earlier bureaucratic offices. Later, in 1899, an imperial proclamation laid the basis for an examination system. Placed on a merit basis, the bureaucracy, which came to embrace half-a-million civil servants, became impervious to the popular or parliamentary will. It enjoyed its own esprit de corps, and cabinets usually included members from its top ranks.

Bureaucrats affiliated with special interests, such as military or industrial groups, could exert influence for good or ill in their autonomous role. In the top rank of the bureaucracy was the cabinet, which pre-dated the constitution. In its early years it embraced the heads of ten departments. Yet the most influential political group was yet another extraconstitutional and advisory body, the *genro-in*, or elder statesmen (as Ito in later life), who derived essentially from Satsuma Choshu ranks. These few men, acting as a closely knit geriatric oligarchy, ruled Meiji Japan in the name of the emperor.

Military leaders, some of them also from genro ranks, assumed prominence in Meiji Japan. Endeavoring initially to separate military and civilian affairs, the constitution had stipulated that the military were not to vote. In 1882, an imperial rescript, going a step further, prohibited military involvement in political affairs. Yet the military conceived itself as protectors of kokutai, the national spirit. The professional soldier, far from eschewing politics, entered into it. Paradoxically, despite the restrictions placed on them, the military in time became more and more important in national affairs. In 1878, in addition to the already existing cabinet post of minister of war, the emperor, under genro advice, created an army general staff headed by a chief responsible to him. In 1893, the same procedure was extended to the navy, and the chief of the naval general staff was also to report directly to the throne. Such organs as the Board of Field Marshals and Fleet Admirals and the Supreme War Council were composed of top-ranking military planners.

A dominant position for the military in Japanese politics was ensured, when, in 1900, an ordinance provided that only generals and lieutenant generals on the active list could be appointed to the traditionally civilian cabinet post of minister of war, reporting directly to the emperor. Similarly, only admirals and vice admirals on active duty could be appointed as minister of the navy. Unlike normal parliamentary governments, in which the prime minister had a relatively free hand in selecting ministers for various portfolios, no cabinet in Japan could be formed after 1900 without military approval of the other posts. A modern-day bakufu had reemerged in cabinet ranks.

The new military man was best exemplified by Yamagata Aritomo (1838–1922). Like Kido and Ito, he was a Choshu clansman. He also benefited from tutelage under Yoshida Shoin. Yamagata was orphaned at the age of five and was raised by a strong-willed grandmother, who was said to have later committed suicide lest he be torn between family obligations to her and patriotic duties to country. In the pre-restoration Western attacks on Choshu, Yamagata had helped to organize clan defenses. He discovered that although the peasant conscripts fought as bravely as the samurai, sheer fighting spirit was no match for modern arms. At the earliest opportunity, Yamagata embarked on a world tour to study the military organization of the advanced Western powers. On his return, he took a leading part in the establishment of the new conscript army, which defeated Saigo's rebels. Yamagata enjoyed a long and honorable government career. His military positions included those of minister of war, chief of general staff, and field marshal. He also participated in politics, serving twice as home minister and as prime minister, and three times as president of the privy council. He

Meiji military figure Yamagata Aritomo

finally became a prince in the new Meiji aristocracy. After Ito's assassination in Manchuria in 1909 by a Korean, he assumed, until his death, the position of senior elder statesman and principal adviser to the throne. Under leadership such as his, Japan commenced its experience with constitutional government.

GOVERNMENT AND PARTY RELATIONS

With leadership consolidated in Satsuma and Choshu civilian and military ranks, constitutional government began with the promulgation of the document in 1889. However, parliamentary machinery did not change the basic nature of Japanese politics, which remained oligarchic. The "in" group, who controlled the government, held at bay the political parties spearheaded by the "out" clans of Tosa and Hizen. The struggle among clan leaders was reflected in the Diet from the first elections of 1890 until World War I, when party government (defined as a system in which the prime ministers generally are chosen from the parties controlling majorities in parliament) was instituted. It remained difficult to reconcile government absolutism with party participation. Government leaders endeavored to maintain the status quo, and they narrowly interpreted the already constricted constitution. The leaders meant to preserve the prestige of the throne, and they shied away from passing liberalizing measures. And while their opponents in parliament pleaded for the extension or provision of more political rights, the degree of this opposition's liberalism was also in question. Often more concerned with individual prestige and party positions than with the extension of popular rights, Itagaki and Okuma followed courses of expediency and of opportunism. Because Japanese politics was dominated by strong personalities, factions that formed around these personalities rather than around political programs became a dominant strain in party alignments and realignments.

In the first parliamentary elections of July 1, 1890, all but 27,000 of 450,000 eligible voters (in a country of some 35 million) went to the polls. In part, voters turned out in large numbers to gain the respect of the Western countries and because of simple faith in the magic of constitutionalism that brought them the right of franchise for the first time. Of those voting, 91 percent were commoners and 9 percent were ex-samurai; the latter were represented in the Diet in proportion to their numbers. Some prefectures elected only commoners. In its report on the election, the government noted that electioneering, considered notorious, was not widespread, and instead candidates depended on family name or position to win votes. Not many speeches were given in campaigns and few issues were discussed. Itagaki's Liberal Party and Okuma's Constitutional Progressive Party won a combined total of 171 out of 300 seats in the lower house of the first Diet. With this mandate, the parties set about to rid Japan of the unequal treaties, and they proposed drastic cuts in the government budget. They envisioned parliament as a means to exercise some control over the government, but government leaders held a contrary view, resulting in rapid estrangement between the parties and the oligarchs.

In the first seven years of the constitution (1889–1896), the government oligarchs worked at cross-purposes with the parties. Yamagata headed the first cabinet (1889–1891) under the constitution. He called on the House of Representatives to act in unison with the government. The parties responded instead by proposing budgetary cuts, including salaries of bureaucrats. The government replied by invoking the legal provisions prohibiting any reduction of fixed expenditures. It went further and resorted to intimidation of party members by hired gangsters, and it bribed weak-kneed members to modify their votes. Yamagata also made a private deal with Itagaki, whose Liberal Party suddenly announced support of the government by requesting only a 6 percent, rather than an original 10 percent, cut in the budget. Disliking the give-and-take of politics, Yamagata resigned office shortly afterward, and Matsukata Masayoshi of Satsuma, a former minister of finance and protégé of Yamagata, became prime minister (1891–1892). No fresh point of view emerged in the government, because the majority of members in the old cabinet were carried over into the new. The same parliamentary controversy arose over the budget, which now had been expanded to include expenditures for naval and shipbuilding programs.

Meeting with continued opposition, the government dissolved the Diet, and in the special election of February 1892, a brutal one, at least 25 people were killed and nearly 400 wounded. Yet the government did not succeed in cowing the House into submission, for in the new Diet the parties won 163 out of 300 seats. This time Ito accepted the premiership (1892–1896) in a cabinet that included several genro. The fight over the budget was again immediately repeated. This time Ito, through a unique stratagem, secured an imperial announcement stating that the emperor was contributing 350,000 yen a year for six years toward military programs and was requesting similarly all civil servants to contribute 10 percent of their salaries to the military budget. Losing face, the Diet voted the budget, and then turned its attacks on foreign policy issues. In 1894, the war with China provided the government with welcome relief from domestic problems.

From 1896 to 1900, the government oligarchy, represented by the three prime ministers from its ranks, cooperated somewhat with the parties. They realized that party support was preferable to party antagonism, and they extended limited political promises as concessions. With backing from the Progressive Party, Matsukata formed his second cabinet (1896–1898), to be followed by Ito's second premiership (1898). By this time, an open break in the genro had emerged between the civilian Ito and his military clansman, Yamagata. Itagaki and Okuma in the summer of 1898, had temporarily settled their differences and had merged their followers into a coalition Constitutional Party (*Kenseito*). In an election that year, the new party won 260 out of 300 seats, and this overwhelming party majority precipitated a serious government crisis. Yamagata advised the emperor to suspend the constitution, while Ito, who had worked so closely with its formulation, rather than terminating or weakening it, recommended that the party take over the cabinet. Ito won his point, and Okuma became prime minister.

The first real Japanese party cabinet was short-lived. The genro and the bureaucracy were not favorably disposed toward it; the two coalition factions themselves could not cooperate. A dispute arose over a vacated cabinet position, and Itagaki resigned when Okuma filled the post with a man from his own faction. Yamagata again stepped back into office (1898–

1900) for the third time. In this period, the government enacted important measures, the land tax was increased, voting qualifications were reduced, the civil service was put on a merit basis, and, as noted, the military took over the cabinet posts of ministers of war and of the navy. These measures were passed in parliament because of their support by Itagaki, who, though in political opposition, was not democratic and enjoyed a working relationship with Yamagata.

In a third phase (1900–1913), the oligarchs took over or directed the political parties. As head of the new *Seiyukai* Party (Association of Friends of Constitutional Government), Ito, for the third time, formed a cabinet (1900–1901). He gave it prestige, and he attached adherents from the ranks of the disintegrating Constitutional Party. But it was his last term in office, and two new genro, Prince Saionjii Kimmochi, a court noble, and Katsura Taro, a Choshu general, proteges of Ito and Yamagata respectively, alternated as premier between 1901 and 1913. Saionji (Seiyukai Party) held the post twice, and Katsura (nonparty) three times. The country finally tired of the seesawing, and with the emperor Meiji's death at sixty in 1912, the accession of a new emperor and of new men as premiers augured changes in the Japanese political scene.

CHRONOLOGY

1827–1877	Saigo Takamori
1830–1878	Okubo Toshimichi
1833–1877	Kido Koin
1837–1919	Itagaki Taisuki
1838–1922	Okuma Shigenobu
1838–1922	Yamagata Aritomo
1841–1909	Ito Hirobumi
1868–1912	Reign of Mutsuhito, the Emperor Meiji (No. 122)
1874	Itagaki founds Public Society of Patriots (*Aikoku Koto*)
1878	Army general chief of staff created, responsible to emperor
1879	Elected prefectural assemblies
1880	Elected town and local assemblies
1881	Okuma's memorial on parliamentary government. Throne promises constitution by 1890. Itagaki forms Liberal Party (*jiyuto*).
1882	Okuma forms Constitutional Progressive Party (*Rikken Kaishinto*); government forms Constitutional Imperial Rule Party (*Rikken Tetseito*).
1889	Constitution promulgated

1889–1891	Yamagata Aritomo prime minister
1890	First parliamentary elections
1891–1892	Matsukata Masahoshi prime minister
1892	Special elections, second parliament
1892–1896	Ito Hirobumi prime minister
1893	Navy chief of staff created, responsible to emperor.
1896–1898	Matsukata prime minister second time
1898	Ito prime minister second tiime; third elections; coalition Constitutional Party (*Kenseito*), Okuma Shigenobu prime minister
1898–1900	Yamagata prime minister second time; military as ministers of army and navy
1900	Ito prime minister third time; heads Association of Friends of Constitutional Government (*Seiyukai* Party)
1901–1906	Katsuro Taro, prime minister (nonparty)
1906–1908	Saionji Kimmochi, prime minister (*Seiyukai*)
1908–1911	Katsura, prime minister second time
1911–1912	Saionji, prime minister second time
1912–1913	Katsura, prime minister third time

11

Meiji Japan

Economics and Society

As Japan modernized its political structure, concurrent changes were proceeding in economic and social life. Light and heavy industries both were developed and helped to lay the groundwork for the country's rapid rise as a world economic power. Supported in part by government policies and financing, private industries grew in number and size, to dominate the economic scene by late Meiji. Rural life continued along traditional lines, but cities expanded, and it was in urban areas that social change was most noticeable.

ECONOMICS

Japan's leaders had achieved a new political structure, and they also turned toward directing an industrial revolution. In typical Japanese fashion, economic changes were initiated by the state. The programs were so large and so basic that only the government possessed the funds and the ability to execute national plans. There was relatively and proportionately little capital in private hands of merchants, daimyo, and samurai. Even if private parties had the funds, they often did not desire to gamble on large-scale undertakings, at least not without official support. In addition to state control and operation of key industries, the government did extend considerable aid and subsidies to encourage the development of certain specified private industries. The government did not adhere to any preconceived concepts of state socialism or of dedication to private enterprise but rather it used pragmatic means to solve immediate economic problems. Noting the situation in China in which foreign loans brought foreign interference, it eschewed loans from abroad. In addition, fearing that foreign assistance might come with political strings attached, it held to a minimum number of foreign economic advisers.

Despite the desire to industrialize, there were several fundamental obstacles to Japan's industrialization. Capital was relatively scarce even for government investments, and the government in the early Meiji decades resorted to deficit financing. Also lacking was the supporting infrastructure for industry, such as adequate systems of distribution, transportation, communication, and marketing. Foreign competition was keen, and the low import duty of 5 percent imposed by the unequal treaties proved a handicap. Political power was potentially weighted against sudden change, for industrial advancement implied dislocations and rearrangements in social and economic patterns.

Yet by 1890, Japan was ready for an economic breakthrough, at least in certain key industrial areas. Cotton spinning mills started the trend, and other fields followed. With Matsukata as minister of finance in the mid-1890s, the transfer of many government enterprises to private hands resulted in the first industrial boom, and cartels expanded their operations. In the mid-1890s, another surge in industry occurred. In part as a result of the war with China (1894–1895), light industry became more diversified, and heavy industry became extensive. Chemical fertilizer plants, cotton weaving mills, electrical industries, coal and steel factories, sugar refining, and the manufacture of machine tools were among the more important industries. Wartime commitment in the campaigns against Russia (1904–1905) accelerated industrial growth. In the second half of the Meiji period, industry had come of age, and Japan registered sustained economic growth.

In line with the general policy to enrich the nation and strengthen its arms, the government directly developed and controlled certain services and public utilities. In 1872, the first railway, only eighteen miles long, was completed between Tokyo and the neighboring port of Yokohama, but it took time to develop a national system of railroads because of the rugged Japanese terrain. The government constructed paper mills, cotton spinning plants, and other light industrial complexes, which were sold in the 1880s to private interests. Besides the liquidation of some interests, government aid to private industry included extending low rates of interest, setting up model factories, giving technical advice, advancing long-term loans, and guaranteeing profits. The phenomenal growth of certain industrial interests resulted, and small fortunes skyrocketed into great economic empires, which branched out in all directions through interlocking companies.

The largest of these new zaibatsu, the Mitsui, traced its origins to merchant interests of the early seventeenth century. After the restoration, the family moved its headquarters from Kyoto to Tokyo, and there embarked on a program of modernization. It diversified its interests, and its directors studied commercial techniques abroad. Mitsubishi, the next largest, was founded by a samurai from Tosa, who had supervised subsidiary operations of that fief in Nagasaki. Subsequently, he transferred daimyo interests to his own company, and, while particularly active in shipping, the firm also diversified its activities. The third-largest zaibatsu, the Sumitomo, grew out of an old merchant firm of the early seventeenth century, which, after the restoration, concentrated on copper mining activities and allied enterprises. Yasuda, the fourth largest, was started by a peasant entrepreneur who, prior to the restoration, ran away from home in western Honshu to Edo, where he became a money changer. After the restoration, he went into banking, railroads, and other businesses. Cartels such as these four were larger than their contemporary counterparts in the West. They were essentially family corporations, their interests were not necessarily confined to any one branch of industry, and they had their own banks and credit facilities to finance their wide-flung operations.

The financing of Meiji economic enterprises had begun precariously. In 1868, official receipts were only a third of expenditures. Government financial burdens were heavy. Military campaigns were expensive, as were the assumption of shogunal and feudal debts and the pension payments to former daimyo and samurai. It took two-thirds of the national budget itself to support the ex-samurai in the early years of the restoration. Deficit financing was practiced, but with expansion in the economy came rising confidence in the new government. Bond issues were floated at home. In 1871, Ito and Okuma standardized the currency, adopted the decimal system, and promulgated the yen as the standard coin. A mint was set up at Osaka. Matsukata's retrenchment policies in the next decade, that involved, among other moves, the privatization of official projects, further helped to stabilize finances. Government industrial enterprises, except for war industries, communications, and public utilities, were sold, usually to insiders, at 11 to 90 percent of original investments. New taxes, a centralized bank system, reduction in volume of paper currency, and lower interest rates helped to solidify the government's economic foundations.

Nevertheless, agriculture remained the chief source of wealth. In the first fifteen years of the Meiji, 80 percent of government revenues came from land. In 1873, the land tax was fixed at 3 percent in money on the assessed value of land rather than on harvest yields, so that the farmer was responsible for the same tax in times of good or bad crops. In Meiji Japan, as in earlier eras, the peasant bore the brunt of taxation. Whether as landowner paying taxes or as tenant farmer paying rent, which usually amounted to between 45 and 60 percent of the crop, a peasant's lot was financially difficult.

Rural life continued with little change. Averaging about two acres, the size of a typical farm remained small. Leading a marginal existence, families of some five to eight members tilled the fields in traditional manner.

Agriculture was mostly unmechanized and involved the use of simple tools and series of hand operations. The main agricultural activity continued to be rice cultivation, which required the use of much water, development of extensive irrigation systems, and cooperative family and village endeavors in planting and harvesting the crop. Conservative rural society emphasized old, traditional, and authoritarian values. Generally the family and village remained self-sufficient, consuming about one-third of the produce and selling the remainder. Isolated from modernization processes, much of agrarian society remained embedded in unchanging ways. Low standards of living persisted, although as both the rural and urban populations grew, some farm hands moved to cities to provide a source of cheap labor in industry.

The cities grew in population and in importance in pace with their commercial and industrial complexes. The capitalist group remained small, and with a concentration of private wealth in few hands, the zaibatsu exerted economic influence far beyond their numbers. The urban middle class was small but growing. Bureaucrats, professionals, intellectuals, and students swelled its ranks. Most numerous were the unskilled industrial laborers, who made the goods but who could hardly afford to buy them, because they lacked adequate purchasing power. These economic groupings in cities affected the political scene. The industrialists, with important commercial and trading interests, expressed their political outlook through conservative parliamentary parties. The growing middle class also reflected its more liberal desires through the Diet, but its interests did not always coincide with those of the government. And as the urban middle class grew, the government had greater difficulty in keeping it in line, because this class displayed a propensity to accelerate changes in Japanese political life.

SOCIETY

The modernization and industrialization of Japan were reflected in its social and intellectual life, known in the early Meiji period as one of civilization and enlightenment (*bummei kaika*). An extensive but orthodox educational pattern was developed by the government. The early Meiji leaders showed wisdom in discerning the importance of education in a modern state. One base for power included a literate, and possibly indoctrinated, population, soldiers who could read and write, and trained technicians. Study abroad was encouraged, and among the two dozen political leaders, only two (Saigo and Okuma) had never been to Europe or to the United States. At first, foreign experts were hired to develop educational systems and were highly respected. These experts proved valuable but expensive, and by the turn of the century only a few of them remained as language teachers. In 1871, the Ministry of Education was formed and embarked on a great program of universal education. It build thousands of schoolhouses and trained tens of thousands of teachers.

By the early twentieth century, six years of primary coeducational schooling had become compulsory for all. Girls could go on in government institutions to middle schools for four or five years, but there their education ended, unless they entered private academies. In the educational structure, after the primary grades, boys could advance through lower technical to higher technical schools, or they could alternatively proceed up through five-year academic middle schools to three-year higher-level schools, and finally to three years at government universities (or four years in medicine). Tokyo Imperial University, with antecedents dating to shogunal schools that combined into one faculty in the year following the restoration, was formed in 1877. That same year, Kyoto Imperial University was opened, followed by universities at Sendai (1907) and Fukuoka (1910). Private mission and secular schools augmented publicly supported ones at various levels of instruction. In 1868, Fukuzawa Yukichi established a school that eventually grew into Keio, and in 1882, Okuma formed an institution that became Waseda. In 1875, a Japanese Christian, trained in the United States, founded Doshisha in Kyoto.

The overall educational system was geared to Japanese requirements. The general populace was taught to read, larger groups of literate people

Tokyo: prestigious Waseda University

found semi-skilled jobs, and a small core of highly educated men entered the professions and the bureaucracy. The Ministry of Education asserted authority over all schools, including private Japanese and Western mission schools. Curricula combined Occidental and Japanese subjects; students pursued Western sciences and used Chinese characters. Foreign languages, notably English, were taught. Books were translated from other languages; newspapers appeared and multiplied.

Universal education transformed Japan into the first Asian country with a literate populace, a fact that helped to explain its concurrent rise to industrial power and military strength. But the Japanese rejected the ideas of democracy and of equality in education. To the Japanese leaders, the purpose of education was not to permit youth to enjoy a richer life, but it was rather to provide competent citizens as a base for a strong state. These official goals prevailed, and, as stated in the Imperial Rescript of 1890, the core of Japanese education emphasized morality, social harmony, and loyalty. Education became an instrument of government that existed for the sake of the country and not for that of the individual. Japan pioneered in authoritarian techniques of using education as a means of political tutelage.

The formulation of state Shinto buttressed political indoctrination. State Shinto was administered by a separate department of religion, which also took charge of the varying particularist Shinto sects that continued to worship individual kami. State Shinto stressed the importance of the imperial shrine at Ise, the royal family, the national heroes, and ancestors. It incul-

Tokyo: Meiji Park, Shinto procession

cated devotion to the emperor and encouraged patriotism by reiterating the time-honored concepts of divinity of the emperor and of Japan as a unique land of the gods, with a benevolent but expansive manifest destiny.

As Shinto returned to the forefront, so did Buddhism and Christianity suffer. Even before the long-standing ban on Christianity was removed in 1873, Protestant missionaries had arrived from England and the United States. At first welcomed, they founded schools and won some converts, but Christianity was not completely adopted by the Japanese. Whereas in the early seventeenth century perhaps 2 percent of the population had embraced Christianity in its Catholic form, in 1889, less than a quarter of 1 percent were converts (40,000 Catholics, 29,000 Protestants, and 18,000 Orthodox). Christian theology made only a limited imprint in Meiji Japan, although Christian principles of social responsibility and of humanitarianism probably had greater, although a more indeterminate, effect.

Secular concepts had varying degrees of impact. Marxism was introduced to Japan later than other Western ideas. The Japanese initially were not interested in, and later not permitted to indulge in, protest movements or unorthodox ideologies. They concentrated on more abstract systems of philosophy. But in the 1880s, students and intellectuals became concerned with social issues resulting from urbanization and modernization. In 1882, a rickshaw men's union protested technological unemployment. It was disbanded, but the union activity attracted wide interest. Articles exposed adverse working conditions in coal mines and factories. There was a slow growth of the social conscience, and books with Marxist flavor were translated into Japanese.

After 1892, Socialist magazines were founded. In 1898, a small group, including some Christians, established the Society for the Study of Socialism (Shakai Shugi Kenkyukai). Early Socialist endeavors bore fruit by the turn of the century, and more labor unions were organized in the railroads and the ironworks. In 1901, the Social Democratic Party (*Shakai Minshuto*) was formed, but the government ordered it dissolved within three hours of its founding. A journal, *Heimin Shimbun* (*Common People's Newspaper*), was founded in 1904. It managed to eke out a precarious six-year existence, although it was suppressed from time to time. Protest action by the lower classes was something novel in Japan, and the government remained alert to any flare-ups of radicalism. By 1922, twenty-three leading Socialists had been tried and twelve executed. Leaders temporarily disappeared, to emerge in the more liberal decade of the 1920s with greater influence in intellectual and academic circles, especially among university faculties, in economics and history.

Other secular aspects of modernization made more visible impact. Foreigners started the first modern press in Japan in English, but, in 1870, in Yokohama, the first regular Japanese daily, the *Mainichi*, was issued. Nine years later, the *Asahi* chain was established, and into contemporary times the two became the zaibatsu of the newspaper industry. To help rid the country of unequal treaties, the government embarked on legal reforms. Individual, rather than joint family, ownership of property was provided for, but census statistics continued to recognize the validity of the old extended family as the appropriate demographic base of society. Laws were publicized, torture was abolished, and law court procedures were modeled after Western practices. Legal reforms proceeded on a piecemeal basis, but those that did not derive from popular acceptance or understanding proved ineffectual and they were dropped. By the turn of the century, the three basic law codes of a modern state—criminal, civil, and commercial—had been adopted. In 1873, the Gregorian calendar with its seven-day week and Sunday holiday was fashioned.

In the earlier decades of the Meiji, a mania for Westernized customs developed in urban society. The Charter Oath stipulation of 1868 that evil customs had to go was taken literally. Buddhists married, raised families, and ate beef. (Sukiyaki was supposedly invented because of the Western taste for meat dishes.) Instead of wearing the traditional long hair done up in a topknot, men cut their hair. Married women stopped blackening their teeth and shaving their eyebrows. Sensitivity to Western opinion and desire to follow the latest fads stimulated extremes, but, by 1885, the irrational imbalance for things Western was countered by a conservative reaction. Superficial Westernized customs, such as ballroom dancing and costume parties, were discarded, while the more lasting and significant imported technological and scientific innovations lost their onus of association with trivial Occidental peculiarities.

Perspective was regained, and, although Western influence continued to be strong, it was opposed in some quarters and more rationally evaluated in others. Meiji literature reflected the impact of Western thought. Translations of European and American classics were popular, although many translators were students rather than professional writers and linguists. A creative native style developed in the novel. During the early restoration years, novelists treated political themes, but with the advent of the constitution they redirected their talents to other ideas. One familiar literary strain portrayed the tensions of modernization. With pressures on individuals and families, cultural schizophrenia resulted in the main characters because modern and traditional values came into conflict. In the late nineteenth century, prominent themes of novels were pessimism and inaction. A typical Meiji novel might portray a hero, a sensitive soul, perhaps an artist with aspirations and individual goals, trying to meet and to resolve conflicting social and family demands made upon him. Self-doubt and self-denial complicated the resolution of his problems, and the hero, brooding on the bitterness and complexity of life, lapsed Hamlet-like into a state of paralysis and indecision.

CHRONOLOGY

1868	Fukuzawa Yukichi founds Keio University
1870	Mainichi, first Japanese newspaper, issued
1871	Ministry of Education established; currency reforms
1872	First railroad, Tokyo to Yokohama
1873	Land tax framed; ban on Christianity removed; Gregorian calendar adopted
1875	Doshisha University established in Kyoto
1877	Tokyo Imperial University founded
1879	Asahi newspaper chain founded
1882	Okuma establishes Waseda University
1888	Society for the Study of Socialism (Shakai Shugi Ken kyu-kai) founded
1890	Imperial rescript on official goals of education
1901	Social Democratic Party (Shakai Minshuto) established; dissolved immediately
1904	Heimin Shimbun founded

12

Meiji Japan

Foreign Relations

The energy devoted to strengthening the nation was also reflected in the creation of the imperial foundations of territorial expansion. Taking the cue from the aggressive tenor of the times at the turn of the century, Japan embarked on two major wars, the first with China (1894–1895), and the second with Russia (1904–1905). As a result, it gained colonies or spheres of influence on mainland Asia and offshore islands. In 1910, after long, careful periods of watchful waiting and careful diplomatic maneuvering, it annexed Korea. It came to diplomatic accommodation with the major European powers as well as with the United States. By 1911, all the unequal treaties had been terminated and replaced by others based on equality.

BACKGROUND

In the latter years of seclusion, prior to the restoration, there were individuals in Japan who had urged a vigorous continental policy. Russia's march eastward across Siberia awakened fears, and some Japanese had early advocated the acquisition of Kamchatka peninsula and Sakhalin Island. Others, including Yoshida Shoin, advocated the seizure of Taiwan, Korea, Manchuria, and the Philippines as well. After the restoration, although the primary concern was with charting domestic affairs, a concurrent military buildup laid the basis for the initial acquisition of territories including the islands surrounding Japan and on the Asian mainland.

Essential in a world of force was reliance on force, some Japanese argued, which could be used either for self-defense purposes or for supporting foreign conquests. The conscript laws of the early 1870s made youths liable for seven years of service: three on active duty, two in the first reserve, and another two in the second reserve. European uniforms were adopted, foreign advisers were hired, and, because of German military successes in Europe, the Japanese army modeled itself after Prussian organization and discipline. The country was divided into six military districts, and an efficient standing army of 400,000 was attained around the turn of the century. In 1869, a naval training station was created in Tokyo with English advisers and instruction in English, because England was the leading naval power of the day. In another six years, Japan had its own naval academy, arsenal, and naval medical facilities. It had constructed the first war vessel at Yokosuka near Yokohama, but it still depended upon the use of foreign ships and torpedo boats against the Chinese and the Russians in later campaigns.

As Japan built up its army, it sought to terminate the unequal treaties with the West. As early as 1872, Iwakura Tomomi, a court noble, was sent abroad to negotiate treaty revision. His mission was not successful, because Japan had not yet by that time taken enough strides toward modernization to placate the Western powers. A decade later, the foreign minister called a conference of interested parties to give up their rights regarding extraterritoriality and tariff controls. This move also was not successful. The foreign office then proceeded to negotiate individually with the respective powers on revisions, and it made some progress.

In 1888, Mexico, although a minor power, surrendered special legal rights and recognized Japan's tariff autonomy. In 1894, treaties with Great Britain and the United States, to be effective in five years if other powers took similar steps, were signed that abolished extraterritoriality and the most-favored-nation clauses, and provided for reciprocal rights of travel, residence, navigation, and religion. By 1899, Japan was the first Asian country to free itself of juridical aspects of extraterritoriality; in 1911, Japan resumed complete control of its own tariff schedules. By now, Europeans and Americans had been favorably impressed with the rapid strides made by the Japanese in modernizing and in quite successfully undertaking two wars; they were willing to give up their rights when the legal and administrative systems in Japan paralleled their own.

The Meiji leaders had won their point. In following Western models, they had eliminated special Western privileges. Japan also turned to overseas expansion. Within a decade of the restoration, Japan's borders had been extended. More complete control was imposed on Hokkaido. Under the Tokugawa, the island had been a daimyo fief, and few Japanese lived there. Now the economic development of the island was encouraged, and American experts were employed to assist in the development of that frontier area. Farther north, Japanese landed on the Kuriles and Sakhalin, where they encountered Russian presence and rivalry. In 1858, temporary accommodation was reached between the two powers in a treaty that declared joint possession of Sakhalin. Later, the Tokugawa shogun proposed a division of the island at the fiftieth parallel, but no agreement was reached on the issue. In the postrestoration period, another compromise was sought. In an 1875 quid pro quo treaty, Japan surrendered its claims to Sakhalin, Russia in turn surrendered its claims to the southern Kuriles, and Japan acquired legal title to part of that island chain. In 1878, the Bonins, a desolate island group in the Pacific but with potential strategic importance, also were annexed. Two years later, they were incorporated into the Tokyo metropolitan prefecture.

JAPAN, KOREA, AND CHINA

Japan then came into collision with China, first in the Ryukyus and Taiwan, and then in Korea. To the south, the Ryukyus, claimed by China, were absorbed into the growing empire. In an anomalous situation, the inhabitants of that archipelago were related to the Japanese by blood, and for two centuries they had been considered as part of the Satsuma fief. But they also had paid tribute to China through their ruler, who, moreover, had entered on his own into independent treaty relations with Western representatives, including Perry. The Japanese forced the complicated issue of sovereignty over the islands. In 1871, fifty-four of sixty-six shipwrecked Ryukyuans were massacred by aborigines on the east coast of Taiwan, which also was claimed by China. The next year, Japan took punitive action against the Chinese by formally annexing the Ryukyus. Only after some delay, in 1874, did it dispatch a force to Taiwan itself. Encountering superior military might, the Chinese settled the dispute by paying Japan an indemnity for the costs of the expedition as well as for the previously murdered Ryukyuans on Taiwan. The Japanese then left the island. China eventually gave up its claims to the Ryukyus, but the Japanese were to return within two decades in force to reoccupy and absorb Taiwan as a colony.

Japan and China had long historic interests in Korea. The ancient Yamato sovereigns had planted colonies on the southern Korean coast. For centuries, there had been close contact and exchange of ideas between China and Japan through Korea as intermediary. In the late sixteenth century, Hideyoshi had tried to conquer Korea and incorporate it into Japan. During the early seventeenth century, and into the nineteenth, Korea enjoyed commercial relations with both Japan and China. Korea always had been important geographically. From Japan, the nearby peninsula commanded the sea approach to Manchuria, eastern Siberia, and north China. From the mainland, in the hands of a strong power, the country could be a "dagger pointed at the heart of Japan."

In early Meiji times, a new wave of interest was directed toward the mainland. Western powers were encroaching in Korea. France, Great Britain, and the United States were interested in trade. Russia, through treaties with the Manchu rulers of China, had extended its borders to the Pacific. Ever-present China was also involved in domestic Korean politics, and, in the first half of the nineteenth century, Korea was more an appendage of China than of Japan, despite the political and military weakness of the former country. China, which had been in and out of Korea since the second century BCE, did not easily surrender its rights and claims of suzerainty. To complicate matters, against the background of international competition for Korea, that country was internally weak. The Yi dynasty, dating to the early fourteenth century, was in its final stages. Its officials were backward, conservative, sterile, and quite unable to discern winds of change. Korea truly lived up to its name as the Hermit Kingdom.

The early policy (1868–1876) of the Meiji leaders was to establish the fact of Korean independence and sovereignty and so eliminate Chinese-claimed paramountcy. They sent commissioners to investigate conditions there, and the mission reported that were China to take decisive action, Korea might become subject to a foreign power. While China disclaimed any responsibility for acts by Koreans, the Chinese declared, paradoxically, that although Korea was nominally a vassal of China, it did retain the unilateral power to make peace and to declare war against third countries. In 1874, Korea, in the nebulous status of a semi-sovereign state, agreed to receive an envoy from Japan and to send one in return. When the Japanese envoy arrived at Seoul, he was refused an imperial audience. Incidents ensued, and in the following years, a Japanese gunboat that was surveying the entrance to the Han River, on which Seoul, the capital, was located upstream, was fired upon. After demonstrations of Japanese naval force in 1874 and 1875, the Koreans were frightened into signing the Treaty of Kanghwa in February 1876. This first Korean treaty of modern times, signed with a country itself still chafing under unequal treaties, asserted the independence of Korea (one that denied Chinese suzerainty); opened two ports to Japanese trade, in addition to Pusan, where the Japanese already resided; and provided extraterritorial privileges for Japan. Other powers, including the United States in 1882, followed in concluding similar treaties with Korea.

China refused to recognize the growing Japanese role in Korean affairs. Over the next decade (1876–1885), a cold war in Korea ensued between China and Japan. Although the Korean king oriented his policies toward the Japanese, China endeavored to reassert its influence through other factions in the Korean court favorable to it. A struggle ensued in Seoul between those who wanted to learn from the West, as Japan had, and those conservatives who desired to resist change, as China was trying to do. Rivalries beset the court; mob demonstrations got out of hand. In 1882, the palace was attacked, and the Japanese legation was damaged.

Japan exacted an indemnity, demanded a mission of apology, extracted new privileges, and stationed an army in the capital. In turn, China began to deal more actively in order to keep Korea in its political orbit. Chinese troop presence was likewise augmented, and, after clashes with Japanese troops, more turbulence followed. Ito was dispatched to China to conduct negotiations to resolve peacefully the conflicting Asian interests in Korea. In 1885, a Sino-Japanese convention was signed. Both countries pledged to withdraw troops, and, if either side found it necessary to return troops to quell disorders, it had to notify the other concerned power.

The following decade (1885–1895) was marked by an uneasy coexistence between China and Japan in Korea. During this interim, more Western powers became involved in Korean affairs, but the chief struggle remained between the two Asian protagonists. Japan was committed to maintain its position in Korea. After the events of the 1880s, no Japanese cabinet could have withdrawn from Korea and survived the consequences. Yet the truce with China could not last indefinitely. In 1894, one of the many sporadic internal uprisings broke out in Korea. Both China and Japan sent in additional troops to suppress it. Although the rebellion ended before the arrival of either foreign contingent, more friction resulted between Japan and China.

Open hostilities between them finally broke out in July 1894, when Japanese ships fired on Chinese gunboats and on a British merchant ship transporting Chinese troops to Korea. Formal declarations of war followed. The war was brief; the Chinese were decisively routed on land and sea within nine months. Their small fleet was smashed, and their armies were quickly expelled from Korea. Japanese troops moved into Manchuria, where they captured the naval base of Lushun (Port Arthur) on Liaodong peninsula in southern Manchuria. They also occupied the naval base of Weihaiwei on Shandong peninsula, opposite Manchuria. Now commanding the sea approaches to northern China, the Japanese were in a strategic position to move on to the Chinese capital of Peking.

Defeated but haughty, the Chinese concluded peace with a people they regarded from ancient times with contempt. They sent a top diplomatic envoy, Li Hongzhang (Li Hung-chang), to arrange treaty terms at Shimonoseki (the former Choshu stronghold) with Japan, which was represented by Ito at the bargaining table. Each delegation had an American adviser. In the course of the negotiations, a Japanese attempted to assassinate Li. Losing face, the Japanese somewhat softened their already severe treaty provisions. In the chief terms of the Treaty of Shimonoseki of April 1895, China recognized the fact of Korean independence. It ceded to Japan the Liaodong peninsula, Taiwan, and the nearby Pescadores, a small group of islands lying some twenty-five miles off western Taiwan. China also paid an indemnity, opened four new treaty ports, extended the most-favored-nation clause, and promised a new treaty of commerce. Japanese troops occupied Taiwan, and in October 1895, a Japanese general set about pacifying the island. The following year, a civilian administration was commissioned, and the island became an integral part of the Japanese empire.

The Japanese were less successful in retaining the Liaodong peninsula. Within six days of the signing of the treaty, Germany, Russia, and France counseled Japan to surrender its claims there, allegedly because Japan's presence would be a menace to Peking and to the independence of Korea. Japan interpreted the act, known in history as the Triple Intervention, as a thinly veiled threat, but it was not strong enough to defy the three European powers. After extracting an additional indemnity from China, Japan acquiesced and withdrew from the Asian mainland. The experience was a bitter one, for it constituted the most humiliating diplomatic defeat for Japan prior to World War II. Relations between Japan and the three powers became estranged, while those with England, which had remained aloof from the problem, continued on a friendly basis.

JAPAN, KOREA, AND RUSSIA

After its defeat in 1895, China was replaced by Russia as the most serious challenger to Japanese interests on the northeastern Asian mainland. Between 1895 and 1904, Russian interests and influence increased in both Manchuria and Korea. Although China had been recently defeated, by the end of 1895, Japan felt less secure in its economic and political interests in China itself because of Russian presence. The Russians were completing the Trans-Siberian Railroad, which terminated in Vladivostok. In the course of Czar Nicholas II's coronation festivities in St. Petersburg in 1896, they concluded a fifteen-year treaty of alliance with China that pledged Russian protection of China against third parties. In turn, China granted Russia the right to construct the Chinese Eastern Railroad through northern Manchuria as a shortcut to Vladivostok. As Manchuria appeared to be moving into the Russian orbit, so did Korea, because its monarchs now looked to Russian support to counterbalance Japanese interests there.

Not desiring war at the time, the Japanese explored alternatives to contain Russia. On this matter, Japanese foreign policy, far from being monolithic or united in outlook, was flexible and was subject to experimentation and debate. Three points of view emerged from policy discussions as to how to contain Russia. One school, which included Fukuzawa Yukichi, advocated an alliance with the British, for England, like Japan, seemed threatened in Asia by Russian expansion. Others, including Okuma, advanced the idea of an alliance with China and Korea. Although it was an unrealistic alternative at the time, Okuma argued that Japan's safety lay not in any alliance with a Western power, which would exploit Japan, but rather with the two mainland powers who also were experiencing problems with Europeans. The trouble was that both China and Korea were backward and weak, although both had great resources and potential strength. Implicit in Japanese thinking was the idea that China and Korea could be developed under Japanese leadership and direction in a type of Pan-Asian movement. The third view, advanced in 1895 by both Yamagata and Ito before their split, was to seek accommodation with Russia itself and to delineate respective spheres of influence.

The third viewpoint initially prevailed. Japan endeavored to reach a modus vivendi with Russia in Korea, which constituted the more immediate consideration. While in Russia in 1896 for the czar's coronation (a year after China's defeat by Japan), Yamagata proposed to the Russians a division of Korea at the thirty-eighth parallel. The Russians declined the offer. But that same year, Yamagata concluded with the Russian foreign minister an agreement to establish a condominium over Korea. The joint protectorate did not work out, and, in 1898, the Japanese foreign minister signed with the Russian ambassador in Tokyo an agreement declaring the mutual nonintervention by both powers in internal Korean affairs.

Meanwhile, the Russians pushed on in northern China and Manchuria. In 1898, as part of a general scramble for concessions, Russia received from China leaseholds at the tip of the Liaodong peninsula in southern Manchuria, where Lushun and Dalian or Luda (Dairen) were located. It also received the right to construct a railroad branching from the Chinese Eastern Railroad and cutting south across Manchuria to Lushun. Now entrenched in an area from which they had helped to force out the Japanese only three years previously, the Russians established a naval base at Lushun, and they moved ominously closer to Peking. There, at the turn of the century, as a result of the Boxer uprising against the Westerners, the Russians participated in an international expeditionary force that marched on the Chinese capital to quell the rebellion. Their troops remained in northern China and in Manchuria until 1902, long after the suppression of the outbreak. Convinced that no accommodation was possible with Russia, the Japanese, who had once advocated a Russian alliance, now began to favor the notion of one with England. Ito held out to the end for an arrangement with Russia.

Desiring to end their isolation, to advance their interests in Korea, and to contain Russia, the Japanese negotiated a treaty with the British, who in turn envisioned Japan as a counterpoise to Russia in Asia. Fearful that Japan might ally itself with Russia against their own interests, the British in 1902 concluded with the newly arising Asian power the ten-year Anglo-Japanese

Alliance, thereby ending centuries of "splendid" British isolation as well. Its terms confirmed the integrity of China and of Korea, although Britain recognized special Japanese interests in Korea. The two signatories affirmed neutrality in the event that one of them was engaged in war with a third party, but each would aid the other if either were attacked by two or more other powers. Three years later, in 1905, in a revision of the alliance, Britain recognized the paramount rights of Japan in Korea, and each now pledged to aid the other should either be attacked by only one other power. In 1911, the treaty was renewed for another decade until it was replaced by post–World War I international security arrangements.

Despite the alliance with the British, in 1903 and 1904, the Japanese continued efforts toward rapprochement with Russia in regard to Korea. They suggested a Russia-in-Manchuria zone for one of Japan-in-Korea, an arrangement recognizing Russian supremacy in Manchuria and Japanese predominance in Korea, but the Russians stalled. The conflicting positions relative to political paramountcy in Manchuria and Korea finally erupted in war. On February 6, 1904, the Japanese severed relations with Russia. Two days later, they torpedoed the Russian fleet at Lushun, and, on the fifth day, they declared war. Segments of the U.S. press headlined the sequence of events as a bold initiative. The Russians augmented troop strength over the newly completed Trans-Siberian Railroad to Manchuria and Korea and dispatched their Baltic fleet halfway around the world to Korea, only to be destroyed by Admiral Togo Nakagoro in a great naval battle in the Tsushima strait off Kyushu. In the eighteen months' war, major battles were fought in Manchuria on Chinese soil. The military engagements, well covered by news correspondents including Jack London, ended in stalemate. The Japanese asked President Theodore Roosevelt to mediate (an act for which he received the Nobel Peace Prize). The Russians accepted the proffered mediation, and both belligerent parties met at Portsmouth, New Hampshire, to conduct peace negotiations.

The Treaty of Portsmouth of September 1905 reflected the stalemated military situation. Japanese demands were not fully met. Japan received not all of Sakhalin as desired but only the southern half. It did not get an indemnity, and it did not acquire the coveted Maritime Provinces along the Siberian Pacific coast. But, subject to China's consent, Japan succeeded to the twenty-five-year (from 1898) Russian territorial, railroad, and commercial leases in southern Manchuria. The Russians also acknowledged the fact of Korean independence (and inferentially Japanese paramountcy there). Despite the restraints of the treaty, Japan's position was strengthened on mainland Asia, and it achieved the status of a world military and political power. Entering the war as the underdog, it emerged with enhanced prestige. Japan fired the imagination of colonial Asia, for here at last was an Asian power fighting a white power on an equal basis and "defeating" it. Asian nationalists took heart, while the Western powers, including the United States, began to reevaluate their positions in a changing Asian international security pattern.

The Japanese 1905 Peking treaty with China confirmed the Portsmouth concessions in southern Manchuria, and the agreement laid the legal foundations for Japanese economic and political growth there and in northern China. In 1906, Japan created the South Manchurian Railroad, which became the chief agent of Japanese penetration into the area. Japan not only operated the railway but also managed mines, hotels, schools, hospitals, ships, and research institutes in the wide accompanying railroad zone in southern Manchuria, known familiarly to the Chinese as Guandong (Kwantung). It stationed troops to maintain security, and over the years, these troops increased vastly in number until they were designated in time as the Guandong Army. A governor-general ruled the leased areas. Lushun became a strong naval base, and in the adjacent free port of Dalian, a Chinese official collected the customs tariff under Japanese aegis. Eased out of Manchuria in 1895 by the Triple Intervention, the Japanese in 1905 returned for a longer, well-entrenched stay.

JAPAN, KOREA, AND WORLD POWERS

The Treaty of Portsmouth recognized Japan's paramount interests in Korea as well. In late 1905, Ito went to Seoul to negotiate a treaty that transformed the country into a Japanese protectorate. Korean foreign relations came under Japanese management, and a Japanese resident general (Ito was the first) was stationed in the capital. Ito launched reforms, but, complaining of the slow pace of modernization, he forced the abdication of the Korean king. In 1907, a new Japanese-Korean agreement was signed that placed in Japanese hands the administration of all important affairs of state, official appointments and dismissals, and all laws. The Korean army was disbanded. Finally, on August 22, 1910, a treaty of annexation terminated Korean sovereignty. The peninsula, now a colony of Japan, was renamed Chosen (derived from an ancient Chinese designation for the country). Japanese divisions were stationed there, and subsequently, the government of the country was placed under a Japanese general. Chosen became the Japanese political and military headquarters on the Asian mainland.

Korea played a key role in the Japanese movement into China, as had Taiwan in southward expansion. To Korea, the Japanese brought law, order, and prosperity, but all efforts were made for Japanese benefits. In the regimented colony, rice production increased, the fish catch in Korean waters quadrupled, and reforestation proceeded. Economic gains were noticeable, but the Koreans did not participate in them. In a double standard of wages and opportunities, the Japanese received the better paying jobs and offices. Study of the Japanese language was made compulsory for Koreans. Some were forcibly sent as labor battalions to southern Sakhalin or to the Japanese home islands. Hatred of Japan became widespread among Koreans at home, but rebellion was impossible because of military controls. Some anti-Japanese leaders, such as Syngman Rhee, left the country in exile. They took up residence abroad, to continue the fight against Japanese colonial rule over their homeland.

Having confirmed its paramount position in southern Manchuria and Korea, Japan came to terms with the leading European powers. There were no problems with Britain, for the alliance sealed diplomatic friendship. There were no disputes with France, although Japan had resented that country's role in the Triple Intervention. After England had signed the Entente Cordiale with France, Japan also came to an agreement with the French. In 1907, a treaty concluded in Paris pledged mutual respect for Chinese independence and territory. Japanese in French Indochina, and Indochinese in Japan, were to be accorded reciprocal most-favored-nation status. No problems existed with Germany.

The Russians did not remain enemies. Japan concluded four agreements with czarist Russia to delineate respective spheres of influence in East Asia. In 1907, two conventions, one public and one secret, were signed. The former constituted a routine reaffirmation of the Open Door policy (equal commercial opportunities for foreign powers) in China, while the latter divided Manchuria into two spheres of special jurisdiction—Japan in the south and Russia in the north. Japan also recognized the primary interests of Russia in Outer Mongolia, while Russia accepted Japan's position in Korea. In 1910, the two parties agreed to consult each other on effective measures in case the status quo in East Asia were threatened. In addition to northern Manchuria, in 1912, Russia was allotted the area of western Inner Mongolia (part of China) as its place of influence, while eastern Inner Mongolia was added to that of Japan. In 1916, with Russia bogged down in World War I, Japan pledged munitions and war supplies to Russia. The signatories promised not to be a party to any arrangement or treaty directed against the other. A secret convention also established a five-year defensive alliance; the two nations pledged mutual assistance should war result from the defense of their interests in China and border areas. By World War I, Japan had swung Russia, as well as England and France, into support of its policy of expansion on the Asian continent.

The story was otherwise with regard to the United States; a turn for the worse took place in Japanese-American relations. Relations had been cordial prior to 1905. The United States did not intervene in the Sino-Japanese War. Its sympathies were with the Japanese in the war with Russia; in 1905, it closed its embassy in Seoul and dealt with the Koreans through the Japanese. In return, Japan looked on the United States as the one great Western power from which it had nothing to fear. Japanese students came to the United States. American markets sopped up Japanese tea and raw silk, and the Japanese in turn bought American cotton, machine goods, and raw materials.

After 1905, the tide turned. Although some Japanese blamed the United States for the compromised terms of the Treaty of Portsmouth, more serious and long-range problems were emerging. The issue of Japanese immigration into the United States, technically a domestic issue, was turning into a diplomatic impasse. Unskilled Japanese arriving on the West Coast, where they received low wages, alarmed American labor leaders, who claimed that their workers could not compete on similar terms. (Census statistics for 1900 revealed some 80,000 Japanese in Hawaii and 24,000 in the United States as compared with 90,000 Chinese in the territorial United States.) In 1900, Tokyo imposed restrictions on emigration to the United States, and, in 1907, the government concluded with Washington a gentleman's agreement to prevent more laborers from emigrating.

Americans formulated more extreme measures. In 1905, in San Francisco, a league to exclude Japanese and Koreans was organized. The next year, San Francisco school officials attempted to segregate Japanese students, who numbered only eighty, from American pupils. President Theodore Roosevelt interfered, and the idea was dropped, but on the stated condition that the federal government would stop immigration of Japanese into the continental United States from Hawaii, Mexico, and Canada. These discriminatory moves occurred at the same time as the San Francisco earthquake and fire of 1906, disasters in which the Japanese Red Cross had contributed materially to relief measures. The next year, the Congress passed an act authorizing the president to prevent further immigration, and the president by proclamation then prohibited Japanese movement from Hawaii, Mexico, and Canada.

Power politics complicated immigration matters. Now committed in the Philippines, wrested from Spain in 1898, the United States was concerned with possible thrusts toward the archipelago, which Roosevelt termed an "Achilles heel." Washington was also pledged to maintain the Open Door policy of equal commercial opportunity and treaty rights in China. In attempting to preserve Philippine territory and Chinese treaty rights, U.S. policies toward Japanese moves became contradictory. Endeavoring to contain Japan's commercial and financial continental expansion, Secretary of State Frank Knox in 1909 proposed the purchase by China of Japanese and Russian railroads in Manchuria with funds provided by those powers that had pledged to uphold the Open Door. The neutralization proposal called for the operation of the railroads by an international board until China could repay the international loan. The Japanese and the Russians found this unacceptable, and the suggestion tended instead to throw the Japanese and Russians closer together. (The 1910 treaty reflected their concern about encroachment on mutual Manchuran interests).

However, American policy seemed to accept Japanese territorial expansion. Agreements in 1905 between Secretary of War William H. Taft and Prime Minister Katsura in Tokyo and, in 1908, between Secretary of State Elihu Root and the Japanese ambassador Baron Takahira in Washington, confirmed Japan's paramount position in Korea, while Japan affirmed that it had no designs on the Philippines. Despite these temporizing arrangements, Japan was coming more and more into conflict with the United States over mutual Asian territorial and commercial concerns. The disparate positions of Americans, who advocated equal treaty rights (implied in the Open Door policy), and of the Japanese, who advanced special rights, in time escalated and finally culminated in war in 1941. Ironically, the country that had introduced Japan to Western ways was to receive the brunt of Japanese modernization in its military form.

CHRONOLOGY

1858	Russian-Japanese joint occupation of Sakhalin
1872	Iwakura mission abroad to end unequal treaties; Ryukyus annexed
1874	Taiwan incident; Ryukyu indemnity paid by China
1875	Japanese-Russian treaty; Sakhalin for Kuriles
1876	Treaty of Kanghwa with Korea
1878	Japan annexes the Bonins
1885	Sino-Japanese convention on Korea
1894–1895	Sino-Japanese war over Korea
1895	Treaty of Shimonoseki; Taiwan annexed; Triple Intervention
1896	Japanese-Russian condominium over Korea
1898	Japanese-Russian abstention in Korean affairs
1899	Japan frees itself of extraterritoriality
1902	Anglo-Japanese Alliance
1904–1905	Russo-Japanese war
1905	Treaty of Portsmouth; Anglo-Japanese Alliance amended; Peking treaty with China confirming Portsmouth terms: Korea a Japanese protectorate; Taft-Katsura note
1906	Southern Manchurian Railway created
1907	French-Japanese treaty on reciprocal rights of citizens; Russo-Japanese treaty on Manchurian spheres; gentleman's agreement with United States

1908	Root-Takahira understanding
1909	Knox proposal of railroad neutralization in Manchuria
1910	Korea becomes a Japanese colony; Russo-Japanese treaty to keep status quo
1911	Japan resumes tariff control; Anglo-Japanese alliance renewed
1912	Russo-Japanese agreement on Inner Mongolia spheres
1916	Japan promises Russia war aid; five-year mutual assistance treaty signed

13

Imperial Japan

World Power

(1912–1922)

The story of imperial Japan in the thirty-three years between the death of the Meiji emperor and the end of World War II is one of political success twisted into military failure. The only non-Western country to meet the modernizing challenge of the Occident, Japan continued its spectacular growth, initiated in the Meiji period, well into the 1930s.

After the death of the Emperor Meiji in 1912, his son Yoshihito ascended the throne and inaugurated the Taisho (Great Righteousness) period. His reign, which lasted to 1926, has been characterized as the Taisho democracy by some Japanese historians because of the relative liberalism of the times. Concurrent with the accession to the throne of a new emperor was the termination of the alternating premierships of Saionji and Katsura. The cycles came to an end in 1913, accompanied by outbursts and rioting by mobs, who surrounded the Diet building and demanded the end of genro rule.

An admiral, Yamamoto Gombei, was next designated as prime minister, but when the navy was implicated in financial scandals relating to battleship construction, the Diet refused to pass the budget, and the prime minister resigned. In 1914, Okuma, now eighty years old, in command of a new coalition party, the Kenseikai, assumed the post. The aging aristocrat, earlier a champion of representative government, led an administration marked by unprecedented chauvinistic nationalism. This included the presentation of the Twenty-One Demands to China, an action that resulted in the strengthening of the military hand in diplomacy.

After two years in office, Okuma was replaced by Marshal Terauchi Masatake, a general and former governor-general of Korea. His term was marked by domestic wartime problems, profiteering, inflated prices, and widespread rioting over the high price of rice. In 1918, his cabinet fell, and Hara

Kei (or Takashi), head of the Seiyukai, the majority in parliament, became prime minister. Except for the brief interlude of the Okuma-Itagaki party coalition in 1898, Hara Kei was the first party man, and the first commoner, to be prime minister. His appointment was epochal, for it heralded the end of rule by the genro and the beginning of rule by party politicians, the men of new Japan in commerce, industry, and finance. Party government, with an interruption between 1922 and 1924, lasted until 1932.

BACKGROUND

Further changes brought with them new and urgent problems and fresh leadership but divided counsels. In the first half of the twentieth century, the sons and grandsons of the nineteenth-century Meiji reformers lived in a world different from that of their forebears. The second and third generations had to face and to resolve such pressing issues as providing employment and benefits for a burgeoning population, increasing food imports, regulating free market economic cycles, achieving military security in an ever-expanding empire, and adjusting to the social and intellectual ramifications of modernization. National wealth increased, but all groups, especially the tenant farmers and factory workers, did not share proportionately in the increase.

As new groups emerged and the political structure was rearranged, a larger and more diverse leadership replaced the smaller, unified Meiji oligarchy. The new elites embraced the military, the bureaucrats, the political parties, the zaibatsu, the middle classes, and the several constitutional and nonofficial bodies close to the emperor. The monarch himself became more symbolic and more removed from decision-making procedures. With no strong and effective mechanism for settling disagreements among the various factions, except for each to claim that it spoke in the name of the emperor, these forces operated in countervailing fashion through the 1920s, although by the end of the next decade, the military had gained predominance.

Plural political elites were accompanied by plural political philosophies. A growing liberal strain of opinion, spearheaded by Minobe Tatsukichi, professor of administrative law at Tokyo Imperial University between 1900 and 1932, implied that the emperor was only the highest organ of the state rather than an absolute independent entity. His theory had some acceptance among intellectuals of the 1920s, but traditional views continued to be strong. Kokutai, or national policy, continued to emphasize the uniqueness of Japan, its strong moral base, its familiar character, and its Shinto statism. This more extreme position eventually won out in the 1930s, because advantages were passing to rightist civilian and military groups at a time when Japan was becoming more responsive both to authoritarian trends in the outside world and to internal reactions to these external forces. For too long, Japan existed in a compromised world of restrictions and of partial freedoms, in a delicate balance of authoritarianism and liberalism.

Japan's economy, despite fluctuations, continued to expand. By the turn of the century, a firm basis had been laid for modern industrial development. A few indices revealed continued expansion. Between 1914 and 1930, production of raw materials went up 46 percent; in the last half of the 1920s, overall increase in economic productivity reached 59 percent. Gains provided an impetus for further growth. From an exporter of raw and semi-processed materials during the Meiji period, Japan was transformed into a producer of finished goods. Newly acquired colonies, leaseholds, and expanding foreign markets, particularly in southern Manchuria and in northern China after 1905, helped to sustain the growing economy. Yet they contributed only a small percentage of total Japanese raw materials and of the ratio of foreign trade.

The psychological awareness, as well as the reality, of economic dependence on overseas areas became more intense as the decades progressed. As Japan industrialized, it became more tied into world trade; it experienced the modern capitalistic phenomenon of booms and recessions. In part because of an overambitious rate of industrial investment and of official expenditures that helped to create a lopsided and top-heavy government sector in the mixed economy, by 1913, the Japanese economy was floundering.

The advent of World War I helped to bail the country out of its economic doldrums. The war diverted the industry of European competitors to production of armaments and industries, while Japan's arms production was considerably smaller. Its military participation was limited and allowed it to continue the industrialization process. Japan was virtually free to produce for Asian markets and to make inroads into European and African markets. It displaced Great Britain as the chief foreign economic power in China, and, by filling Allied war orders, it changed from a debtor to a creditor nation in international trade. But a year or so after the end of the war, deflation set in, prices collapsed, and government expenses declined.

As Japan broadened its domestic base, so it expanded abroad. Imperial Japan capitalized on its preeminence in Asia to consolidate either forcibly or peaceably territorial and diplomatic gains achieved during World War I. It displayed tractability in foreign affairs of the 1920s in several major instances. It pulled out of Siberia after the Russian Revolution and the Allied intervention there. It agreed to the arrangements of the Washington Conference of 1921–1922, which reduced its naval strength considerably (as elaborated later in this chapter).

The foreign policy of imperial Japan was concerned essentially with China. Japan's paramount interests were centered on the Asian mainland, where they were facing crises by the end of the Meiji period. In China, the two-and-a-half-century rule of the Manchu, the last of two-dozen traditional dynasties dating back to around 2000 BCE in Chinese history, was coming to an end. China's political order, weakened in the nineteenth century by internal decay and external forces, was collapsing. In 1912, the ancient empire abruptly came to an end. The Manchu were replaced by a nominal republic, headed by a warlord, established in Peking that same year.

Recognized by Japan and the Western powers, it did not command universal Chinese loyalty. In southern China, a rival government was established, and other warlords operated independently throughout the country. Instability in Chinese politics implied difficulties in the preservation of Japanese economic privileges in the chaotic country. The Japanese had great interest in China and in Manchuria, considered a territorial part of China but under the autonomous rule of a warlord. One-fifth of Japanese capital was invested in Manchurian industries, and the same proportion of Japanese imports, including necessary iron and coal, came from China. Extensive investment was augmented by psychological commitment as well, for the Japanese envisioned limitless resources and endless markets in China.

In order to preserve Japanese economic rights in a politically confused China, several possibilities were open to Japan. It could practice, on the one hand, a policy of nonintervention in internal Chinese affairs and wait "until the dust settled." The advantage of such a policy was to avoid identification with any of the several Chinese factions contending for eventual mastery over all of the country. The disadvantage was that Japanese interests might suffer in a chaotic interim of indefinite tenure. However, Japan could pursue a policy of intervention. It could encourage revolution or political change in China, and, by backing some Chinese party, it might shift the balance of power in its favor. As a third tactical move, a combination of the two policies could be achieved by treating China and Manchuria separately: noninterference in China, but involvement in a more important economically Manchuria. The last policy eventually won out in the 1920s, but prior to that time, in the course of World War I and in the postwar settlements, Japan fished most extensively in the muddied Chinese waters.

JAPAN AND WORLD WAR I

Japan entered World War I essentially for two reasons: broadly to extend its Asian interests, and specifically to honor what it interpreted as a commitment under terms of the Anglo-Japanese alliance. According to the treaty, as amended in 1911, each signatory was to support the other if it were attacked by a third party, but not necessarily to the extent of also declaring war. When Great Britain entered the conflict, the Japanese, recalling their obligation, as well as Germany's role in the Triple Intervention of 1895, pressed for war. But Britain, realizing that Japan could expand its Asian operations (which materialized, because Japan took over the German islands in the central Pacific), was cautious about invoking the alliance.

Acting unilaterally, Japan went ahead and served an ultimatum to Germany, demanding the surrender of German interests in Shandong (a peninsula and province in northern China opposite southern Manchuria). Britain could not restrain Japan, and neither could the protesting and powerless Chinese. The Americans remained neutral. An unwanted ally, Japan declared war on Germany. Hostilities erupted in one-sided engagements in China and in the Pacific. The Japanese appropriated German holdings in China, granted to Germany through earlier unequal treaties by a weak country. Germany's rights in Shandong were extensive. The more important provisions included a ninety-nine-year lease on Jiaozhou Wan (Kiaochow Bay) from 1898, with its fine modern port city of Qingdao (Tsingtao); an approximately thirty-mile-wide belt around the bay, where foreign troops could be deployed; the operation of a railroad between Qingdao and Jinan (Tsinan), the inland capital of the province; the right to mine coal within ten miles of the railroad; and the previous consultation of China with Germany, and now Japan, on any decisions affecting Shandong. Firmly ensconced in Shandong, a province particularly important to the Chinese because it was the ancient home of Confucius, their greatest sage, Japan made further demands on China.

The most extreme of these were presented in January 1915 by Okuma's cabinet to the Peking warlord government at a time when the Western powers were diverted by conflict. Known collectively as the Twenty-One Demands, they indicated the extent of Japanese interest in dominating China. Had they all been granted, China would have become a Japanese protectorate. The demands were grouped into five categories. Group One confirmed Japan's newly won rights in Shandong, and Japan was to consent to any future disposition of them. This demand precluded a German return to Shandong after the war. The Japanese were adamant on this point because the previous humiliation of the Triple Intervention and the compromises of the Treaty of Portsmouth still rankled Japanese foreign policymakers. Group Two related to Japan's position in southern Manchuria and in eastern Mongolia. Japan demanded that the leaseholds, shortly to expire, of Lushun, Dalian, and the South Manchurian Railroad, be extended from twenty-five to ninety-nine years. It also sought more extensive economic and residential rights for its citizens in eastern Mongolia and in southern Manchuria. (Russian control of the Chinese Eastern Railroad continued in northern Manchuria until 1935.)

Group Three of the demands dealt with a program to promote Japanese industrial activity in the central Yangtze valley by giving the Han-Ye-Ping

Company, a Sino-Japanese concern, the mining monopoly of iron and coal property in central China. Group Four concerned the nonalienation of Chinese coastal territory opposite the Japanese island colony of Taiwan. Group Five consisted of a variety of demands, designated by the Japanese as "requests": the hiring of Japanese as advisers, the granting of interior lands to Japanese individuals and groups, the placing of Chinese police under joint administration in designated areas, Chinese purchases of arms from Japan, the extension of railway concessions in southern China, and the "right of preaching" in China.

Presented secretly, the terms of the demands were leaked by Peking and resulted in strong world reaction. But the European powers were engaged in a desperate conflict, and while the Chinese protested, they could modify only some of the demands. From Washington, Secretary of State William Jennings Bryan informed both Japan and China that the United States would not recognize any agreement that impinged upon the political or territorial integrity of the Republic of China or that abrogated the international policy relative to China commonly designated as the Open Door.

Faced with some opposition in China and abroad, the Japanese in an agreement of May 1915 received only part of their demands. Of these, the more important included the German leaseholds in Shandong, which were to be returned to China after the war but on the condition of the recognition of Shandong as a Japanese sphere of influence. They extended the Manchurian leaseholds to ninety-nine years. Japan received the right to be consulted first in case China required foreign capital to develop railways or harbors in Fujian (Fukien) province, across the strait from Taiwan. By pressing extreme demands and realizing only part of them, the Japanese lost face in China and redirected their efforts toward Manchuria. On the other hand, the demands helped to crystallize Chinese national consciousness and heightened Chinese distrust of Japan.

Buffeted in China, Japan pressed for advantages at the Versailles Conference after the war. There the Japanese delegation presented at least three items for the agenda that were of paramount importance to them: the cession of the former German islands in the Pacific that Japan was occupying (the Marianas, Carolines, and Marshalls), the confirmation of claims to the former German rights in Shandong, and a declaration of racial equality in the Covenant of the proposed League of Nations. In none of these areas did the Japanese wholly succeed. At Versailles, President Woodrow Wilson, unhappy over the necessity of granting Pacific islands to Japan, agreed to a league mandate system. This system gave Japan supervisory control, subject to league approval, over the islands.

Wilson compromised on mandates rather than colonies for Japan, because he had been forced by the insistence of Australia and New Zealand that they be awarded some of the German territories, which they occupied, preferably also as colonies. Japan's position was strengthened by the fact that in early 1917, it had concluded secret agreements (of which Wilson may not have had any knowledge) with Great Britain, France, Italy, and Russia, all of whom promised to support Japan's claims at the peace table. The administrative distinction was fine, but despite Allied support, in the end Japan got mandates, with theoretical responsibility to the League for their administration (although the islands did in effect become Japanese colonies).

Japan also wanted to confirm the former German rights in Shandong. The problem became complicated, for although Japan was determined to retain these rights, the Chinese were equally determined not to transfer them. The Chinese delegation, while representing divided political factions at home, were united at Versailles on this issue. The members of the delegation, drawn from a young, progressive, nationalistic, and revolutionary China, were adamant in opposing the Japanese claims. Japan's legal position in Shandong, on the other hand, had just been bolstered by an agreement (September 1918), not concluded under duress, with the conservative warlord Peking government, which explicitly consented to the transfer of Jiaozhou to Japan on the understanding that Japan would restore the leaseholds to China and would retain only certain rights. Caught between both Chinese and Japanese inflexible positions, Wilson took a middle stand on the issue. The Shandong properties were awarded to Japan, but, under Wilson's insistence, Japan declared that it would return them to China and would retain only certain of the rights. Japan remained unsatisfied, and China, annoyed, refused to sign the Versailles Treaty. It concluded a separate peace treaty with the defeated Central Powers.

Finally, Japan, a rising nonwhite world power and spokesman for colonial Asia, was sensitive to racial slights and requested that a declaration of racial equality among states be posited as a basic principle of the League of Nations in its Covenant. This proved to be a controversial issue. Initially, Wilson appeared to favor its inclusion, as did France and Italy. But Australia, which excluded nonwhite immigration, vigorously opposed it. Britain, caught between ties of empire and the Japanese alliance, supported the former. Moreover, Wilson had second thoughts, because some state laws, such as those of California, forbade ownership of land by aliens ineligible for citizenship, which included the Japanese and other Asians. In Washington, senatorial resistance to granting Japanese racial equality might defeat the Covenant, the president argued.

The Japanese, encountering a mixed international response, then modified their request by asking for the endorsement of the principles of equality and just treatment of nations in the preamble, rather than in the operative text of the Covenant. The amendment to effect this change was passed, 11 to 6, by the commission preparing the Covenant, but Wilson, the chairman, ruled that because the vote was not unanimous, the amendment did not carry. Japan did not get the declaration, and the racial rebuff struck a deep resentful chord. Yet, despite setbacks, it gained appreciably from participating in World War I. It expanded territory and acquired more rights, however temporary, in China. With no great expenditure of troops or of armaments, and with limited fighting confined to the Far East, Japan gained much at little cost.

As the war came to an end, international complications concurrently arose in Manchuria and in Siberia as a result of the Russian Revolution. In July 1918, Japanese troops marched into northern Manchuria to take over the Russian-administered Chinese Eastern Railroad on the pretext that peace in the region was threatened by possible attacks by the Bolshevik or White Russian forces that had fled there. The United States protested Japanese actions, but not desiring Chinese sovereignty over the railroad either, it solved the dilemma by participating in an interallied board, headed by a distinguished American engineer, to administer the railroad on an interim basis.

Siberia proved stickier. Several White Russian governments in exile, as well as self-appointed empire builders, operated independently in eastern Siberia. Into the political confusion came some 50,000 Czech troops, who had been prisoners of the Russians or who were deserters from the Austrian armies, wending their way back to Europe via Siberia. On their retreat, they clashed with the Bolsheviks, and although they probably were never in danger of recapture by the Austrians or by the Germans, the Allies thought them endangered, and they tried to enlist them in the Allied side in the European war.

Into this chaotic state of affairs, in July 1918, Wilson reluctantly permitted American participation in the Siberian intervention, ostensibly to save the Czechs but more realistically to prevent Japan from absorbing eastern Siberia. He disavowed intervention in internal Russian affairs. Some 9,000 American troops landed at Vladivostok, as did a small number of British and some Annamese from Indochina under French command. The Japanese dispatched 72,000 men. The Allies took over the management of the Trans-Siberian Railroad, but the American attempts failed to stop effectively the buildup of Japanese troops. In the touch-and-go situation in Siberia, Japanese were killed by Russians in various incidents. The aftermath of one such incident resulted in the Japanese occupation of the northern half of Sakhalin and a demand for reparations from Russia. Gradually, the Bolsheviks consolidated their hold eastward through Siberia, and, in 1922, it was incorporated into the Soviet Union. By that time, the Americans had long since withdrawn (April 1920), but the Japanese left only under pressures generated that year at the Washington Conference.

THE WASHINGTON CONFERENCE

By the time the Washington Conference was convoked in late 1921 to settle Pacific issues generally and to accommodate conflicting Japanese-American problems specifically, many sources of tension had arisen between the two countries. The immigration issue, commercial and naval rivalry, and political problems were the outstanding causes of conflict. In 1917, there had been momentary accommodation when Secretary of State Robert Lansing and the Japanese Ambassador Viscount Ishii Kikujiro, in a controversial exchange of notes in Washington, acknowledged that Japan had priorities in China, because "territorial propinquity creates special relations."

But the bulk of American policies in Asia seemed instead to aim at the containment of Japan. In 1910, Secretary of State Frank Knox had proposed the neutralization of Manchurian railroads, as noted previously. From 1911 to 1913, and again in 1920, the United States had joined multinational railroad consortiums in China to build railways there and to block further Japanese commercial and financial programs. In 1915, Secretary of State William J. Bryan had proclaimed the nonrecognition of the Twenty-One Demands. At Versailles, Wilson did not fully endorse Japanese claims to racial equality, Shandong rights, or Pacific colonies. In 1918, the interallied board was created to manage Manchurian railroads, and the Siberian intervention was joined with the aim of containing Japan.

To resolve peaceably the conflicting national interests in East Asia, the Washington Conference, which met during three months, from November 1921 to February 1922, under the Harding Administration, resulted in seven treaties and twelve resolutions relating to Pacific and Asian affairs. The Five Power Naval Treaty concerned itself primarily with naval ratios for capital ships (battleships), with some reference to aircraft carriers, newly emergent on the naval scene. Overall total strengths of battleships were limited to a 5:5:3:1.75:1.75 ratio, respectively, for the United States, Great Britain, Japan, France, and Italy. Japan insisted that because its navy was especially reduced by this formula, the United States and Great Britain should join it in nonfortification programs to ensure Pacific, and, especially, Japanese security. (As it was, this was the first international treaty to recognize that U.S. naval strength, let alone Japanese, was equal to Great Britain's.)

Accordingly, the three governments incorporated into the Five Power Treaty other provisions prohibiting construction of any additional fortifications on certain Pacific islands. The relevant U.S. possessions included Wake, Midway, the Aleutians, Guam, Pago Pago on Samoa, and the Philippines. The British areas that were covered by the treaty were Hong Kong and insular possessions in the Pacific east of the 110 east longitude meridian, excepting the islands adjacent to Canada, Australia, and New Zealand. The Japanese islands included the Kuriles, Bonins, Ryukyus, Taiwan, and the

Pescadores. The United States and Great Britain could still fortify the major naval bastions of Hawaii and Singapore, but because of their distance from Japan, the arrangement practically ensured Japanese security in the western Pacific. The Five Power Treaty was to run initially until the end of 1936, at which date any of the contracting parties could terminate the agreement by giving two years' prior notice.

A second treaty, the Four Power Treaty, replaced the Anglo-Japanese alliance. This alliance, initially aimed at Russia in 1901 and then Germany in World War I, by 1921 could be interpreted as now directed against the United States. Americans denounced the existence of the alliance, and strong Canadian protests were added to those of Americans. Canada feared both Japanese immigration and the specter of involvement in war as a member of the empire on the side of Great Britain, allied with Japan, against the neighboring United States. Canada was not represented at the conference, but the United States, Great Britain, Japan, and France signed the treaty. The signatories pledged to respect one another's rights in Pacific island possessions, to call joint conferences to solve area questions, and to take common action against any aggressive party. The Four Power Treaty endeavored to freeze the extent of colonial possessions, at least to the extent of its ten-year period of effectivity, as the Five Power Pact had frozen certain naval categories and fortifications.

Finally, the Nine Power Treaty, although relating primarily to China, affected Japan. The treaty internationalized the Open Door policy, which stood for equal rather than any special treaty rights of one country in China. Additionally signed by four other parties with Asian interests at the conference—China, Belgium, the Netherlands, and Portugal—the nine powers agreed to respect the sovereignty, the independence, and the territorial and administrative integrity of China. This was as strong a statement as Japan would commit itself to. The Open Door, a traditional plank in the U.S. Asian foreign policy, was now written into international law, and Americans were to make much of its enlarged diplomatic definition in future disputes with the Japanese.

Other miscellaneous agreements were concluded at the Washington Conference. The Shandong issue, not directly on the agenda, again cropped up. After three dozen separate Sino-Japanese meetings, at which American and British observers were present, a bilateral treaty between the two concerned powers, signed in February 1922, promised the return of Jiao-zhou to China, although Japan was to retain control of the Jinan-Qingdao railroad for another fifteen years. China received some territory back, but the Japanese retained a measure of economic and political control on the peninsula.

Prime Minister Hara weathered the setbacks of the Versailles Treaty, but in late 1921, before the convocation of the Washington Conference, he was assassinated by a young fanatic with no clear stated purpose in mind as to what he wanted to achieve by the act. Finance Minister Takahashi Korekiyo assumed top post, but, an ineffectual politician, he resigned in mid-1922, when Seiyukai party defections relegated the post to a minority position in the Diet. In the larger international arena, despite political changes in Japan, the Washington Conference eased tensions for a decade in the Pacific and in Asia. However, the implementation of its terms was predicated on good faith, and it was only a matter of time until one party would first unilaterally terminate the agreements. As it turned out, Japan did end the treaties, but legally and correctly as provided for in their terms, in a changing world of the mid-1930s.

CHRONOLOGY

1912–1926	The Emperor Taisho (No. 123)
1913–1914	Yamamoto Gombei, prime minister
1914–1916	Okuma Shigenobu, prime minister
1914–1918	Japan in World War I; acquires German Pacific and Chinese rights
1915	Twenty-One Demands presented to China; Bryan's nonrecognition doctrine
1916–1918	Terauchi Masatake, prime minister
1917	Lansing-Ishii notes
1918	Hara Kei (Takashi) party, prime minister (to 1921); Siberian intervention; interallied board takes over Chinese Eastern Railroad; agreement with Peking to retain Shandong rights
1919	Versailles Conference
1921–1922	Takahashi Korekiyo, prime minister; Washington Conference with Four, Five, and Nine Power Treaties; Japan-China understanding on Shandong

14

Imperial Japan

Peace and Conflict

(1922–1937)

After making necessary postwar readjustments, Japan experienced again new economic growth in the 1920s, which saw further advances in technology and diversification of industry. The renewed economic expansion permitted gains in both military and civilian industrial productivity. Industry was able to support a program of both "guns and butter." Japan recovered from the world depression fairly quickly, in part through the resumption and expansion of foreign trade, the acquisition of more Asian territory to provide more raw materials and absorb more markets, and the increase of military expenditures. Japan became the third naval power in the world. The zaibatsu, as a handful of giant combines, continued to dominate Japan's trade, industry, and commerce at home and abroad, but thousands of small workshops, grinding out traditional wares, undergirded what has been called the "double structure" of the Japanese economy: huge cartels coexisting with modest entrepreneurial enterprises. As the country entered the latter years of the 1930s, the economy became more based on a war footing; it came to fulfill the Meiji slogan of not only enriching the nation but also strengthening its arms.

THE 1920s: DOMESTIC DEVELOPMENTS

Paralleling political and economic changes in Japan in the early decades of the twentieth century were liberalizing and modernizing trends that were proceeding in society and in culture, particularly in urban areas. The great Tokyo earthquake and fire of September 1923 abruptly quickened the rate of social and physical change in the capital. A tremendous cataclysm, in three days the holocaust exacted 100,000 lives, obliterating half of the city and most of neighboring Yokohama. It helped to eradicate the old urban areas, and at the same time it laid the groundwork for a new megalopolis. The rebuilt central Tokyo area was transformed into a city of broad boulevards flanked by massive steel and reinforced concrete buildings. Other cities followed Tokyo's lead in a countrywide outburst of urban construction.

Despite modernization, however, in Japanese society, particularly in rural areas, some old characteristics survived, such as the importance of family ties, the exercise of paternal authority, and the dominance of the male. Yet in increasing numbers, the younger generation in the cities challenged these traditional social customs. Youth contracted its own marriages rather than accept those arranged by families, and women joined the ranks of career workers. The *moga* (modern girl) and *mobo* (modern boy) enjoyed Hollywood movies, jazz, and Western-style dancing. Western sports became the rage. Tennis, track and field sports, swimming, and baseball, the great national sport, became common in Japan.

City people began to share in new intellectual and cultural life, but social currents in urban areas reflected the disruptive forces of modernization. Neither completely traditional nor modernized, the generation of the 1920s experienced the pangs of cultural dysfunction. As the group most

Tokyo: Frank Lloyd Wright's Imperial Hotel, which survived the 1923 earthquake

affected in the cultural conflict, intellectuals tended to become alienated from society and from contemporaneous political life. Naturalism, realism, socialism, and anarchism were some of the philosophies of the day, and these were reflected in literary output. Natsume Soseki, probably the greatest of Japan's modern novelists and professor of literature at Tokyo Imperial University, sought to blend Western ideas with indigenous values. But few liberal, positive, and hopeful strains appeared either in his novels or in those of other authors. The course of individual action did not lead to freedom and to control of forces of natural desires but rather ended in fear, despair, and loneliness.

At the head of the realm, the Emperor Taisho, after several years of mental ill health, died in 1926, and his son, Hirohito, who had been acting as regent, assumed the throne as Emperor Showa (Enlightened Peace). Political life revolved around the fortunes of two conservative parties, the Seiyukai and the Kenseikai, renamed the Minseito in 1927. In the decade between 1922 and 1931, nine cabinets were formed (with two repeating prime ministers). The first three, between 1922 and 1924, were nonparty "transcendental" cabinets; of the remaining six, two were Seiyukai and four were Kenseikai/Minseito.

Both parties represented identical interests, consisting of a fusion of landlords, agrarian capitalists, big business, and the rising middle class. The landlord class was probably somewhat stronger in the Kenseikai/Minseito, but fundamentally both parties were the same in ideology and platform. The difference lay in that each was composed of different factions within the same classes. The Mitsui group was more pronounced in the Seiyukai, and the Mitsubishi dominated the other. This period was the most democratic of Japanese political history to that time, but the degree of democracy should not be overrated. In 1925, suffrage was extended to all males twenty-five years of age and over, and for the first time, no property tax requirement was stipulated. That same year, the Diet enacted the Peace

Prime Ministers (1922–1932)

	Nonparty	*Seiyukai*	*Kenseiko/Minseito*
1922–1923	Kato Tomosaburo		
1923–1924	Yamamoto Gombei (earlier, 1913–1914)		
1924	Kiyoura Keigo		
1924–1926			Kato Komei (or Takaaki)
1926–1927			Wakatsuki Reijiro
1927–1929		Tanaka Giichi	
1929–1931			Hamaguchi Yuko
1931			Wakatsuki Reijiro (second time)
1931–1932		Inukai Tsuyoshi	

Preservation Law, which permitted the arrest of subversives and of radicals and which muzzled free speech. The relative freedoms of speech and of political activity that were extended were contained within orthodox bounds as defined by the government, because parties and individuals could not be fundamentally critical of the Japanese economic, political, or social system.

The left movement, growing but illegal, was forced to operate outside the pale of the law. As noted, Marxist ideas had begun to percolate into Japan in the late nineteenth century. By the end of the Meiji period, some Japanese intellectuals were acquainted with the general outlines of Marxism. After the 1917 Russian Revolution and the establishment of the Communist International (Comintern) two years later, Communist ideas entered Japan. Japanese began to attend international conferences in Russia, and Japanese representatives, returning from one such conference, founded the Japanese Communist party in July 1922, the third-oldest Communist party in Asia (after the Indonesian, established in 1920, and the Chinese, formed in 1921). The police acted quickly, and within a year there was only a small handful of party members.

In 1925, after a strategy conference in Shanghai with Comintern members, the party was reactivated and mass activity was emphasized. But few Japanese were attracted to the cause of militant communism, and another meeting was called in 1927 to discuss the poor progress of the party. Members analyzed the nature of the class struggle and of the Japanese nation. Operating rigidly within the prescribed Marxist interpretation of the evolution of man through five inevitable stages as based on the economic modes of production (the primitive, slave, feudal, capitalistic, and socialistic), they placed their country, which contained both strong agrarian and industrial interests, between the feudal (with wealth derived from landholdings) and the capitalistic (income from industry) Marxist eras. They proposed, through a double revolution, to destroy first the feudal elements, which they considered to be the weaker of the two stages, and then turn their attention to the capitalistic.

Because the revitalized party was illegal, the Communists worked through the Farmers and Workers party in the general election of 1928, the first one to be called after the new electoral laws of 1925. Great progress was made, and the front party won a quarter of a million votes. In that same election year, however, the police embarked on another wave of arrests and drove party members into hiding. Police vigilance carried over into the depression years, and, by the early 1930s, it was impossible for party members to operate politically. Prior to the disbanding of the party in 1932, the members reiterated the necessity of the double revolution on the road to socialism, or communism. But now they switched priorities and pronounced the feudal elements as the stronger because they had not yet been eradicated. To gain their ends, the party also approved a united front policy of continued cooperation with all bourgeois parties. The Communist strategies were important, because they surfaced again as party directives in a postwar Japan.

THE 1920s: FOREIGN POLICIES

Although a degree of liberalism existed at home, Japanese foreign policies basically were not altered abroad. After World War I, as in prewar times, liberals, or party men such as Hara Kei, tried to maintain the nation's privileged status on the Asian mainland, although they did give ground at the Washington Conference. Yet the goal remained the same—the maintenance of a paramount position in Manchuria and, by extension, in bordering northern China. The means to the end differed; the military relied on direct action, and the liberals advocated the use of diplomacy and of negotiation in maintaining a primary continental position. Yet the overall peaceful record of Japanese foreign policy in the decade of 1922–1923 compared favorably with that of other great powers. Secretary of State Henry Stimson of the Hoover Administration declared that the Japanese government in that decade had evidenced an exceptional record of good citizenship in international affairs.

But the immigration issue with the United States continued to rankle. In 1924, the question of Asian immigration came up when the Congress debated a general immigration law. Some legislators, includng senators from western states, voted for exclusion of Asians. Others opposed any type of discriminatory law. Secretary of State Charles Evans Hughes of the Harding Administration pointed out that such a bill would undo much of the goodwill created by the Washington Conference (over which he had presided). He wrote to a congressman asking that the Congress not take any strong action. The Japanese ambassador in Washington added his unsolicited protest, for he communicated to the Department of State that grave consequences would result should the bill pass. Mistakingly judging that the threat would add to his cause, Hughes passed the note on to the Congress, which reacted strongly in the negative.

In part, because of Japanese interference in a domestic American issue (which had foreign policy ramifications, however), senators and congressional representatives voted for the immigration bill with its exclusion provisions. The House approved it, 308 to 62, and the Senate, 68 to 9. The reaction of the Japanese press was bitter but restrained. The Japanese foreign office sent along another note of protest. It was particularly difficult for Japan to accept the act in view of the extensive American aid rendered the year before during the Tokyo earthquake and fire. The fact that the immigration law, had the exclusion clause not been contained, would have provided for immigration of a total of only 250 Japanese under the national origins quota was also used by Japanese militarists to arouse anti-American hatred in the years prior to World War II.

Accommodation was the keynote in Japan's relations with other countries. A rapprochement developed toward the Soviet Union. In 1922, the last of the Japanese forces left Siberia, in part because of opposition at the Washington Conference deliberations, and in part because of heavy occupation costs. In search of allies and friends, Japan, in order to end its semi-isolated position, turned to the Soviet Union in the mid-1920s. The U.S. immigration act had produced bitterness; no Chinese party or leader whom Japan could decisively support had yet emerged on top of the muddled political situation in that country; the psychologically comforting alliance with Great Britain had terminated. Although Japan disliked Communists and their ideology that precluded emperor worship and ownership of private property, and although it cracked down on communism at home, Japan began negotiations with the Soviet Union to normalize diplomatic relations, which had been cut off at the advent of the Russian Revolution in 1917. In 1925, after nearly two years of negotiations, Japan and the Soviet Union signed a treaty of recognition, pledged an exchange of diplomatic representation, and regulated matters of mutual concern, including the adjustment of fishing rights in contiguous waters. It was ironic that Japan, probably the most effective bulwark against communism in prewar Asia, came to agreement with the Soviet Union and eventually went to war with the United States, which also maintained a similar antipathy to communism. Asian power politics proved stronger than international ideological niceties.

Both soft and hard approaches were advocated toward a politically muddled China of the 1920s. The former was typified by Baron Shidehara Kijuro, the foreign minister between 1924–1927 and 1929–1931 in the Kenseikai and Minseito cabinets. Related to the Mitsubishi family and supported by business interests that advocated peaceful measures in Manchuria and China, Shidehara outlined his accommodating policies before the Diet early in 1927. Japan was to respect the sovereignty and the territorial integrity of China (as formulated in the Nine Power Treaty), promote solidarity and economic relations between the two countries, help the just aspirations of the Chinese people, tolerate the China situation, and protect legitimate Japanese rights by reasonable means. The essence of his approach was to reconcile China's aspirations with Japan's interests. Yet in the course of his first term of office as foreign minister, Shidehara twice dispatched Japanese troops into both Manchuria and China to protect Japanese rights. On the other hand, in March 1927, he did not commit Japan to the Anglo-American bombardment of Nanjing (Nanking) on the lower Yangtze River in central China, where several Japanese nationals had been wounded by Chinese in the course of anti-Western demonstrations and rioting in that city.

The so-called hard China policy was supported by a general, Baron Tanaka Giichi, prime minister between 1927 and 1929. He reemphasized special Japanese interests in Manchuria and eastern Mongolia and deemed it his duty to protect those areas were they to be threatened by disturbances affecting Japan. He sent troops to Shandong to check the northern advance of the Chinese Nationalists under the young rising general Chiang Kai-shek, who aspired to unify China and who achieved some success when, in October 1928, he proclaimed a reconstituted Republic of China at Nanjing with himself as president. Tanaka, and some of his successors, began to fear the possibility of a reunified China under Chiang, a development that could presage the termination of special Japanese interests.

Adjusting its policies toward China and the Soviet Union, Japan expanded its role in international life as a member of the League of Nations. A number of Japan's ablest statesmen, jurists, and diplomats served with the League, and two Japanese occupied the post of under secretary general. They also were active in the field of arbitration and in the adjudication of international disputes. They signed the Convention for Pacific Settlement of International Disputes, and a Japanese jurist helped to draft the statutes for the World Court (which the United States officially declined to join), of which a Japanese was one of the original eleven judges and of which one Japanese was later president.

The cooperative spirit carried on into further naval agreements. After the Washington Conference, naval rivalry was possible in auxiliary ships, because the Washington ratios applied only to battleships and aircraft carriers. A naval race between Japan and Great Britain was already shaping up in categories of vessels not regulated by the conference (as cruisers, destroyers, and submarines), and multilateral efforts were expended to solve the problem. In 1927, at Geneva, the United States, Great Britain, and Japan in preliminary conferences attempted to extend the Washington agreements on a 5:5:3 basis to other ships, but no agreement was reached. In 1930, another effort was made in London, in which France and Italy participated, although they did not ratify the resulting agreements. The presence of new men as national leaders who were more amenable to the settlement of disputes, such as President Herbert Hoover, Prime Minister Ramsey McDonald of the British Labour Party, and Foreign Minister Shidehara, contributed to the agreement concerning maximum ratios for auxiliary naval vessels to be attained by the end of 1936.

Four types of vessels were affected by the London naval treaties. In regard to heavy cruisers, the United States was allocated eighteen ships, the British fifteen, and the Japanese twelve. For light cruisers, the overall limitations were respectively set at 143,500 tons, 192,200 tons, and 100,450 tons. Destroyers were allocated to the United States and Great Britain on a parity basis, each provided with a total tonnage of 150,000, but Japan was limited to 105,500 tons. In submarines, all three parties achieved parity, with maximum overall tonnages set at 52,700. The Japanese insisted on a more favorable ratio in heavy cruisers, but the cabinet of Prime Minister Hamaguchi Yuko of the Minseito party compromised on the issue. The acceptance of the London Naval Agreement in Japan, despite strong military objections to freezing long-range military programs, constituted a high point in Japan's march toward responsible government. It was a victory for the civilian and moderate point of view. But the victory proved short-lived in Japan, for there was no deep-rooted unified public opinion or popular backing for a government that was striving to maintain a responsible and viable party government.

THE MANCHURIAN INCIDENT, 1931–1933

In the 1930s, the pattern of civilian ascendancy in politics and of international cooperation was reversed with the growth of militarism and of authoritarianism at home. Enjoying independent status since the turn of the century, the military by World War II had emerged as the key foreign policy maker. Even in politically quiescent times, there had been precedents for military intervention in home and foreign affairs. In 1912, the minister of war toppled Saionji's second cabinet. The army helped to commit the country to the Siberian expedition and had prolonged its stay there. Army leaders continually sought a greater portion of national budgets for military expenditures. On occasion, even its junior grade field officers exercised independent action. They assumed initiative in planning Japanese moves into Mongolia in 1915–1916, hatched plots during the Siberian expedition with White Russian officers, and propelled the army in taking over all of Manchuria in 1931–1932. They, as did other political activists, purported to act in the name of the emperor. Although foreign ministry officials and some high army and navy figures at home questioned the feasibility of direct military solutions to foreign policy issues, no top Japanese leader disagreed with the basic foreign policy goal, which was Japanese hegemony on the Asian mainland. Internal quarrels developed not over policies but rather over the control and nature of policymaking decisions.

Rightist groups, military and civilian, were in the background ready to capitalize on opportunities for the advancement of their views. These groups were successful in the 1930s, a period of gradual growth of totalitarianism in Japan. They took positive action at home and abroad to destroy and to discredit representative government. The spiral of events that consolidated authoritarianism at home began abroad in southern Manchuria, where young Japanese army officers in the Guandong Army began to act independently of both the military and the civilian authorities in Tokyo.

The nature of Manchurian affairs helped their cause. The nominal Chinese ruler of Manchuria was a warlord, Zhang Zuolin (Chang Tso-lin). Known as the Old Marshal, he was assassinated in 1928 in a plot by young Japanese officers when he tried to cooperate with Chiang Kai-shek as the latter moved north toward Peking in an effort to reunify China.

Upon his death, his son, Zhang Xueliang (Chang Hsueh-liang), took the reins. The Young Marshal proved even less satisfactory to the Japanese army than his father had, for he recognized the Nationalist regime at Nanjing under Chiang Kai shek, who confirmed him as governor-general of Manchuria. The many Chinese residents in Manchuria, who had immigrated there in great numbers after the fall of the Manchu in 1912, were becoming increasingly nationalistic and desired closer ties with China. Moreover, the Chinese had built railroad lines parallel to the South Manchurian Railroad, and the Japanese objected to this competition. The Chinese in Manchuria also instigated effective boycotts against Japanese goods. Against a background of growing Chinese restiveness, the Japanese army in Manchuria decided to act.

The Guandong Army forces had grown in numbers and independence over the years. Originating as troops to guard the South Manchurian Railroad, they became in time the Japanese army in south Manchuria. The general in charge of the army, since 1927, also had been the governor-general of the leased Guandong territories. In this situation containing an independently minded Chinese warlord, growing Chinese restlessness, and expanding Japanese military might and commitments, the incident of September 18, 1931, occurred. That evening at Mukden, the Manchurian capital, the tracks of the South Manchurian Railroad were blown up (by the Japanese themselves, as was later proved). Although the express train due in Mukden arrived on time in spite of the damaged tracks, the Japanese blamed the Chinese, who were supposedly protecting the zone, for the explosion. Using this as a pretext to commence large-scale military operations (and this was only one of any number of pretexts that might have been used), the Japanese troops clashed with Chinese troops under Zhang Xueliang, who was pushed out of Manchuria into northern China. Within several months, the Guandong Army eventually took over all of Manchuria. In February 1932, it promulgated the puppet state of Manchukuo with Henry Pu Yi, the last of the Manchu emperors, as the new chief of state. The Soviet Union continued to be tolerated, however, in its operation of the Chinese Eastern Railroad for several more years.

Disapproving but not disavowing the acts that led to the formation of Manchukuo, the foreign office in Tokyo reluctantly recognized the new state eight months later. The commanding general of the Guandong Army, in addition to other duties, became the Japanese ambassador to the state. In Tokyo, tensions developed between the military and the foreign office as well as between the military and big business, which opposed the direct army action in Manchuria. In the spring of 1932 in Tokyo, discontent among the younger and lower-ranking officers over opposition to militaristic Manchurian moves was reflected in a series of assassinations aimed at the governor of the Bank of Japan and the head of the gigantic Mitsui company. On May 15, 1932, young naval officers and army cadets, claiming to free the Emperor Showa from "evil influences," killed Inukai Tsuyoshi, the prime minister. The army demanded the end of party government; the bureaucrats tacitly supported the idea. Saito Makoto, an admiral of moderate leanings, in 1932 was chosen prime minister in a compromise, nationalistic nonparty cabinet. Two years later, he was succeeded by Okada Keisuke, whose cabinet, in an atmosphere of increasing ultranationalism, sacked Professor Minobe from the Tokyo Imperial University for his stand that the emperor was only an organ of the state and not the absolute sovereign of the land. In 1936, a nationalistically inclined Hirota Koki, supported by the army, assumed the top cabinet post. The balance of power was shifting in favor of the military, and the role of political parties grew progressively weaker in the thirties.

The United States protested the unilateral Japanese takeover of Manchuria. Continuing the doctrine of nonrecognition of special Japanese interests, Secretary of State Henry Stimson, like his predecessor Bryan on an earlier occasion, objected to violations of American treaty rights. The United States never recognized Manchukuo, although both Washington and Tokyo permitted American businessmen to operate there. The League of Nations dispatched a commission under Lord Lytton to Manchuria to investigate the chain of events. Its report, in effect, blamed the Japanese for aggression. Japan's reply in March 1933 was to walk out of the League when its members accepted the findings and report of the commission. Manchuria was swallowed up as a Japanese possession, and only the fiction of an independent state was maintained. But there were even further implications in the matter. The Chinese considered Manchuria an integral part of territorial China, but they were in no position under Chiang Kai-shek to reconquer the region. He had a multitude of problems to contend with closer at hand. Yet they went on record to object continuously to Japanese domination there. By 1933, neither China nor Japan could separate Manchuria from China. Manchuria became the pivotal area in the foreign policy of both contending countries.

THE 1930s: GROWTH OF AUTHORITARIANISM

As Manchuria went into Japan's orbit, Japan moved toward becoming an autocratic state that sanctioned unilateral acts by the army. Support, tacit or overt, for militarism came not only from the bureaucracy and the middle classes but also from a growing group of rightist civilian societies. Reactionary factions were not new in Japan, but their doctrines at this time found a degree of intellectual acceptability. Right-wing civilian movements gathered strength in Japan shortly after World War I. A number of small but disorganized groups appeared, generally in reaction against postwar proletarian movements. Their names indicated their character—the Imperial Way Society (Kodokai), the National Purity Society (Kokusuikai), the Anti-Bolshevik League (Sekka boshidan), the National Foundation Society (Kokuhonsha). They propounded a fascistic way of life, with its connotations of the glorification of war, of extreme nationalism, and of a one-party government operating above and beyond the will of the people. Symptomatic of this postwar trend of thought was Kita Ikki, who has been termed the intellectual father of Japanese fascism. As early as 1919, his book, *The Reconstruction of Japan* (*Nihon kaizo hoan taiko*), advocated, among other ends, the dissolution of parliamentary parties, the enhancement of personal imperial rule, and the nationalization of the means of production.

Held in the background during the more liberal atmosphere of the 1920s, in the course of the following decade the right-wing civilian movement joined forces with segments of the military, particularly those of junior rank, who became the motivating center for action. Agreeing with the civilian rightists, these younger officers proclaimed the so-called Showa Restoration (or Second Restoration, the first being the 1868 Meiji Restoration), aimed at enhancing imperial rule and prestige. Propagating a violent brand of fascism, they performed terroristic acts and carried to an extreme a policy of radicalism, as they had in 1932. Anticapitalistic as well as anticommunist, they demanded the abolition of both capitalistic societies and left-wing movements.

Their double attack attracted leaders from the middle class, which had been affected more by the depression than had the zaibatsu. By the mid-1930s, some of the middle class saw themselves as squeezed in between fancied or real oppressive Marxist and capitalist pressures. With newfound strength, a group of young officers from a Tokyo regiment took direct action on February 26, 1936. Leading enlisted men, the mutineers made attempts on the lives of prominent statesmen. They tried to assassinate the premier and aging genro, Saionji, and succeeded in murdering a former prime minister, Admiral Saito Makoto, now the lord keeper of the privy seal. Holding out for three days in downtown Tokyo, the rebels were eventually subdued, tried, and some executed. This time, those around the throne and the elder military took decisive action against the younger rebels. But in the process of repressing extremism with forceful measures, they themselves were drawn into the vortex of extremism and contributed even further to the institution of dictatorial government in Japan. By 1936, fascism had become the form of the Japanese government.

Japanese fascism bore certain ideological similarities to the European brand as evidenced in prewar Germany, Italy, and Spain. These similarities included rejection of individualism and of representative government, idealization of war, disallowance of the class struggle concept, and insistence on the unity and indivisibility of the nation. Yet the Japanese form had its own peculiarities. For one, the unitary society was based not so much on race as on the idea of the family. Japan was an extended patriarchal family; the emperor was the father of the Japanese and the individual was only a single element in the whole body politic.

Second, agriculture assumed a mystical but leading role in society. European fascism emphasized state power to control modes of production, and while the same emphasis was found in Japan, it was effected with inconsistencies. State ownership was advocated in industry and commerce, but in Japanese fascism less control was exercised over the peasants, who were to be respected and were not to be exploited at the expense of urban groups. This special role of agriculture in Japanese fascism arose in part because the young military leaders had a close affiliation with the countryside where many of them grew up, in part because Japan was still the most agrarian of all the highly industrial countries, and in part because rural interests had felt themselves sacrificed to industry ever since the Meiji Restoratiion. Third, Japanese fascism involved a Pan-Asian concept. It was Japan's sacred trust to free Asia from the West, to expel colonial powers, and to guide Asian countries to national and collective strength. The foreign policy advocating Asia for Asians under Japanese hegemony, was the Japanese version of the American manifest destiny.

These young military men who espoused Japanese fascism often turned to acts of heroism to promote their cause. Such a young man was termed a *soshi*, one who dedicated himself to the nation. In the tradition of Yoshida Shoin and of Saigo Takamori, the heroes of the right performed self-sacrificial, dramatic acts and offered themselves to the nation. In a peculiar psychology of heroism, as evidenced in the attempted Showa Restoration, the young men believed themselves to be following in the footsteps of the leaders of the Meiji Restoration. Yet there was a degree of irrationality involved in implementing their ends. They possessed no precisely outlined program of action, nor did any blueprints exist on how to put an end to parliamentary government other than to assassinate persons considered unfriendly to the cause. Intuition, they argued, would outline definite plans and ends at a later time, for truth was not to be revealed by formal logic or through book learning. Intuition and action were the limited sequence of reasoning.

By the late 1930s, the net result of a wider acceptance in Japan of the tenets of fascism had been to increase both authoritarianism and militarism. Each strain interacted with and enhanced the other. The reason for their growth and, conversely, for the failure of parliamentary government, might be attributed to several factors. In Japan there had always existed a degree of government suppression of criticism, termed "dangerous thoughts," a tendency that was not conducive to a free exchange of ideas and philosophies. Dissent from the existing order was tolerated only within stipulated bounds, which were defined by the government.

Moreover, Japan had no strong and deeply rooted tradition of democratic parliamentary government. By 1932, when nationalist, nonparty transcendental cabinets replaced party cabinets, the Meiji constitution had been operative for only forty-two years, and in this period there had been only one decade of a semblance of parliamentary responsibility. One generation had been too short a period to implant democratic procedures. The Japanese, strong traditionalists, probably understood the intellectual content of democracy but had little emotional attachment to it. When war came, Japan was still too close to authoritarianism for democracy to survive. Related to this lack of a liberal tradition was the structural weakness of the Diet, which could not control the government, although it tried, in the face of the military independence and the retention of the idea of imperial divinity. The weakness, although temporary, of the economic base in early depression years acerbated social and political tensions. In the brittle domestic situation, rightist extremism was able to flourish.

Other economic developments of the mid-1930s contributed to the growth of centralized, militarized operations. Economic activity was increasingly oriented toward Manchuria and China. A new group of zaibatsu called the *shinko* developed, whose plans and wealth were located chiefly in Manchuria. Closely linked to Guandong Army interests, they were not so large as the traditional cartels, but they proved effective in implementing military rule overseas. Raw materials from the Asian mainland, including coking coal, iron, and industrial salt, also flowed to home factories. More industries produced more goods and required more outlets, at home and abroad. The dependence on foreign trade, a necessary feature of Japanese economic structure, did not alter during this time.

Economic affairs were also characterized by increased state intervention. The government, now under greater military control, saw military expenditures as one solution to internal problems brought about by the depression. Military allocations went up from 31 percent of the total budget in 1931 to 47 percent in 1936. Deficit spending resulted in doubling of the government debt in the same five-year period. The economic and industrial consequences of government outlays for armaments were registered in an enormous expansion of heavy industry. By 1936, Japan was industrially self-sufficient and prepared for war. Control boards for each major industry were set up, and these boards fixed prices and allocated raw materials. Increased armaments put new strains on foreign relations, and the Washington and London naval agreements lapsed at the end of 1936.

Paralleling its role in domestic affairs, the army emerged as top policymaker in foreign relations. The Guandong Army controlled Manchuria, at home the fascist movement resulted in increased military control, and economic developments made industrialists and capitalists increasingly dependent on the military. Between 1932 and 1937, while busily consolidating gains in Manchuria, Japan pursued a generally quiescent policy toward China, and only gradually in those years did it extend its zone of control into northern China. Japan began to ally itself with European fascist powers, and strove to secure its borders with the Soviet Union. But after 1937, when renewed aggression broke out in northern China, Japan was placed in direct confrontation on the mainland with Western powers, including the United States.

CHRONOLOGY

1919	Kita Ikki, *The Reconstruction of Japan*
1921–1922	Washington Conference
1922	Japanese Communist party formed
1922–1923	Kato Tomosaburo, prime minister
1923	Japanese earthquake and fire, Tokyo-Yokohama area
1923–1924	Tamamoto Gombei, prime minister
1924	Kiyoura Keigo, prime minister; U.S. immigration law excludes Japanese
1924–1926	Kato Komei, prime minister
1925	Universal male suffrage; Peace Preservation Act; Soviet Union treaty
1926–1989	The Emperor Showa (Hirohito, No. 124)
1926–1927	Wakatsuki Reijiro, prime minister
1927	Unsuccessful Geneva Naval Conference
1927–1929	Tanaka Giichi, prime minister
1929–1931	Hamaguchi Yuko, prime minister
1930	London Naval Conference
1931–1932	Prime ministers Wakatsuki Reijiro and Inukai Tsuyoshi
1931–1933	Japanese army takes over Manchuria, creates Manchukuo state
1932	Uprisings of young officers in Tokyo (May 15), nonrecognition of doctrine of Stimson
1932–1934	Saito Makoto, prime minister
1933	League condemns Japanese record in Manchuria; Japan walks out of League
1934–1936	Okada Keisuke, prime minister
1936	Army mutiny in Tokyo (February 26); Washington and London agreements end
1936–1937	Hirota Koki, prime minister

15

Imperial Japan

World War II (1937–1945)

In 1937, as Japan began to expand on the Asian continent, its leaders stepped up the diplomatic offensive. They buttressed their international position through treaties with the Axis powers of Germany and Italy and through neutrality with the Soviet Union. They engaged in extensive military operations in a domestically weak and divided China. By the end of 1941, the leaders expanded their scope of operations into open conflict with the United States and the Western European powers. Subsequent to Pearl Harbor, spreading into Southeast Asia and islands of the western Pacific, Japanese forces created temporarily one of the largest empires in history. But the imperial structure, based on force, collapsed within a few years. In 1945, after a century of expansion, the political entity of Japan essentially reverted to its traditional pre-Perry territorial limits of the mid-nineteenth century.

JAPAN, THE AXIS POWERS, AND THE SOVIET UNION

In the years immediately preceding World War II, through a combination of political and economic factors at home and abroad favoring expansion, Japan moved toward total mobilization for war. At home, the seven non-party cabinets between 1937 and 1941 fell in step with the increasingly militant outlook: Hayashi Senjuro (1937); Konoe Fumimaro (1937–1938, in the first of three premierships); Hiranuma Kiichiro (1938–1939); Abe Noguyuki (1939–1940); Yonai Mitsumasa (1940); and Konoe again twice (1940, 1941). Abroad, the leaders aligned the country with the Axis powers, who possessed similar ideology and expansionist tendencies in Europe. In

205

the Anti-Comintern Pact of November 1936, Japan and Germany pledged to counteract Soviet propaganda, and in an appended secret protocol, they promised not to help the Soviet Union if either signatory were attacked by it. The following year, Italy joined the pact. Nearer to home, Asia for Asians turned out to be more appropriately Asia for the Japanese. The conquerors, who through their enunciated Greater East Asia Coprosperity Sphere sought domination in East and Southeast Asia, with local support toward this end; instead, they reaped the ill will of a disenchanted populace.

In September 1940, after the fall of France and fresh German successes in Europe, the three states of Japan, Germany, and Italy concluded the Tripartite or Axis Pact, directed essentially against the United States. Its terms provided that if one of the three contracting states were to be attacked by a power not then involved in the European war or the Chinese-Japanese conflict, the other two signatories would assist the partner with all political, economic, and military means. Because at the time only the United States and the Soviet Union, among the major states, were neutral, another article of the treaty stated that the terms did not affect the status then existing between each of the three parties and the Soviet Union. Despite these multilateral treaty arrangements, Japan's relationship with the Axis powers in Europe was not a happy one. They were never really united in common outlook and planning. The European and Asian parties went their respective separate ways and each neglected to inform the other of basic war plans and strategies.

Japan endeavored to secure its northern flank from Soviet advances. In 1935, the Soviet Union sold the Chinese Eastern Railroad to Japan and kept out of Manchuria and China, but on several occasions, large-scale military clashes along mutual Asian borders erupted between Japan and its neighbor. Between 1937 and 1939, fighting broke out over islands in the Amur River, which formed much of the Manchurian-Siberian border, at Zhangufang (Changkufeng) hill near the Korean-Manchurian border, and in the Nomonhan border region in Inner Mongolia. Tens of thousands of troops were employed in these campaigns, especially the last one, by both sides, but war was not declared. Then, with the conclusion of the surprising and unexpected German-Soviet neutrality pact between Hitler and Stalin signed in July, 1939, Japan, fearing a Soviet attack, halted its aggressive action. Two years later, when Hitler, unilaterally ending the treaty, attacked the Soviet Union, Japan felt safer and it redirected efforts southward. Japanese military counsels decided against moving into eastern Siberia with its relative paucity of known natural resources at the time, including a lack of oil, essential for military and industrial operations. But to make doubly sure of Soviet intentions, Japan concluded with the Soviet Union in April 1941 a five-year neutrality pact in which each party pledged not to go to war with the other during that interim.

JAPAN IN EAST ASIA

Japan meanwhile had expanded military operations along the far-flung Chinese coastal areas and plains. On July 7, 1937, at Luguoqiao (Luku-chiao, the so-called Marco Polo Bridge) near Peking, shots were exchanged between the Chinese garrison and Japanese forces in maneuvers there where they had no treaty right to be. Although the Chinese apologized, the tense situation persisted, and the Japanese military used the incident, one of any number that had broken out in the area, as a pretext for continued expansion.

There was now no stopping Japan's military expansions in China in these prewar Pearl Harbor years (1937–1941) collectively known as the China Incident. By the end of July, Japanese troops occupied Peking. They fanned out over the northern China plain until they were met and contained by the independently operating Chinese Communist guerrilla armies near the last great bend of the Yellow River. In Central China, along the broad Yangtze River, in another operation, the Japanese, in 1937 and 1938, also spread out from Shanghai, where they, like other major Western powers, had extensive economic interests and troops protecting them.

The Japanese captured Chiang Kai-shek's capital of Nanjing, where they killed inhabitants (known to the Chinese as the Nanjing Massacre but denied by the Japanese) and proceeded up the broad river valley. The Nationalist Chinese regime fled upstream to Chongqing (Chungking), located in the Yangtze River gorges nearly impregnable to invading enemy land forces. Chongqing remained China's capital throughout the war years. In southern China, in a third operation, Japanese forces occupied the large city of Guangzhou (Canton) near Hong Kong and moved inland along narrow river valleys and railroad lines. They occupied coastal enclaves between Shanghai and Guanagzhou but never penetrated the rugged hilly terrain of interior south coastal China. Several years before Pearl Harbor, the Japanese in China had absorbed most of the Chinese territory they were ever to secure.

No formal declaration of war followed any of these Japanese military operations. As in the case of Manchuria, Japan tried to set up puppet governments in occupied China. In December 1937, it established in Peking, a traditional capital of later Chinese dynasties, the provisional Government of the Republic of China with elderly experienced Chinese, hostile to Chiang Kai-shek's regime, as head officials. But the Japanese desired some outstanding Chinese to form a national government that could be recognized as legitimate for all China. They brought pressure to bear on a few warlords without success until they managed to obtain the services of Wang Jing-wei (Wang Ching-wei), who had held high civilian positions under

Chiang Kai-shek but who had become dissatisfied with a perennially secondary position under the generalissimo.

In March 1940, the Japanese proclaimed the return of the national government to Nanjing under Wang, who remained subservient to the Japanese until his death in 1944. The Japanese gave diplomatic recognition to his government and concluded a treaty of friendship with it, which was eventually recognized by Japan's totalitarian associates in Europe. Political reorganization was accompanied by a new economic plan, the coprosperity sphere, enunciated earlier by the Japanese cabinet in 1938. Japanese companies and corporations controlled either directly or through subsidiaries the economic life of occupied China. Cultural redirection also was ordered. Schools were reorganized and textbooks were revised; history was rewritten. The Japanese attempted to impose total administration of subjugated areas. Through such wide-ranging and thorough policies, prior to the outbreak of the Pacific War in 1941, Japan was already well-versed in the establishment and techniques of controlling puppet governments.

Japanese expansion infringed on Western rights, particularly those of Great Britain, which retained strong economic interests in occupied China. The Japanese disliked the British, who through Hong Kong and Burma permitted aid, albeit a trickle, to flow to the capital of free unoccupied China at Chongqing. Walking a tightrope, the British, under Japanese pressure, closed the Burma Road for three months in mid-1940, but then reopened it. In China, British subjects and diplomats suffered indignities and maltreatment. The Japanese seemed to delight in insulting the British to reveal the latter's impotence to take retaliatory action. With comparatively few troops committed to Asia, particularly after the outbreak of the European War, the British were constricted in the possibilities of taking positive retaliatory action and the Japanese were well aware of this.

Similarly, the Japanese pushed into Indochina after the fall of France in June 1940 and met with little resistance there. With the conclusion of the Hanoi Convention later that year, Japan received the right to station troops in northern Indochina. In July 1941, Japanese troops marched into Saigon. For all intents and purposes, Japan also had occupied Indochina prior to Pearl Harbor. Coveting the valuable oil, rubber, and tin of Indonesia after the fall of the Netherlands to the Nazis in spring 1940, Japan sent delegations to Batavia, the capital of the East Indies, to negotiate for concessions. The Dutch, more secure in their archipelago from the Japanese than the hapless French on the continent, refused to extend any rights until their Asian possessions were also occupied by the Japanese after the advent of open hostilities there in early 1942.

JAPAN AND THE UNITED STATES

As the United States had done on previous occasions, it protested the infringements of its treaty rights in China. It refused to recognize the puppet Wang Ching-wei, and, for the record, continually protested individual and collective private and official insults and attacks on Americans by the Japanese. Washington participated in attempted collective security measures to restore peace on the Asian mainland, and although not a member of the League of Nations, the United States cooperated unofficially with the Lytton Commission, on which it had an observer, investigating the Manchurian Incident. In 1937, the Roosevelt Administration participated in the Brussels Conference called by Belgium for the nine powers of the Washington Conference to deal with Japanese actions in China. Because Japan, the most directly concerned foreign power, did not attend, the conference was unsuccessful. Upon the termination of the Washington and of the London naval arrangements at the end of 1936, military escalation among Pacific powers became a reality.

The United States extended to Chiang Kai-shek air support and loans, but more effective were U.S. economic sanctions, growing ever tighter against Japan. Although these sanctions were adopted to deal primarily with the growing European embroilment, they affected U.S. economic relations with Japan as well. To keep the United States out of potential foreign conflicts, Congress enacted a law in 1935 to the effect that should the president declare the existence of a state of war between foreign powers, an embargo on the sale and transportation of arms would be imposed on all belligerents involved. The following year, provisions were enacted to forbid the extension of loans to countries at war. In 1937 and in 1939, after the outbreak of the European war and the Sino-Japanese conflict, Congress in effect reversed itself and repealed the embargo on arms, ammunitions, and implements of war to such foreign nations, belligerents or neutrals, who could cross the seas to buy for cash and take away anything they wanted, in the so-called cash-and-carry policy. This was done principally to try to extend help to the chief allies, Britain in Europe and China in Asia. The laws paradoxically enhanced the position in the Pacific of a belligerent Japan, which had the cash and the ships that China did not.

In July 1938, the United States invoked a moral embargo, in effect an appeal to the consciences of exporters, on the sale of airplanes to Japanese importers because, it was argued, these planes, some with U.S. made parts and using U.S. oil, were used to bomb hapless Chinese civilians. In December 1939, the moral embargoes were extended to cover shipments of oil and petroleum products to Japan. Earlier, in July of that year, the United States announced its intention to terminate the 1911 Japan treaty of commerce with its clauses of nondiscriminatory treatment. Japan's place in normal bilateral trade channels would then halt and legal obstacles could be imposed should the United States desire to restrict further trade with Japan. Following this more effective policy, in the following July and December, stringent export controls were invoked on a worldwide basis. These controls particularly affected Japan, which relied on imports of U.S. oil and items of war for its military machine. The import controls were imposed on scrap iron, aviation gas, munitions, and other implements of war. In July 1941, after the occupation by Japanese troops of Saigon following an American presidential warning, the United States froze Japanese financial assets and embargoed all oil exports, so essential to the dwindling stocks of the ever-expanding Japanese military machine.

The U.S. and Japanese positions had become irreconcilable. Yet the U.S. government was hard put to formulate a consistent China policy. Washington had to protect U.S. nationals, but it did not wish to provoke war. It tried to restrain Japan, but it had to work for peace, because a substantial segment of American public opinion, still affected from the lingering depression of the 1930s, supported isolation. It pledged to enforce orderly processes, but it would not tolerate aggressive action by Japan. It continually protested Japanese actions by words, but it could not back the protests with force. Roosevelt's secretary of state, Cordell Hull, continually enunciated like a pious litany Japan's necessity to adhere faithfully to international agreements and to settle differences through peaceful negotiations.

He sought conciliation with Japan on terms that the Japanese found unacceptable, such as the conclusion of a multilateral Asian nonaggression agreement, the complete withdrawal of Japanese troops from China and Indochina, and the recognition of Chiang Kai-shek as the legitimate head of the Republic of China. In return for such Japanese concessions, Hull promised that the United States would negotiate a new commercial treaty with Japan to restore normal economic relations. Japanese in Tokyo and their delegations in Washington rejected the basic terms, for they desired the recognition of growing territorial and economic rights and free access to stocks of essential natural resources, especially that of oil, which were now more than ever necessary for inflated military and industrial commitments. Against the backdrop of irreconcilable positions, Japan took the decision to go to war.

As early as July 2, 1941, an imperial conference decided on a drive into Southeast Asia, where valuable natural resources could be obtained. Subsequent conferences reiterated the strategy. In October, General Tojo Hideki, as one of the top-ranking Japanese militarists, became prime minister and expansionist plans swung into action. On November 1, Admiral Yamamoto Isotoku issued the orders for an attack on Pearl Harbor, which was meant to immobilize the U.S. Pacific Fleet temporarily while the Japanese could consolidate their gains in Southeast Asia. On November 17, the admiral designated December 7 as the attack date. On November 26, under Vice Admiral Nagumo Chuichi's command, the Pearl Harbor Striking Force composed of dozens of vessels including six carriers protected by two battleships, three cruisers, and nine destroyers sortied from Etorufu in the Kuriles.

On the same day in Washington, Hull reiterated his final proposals for peace to a special Japanese delegation. On November 17, Washington, which had broken the secret Japanese diplomatic code (but not the military ones) sent warnings to posts abroad including Pearl Harbor. These warnings, however, indicated possible aggression in the Philippines or in Malaya rather than in Hawaii. In the meantime, the Japanese striking forces, undetected with radios silent, approached Hawaii by a circuitous route across the north Pacific Ocean. In the early hours of Sunday, December 7, the Americans sunk a midget Japanese submarine and a U.S. Army radar picked up on its screen planes that turned out to have been launched from Japanese carriers. The first Japanese air attack at 7:55 AM (and a second assault forty-five minutes later) caught Hawaiian forces unprepared. In less than two hours, six U.S. battleships were disabled, 120 planes were destroyed, and 2,400 men, mainly naval personnel, were killed. Japanese losses were minimal.

THE PACIFIC WAR

Pearl Harbor united a previously divided American people, but the first year of the Pacific War proved successful for the Japanese (who now escalated the China Incident into the Greater East Asia War, but postwar, it was called by many, as in the United States, the Pacific War). Japanese won all major objectives in Asia and the Pacific. In the flush of "victory disease," it established control over land and sea areas from the Aleutians in the north to Indonesia in the south, and from Burma in the west to the central Pacific archipelagoes. Japan's initial successes made a great psychological impact on Asian peoples, for an Asian country had defeated Western nations. The myth of the invincibility of the white man had again been exploded (as in the Russo-Japanese War) as he was paraded through Asian streets as a prisoner of war. Colonial regimes of Southeast Asia toppled, and native nationalism received promises of self-government.

The Japanese set up autonomous indigenous governments that claimed independence from the colonial powers. But as the war wore on, friction developed between the Japanese and their sponsored native governments. By the end of the war, the Japanese, because of their many brutal and tactless actions, became as discredited as the earlier colonial powers. Asia for Asians turned out to be more appropriately Asia for the Japanese. The conquerors, through their enunciated Greater East Asia Coprosperity Sphere, had ended white domination in East and Southeast Asia and had courted local support for this end; instead they reaped a disenchanted populace.

Despite extensive losses at Pearl Harbor, the United States recovered and made use of its remaining fleet, including aircraft carriers, until U.S. industry could replace and augment the military losses. The British fleet was decimated, because Singapore, the important naval base, had been taken and the British battleships sunk. The Japanese navy was in prime condition, but it began to receive setbacks after initial victories through a combination of unimaginative strategy and some bad luck. In the Battle of Coral Sea, May 4–8, 1942, off Australia, the Japanese tried to secure Port Moresby, on the southern coast of New Guinea, as a southern anchor point. It was a unique naval battle, because all fighting was done by carrier planes against enemy planes, or by planes against enemy ships. Turned back, the Japanese failed to take the port.

The Battle of Midway (June 4–6, 1942) was conceived by Admiral Yamamoto as a frontal attack on Hawaiian positions. It was partially concealed by Japanese operations farther north in the Aleutians (where the United States temporarily lost Kiska and Attu islands). But Admiral Chester Nimitz, now taking advantage of decoded Japanese military messages, saturated the Japanese navy with air attacks from land- and carrier-based planes. The Japanese failed to gain Midway, and in the battle, which constituted the first major defeat of the Japanese navy, Japan lost four of its best aircraft carriers. Subsequently, in the south Pacific operations in the Solomon Islands, mainly Guadalcanal, the Japanese failed in their strategy to achieve a strong southern position in order to cut off the heavily used U.S.-Australian supply lines. The tide of war was changing in the Pacific. The Allied cause in 1943 slowly advanced northward, island-hopping under General Douglas MacArthur. He had withdrawn from the Philippines early in 1942 to Australia, which became his headquarters and base of military operations, and moved Allied troops, chiefly U.S. and Australian, up the north New Guinea coast to capture Japanese outposts.

Complementing MacArthur's military drive up the southwest Pacific island chains, which aimed at retaking the Philippines, were engagements across the central Pacific Ocean under Admiral Chester Nimitz, with principally naval action. In March 1943, the two Aleutian islands of Attu and Kiska were retaken. By mid-1944, intensive but costly operations in the Pacific regained the Gilberts, including Makin and Tarawa atolls, the Marshalls, including Kwajalein and Eniwetok; and finally the Marianas, among which were Guam, Saipan, and Tinian. The fall of Saipan in July 1944 proved a turning point in the Pacific War. From the Marianas, Japan could easily be reached in round-trip saturation bombing raids (fields in China were too distant for the same purpose). Tojo's cabinet fell in mid-1944, and in the course of the hectic war's end, it was succeeded by four others within a year into the days of surrender: Koiso Kuniaki, 1944-1945; Suzuki Kantaro, April 1945; Prince Higashikuni, August 1945; and Shidehara Kijuro, October 1945.

Although no Japanese openly talked of defeat, some leaders were privately considering the possibility of a negotiated peace. The Allied troops, drawn from both the southwest and central Pacific theaters of operation, converged on the Philippines in October 1944. The final campaigns in the first half of 1945 included those at Iwo Jima and Okinawa, which were to be used as a staging area for the invasion of Japan.

During the war, military problems had taken precedence, for victory was the main objective. But international problems affecting Japan's postwar status persisted, and although those problems were temporarily subordinated to military concerns, they spawned complications. Long-range diplomatic and political issues could not be separated from the immediate military considerations, and there were several Allied conferences held in the course of World War II to consider postwar problems relating to Japan.

In January 1943, Roosevelt met with British Prime Minister Winston Churchill in Casablanca, where they issued the unconditional surrender ultimatum. The Allies, they pledged, would fight until the unconditional surrender of their enemies in Europe and in Asia. There was to be no repetition of any of Wilson's Fourteen Points at Versailles implying accommodation of the enemy. The insistence on unconditional surrender was controversial, for it spurred the Japanese militarists to fight to the bitter end, in the absence of any other mitigating alternative. The demand probably delayed the Japanese surrender, for the army used it in their arguments against the foreign office and the navy to conclude peace. In the case of Japan, unconditional surrender turned out anyway to be conditional, for the Japanese requested and received the right to retain the emperor, who was made subject to the directives of General MacArthur, designated by the Allies as the Supreme Commander of the Allied Powers (SCAP) in Japan.

In November 1943, Roosevelt and Churchill met with Chiang Kai-shek at Cairo. There they agreed on the course of future operations against Japan and issued a joint statement of purpose. In the Cairo Declaration of November 26, four general areas of intent were announced. First, Japan was to be stripped of all islands in the Pacific seized or occupied since 1914. This essentially meant that the League mandates of the ex-German territories would be terminated. Second, all territories that Japan had "stolen" from China were to be returned to the Republic of China. These included Manchuria, other occupied areas on the continent, Taiwan, and the Pescadores. Third, Japan was to be expelled from all other territories taken by "violence and greed."

This covered much territory. It was understandable in terms of mainland and insular Asian holdings taken by force, but not in the case of South

Nuclear cloud over Hiroshima, August 6, 1945

Sakhalin and the southern Kuriles, which Japan had obtained from czarist Russia in the course of legally concluded and internationally binding treaties. Finally, with reference to Korea, the Japanese colony in due course was to become free and independent. The Cairo Declaration meant to turn the clock back to pre-Perry times as far as Japanese territory was involved. In February 1945, at Yalta, in order to gain Soviet support of the projected invasion of the Japanese homeland later that year, Roosevelt promised to restore to the Soviet Union pre-1904 Russian rights in Manchuria, and gave to it titles to the Kuriles and to South Sakhalin.

By 1945, with tightened submarine warfare and air raids against the home islands themselves, the war had definitely turned against Japan. Japanese merchant ships had difficulty getting raw materials and importing food. Manpower was shifted from agriculture to military needs. The war effort was adversely affected by hasty reallocations of human resources. After the conclusion of the war in Europe, Harry S. Truman, the new American president who took over after Roosevelt's death in April 1945; Clement Attlee, who had succeeded Churchill as the British prime minister; and Marshal Stalin reiterated the Yalta agreements at Potsdam. They outlined the zones of occupation in Asia. The Americans were to receive the Japanese surrenders in Japan, the Philippines, the Pacific islands, and Korea south of the 38th parallel; the Soviets, in northern Japanese islands, North Korea, and Manchuria; the Chinese under Chiang Kai-shek, in China and Indochina to the 15th parallel; and the

Hiroshima, monument marking the epicenter

British, in Southeast Asia. The Potsdam Declaration called for the elimination of militarism in Japan, the occupation of Japan, and the territorial limitations of Japan to its four main islands and adjacent minor ones.

The terms of the Potsdam Declaration were relayed to Tokyo, where, in the ensuing weeks, debates raged around the emperor as to their acceptance

Nagasaki Peace Monument noting the atomic bomb drop of August 9, 1945

or rejection. The conclusion of the war was hastened by three factors: the two atomic bombs dropped on Hiroshima and Nagasaki on August 6 and 9, respectively, and the entrance of the Soviet Union (which prematurely scrapped the five-year 1941 neutrality treaty) into the Pacific War on August 8. The Japanese, despite last-ditch opposition from the army, followed an imperial rescript on August 15 (Victory in Japan or V-J Day) to lay down their arms.

Two weeks after the call for capitulation, on Sunday, September 2, 1945, the instrument of surrender was concluded on the U.S. battleship *Missouri*, in Tokyo Bay. It was signed by representatives of the military and foreign office in Tokyo, General MacArthur on behalf of all the Allies, and a battery of signatures from individual participating countries in the Pacific War. As stipulated in the Potsdam Declaration, additional surrenders were confirmed in occupied countries. In the holocaust over the years 1937 to 1945, 3.1 million Japanese had lost their lives: 2.3 million soldiers died on the various fronts; 300,000 civilians were overseas casualties; and 500,000 others, including atomic bomb victims in Japan, perished. Casualties of other involved nationalities totaled into unnumbered tens of millions of lives.

Japan was defeated, militarism was eradicated, and, for the first time in modern Asian history, there appeared the spectacle of a weak, occupied Japan. A transformed situation in Japan was matched by a new Asia. China continued divided and weak, but now the Chinese Communists, located in strength in northern China, were contending for the mastery of the country from Chiang Kai-shek. Prewar colonial arrangements in South and Southeast Asia were collapsing, because a defeated Japan had left in its wake a colonial Asia in ferment. Some metropolitan powers, as the United States and Great Britain, read the signs of nationalism correctly and gave up their colonies. Others, as the French and Dutch, retreated only after a show of nationalist force.

Until Japan's defeat, no power in world history had achieved in Asia precisely the same extended imperial stature and the same widespread imperial boundaries. But Japan's temporary wartime supremacy was gained only at a great human cost to all parties concerned, built as it was on force and servitude. In 1941, Japan's position in Asia and the Pacific was paramount; in 1945, it became minimal. But like the proverbial phoenix rising from the ashes, Japan, in the ensuing postwar decades, in a striking irony of the terrible war years, reached greater heights of affluence, economic strength, and international respect, but this time, the success story was based on peaceful foundations.

CHRONOLOGY

1935	Soviet Union sells Chinese Eastern Railroad to Japan; U.S. neutrality laws
1936	Anti-Comintern Pact (Japan and Germany)
1937	Hayashi Senjuro, prime minister; Brussels Conference
1937–1938	Konoe Fumimaro, prime minister; Japan moves into northern, central, southern China
1937–1939	Fighting with the Soviet Union on border areas; U.S. "cash and carry" laws
1938–1939	Hiranuma Kiichiro, prime minister; U.S. moral embargo laws
1939	Soviet-German treaty; U.S. declares intent to terminate 1911 Japanese trade treaty
1939–1940	Abe Nobuyuke, prime minister
1940	Yonai Mitsumasa and Konoe, prime ministers; Tripartite, or Axis, Pact; puppet Chinese republic at Nanjing; U.S. export controls; Japan in northern Indochina
1941	Konoe, prime minister, and Gen. Tojo Hideki (to 1944); Soviet-Japanese five-year neutrality pact; Hitler invades the Soviet Union; Japanese in Saigon; U.S. freezes Japanese assets, embargoes oil; Japanese imperial conference on war strategy; Pearl Harbor
1941–1945	Pacific War
1943	Casablanca (January) and Cairo (December) conferences
1944–1945	Koiso Kuniaki, prime minister
1945	Yalta conference (February); Suzuki Kantaro, prime minister (April); Potsdam conference (July); atomic bombs on Hiroshima and Nagasaki (August 6, 9); Soviet entry into war (August 8); Japanese surrender (August 15); Prince Higashikuni, prime minister (August 17); Japanese instrument of surrender signed (September 2); other surrenders elsewhere; Shidehara Kijuro, prime minister (October)

IV

POSTWAR JAPAN

(1945 TO PRESENT)

Defeated and shattered at the end of World War II, the Japanese experienced, for the first time in their history, the presence of a foreign occupying power, that of the United States. During the seven years of occupation (1945–1952), measures of reform and recovery were effected, so that by the return of sovereignty in the latter year, Japan once more came into its own political identity. Despite the severance of formal bonds, however, the course of the rest of the decade was marked by continued Japanese dependence—economic, political, and military—on the United States. But then, as the 1960s progressed, the Japanese increasingly tapped their own sources of strength and independence. In the course of the ensuing latter decades of the twentieth century and into the twenty-first, they rose to a position again as a world political power and to unprecedented heights as an economic superpower, accomplishments attained this time through peaceful means and international cooperation.

16

Occupied Japan

(1945-1952)

Japan, crushed at the conclusion of World War II, soon regained a sense of direction. In the remarkably short period of seven years of occupation, it recovered to a great extent its economic productivity and political viability. This was due in part to the nonvindictive, constructive policies of the occupation and in part to the remarkable ability, resilience, and creativity of the Japanese in adapting to changing conditions. As an attempt to transform Japan into a democratic society as defined by American norms, on the theory that democracies do not threaten the peace of the world, the occupation was an ambitious undertaking. The Americans accomplished much, but it was the Japanese themselves who made the occupation work. Reforms and recovery were implemented with the restoration of political parties (mainly the Liberal and Democratic), elections (from April 1946), and parliamentary governments with cabinets headed by three prime ministers: Yoshida Shigeru, 1946-1947 (Liberal); Katayama Tetsu, 1947-1948 (Socialist coalition); Ashida Hitoshi, 1948 (Democratic); and Yoshida again, 1948-1954.

NATURE OF THE OCCUPATION

The occupation was not a complete break with the past. Those years might be interpreted as a catalyst that speeded up certain limited prewar liberal trends, held back during the years of conflict, such as universal male suffrage, the gradual emancipation of women, party politics, and the partial freedom of the press. Occupation reforms implemented by the United

States that were favorable to concepts already initiated by the Japanese tended to be more enduring, while others were eventually discarded. Had Japan been occupied by an authoritarian regime, such as the Soviet Union, its national life conceivably might have been redirected toward a totalitarian goal by following another set of prewar authoritarian traits.

The chief planning for the occupation, which was in essence an American show, was done in Washington, for the United States alone possessed the military forces, the transportation facilities, and the economic assets to undertake the job. It was, moreover, the major Allied participant in the Pacific War, in which it expended great manpower and unbounded technical prowess. In early 1945, the United States had drafted the U.S. Initial Post-Surrender Policy for Japan, which was sent to General MacArthur, the Supreme Commander of the Allied Powers (SCAP), in Tokyo, as the overall guiding philosophy of the occupation. The two broad policy objectives were to be the demilitarization and democratization of Japan. To achieve these ends, specific tactics were outlined: a purge of war criminals, encouragement of political parties, extension of civil liberties, and breakup of the zaibatsu. Toward these ends, the machinery of the occupation swung into operation.

In contrast to their record in Germany, the U.S. administrators in Japan utilized the Japanese as much as possible inasmuch as there was a dearth of Japanese-speaking Americans. The Japanese government, although it was subordinated to MacArthur, was left in a position to implement U.S. operations. This necessary approach also was based on the prohibitively high costs of direct U.S. government that would necessitate huge staffs. The Japanese state remained a constitutional monarchy, headed by the emperor, but he was stripped of his sanctified aura. In a rescript issued on New Year's Day 1946, under the prodding of MacArthur, he himself renounced the idea of imperial divinity. The U.S. decision to retain the emperor, strongly supported by the Japanese, was a wise one, for it left the country with an institution through which to implement change. Continuing in the native tradition of indirect rule, MacArthur simply acted as a twentieth-century shogun or military adviser.

Yet because of the existence of double U.S. and Japanese administrative machinery, a serious handicap in effecting reforms existed, for the implementation had to be left to the Japanese themselves. The actual enforcement of the laws depended in the final stage on the Japanese, and although there existed some procedures to evaluate results, these sometimes were difficult. Until 1948, occupation authorities worked through a Japanese liaison office, after which direct contact was substituted with individual branches of government.

The occupation was run by predominantly military personnel. At the head was General MacArthur, responsible to the War Department in Washington, and not to the Department of State, which assumed a subordinate role in these years. He was the Supreme Commander of the Allied Powers; SCAP was a term that was variously used to designate the general himself, his headquarters in Tokyo, or the total occupation machinery throughout the country. MacArthur performed in two capacities. As a military figure, he endeavored to effect changes in a civilian Japanese society. These duties were clearly outlined in the Post-Surrender Policy for the reformation of Japanese society and government. He was, secondly, responsible for the various military commands of U.S. forces strung out throughout the Pacific and Eastern Asia and for the United Nations forces in Korea after war broke out there in mid-1950. As commander of the U.S. troops, his military duties were to safeguard U.S. rights and to interpret the needs of U.S. security, particularly with the escalated presence of the Cold War in 1948. With his sense of mission and his flair for destiny, he fitted the dual posts admirably.

The occupation was an overwhelmingly American affair, with some participation by the British Commonwealth. Yet the terminology of SCAP implied association with other concerned parties. The allies of the United States in the Pacific War operated through two nominal advisory multilateral agencies. Representing initially eleven, then thirteen, countries that had participated in the war, the Far Eastern Commission (FEC) met in Washington periodically to issue policy directives to MacArthur. Because the United States could veto any commission directive, and because it also could issue interim directives pending any commission action, the United States was guaranteed a primary position in deliberations of that organ.

In Tokyo, the Allied Council for Japan (ACJ), consisting of representatives of the United States, the Soviet Union, China, and the British Commonwealth, consulted with MacArthur on terms and implementation of policies. It was unsuccessful in its operations, and council meetings degenerated into debates between the representatives of the United States and of the Soviet Union. Unlike the shared occupation of Germany and Austria, but like the unilateral occupation of Eastern European countries by the Russians, the United States enjoyed on its own terms the luxury of negligible international complications in administering Japan.

THE FIRST PERIOD: REFORM

The occupation can be conveniently divided into two periods, the first stressing reform between 1945 and 1948, and the second emphasizing recovery from 1948 to 1952. In the first period of reform, at least six basic sectors of Japanese life and society were affected by occupation directives. First were the purges, military and civilian, of those high-ranking Japanese in official and private life who were associated with the prosecution of the war. An allied International Military Tribunal for the Far East (IMTFE), representative of the powers involved in the Pacific war, was set up in Tokyo. For almost two years, the tribunal tried top Japanese military and civilians on general charges of conventional war crimes, crimes against peace, and crimes against humanity, as well as on individual charges of specific acts committed in the course of the conflict. Of the twenty-five tried, seven, including Tojo, were hanged. The rest were sentenced to imprisonment for terms varying between seven years and life, although these sentences were later commuted. In addition, individual Allied countries, in Japan or on their own soil, tried certain Japanese whom they considered war criminals in cases against their nationals.

Although the international court was authorized by the Potsdam and other Allied agreements (which had also provided for the Nuremburg trials of Nazis), its propriety aroused controversy and criticism because of its ex post facto nature (the laws were made after the acts were committed and applied retroactively) and because only nationals from the country that lost were tried. Proceeding on the debatable conclusion that some civilian economic and political figures also were automatically allied with prewar and wartime militaristic expansion, the occupation purged by category, rather than by individual, some 200,000 bureaucrats from their jobs and managerial positions, ones who were in the best position to help reconstruct a devastated postwar Japan.

A second significant reform was the promulgation of the constitution of 1947, which replaced the Meiji constitution of 1889. In many ways written in terms similar to those of the U.S. Constitution, the new document broadened the political life of Japan and provided for a parliamentary state. A draft prepared by the Japanese proved unsatisfactory to SCAP, and it was revised with its advice and then adopted by the Diet. The position of the emperor was transformed from divine ruler to symbol of the state. He continued to represent the unity of the people, but now he derived his position from the popular will, in which sovereign power resided. Although the emperor and the royal family were retained, the peerage was abolished.

The constitution eliminated the political priority of the prewar elites over the cabinet, which now became, in true parliamentary form, a committee of the majority party, or a coalition, from which the prime minister was selected. The Diet was made the highest and sole law making organ of the state. Both houses of the Diet became fully elective, and the franchise was extended to all men and women over the age of twenty. The lower and more powerful House of Representatives consisted of 467 members elected to four-year terms, with three to five chosen from each of 118 electoral districts as in prewar days. The upper House of Councillors had 250 members sitting in six-year terms, of whom 100 were chosen at large and the rest in varying numbers from the prefectures.

The judiciary, formerly subordinated to the Ministry of Justice, was made independent. A Supreme Court, like its counterpart in the United States, became the final adjudicator of constitutional matters. Approval of the membership of the Supreme Court was to be submitted every decade to popular vote. Local self-government was strengthened, for the constitution specified that the principal local officials, such as mayors, governors, and members of local assemblies, be elected by their respective constituencies. The constitution guaranteed the rights of life, liberty, and equality, as well as the more modern ones of academic freedom, collective bargaining, and higher standards of living.

The constitution was far ranging, but it had some weak points. The document did not originate with the Japanese themselves (it was originally written in English). Conceivably, should occasion arise, the Japanese could claim provisions as nonbinding or alterable. Moreover, troublesome Article Nine, insisted upon by SCAP, renounced war as an instrument of national policy, and it prohibited armed forces in the country. This constituted an idealistic and pacifistic proposition that appealed to many Japanese, but SCAP after the outbreak of the Korean War was to reverse itself on the question of Japanese defense forces.

In keeping with constitutional provisions to ensure greater responsibility and more democratic procedures at the local level, another occupation reform revised the highly centralized relations existing in Meiji and imperial Japan between Tokyo and subordinate political units. Local authorities were granted far greater powers of taxation, education, police, and legislation than they had previously enjoyed. Control of the police was transferred from the Home Ministry to municipal and prefectural authorities. The local units hired educators, police, and bureaucrats, but problems soon arose from such decentralized patterns. The local administrative units had to tax themselves to discharge their functions, and they soon discovered that democracy required expendng large funds and levying higher taxes. Tokyo stepped in with informal grants-in-aid, but with the extension of funds there returned a degree of centralized control. Because of the existence of multiple and confusing jurisdictions, the Japanese restored some measure of centralized control, particularly in police affairs. In their small and highly unified country, the Japanese preferred a pattern of political centralism.

SCAP reforms further emphasized the extension, the liberalization, and the equalization of educational opportunities for all. They stressed the importance of teaching students how to think rather than what to think. Textbooks were rewritten to eliminate nationalistic propaganda, and the traditional courses on ethics and morality were replaced by newer ones in the social sciences. In the prewar system, students had been marked for either vocational or general training; postwar reforms standardized levels of education for all. Compulsory education of nine years was prescribed, and the academic structure came to resemble the American school system—six years of primary school, three years of junior high school, three years of senior high, and then two years of junior college or four years of college. In the occupation's zeal for extending the general educational level of the populace, which was presumed to be a prerequisite of democracy, educational facilities at higher levels particularly proliferated. A university, feasible or not, was established in every prefecture. Japan experienced a growth of private and state-supported junior colleges and universities. The new system offered new educational opportunities for both sexes, but many Japanese felt academic popularization was accompanied by deterioration in intellectual standards.

Occupation authorities devoted efforts to breaking up the great zaibatsu on the controversial thesis that the cartels had been allied with Japan's military imperialists and on the more tenable proposition that such imbalanced accumulation of wealth in a country was detrimental to the development of a viable democracy. Besides purging members of zaibatsu families and their top-ranking managerial staffs, SCAP froze company accounts. It took over the greater bulk of financial holdings through capital levies, and it redistributed assets. In the first wave of reform, eighty-three holding companies were broken up into their components. An antimonopoly law was passed at the same time to preclude their recombination. In December 1947, a law was enacted to provide for the further deconcentration of 1,200 companies, but by that time the emphasis of occupation policy was changing from reform to recovery, and only nine companies were affected.

As SCAP broke up the zaibatsu, so it encouraged labor organizations. It proceeded in the belief that the creation of bona fide labor unions would abet the process of democratization in Japan, that unions would tend to diminish the strength of the zaibatsu, and that unions would help lower urban income groups to participate in politics and mature through political experience. In December 1945, a Trade Union Law gave workers the right to organize, bargain, and strike. A Labor Relations Board was created to enforce the act. At the same time, SCAP ordered all political prisoners released, and these included labor leaders. Unionism experienced a phenomenal growth, and within a year of the passage of the law, union membership had jumped from 1 million to 4.5 million. But the movement was not so powerful as numbers indicated, because most Japanese were inexperienced in the matter, and employers set up unions without knowing their own rights and duties or the purposes for organization. The vigor of labor's response at first delighted occupation reformers. However, their enthusiasm was soon dampened as the movement grew into a leftist political force, controlled in large measure by Communists, now a party legalized by occupation reforms to broaden the indigenous political spectrum.

Finally, a major achievement of the occupation was land reform. At the end of the war, probably one-half to two-thirds of Japanese arable holdings was worked by tenants paying exorbitant rents in kind. On the assumption that an agrarian pattern structured on semi-feudal ownership of large holdings by a few landlords hindered democratization, land reforms were instituted. In 1946, legislation was passed, in part to check the evils of absentee landownership as well as of tenancy, which set maximum ownership limits of two-and-a-half acres for noncultivator owners and seven-and-a-half acres for cultivator owners. The government purchased all remaining land at 1939 prices and sold it to former tenants at the same prices, but at inflated 1947 rates. This was tantamount to expropriation, but by the end of the reform only 10 percent of the land was worked by tenants, and rents in kind were virtually eliminated. Some five million acres of arable land were redistributed within two to three years. Although the peasant enjoyed pride of ownership, the land reforms did not necessarily result in increased food production because of the continued utilization of uneconomical small plots, the marginal existence of many of the new owners, and the ever-recurring possibility of agrarian debt in the event of crop failures.

THE SECOND PERIOD: RECOVERY

Within the first few years of the occupation, most of the basic reforms had been outlined and implemented. But a change of attitude in 1947 and 1948 occurred in SCAP that shifted emphasis from reform to recovery. Internal developments in Japan favored the tapering off of reform measures, and as early as 1947, MacArthur declared that Japan was ready for a peace treaty. Factors outside Japan effected the change in occupation philosophy, now to build up the country. Japan's role was reconsidered as an ally to help contain communism in the emerging Cold War confrontations, and the zealous reforms were slowed down. In the late 1940s, tension was apparent in Europe and Asia, and the wartime alliance seemed to be splitting apart. The Berlin airlift, the Trieste problem, Czechoslovakia's entrance into the Communist orbit, and the Marshall Plan were some of the major developments in the East-West conflict in Europe. Signs indicated that after the fall of Manchuria to the Communists in November 1948, Chiang Kai-shek's regime on the China mainland was disintegrating in the face of stepped-up Chinese Communist activity. More than ever, the United States became concerned with the maintenance of political and economic stability in Japan and the necessity of Japan as an ally. The new emphasis on economic recovery sometimes conflicted with earlier SCAP policies of democratization.

Occupation authorities cracked down on left-wing radicals, including Communists. Labor union demands for higher wages and the right to strike were checked. In 1948, the Diet passed a no-strike law for both civil service and industrial workers. As a substitute for the lost right to strike, the government appointed an official employer-union Public Arbitration Board. The first important test of the board was the case of a demand for higher pay by railroad workers on government lines. For six months, the board studied the case. After it decided to raise salaries by 25 percent, the government refused to accept the recommendation and advocated instead a 3 percent raise. The unions informed SCAP that the repeal of the right to strike was unfair; SCAP replied that the negotiations constituted a domestic affair. The railroad workers did not get the pay raise.

In 1949, the government embarked on a policy of fiscal retrenchment to cut the budget, a policy advocated by SCAP on the recommendation of an economic survey mission from the United States the year before. To reduce expenditures, the government laid off as many as 100,000 employees, including labor union leaders. On the other hand, SCAP now permitted some purged economic leaders to return to their original industrial and zaibatsu posts. The FEC stopped reparations shipments and the dismantling of plants, which it had permitted to a limited extent, although this action occasioned the particular wrath of the war-devastated Philippines, which felt entitled to extensive reparations. The United States started preparations for a Japanese peace treaty to return full sovereignty to Japan as an ally of the United States, a matter of urgency particularly after the outbreak of the Korean War in June 1950.

PEACE TREATY NEGOTIATIONS

As early as the summer of 1947, the United States extended an invitation to the FEC powers to draft a peace treaty that would be accepted by majority rule. Stalin and Chiang Kai-shek objected, because they desired to retain the veto as stated in the provisions of the Potsdam Declaration. The Soviet Union also pointed out that the United Nations Declaration of January 1, 1942, to which the United States had adhered, forbad any separate peacemaking procedures. Finding it impossible to work through divided FEC councils, making no headway on a German peace treaty either, and deeming it imperative to strengthen Japan as early as possible, the United States began individual negotiations for a peace treaty with as many of the involved states as possible.

In September, 1950, President Truman named a Republican, John Foster Dulles, who had an extensive background in procedures of international law and public conferences, as his special ambassador in charge of peace-making with Japan. For almost a year, Dulles and his assistants, traveling to Tokyo and at least ten world capitals, worked at arriving at agreeable terms. In the course of negotiations for a peace treaty, in April 1951, in a final lesson of democracy that impressed the Japanese, Truman fired Mac-Arthur from all his posts because of the general's insubordination resulting from policy differences in the conduct of the Korean war, which MacArthur wanted to extend into Manchuria. Truman replaced him with General Matthew Ridgway, who served out the remainder of the occupation as SCAP.

The initial U.S. proposals for peace were aimed at bringing a fully independent Japan back into the family of nations. Japan was to enter the United Nations, which was to establish a trusteeship for the Ryukyus and the Bonins. Japan was to recognize Korean independence and accept a later decision of the concerned powers regarding the disposition of Taiwan, the Pescadores, South Sakhalin, and the Kuriles. In commercial agreements, Japan was to receive the usual most-favored-nation treatment. With respect to security measures, the United States advocated bilateral arrangements with Japan. The United States also pondered the advisability of including in the peace treaty clauses binding Japan to continue the occupation reforms. This proposal was rejected, and it was hoped that the reforms would hold.

Reactions to the U.S. peace proposals varied. The Soviet Union continued to question the feasibility and legality of a separate peace. Moscow wanted Communist China to get Taiwan, and it desired confirmation of titles to the Kuriles and South Sakhalin, which it was already occupying. The Russians advocated that all troops leave Japan and wished Communist China included as a party in all discussions. The Chinese Communists, not consulted, seconded the request for participation, and the British, who now recognized their regime, concurred. In reply, the United States, continuing to recognize Chiang Kai-shek, stated that no single nation through the exercise of the veto should hold up peace negotiations. Washington maintained that wartime agreements on dispositions of Japanese territory were not final and claimed that the trusteeship status advocated for the Ryukyus and the Bonins was not identical with territorial expansion.

From Taiwan, where Chiang Kai-shek's regime had retired in December 1949, after the fall of mainland China to the Communists, Nationalist China demanded foreign control of Japan for at least fifty years. Also with bitter memories of Japan, the Philippines and Australia wanted strong guarantees against possible resurgence of Japanese militarism, and they questioned the depth of Japanese democracy. Korea was not consulted on peace terms, because as a colony, it was technically never at war with Japan. Japan had nothing to say on peace terms. Tokyo objected to the terminology of certain wartime agreements and condemned Cairo's "violence and greed" provision, but Prime Minister Yoshida Shigeru, in his second tenure of office and who presided over the transition from occupation to resumption of sovereignty, committed Japan definitely and irrevocably to the side of the free world. In an exchange of communications prior to the peace conference, Yoshida assured Dulles that Japan would recognize Chiang Kai-shek's government. Yet Yoshida claimed that Communist or not, mainland China remained Japan's next-door neighbor and that geography and economic laws would prevail in the long run over ideological differences and artificial trade barriers.

In August 1951, the final text was drawn up by the British and Americans, who served as cohosts at the peace conference that met in San Francisco September 4–8. The conference was unique, for the discussions of treaty terms essentially had been concluded prior to its convocation instead of being discussed for the first time extensively at a conference. The concerned parties were invited to come to sign the treaty on a take-it-or-leave-it proposition. Fifty-two countries attended, including the Soviets and two other Communist states. Not invited were neutrals such as Sweden and Switzerland and former enemies such as Italy and Germany. Burma was invited but did not attend because it believed that the treaty terms were too lenient. Invited India declined to come for precisely the opposite reason—India felt the terms were too severe. Neither rival Chinese government was represented, because the conference cohosts each recognized a different Chinese regime. Communist China stated that the treaty infringed upon Chinese interests and that it threatened the peace and security of Asia. Nationalist China generally approved the terms and felt that it should have been invited to sign.

President Truman opened the conference, Secretary of State Dean Acheson presided, and Dulles acted as peacemaker among the representatives. Endeavoring to confuse, disrupt, and divide the conference, the Soviet bloc offered nine objections and thirteen amendments to the treaty, none of which were adopted. In commenting on the terms, most delegations limited themselves to statements of special interest. Asian delegations generally welcomed Japan back into the family of nations, but Indonesia and the Philippines insisted adamantly on their right to repatriations. On September 8, 1951, forty-nine of the fifty-two states signed the treaty, but some with reservations. Yoshida characterized the treaty as fair and generous, but he pointedly recalled Japan's extensive territorial losses, the bleak international economic outlook, and the third of a million Japanese not yet repatriated from the Asian mainland. He apologized for Japan's prewar militaristic role, paid tribute to Generals MacArthur and Ridgway, and envisioned a reborn Japan.

PEACE TREATY SETTLEMENT

The treaty of peace was a treaty of reconciliation. It was nondiscriminatory, nonpunitive, and motivated by enlightened self-interest. The preamble contained a general statement of objectives and principles. Japan was to apply for U.N. membership (which it did, although Soviet vetoes held up Japanese entrance until 1956), and it was to maintain the new ideals of human rights and freedoms expressed in the constitution. The treaty ended the state of war and recognized the full sovereignty of the Japanese people, but the terms relating to territorial dispositions were vague and unclear. As the Potsdam Declaration had provided, Japan was limited to the four main home islands and some minor islands.

Japan renounced all rights, titles, and claims to Taiwan, the Pescadores, Kuriles, South Sakhalin, the former Pacific mandates, Antarctic areas, and the Spratley and Paracel Islands in the South China Sea that it had occupied in the course of taking over Indochina. Yet the treaty remained silent on the new ownership of these territories, for it did not provide for their disposition or the transfers of titles to any other parties. In the Ryukyus, Japan retained residual sovereignty, but the United States administered the island chain as well as the Bonins (the trusteeship idea had been dropped), which had been built up into a vast military complex.

Japan was to refrain from the use of force in international relations, but the treaty recognized that Japan, in keeping with the U.N. Charter, possessed the right of individual or collective self-defense. All occupation forces were to be withdrawn within ninety days after the treaty went into effect, but the treaty provided that some of the forces might be retained and stationed in Japan according to special agreements between one or more of the Allied powers. Otherwise, the argument went, Japan would be defenseless in the face of any possible aggression. In its economic and political clauses, the treaty provided for nondiscrimination in relations with Japan and pledged Japan to a free economy and an unlimited right to trade. Permanent agreements regarding specific issues were to be negotiated between interested parties. Japan renounced all rights and privileges in China.

The issue of reparations proved sticky. The treaty implied that nations that had suffered at the hands of the Japanese were to get reparations, but it stated that Japan at that time could not meet extensive reparations demands and still keep the economy going. Voluntary rather than mandatory reparations were implied. On this point, Indonesia and the Philippines signed the peace treaty with reservations, for they maintained that Japan had a legal as well as a moral obligation to pay reparations. Other treaty provisions related to Korea, which was treated as an Allied power rather than as a former colony of Japan. Nationalist China was given the right to conclude a separate peace treaty with Japan on the same terms as the general peace treaty.

When the final terms were released in Japan, the Japanese, a disciplined people, received them with great restraint. They feared the future with its imponderable economic and security problems. They simply wanted to be left alone, yet 85 million people could hardly enjoy the luxury of nonparticipation or noninvolvement in world affairs. They feared that too close ties with the United States could embroil them in a war with the Soviet Union or the People's Republic of China. They wanted a demilitarized utopia, and although Article Nine of the constitution might have provided this condition in Japan, strong neighboring countries did not have similar constitutional stipulations restraining the use of force.

Despite some qualms, both houses of the Diet approved the peace treaty by great majorities. The emperor ratified it, and the instrument of ratification was deposited in Washington. The U.S. Senate consented to the approval of the treaty with only a small negative vote. Other countries followed suit. On April 28, 1952, once the majority of signers, including the United States, had ratified it, Japan recovered its independence. On the same day, Chiang Kai-shek concluded a peace treaty with Japan, which recognized Nationalist China as sovereign authority over Taiwan and the Pescadores. Other powers, which did not sign the San Francisco peace treaty or had signed it with reservations, in subsequent years entered into normal relations with Japan: India in 1952, Burma in 1954, the Soviet Union in 1956 (with diplomatic recognition but no separate peace treaty), and the Philippines and Indonesia in 1956 and 1958, respectively, after both countries had at the same time concluded reparations agreements.

To supplement idealism with practical security arrangements, the United States negotiated additional treaties with Japan. On September 8, the day that the peace treaty was signed in San Francisco, the United States and Japan also signed a Security Treaty. In this short but basic agreement, Japan granted to the United States the sole right to maintain forces in and about Japan. The forces were to guarantee peace and security in the Far East as well as to preserve the security of Japan both from external attacks and from internal subversion. This right to station forces, which was to continue indefinitely until other arrangements were made, was granted exclusively to the United States. To implement the details of the Security Treaty, the Administrative Agreement, signed February 28, 1952, minutely stipulated for the disposition of such forces, the use of facilities, the sharing of costs, and the privileges and exemptions of, and jurisdiction over, U.S. troops. The Diet approved the Security Treaty, but many Japanese worried about the dangers, costs, and extent of rearmament as well as its constitutionality.

In the wake of Japan's recovery of independence, the United States made other security arrangements with its uneasy allies to placate them in their fears of any possible resurgence of Japanese militarism. To calm Philippine fears, the United States signed a mutual assistance treaty with the ex-colony on August 30, 1951. To reassure Australia and New Zealand regarding a similar fear of future Japanese military intransigence, the ANZUS pact was concluded two days later. These arrangements, designed primarily for protection against Japan, later were to be the bases on which the United States was to build groupings against perceived militant Communist forces in Asia. The Japanese peace settlement was comprehensive. It included not only the multilateral San Francisco peace treaty but also a series of other bilateral or multilateral arrangements with Japan and third countries. The settlement ended one era in Asia and presaged another.

CHRONOLOGY

1945	MacArthur designated SCAP; Initial Post-Surrender Policy; Trade Union Law; purges in industry and military
1945–1948	First phase: reform
1946	Emperor renounces divinity; land reform law
1946–1947	Yoshida Shigeru, prime minister (Liberal)
1947	New constitution promulgated
1947–1948	Katayama Tetsu, prime minister (Socialist coalition)
1948	No-strike law; Ashida Hitoshi, prime minister (Democratic)
1948–1952	Second phase: recovery
1948–1954	Yoshida, prime minister again
1949	Fiscal retrenchment
1950	Korean war erupts (June 25)
1951	MacArthur fired, replaced by Ridgway; signing of Peace Treaty at San Francisco Conference (September 4–8); Japan-U.S. Security Treaty (September 8)
1952	Administration Agreement signed (February 28); Japan recovers independence (April 28); separate treaties with Nationalist China, India
1954	Peace treaty with Burma
1956	Restoration of relations with the Soviet Union and with the Philippines
1958	Peace treaty with Indonesia

17

Contemporary Japan (Since 1952)

Domestic Affairs—Politics

The occupation of Japan was followed by a transitional phase in the 1950s after the peace treaty, in which many of the reforms of the occupation persisted but some others were phased out. Then, after the riots in the spring of 1960 over the revision of the U.S. Security Treaty, Japan entered a period of a dozen years in which it began to initiate new programs and purposes in domestic and foreign affairs. The end of 1972 witnessed the return to the country of administrative control of Okinawa and the Ryukyus, the normalization of relations with the People's Republic of China, and the resolution of some other basic issues resulting from wartime conditions. Japan entered a period of yet another and greater degree of freedom of action and international standing.

In political life, into the twenty-first century, Japan continued to experience one-party domination (the Liberal-Democratic) and a succession of prime ministers drawn from it. Parties from the left were perennially relegated to a secondary position. On January 7, 1989, Emperor Hirohito, as the longest-reigning monarch, on the throne since 1926, died after a lingering illness. He was number 124 of the Japanese imperial lineage, the longest continuous one in history, its origin dated by myth to February 11, 660 BCE. (Only seven sovereigns were women; the last one, Empress Meisho, ruled from 1629–1643.) With Hirohito departed the last major international figure associated with World War II. His eldest son, Akihito, born in 1933, ascended the throne. After a suitable extended period of national mourning, he was enthroned as Japan's 125th emperor on November 12, 1990, in a Tokyo ceremony witnessed by dignitaries from 156 countries. In his reign, known as Heisei (Achieving Peace), he fell heir to continuing debates over the issues of national wartime guilt and the precise nature of the ongoing imperial house.

THE POLITICAL SYSTEM

The 1947 Constitution (Shijitai/Kyujitai), also known as the Peace Constitution (Heiwa Kenpo), is the founding legal document of postwar Japan. The prewar emperor, once considered a divinity, was relegated to a ceremonial role. Like European monarchs, he reigns but does not rule; he is not officially considered the head of state. Emperor Hirohito and cabinet members were reluctant to replace the former Meiji Emperor's constitutional document with a more liberal one. To appease Japanese sensitivities, the new document was considered an amendment to the previous one and entitled "Bill for Revising the Imperial Constitution." In late 1945, Prime Minister Shidehara Kijuro appointed Joji Matsumoto, a state minister without portfolio, as head of a committee of constitutional scholars to make the revisions. Made public in February 1946, the recommendations were rather conservative. MacArthur rejected them and ordered SCAP to draft a new version. Rewritten in English, translated, and submitted to the government, it met some objections, but the emperor approved it as did both houses of the Diet, the upper House of Councilors, and the lower House of Representatives. There were only five negative votes in the latter, the first election in which women voted. The emperor formally sealed his approval, and the constitution came into effect on March 3, 1946.

The constitution, of some five thousand words, sponsored by the Americans, and written in colloquial rather than literary language, lacks semantic eloquence. Its eleven chapters with 113 articles are brief and to the point. The chapters are: (I) Emperor, 1–8; (II) Renunciation of War, 9; (III) Rights and Duties of the People, 10–40; (IV) The Diet, 41–64; (V) The Cabinet, 65–75; (VI) Judiciary, 76–82; (VII) Finance, 83–91; (VIII) Local Self-government, 92–95; (IX) Amendments, 96; (X) Supreme Laws, 92–99; and (XI) Supplementary Provisions, 100–103.

As head of the imperial family (*koshitsu*), the emperor (I:1–8) was the symbol of the state and the unity of the people, deriving his position from the will of the people with whom resided the sovereign power. The imperial throne was to be dynastic, with succession in accordance with the Imperial House Law as passed by the Diet—through the eldest male heir. The emperor's advice and approval was required for cabinet matters and he could perform duties of state as provided for in the constitution, although he could delegate performance of acts as provided by law. He appointed the prime minister, leader of the majority party, whose name was submitted by the cabinet, as well as the chief judge of the Supreme Court. He had ten specific duties to perform with the advice and approval of the cabinet, including to promulgate amendments to the constitution and other legal acts, convoke the Diet, dissolve the lower house, appoint and dismiss ministers of state, receive foreign diplomats, and perform ceremonial functions. He could not receive any property or gifts without Diet authorization.

Born in 1901, Prince Hirohito attended the Gakushuin Peers School (1908–1914) and then studied at a special imperial institution (1914–1921). In 1914, he became the first crown prince to travel abroad when he embarked on a six-month European tour. In 1921, he assumed the regency when his father, Emperor Taisho, became mentally ill. After this father's death five years later, Hirohito assumed the throne in 1926 as the Showa Emperor, by which designation he was known in his imperial position and posthumously. Earlier, in 1924, he had married his distant cousin, Princess Nagako; the couple eventually had two sons and five daughters. Crown Prince Akihito was the first son but fifth child. Hirohito's reign began during the peaceful 1920s, but in the 1930s was characterized by the rise of the military at home and its expeditions abroad. In 1931, the army annexed Manchuria; in 1937, it occupied North China; by the time of the attack on Pearl Harbor, it was entrenched in coastal China and in Vietnam.

Debate has raged through the decades over the emperor's responsibility for Japan's wartime record. The military leaders informed him of all actions abroad, to which he gave tacit consent. Although all war actions were effected in his name, he escaped any culpability after the war. He was vindicated (for political reasons) when MacArthur, as an American shogun, permitted Hirohito to remain on the throne, allowing MacArthur to effect SCAP measures through the emperor to ensure peaceful continuity in the country and loyalty of the people, which made reforms all the easier. Japanese history fused with foreign occupation.

For the rest of his life, Emperor Showa was active in national concerns and performed the many ceremonial duties delegated him by the constitution. The imperial family kept a strong political presence, although the protective Imperial Household Agency (not mentioned in the constitution), a 1,300-year old, powerful institution, filtered out any unfavorable information concerning the royalty. In 1978, after learning that fourteen Class A war criminals were buried in the Yasukuni Shinto shrine, Emperor Showa boycotted the site. He also played an important role in the country's re-entry into international life. As the first emperor to travel abroad, he visited Great Britain in 1971 and met with Queen Elizabeth II. Four years later he went to the United States, including Washington, D.C., where President Gerald Ford entertained him and the empress at a state dinner. In the palace, he occupied himself with his hobby, marine biology, and published nine scientific articles relating mainly to jellyfish. After he died of cancer in

1989, he was entombed in the imperial mausoleum at Hachioji, alongside his father, Emperor Taisho.

Hirohito's son Akihito, Emperor Heisei, succeeded him. As a youth, Akihito attended the Gakushuin Peers School and was tutored in English by Elizabeth Gray Vining, a Quaker teacher. In 1959, he took a wife, Michiko Shoda, the first commoner to marry into the imperial family. They have three children: Crown Prince Naruhito, Prince Akishino (Fumihito), and Sayako Kuroda. While still crown prince, Akihito and his wife journeyed to thirty-seven countries. After he was enthroned, he and his wife continued to make official visits to eighteen more states as well as all forty-seven home prefectures. In 1996, during a state visit to the United Kingdom, he was made Knight of the Garter, the only non-European to receive the honor.

Despite constitutional restraints and because of continued Asian agitation, Emperor Heisei proffered regrets (but not outright apologies) for the Japanese occupation and wartime record in Asian countries. He particularly noted the legacy of Japan in Korea and offered continued remarks of remorse to China, from 1989, just after his father's death. In 2002, he and the empress visited Saipan in the Marianas, the site of particularly vicious World War II battles, and offered prayers to all those killed. Like his father, he boycotted the Yasukuni shrine. Extending his father's hobby, the emperor also pursued an interest in marine biology, especially ichthyology, on which he published scientific papers in both English and Japanese journals.

Following the section of the constitution outlining the role of the emperor, statements on defense were contained in the short, controversial Chapter II, article 9, on the renunciation of war:

> 1. Aspiring sincerely to an international peace based on justice and order, the Japanese people forever renounce war as a sovereign right of the nation and the threat or use of force as means of settling international disputes. 2. In order to accomplish the aim of the preceding paragraph, land, sea, and air forces, as well as other war potential, will never be maintained. The right of belligerency of the state will not be recognized.

The source of this renunciation is in dispute. One theory suggests that Prime Minister Shidehara Kijuro wanted it as a military stance to protect Japan and accordingly passed the idea on to MacArthur, who approved it. Others maintained that the government section of SCAP originated it. Whatever the source, the Diet endorsed it. Its acceptance was rationalized in part by the wish to protect the emperor—considered by some to be the architect of the country's wartime policies—from being tried as a war criminal.

History shortly rendered this renunciation outmoded. After 1947, the Cold War was developing between the United States and the Soviet Union.

In 1949, the Chinese Communists established their regime over their country. The United States was now searching for allies, including in Asia, as a bulwark against the further geographical expansion of communism. In 1950, following the outbreak of the Korean War (which lasted to 1953), MacArthur ordered the creation of a 75,000-strong National Police Reserve (NPR) to repel any possible invasion. In 1952, the new National Safety Agency (NSA) was formed to supervise the NPR. Two years later, the NSA morphed into the Japan Defense Agency (JDA) and the NPR became the Japan Self-Defense Force (JSDF, the *jieitai*). In several cases, the Supreme Court has upheld the constitutionality of this renunciation of the use of force.

In the chain of command of the civilian-controlled JSDF, the prime minister is in operational control. The minister of defense presides over administrative matters. Conscription is forbidden. Volunteers are aged eighteen to twenty-five and some three thousand women are enlisted. The JSDF is divided into three military components: the army (Japan Ground Force) with five armies; the navy (Japan Maritime Defense Force) with five maritime districts; and the air force (Japan Self-Defense Air Force) with three air defense forces. In 2005, the JSDF totaled 249,330 personnel with 147,732 in the army, 44,327 in the navy, 45,517 in the air force, and 1,849 in the Joint Staff Office. The head of the agency is required to be a civilian, a post not sought by ambitious bureaucrats who want to move on to higher political or business posts. Only one prime minister, Nakasone Yasuhiro (in three cabinets 1982–1987), has served as chief of the JSDF.

Technically all JSDF are volunteer civilians and are subject to civil courts in appropriate jurisdictions. Obviously, no nuclear weapons are allowed and they are forbidden to be imported or to transit within the country from abroad. Moreover, exports of arms are similarly prohibited. The budget for the military runs at approximately 1 percent of the gross national product (GNP, also known as the gross domestic product, GDP), the sum total of goods and services produced. With such a low percentage devoted to the military (much of which expense is borne by the United States), the overwhelming bulk of national effort was concentrated on the civilian sector, a fact that helped propel Japan into its enviable position as the second richest country in the world, and third, after China, in purchasing-power parity (PPP, the price variations of the same commodity in different currencies).

The JSDF have been actively involved in alleviating domestic natural disasters. They have conducted several joint exercises with United States military components within territorial boundaries. Because of the strong anti-war feeling in the country, the naval forces were cautious in beginning to expand operations within the economic territorial zone (defined internationally as 200 miles from shore). In 2001, they sunk a North Korean spy ship and several years later chased a Chinese nuclear submarine out of the zone. Just as gingerly, they then extended their operations into international waters in humanitarian and peacekeeping roles. In 1991, they participated in the Cambodian talks that led to the Paris Peacekeeping Accords.

In 1992 the Diet passed the UN Peacekeeping Cooperation Act to provide for participation in refugee repatriation, logistical support, infrastructure reconstruction, and election monitoring abroad. It took on the task of minesweeping in the Persian Gulf during the first war there. In 1993, fifty-three members went to Mozambique for peacekeeping functions. However, without UN involvement but upon U.S. request, in 2004 some armed troops, protected by Australians, were involved in the Iraq war. This was the first time in the postwar decades that the supposed self-defense forces were actively involved in non-peacekeeping activities abroad. Opposition at home was vociferous to this open-ended, ongoing commitment. But the Diet authorized refueling duties in Operation Enduring Friendship in the Sea of Bengal during the course of the Afghanistan domestic strife. In 2007, seven officers were dispatched to Nepal for peacekeeping duties there. Debate over an amendment to allow Japan's active military participation in international issues has raged for decades. Ironically, the group that desires to maintain the prohibitive clause is the left wing, critical of the SCAP-imposed restriction. The ones who favor a change are grouped around the right wing, notably the Liberal Democrat Party (which has been in power for most of the past half century).

Peaceful and scientific space exploration was also on the government agenda. In 2003, three independent agencies were united to form the Japan Aerospace Exploration Agency (JAXA) to send satellites into orbit. The "Reaching for the Skies, Exploring Space" program examined asteroids and with NASA jointly probed the effects of carbon dioxide in space and the nature of global rainfall. They launched communication and climate observation satellites. No spacecraft with personnel abroad has been launched. The only Japanese astronaut to reach space was part of a Soviet shuttle mission in 1992. A manned mission to the moon is on the future agenda.

The constitution goes on to formulate the executive branch of the government, centered on the prime minister and his cabinet, the duties of which are outlined in Chapter V (65–75). The emperor, above politics, is not considered a part of this political component. Created in 1885, four years before the Meiji Constitution, the position of the prime minister is designated from among the members of the Diet. Usually, the post is held by the president of the majority party in power (all of them men to date), which, as noted, has for decades been the Liberal-Democrats. In office normally for four years, the prime minister can lose office if the Diet rejects any act or if he receives a vote of no confidence. In addition to the prime minister's administrative functions, the constitution lists seven particular duties of his that involve both domestic and foreign affairs.

The prime minister's office encompasses a dozen agencies (in alphabetical order): Defense Agency, Economic Planning Agency, Environment Agency, Environment Disputes Coordination Commission, Fair Trade Commission, Hokkaido Development Agency, Imperial Household Agency, Management and Coordination Agency, National Land Agency, National Public Safety Commission, Okinawa Development Commission, and Science and Technology Agency.

The four years in office is often too short a period for the prime minister—usually a former career bureaucrat—to leave a personal stamp on government. These brief tenures in office weaken the prime minister's influence and render it difficult for him to effect long-term policies and conduct effective international diplomacy. He is often dependent on his cabinet and the bureaucracy for advice in matters of policy. After retirement, he might accept a plush top executive position in business or industry.

The prime minister appoints a cabinet, which, late in the first decade of the twenty-first century, consisted of ten ministries. These were (in alphabetical order) the Ministries of: Agriculture, Forestry, and Fisheries; Economy, Trade, and Industry (METI); Education, Culture, Sports, Science, and Technology; Environment; Finance; Foreign Affairs; Health, Labor, and Welfare; Internal Affairs and Communications; Justice; and Land, Infrastructure, and Transport. Of these, the most important are the Ministries of Finance and METI, which are concerned with fundamental economic matters of state. At least half of the cabinet must be members of the Diet.

Coordinating ministerial activities is the chief cabinet secretary, who integrates measures, conducts policy research, and assimilates material for meetings. The Cabinet Legislative Bureau advises on legislation. An independent board of audit examines government expenditures; a security council advises the prime minister and cabinet on salaries and national civil matters. Additionally, there exist almost one hundred semi-autonomous public and seven privatized corporations that deal with matters relating to housing, finance, communications, transportation, and other national concerns. Cabinet members are drawn from the upper ranks of the bureaucracy and dominating political party personalities and factions. The short terms of cabinet members make them unusually dependent on bureaucrats for advice in matters of policy. Most bills originate in chambers of various ministries and then are presented to the parliament.

The central bureaucracy, an essential part of the executive branch of government, numbers around one million employees, 40 percent of whom are in the postal service, which has been privatized. Civil servants are divided into two groups. The "special" category does not enter by competitive examinations. From this rank come cabinet members, heads of independent agencies, members of the JSDF, Diet officials, and foreign service personnel.

Most of the national civil servants are in the "regular" category, recruited through competitive examinations.

In turn the "regulars" are further divided into junior and professional ranks, the latter a well-defined elite. Over the centuries, persisting into modern times, the bureaucrats have been both revered, because of their privileged status, and resented, because of their social superiority and aloofness from the public. They are reputed to be diligent and hardworking; they take periodic tests for promotion. Some retire early and take lucrative higher jobs in politics or private and public corporations. Ties between the bureaucrats, politicians, and business interests are close, especially if they come from similar good family backgrounds and graduate from prestigious universities. Roughly a third of all employees graduate from Tokyo University and some 15 percent from Kyoto University. Many have been trained in law.

Chapter VIII (92–95) of the Constitution generalizes about the nature of local government; details were left for the Diet to outline. All prefectural and municipal units were organized according to the Local Autonomy Law passed in 1947. Under the central bureaucracy in the executive administration ladder are the forty-seven prefectural divisions; forty-three are designated as rural. The other four are named: Tokyo (one metropolitan district); Osaka and Kyoto (two urban prefectures), and Hokkaido (a district). Large cities are divided into wards and further split into towns, precincts, subdistricts, or counties. Each of the forty-seven jurisdictions, responsible for varying and wide-ranging duties, is headed by a governor and has a unicameral assembly, both elected by popular vote every four years. The governor is responsible for projects funded both by local taxation and the national government.

At the lowest level of organization are the some 32,000 municipalities that encompass cities, towns, and villages. Cities are self-governing units, independent of the greater authorities in which they are located. To attain this type of city status, it must have a population of at least 30,000 inhabitants. A mayor heads the government, elected for a four-year term, with popularly elected assemblies. In this lowest level of government are the many self-governing towns and villages. Under these two fundamental administrative centers are the twenty-three wards of Tokyo, and in addition to the smaller cities, there are eleven large "designated" urban areas. These cities are identified as having approximately one million inhabitants. There are eleven: Fukuoka, Hiroshima, Kawasaki, Kita-Kyushu, Kobe, Kyoto, Nagoya, Osaka, Sapporo, Sendai, and Yokohama.

Although the governing system is tiered, Japan is a unitary rather than a federal system. Local jurisdictions are dependent largely on the national government in administrative and financial matters. The Ministry of Internal Affairs and Communications (formerly the Ministry of Home Affairs) and other cabinet ministries have the authority to intervene in local affairs. The term "thirty percent autonomy" is often used to describe local government because that is the lesser amount of revenues derived from local sources. Nevertheless, townsfolk have a strong sense of local community, and some of the more progressive jurisdictions such as Tokyo and Kyoto have adopted policies in their areas that were later copied by the national government.

The second branch of government is the legislative, or parliament (*kukkai*). Known as the Diet (from the Latin for a consultative assembly), it is a bicameral body (Chapter IV:41–64). It is the highest organ of state power and sole law-making body of the country. The Upper House of Councilors (*Sangi-in*) consists of 242 members, 146 held by the 47 prefectural constituents, the remaining 96 elected by parties from a single national list. All sit for six years, half from staggered terms elected every other three years. The prime minister cannot dissolve this House, which can reject bills from the lower chamber that in turn can override the veto by a two-thirds majority. The lower House of Representatives (*shugi-in*) is the more powerful of the two. It has 480 members sitting for four years, of whom 300 are elected from single member districts, and the other 180 positions are filled by proportional representation from eleven electoral blocs under the party-list system. Among other duties, they elect the prime minister, pass laws, formulate the budget, and conclude treaties. They rarely fill out their full terms because of turbulent politics that necessitate more frequent turnovers of personnel.

The third branch of the government is the judiciary (Chapter VI:76–82). The whole judicial system is vested in a supreme court and in such inferior courts as are established by law (three ranks of lower courts). The Supreme Court consists of a chief justice and such number of judges as may be determined by law (fifteen). The Supreme Court is the court of last resort with power to determine the constitutionality of any law order or regular or official act. Trials are conducted publicly unless deemed dangerous to public safety. Juries were not introduced until 2004. A century ago, the Japanese decided to adopt continental European codes. In addition to the Constitution, there are five: Civil, Civil Procedure, Criminal, Criminal Procedure, and Commercial.

The chief justice is appointed by the emperor following selection by the cabinet. The fourteen other judges are also appointed by the cabinet. Every ten years, a justice's tenure has to be confirmed by referendum. In practice, the justices are almost always reelected and allowed to serve until the age of seventy. Historically, the Supreme Court has played a low-key role. In avoiding controversy and publicity, the judges are practically unknown to the general public. As is the case of the elite bureaucracy, the judges naturally have a law background and attended prestigious universities. In 2009, six supreme court judges were graduates of Tokyo University and three were from Kyoto University. The chief justice and the fourteen associate judges are known as the "Grand Bench." This is divided into three "Petty Branches" of five justices apiece, who hear incoming appeals and recommend them before the Grand Bench.

The Supreme Court is the only one empowered to review the constitutionality of laws. It is generally reluctant to exercise the power of judicial review because it is reluctant to become involved in political affairs. When decisions are rendered, as on the constitutionality of the JSDF, the sponsorship of Shinto ceremonies by public authorities, or the authority of the Ministry of Education to determine the content of school textbooks, the Court generally defers to the government.

The next subordinate judicial level comprise the eight High Courts in Fukuoka, Hiroshima, Nagoya, Osaka, Sapporo, Sendai, Takamatsu, and Tokyo. These serve as circuits of several prefectures each. A special branch of the Tokyo High Court is the Intellectual Property High Court. Additionally, six branch offices exist, in Akita, Kanazawa, Matsue, Miyazaki, Naha, and Okayama. Then follow the District Courts, one in each prefecture, except for Hokkaido, which has four. These have original jurisdiction in felony cases and in civil cases where the disputed amount is over ¥1.4 million. They also handle bankruptcy litigation. A judge presides over each District Court, although two associate judges are consulted for appellate cases or criminal cases where the maximum penalty is more than one year in prison.

Each District Court has a Family Court as well in over two hundred branch offices throughout the country. These deal primarily with divorce and juvenile delinquency cases, but they hear all types of domestic disputes. Lowest are the 438 Summary Courts scattered around the country. They handle mostly small claims civil suits and criminal offenses. A judge presides over each court. Civil cases from here are appealed to the District Court, while criminal cases proceed directly to the High Court.

The four-tiered judicial system of Japan offers a high degree of governmental continuity and stability in society (along with the central bureaucracy). Politics are ephemeral. Prime ministers come and go through revolving doors (thirty-one from 1945 to 2009, as contrasted with twelve presidents for the United States and twelve prime ministers for the United Kingdom, one elected twice). These many judges, in unitary, fair, and accessible avenues of legal recourse, helped to anchor the structural strength of the Japanese nation. While the country's imperial family functioned mainly behind closed doors as a unifying symbol, these dedicated civil officials and bureaucracy rendered visibility, security, and stability but at a cost of conformity, aversion to risk taking, and innovation in public life.

POLITICS: THE RIGHT

After the initial political uncertainty that followed the surrender, conservative parties of the right (*Uyoku Dantai*) notably the Liberal-Democratic Party, came into power in Japan and consistently remained in office. Usually receiving two-thirds of the popular vote, they were proportionately represented in the Diet. They constituted a permanent majority, and although they were periodically divided into factions, they reunited within the formal party organizations. Until 1950, there were two main streams of conservative parties. The Liberals built on the prewar Seiyukai Party, and the Progressives and Democrats evolved from the Minseito. United in 1950 to form the Liberal Party, the factions coexisted uneasily until they split three years later. For another two years, the two conservative factions existed independently until they again reunited in 1955 to form the Liberal-Democratic Party (Jiyu Minshuto), which has dominated political life into the twenty-first century.

Within the majority party, factionalism, based on personalities rather than on divisive issues, continued; leadership proved ephemeral. As many as nine different groups existed in the nominally reunited conservative cause. Consisting of several factions but having purported common programs, appeals, and slogans, the conservatives faced the dilemma of trying to satisfy all leaders and yet distribute equitably the positions of power, especially that of the president of the party, who automatically was designated as prime minister. Unfortunately, there could be only one prime minister selected out of the several party bidders. In order to stay in top position, the one chosen had to enjoy not only the support of his own faction but also the cooperation of others. Another basic dilemma of the conservatives was the problem of reconciling foreign and domestic policy planks, for their acceptance of U.S. aid and trade ties ran counter to strong Japanese wishes for neutrality in world affairs.

Supporters of the conservative cause included the older generation. Traditionally more conservative and adhering to old customs and old family and political ties, this age-group provided a solid basis for the conservative electorate. The upper- and middle-income urban groups, desiring economic and political stability, also tended to cast their votes for conservative candidates. The rural class overwhelmingly voted conservative. Constituting about two-fifths of the total electorate, it usually cast four-fifths of its votes for the conservative cause. There were several reasons for such strong agrarian conservatism. Tradition was a partial answer. In Japan, as in most societies, the agrarian sector has been conservative, and it adhered more strongly to concepts of hierarchy and of obedience to authority than inhabitants of urban areas. In the countryside, conservatives had a heritage of local party organization that they maintained in spite of social and economic changes. Relatively satisfied with Japan's peace, prosperity, and ample subsidies, the farmers had shared in the unprecedented economic growth of Japan after the war. Because the opposition of the left, which was predominantly Socialist, was not able to formulate any program with more appeal to rural voters, this group in society maintained its conservative political complexion.

The conservative postwar prime ministers, as presidents of the Liberal-Democratic Party, working up through party ranks, came principally from the bureaucracy, especially the Ministries of Finance and Foreign Affairs. Yoshida Shigeru, who held office in two separate tenures for a total of nearly eight years (1946–1947 and 1948–1954), presided over the transition stage from the occupation to independence. Having opposed the war, he had not been purged and thus was eligible for office. Vigorous and competent, he controlled the Liberal Party with a firm hand. Assailed as both a dictator of Japan and a puppet of SCAP, he followed a pro-Western foreign policy, although in his determination to modify occupation reforms he showed his independence.

Walking on a tightrope during the early years, he could not ignore either MacArthur's edicts or the Japanese people's feelings on any given issue. But he did modify some of the occupation laws, and he regained Japanese sovereignty in the peace treaty. Yoshida managed to have the Diet pass the Subversive Activities Prevention program. He secured revision of labor laws to provide for compulsory arbitration of disputes that seemed to threaten the national economy. Despite Socialist opposition, he obtained more central control of the police force. He also helped to resurrect the zaibatsu.

The recovery of independence was followed by approval of the U.S. Security Treaty, which required great skill and courage for Yoshida to accept and to implement because of the continued presence of U.S. forces in the country. He pressed for U.S. trade ties, but he also desired commercial relations with Communist China. In regard to rearmament, the prime minister was cautious. He refused to seek an amendment (which required a two-thirds majority in the Diet) to the constitution to permit Japan to rearm, but he had previously created the National Police Reserves during the occupation to conform with MacArthur's interpretation that the constitution permitted self-defense measures.

Yoshida was succeeded by his most powerful rival, Hatoyama Ichiro (1954–1956). A prewar legislator who opposed the militaristic policies of the Seiyukai and who then withdrew from politics, Hatoyama was nonetheless purged under the occupation for having defended Japan's policy of expansion during the war. Before he was purged, he had formed the Liberal Party in an effort to unite antimilitarist conservatives. When he was purged in 1946, he turned over party leadership to Yoshida, who, by the time of Hatoyama's release in 1952, wanted to remain in office. Hatoyama promptly split the Liberals and formed his own party (Japanese Liberals, then Japanese Democrats). With factionalism at its height in conservative circles, Hatoyama finally caused Yoshida's downfall and became the next prime minister.

Hatoyama followed a more independent nationalist line. Desiring a partial return to the old order, Hatoyama wished to revise the constitution to permit a more extensive program of rearmament and to reestablish the theory of imperial rule. He established a Council for Constitutional Research to suggest changes. He wanted to hold down the budget, but he extended generous government aid to relieve the housing shortage. His desire to strengthen the control of the Ministry of Education over "subversives" led to the replacement of elected school boards by appointees of prefectural governors. To achieve a more independent foreign policy, he sought modifications in favor of Japan in the treaties with the United States. During his tenure, trade with Communist China increased, and Japan normalized relations with Soviet Russia, which withdrew its opposition to Japan's entrance into the United Nations. Hatoyama presided over the birth of the united Liberal-Democratic Party in November 1955. Advancing in age, he lost his grip over the party, and the next year, he surrendered the leadership.

After an interim of several months in which Ishibashi Tanzan, another conservative prime minister, held office (1956–1957), Kishi Nobusuke (1957–1960) took the helm. A dominating personality, he had been a bureaucrat in occupied Manchuria, and he had held a post in Tojo's cabinet. But he was not tried as a war criminal, and, in time, he emerged as president of the Liberal-Democratic Party. It was remarkable that he lasted as long as he did, because he did not personally endear himself to many of the Japanese, much less to conservative supporters. He sought to further the process of centralization in education and police matters. Despite great criticism for infringing on academic freedom, in 1958 he introduced a new efficiency rating scale for teachers administered by the Ministry of Education. The same year, he pushed for the further extension of centralized police power.

On other issues he went along with traditional conservative platforms, such as the recovery of Japanese administration of U.S.-governed Okinawa, the ending of nuclear weapons tests, and trade with Communist China. Kishi fell from office after ramming through the Diet the revised Security Treaty in the spring of 1960, an act that resulted in widespread leftist demonstrations in Tokyo and that caused the cancellation of President Dwight Eisenhower's imminent official visit to Japan. The press and many Japanese believed that the prime minister was utilizing the U.S. president's visit for his own prestige and advancement, so the resulting demonstrations were probably as much against Kishi as against the revised Security Treaty.

The next incumbent, Ikeda Hayato (1960–1964), promised a "new forward" look. A career bureaucrat with homespun manners and down-to-earth speech, he entered politics comparatively late in life as minister of finance in one of Yoshida's cabinets. Leaving behind the controversies of the past, he refused to toy with occupation reforms, and he closed that postwar chapter of Japan's history. Accepting the permanence of the reforms, he desired to build a new parliamentary framework within which both the conservatives and the Socialists could operate harmoniously. Concerned chiefly with economic progress, he advanced a ten-year program to double Japan's national income. On the foreign front, he practiced cautious conservatism and a "low posture," which to many Japanese meant the diminishing of newly earned prestige and gains abroad. He resigned in late 1964 after the Tokyo Olympiad because of illness.

His successor, Sato Eisaku (1964–1972), promised to display a higher posture and a more strident voice for Japan in world affairs. A younger brother of Kishi, the prime minister continued through the dominant right wing of the party a stronger defensive pro-Western posture, oriented toward ties to the United States. Yet he was also a nationalist and endeavored to follow an independent path by admitting that as "an Asian nation ourselves, we know the heart of Asia." But problems simmered. His party split over détente with China, the American role in the Vietnam War, and growing economic pressures generated by inflation, pollution, and other industrial issues. A cautious administrator with little initiative, his position eroded in the last year, particularly because of both the "Nixon shock" over the planned U.S. presidential visit to the People's Republic of China without informing the prime minister beforehand and U.S. economic policies.

Next assuming the premiership, Tanaka Kakuei (1972–1974) was a departure from the usual mold of office. With not even a high school education, and as a onetime construction worker, he presaged a change in leadership style. As former secretary-general of the party, he maneuvered to defeat rivals for the top position. A man of action, he was faced, however, with spiraling economic problems resulting from Japanese affluence at home and involvement abroad. In 1974, these issues, as well as involvement in Lockheed Aircraft bribes (in 1983 a Tokyo court sentenced him to a four-year jail term), forced him from office, but he kept a high political profile in behind-the-scenes manipulations of party debates over prime ministerial candidates.

The following years (1974–1991) saw in office nine prime ministers, some cabinets affected by scandals, and almost all subjected to electoral dissatisfaction in regard to constricting economic and financial measures. Tanaka's successor, Miki Takeo (1974–1976), a fairly liberal politician but who had to include among his associates conservative hawks, failed to realize the passage of major bills, including an anti-monopoly law. In the year-end 1976 lower house elections, his party for the first time lost an absolute majority, and Miki resigned, to be followed by Fukuda Takeo (1976–1978), who, though not an economic wizard, faced these issues. Next came Ohira Masayoshi (1978-1980), earlier the party's secretary-general and the first prime minister to die in office. Succeeded by Suzuki Kenko (1980-1983), formerly a Socialist, the next premier, a low-key compromiser not tainted by personal rivalry, still had to cope with persistent economic problems of inflation, increased taxation, and discontent over the unevenly distributed benefits of an affluent state.

Nakasone Yasuhiro (1982-1987), third-longest in office to that time (after Yoshida and Sato), was a mainstream party man wielding power in a self-described presidential style. A dynamic, forceful personality, he tried to push through an unpopular sales tax, preserve the wealthy national status, and concurrently achieve a more influential role in world affairs. In an unusual but successful ploy, he picked his successor, Takeshita Noboru (1987-1989), whose cabinet was involved in scandals that related to receiving donations, stocks, and loans from a prominent real estate company. Uno Sousuke (1989), in office only three months, resigned after the press revealed previous liaisons with geishas. Kaifu Toshiki (1989-1991) was a cautious, pragmatic leader with a few clearly spelled-out views. He held precariously to the reins of power until late 1991, when veteran politician Miyazawa Kiichi succeeded him. After only months in office, Miyazawa's popularity plummeted because of his aloof personality, indecisive domestic policies, and uncertainty in taking firm grip of international issues.

In the following fourteen years, 1993-2007, in a kaleidoscopic fashion, nine men held the prime ministerships, most of them for short terms. Four held office for a year or less: Hosokawa Morihiro, 1993-1994; Hata Tsutomo, 1994; Mori Yoshiro, 2000-2001; and Abe Shinzo, 2006-2007. Three in succession were in for about two years: Murayama Tomiichi, 1994-1996; Hashimoto Ryutaro, 1996-1998; and Obuchi Keizo, 1998-2000. Longest lasting was Koizumi Junichiro, 2001-2006, a popular figure. Fukuda Yasuo assumed office in 2007.

In 1993, Hosokawa Morihiro won the top position with the coalition of new parties. He introduced new political financing and made changes in the electoral system, which passed in 1994. That same year, Hata Tsutomo of the Renewal Party replaced him, as the first minority leader in forty years, but he lasted in office only two months. Next came Murayama Tomiichi, who in the same year through a coalition of the LDP and his Japan Socialist Party and a third small party presided in the position, a surprising coalition since the two parties had been bitter rivals. Then came Hashimoto Ryutaro in 1996 who stayed in power for two years until two small parties pulled out of the coalition.

Obuchi Keizo succeeded him in 1998 with his LDP and support of two other groups, the Liberal Party and the New Komeito Party. In 2000 he suffered a stroke and was replaced by Mori Yoshiro. The Liberal Party left, but a splinter group, the New Conservative Party coalesced with his as well as the New Komeito for a year. In 200l, maverick Koizumi Junichiro assumed top office and was reelected twice as party president which assured him the continued position as prime minister.

The elections of April 2001 swept the Liberal-Democratic Party (LDP) into power, which it had held except for eleven months for more than forty-six years. As party chairman, Koizumi automatically became prime minister. He shook up the party's faction system and the "iron triangle" of government bureaucrats, big industry, and banks. "Change the LDP and change the country" was the slogan. During his three terms of office, he shook up the party, especially its aging closely knit factions, and replaced the aging generation with younger, ambitious, and talented ones. He filled cabinet posts by merit, not factions. In 2003, he named Takanaka Heizo, a young economic expert, to shake up the banks. The biggest banks were to repay defaulted loans and extend credit to the solvent parties. Bad loans, which in 2002 had reached 8 percent of the GDP, dropped to 2 percent five years later. Although a loner, his direct approach to problems won public support, as well as opposition from entrenched sources, but the public media generally supported him. The "lost decade" of the 1990s with its falling prices, insolvent banks, and politics, especially in the postal industry and construction sector, among other problems, gradually morphed into the brighter years of the new century.

When Koizumi came into office, scandals, corruption, and lack of transparency in public entities plagued domestic politics. Banks extending bad loans were collapsing. Interest groups, especially those in the postal service, opposed any privatization of the company. With its savings and insurance components, the Post Office was the largest financial institution in the country, with 320 trillion yen ($42.8 trillion). Koizumi pushed through a privatization bill to separate the two functions, but he encountered parliamentary opposition that delayed the move. Another source of strong opposition came from the construction industry that wanted to expand the infrastructure by 5,000 miles of expressways at a cost of three trillion yen.

Then in his last year of office (2006), the prime minister seemed to have a more relaxed manner and did not strongly oppose this program. The succession of coalition governments proved unwieldy over the decades, but Koizumi managed to introduce basic political reforms, in part because he was in top office for six years, beyond the usual one-to-two years tenure of his predecessors. Whether his reforms would outlast him was problematic. Abe Shinzo followed as prime minister for a year, 2006–2007. Faced with party disenchantment and that of the public, he resigned, replaced by Fukuda Yasuo, in power 2007–2008. In opposition to the Upper House, with his great majority in the Lower House, he managed to pass an act to authorize refueling of ships in the Bay of Bengal in the Afghanistan operations. He in turn was succeeded in 2008 by Taro Aso, grandson of Yoshida Shigeru. His popularity did not last long. With his gaffes, such as misreading written Japanese characters, he seemed out of touch with the public. A scion of a rich family, his high style of living alienated many.

Politics by now had become particularly muddled. In July 2008, the Democratic Party of Japan (DPJ) under Ozawa Ichiro won the general elections for the upper House of Councilors. This was unprecedented; for decades the Liberal-Democratic Party (LDP) had emerged victorious, overcoming its own factional differences that remained ever present in the temporary accommodations with minor parties. A coalition between the two major parties was unthinkable; it was difficult enough to reconcile intraparty differences. Suddenly, after victory, an unpredictable Ozawa bolted his party, terming it unfit to govern, only to return shortly afterward. Unsuccessful backroom dealing among party bigwigs (*kokutai seiji*) resulted in stalled legislation; not a single law was passed for months. On the docket were bills that aimed to correct the various disparities in the pensions and, more importantly, the role of Japan's self-defense forces in refueling operations in the Indian Ocean to support Afghanistan anti-terrorist operations, passed by the Lower House.

The course of future elections (one was scheduled for the lower house in September 2009) was problematic. The majority Liberal-Democrats, one of the longest ruling parties in the democratic world, was founded during the Cold War as an ally of the United States to contain communism. In later decades, the party seemed to lack ideological focus. Stuck in old ways and guided by outmoded traditions and personalities, the party appeared stagnant. It had spent great sums on infrastructure and had built projects that were conceived as frivolous. Encompassing varying political views, leadership was often at odds with itself. The Democratic Party, as an alternate, also held out little promise for improvement. Similarly ideologically adrift, it was inexperienced in politics at the national level, an aspect that many voters viewed as an unattractive choice.

The extreme right, which included the ultranationalists and the militarists, was relatively impotent in postwar Japan. It lacked sources of financial support, it could not advocate expansion on the Asian mainland where a strong People's Republic of China flourished, and chauvinism was out of fashion even among the youth of Japan. Its proponents, like its prewar predecessors, lacked coherent programs. Rightist dissidents, such as the young militant Red Army committing terroristic acts abroad, also registered their protests at home through irrational assassination attempts on Japanese leaders and other personalities. Within three months in 1960, they instigated three political stabbings—one on Prime Minister Kishi prior to his resignation and two on Socialist leaders, one of whom was killed. In 1964, an attempt was made on the U.S. ambassador's life.

More important and in a different category was the rise of the Soka Gakkai (Value Creating Association), a modern-day variant of Nichiren Buddhism, which in the mid-1960s claimed more than four million families as members. It appealed in its authoritarianism and discipline to certain economic and social groups that felt excluded from Japan's rising prosperity. Its creed was utilitarian, and its goal was to give absolute happiness to each individual. Politically active, the Soka Gakkai through its political arm, the Komeito (Clean Government Party), elected members first to local assemblies and then to the House of Councillors, where in the 1962 election it received more than 11 percent of the vote. Over the following decades, it became the third-largest party (after the Liberal-Democrats and the Socialists) in the lower House of Representatives. Its political platform included such popular Japanese issues as peace, honest elections, and outlawing of nuclear weapons. Now known as the New Komeito Party, it is part of the Liberal-Democratic Party coalition in 2008 in parliament. But its dogmatic style of proselytizing for members and its electioneering tactics left an adverse mark on some of the electorate, who preferred more nonconfrontational tactics.

POLITICS: THE LEFT

The parties of the left, chiefly Socialist, commanded the support of a third of the Japanese voting strength. Like the conservative majority, Socialist groups in Japan were not united in outlook; as many as seven factions existed at a time. Though constituted of multiple factions, divided more by ideological variations than by personal groupings, within the formal party structure of the Socialist movement there were, in general terms, a right and a left wing. The former, constituting perhaps 30 percent of the strength, was less disciplined, more opportunistic, and closer to the conservative cause. The latter, some 70 percent, was the more vigorous and Marxist, with its extremist flank allied to Communists.

As in the conservative movement, in the postwar era there were phases of formal party cooperation and splits between the two main Socialist wings. Initially there was party unity (1945–1951) as the Social Democrats. In this period, Japan had its only Socialist prime minister in a coalition government: Katayama Tetsu, a Christian. He derived power from a Socialist plurality within this coalition that included conservative Democrats and another minor party. The coalition was unworkable and fell apart, to be followed by a four-year period of party disunity, split into two factions, the Right Socialists and the Left Socialists. Reunited in forced companionship to contest elections in October 1955 (a month before Hatoyama reunited the conservatives), the unstable cooperation as the Social Democratic Party endured for five years (1955–1960). Then another split occurred with the formation of the right-wing Democratic Socialist Party and the left-wing Social Democratic Party. The latter maintained its strength in the lower house of parliament as the second-strongest party. In 1986, it elected, in a precedent-shattering move, Doi Takako, a woman who had worked her way up through the ranks, as chairman of the Japan Socialist Party. In office five years, in 1991 she resigned after a string of political defeats in local elections and lack of any coherent programs relating to domestic. By 2004, the Social Democratic Party itself had only five members in the upper house and six in the lower.

In their programs, the right-wing and left-wing streams of Japanese Socialism differed in point of degree rather than in principle. In domestic affairs, the left advocated a proletarian state and extensive nationalization. The right, in a type of evolutionary Christian or Fabian socialism, espoused popular democracy, a mixed economy of government and private interests, and civil liberties. But both desired the traditional Socialist program of more state control of industry and transport, strong local rather than national controls of police and education, and retention of land reforms to ensure possession of land for peasants. In foreign affairs, Socialist views ranged from neutralistic to communistic extremes, but unlike the conservatives they did not favor close military and economic ties with the United States. Supporting the strong feelings of neutralism and pacifism in Japan, the Socialists were in sympathy with popular causes.

Yet their political fortunes were not so high as those of the conservatives. In spite of their support of popular ideas, they contributed to their own weaknesses. Factionalism was prevalent, and although this was also the case among the conservatives, it made a weak movement weaker. Party organization was not uniformly strong, and it was represented in only one-third of Japan's four thousand political subdivisions. It was top-heavy, for it tended to concentrate its greatest efforts at the national rather than local level. Socialists held about a third of the total seats in the Diet, but the percentage dropped precipitously at the prefectural, city, and district council levels and in the town and rural units. Moreover, their frequent parliamentary tactics of discourtesy, militancy, and volubility were not conducive to gaining support for them or their causes.

Despite its weaknesses, Socialism could count on certain sectors of Japanese life and society for support. Labor unions were traditionally allied with the Socialist cause, and they sponsored candidates who were expected if elected to further the program of trade unionism. Unions contributed funds to the party, and they campaigned in the hustings for Socialist candidates. Approximately half of the party members were from unions, and many Socialist members of the Diet rose through union channels. Some intellectuals also supported the party. The youth, a traditionally alienated group, perhaps more through emotion than reason, supported Socialist parties or causes. Finally, the urban lower classes, although assured of a degree of economic stability and job security, voted Socialist as a protest against their more fortunate fellow urbanites in the middle- and higher-income brackets.

The postwar Japanese Communist movement, despite its legalized status, was weak. When SCAP released political prisoners after the war or permitted their return from abroad, Japanese Communist leaders reactivated the party. Until 1950, their strategy was one of peaceful revolution, which followed from the 1932 thesis that called for the destruction of feudal elements (both agrarian and capitalist) through a democratic revolution in cooperation with bourgeois groups. Also, the presence of occupation forces made this approach the only practical one. Invoking a policy of moderation, the Communists regarded the occupation as an ally, because both aimed for a democratic, peaceful revolution at home. The party set out to win the allegiance of two particular groups of people, small business and the peasants, and it posed as their benefactor. During this period, there were parliamentary gains for the party, and in the early postwar years for the first time in Japanese history, Communists were elected to the lower house of the Diet.

In 1950, the moderate and cooperative line changed because of outside pressures. The January issue that year of the *Journal* of the Cominform (or Communist Information Bureau, which in 1948 had replaced the Comintern, abolished by the Soviets in 1943) violently attacked the theory of peaceful revolution and its Japanese proponents. The article, formulated in an escalating Cold War atmosphere, declared that the occupation was in effect turning Japan into a military base. The moderate attitude of the party, the article stated, constituted collaboration with the United States, from which the party was immediately to remove itself. The change, aligned with that of the Cominform, placed the Japanese Communist Party in a difficult position, because it was not eager to take on the occupation single-handedly in a confrontational manner, and the program of violence would alienate many of the groups it was endeavoring to win over.

After secret meetings, the party issued a compromise statement. It acknowledged errors, but it claimed that it was not altogether wrong in its tactics. In spite of this clash between national and international Communist tactics and judgment, the party after 1950 entered a phase of direct action. Incidents, demonstrations, and riots were perpetrated during the last years of the occupation and immediately after it ended. The Cominform advice proved harmful, because the militant policy failed. The acts of violence terrified elements that had previously been sympathetic to the Communist cause. The Japanese government cracked down on party activity, and it registered those leaders it could round up. By 1953, the party had lost every one of its seats in the Diet and its membership fell off. In time, because of severe setbacks, the party reverted to peaceful procedures. Though continuing as a legal party, it remained weak, and it captured only 2 to 3 percent of the popular vote in elections for seats in the lower house of the Diet. In the 1972 elections, the Communist Party peaked in strength at thirty-eight in the lower house, then dropped off in the next two decades, and in the 1990 elections numbered sixteen, approximating the 1969 strength. At any rate, the Communist Party provided some ideological spread to the normally unexciting mainstream political life.

The presence of ideological variations in Japanese political thought was a new phenomenon. The postwar political spectrum had broadened, and a radically different constitutional system was in operation. Increased mass participation in public affairs provided a greater base for a new political consciousness. More groups tended to support the democratic experiment, yet the voters continued to return to office consistently conservative candidates. A perennial minority, the left seldom enjoyed the higher offices.

Stability was also assured by the royal family. The Imperial Household Law, as approved by the parliament, stipulated that succession to the throne could be only by males. Unless princesses married into the imperial family, they lost their pedigree, as did three of five daughters of Hirohito, two daughters of his brother Prince Mikasa, and a sister of Akihito. Hirohito's younger brother Prince Chichibu married into the Tokugawa clan, whose fame and fortune was wiped out by the Meiji Restoration but which went on to great financial strength and certainly into political status with this marriage into the imperial family. A crisis occurred when the wife of Akihito's elder son, Prince Naruhito, gave birth to a girl, Aiko, in 2001. Debate ensued about the possibility of amending, through Parliament, the Imperial Household Law to permit female accession. The impasse was fortuitously resolved when the wife of the emperor's younger son Fumihito gave birth to a son, their third child, in 2006. Tradition and law were upheld; Japan continued to coalesce around the imperial family as a symbol of national unity.

CHRONOLOGY

1948–1954	Yoshida Shigeru, second tenure as prime minister
1950	Japanese Communist Party adopts activist line
1954–1956	Hatoyama Ichiro, prime minister
1955	Liberal-Democratic Party formed; Socialist movement breaks up
1956–1957	Ishibashi Tanzan, prime minister
1957–1960	Kishi Nobusuke, prime minister

1960	Anti-Kishi, anti-American demonstrations; President Eisenhower cancels visit
1960–1964	Ikeda Hayato, prime minister
1964	Tokyo Olympiad; assassination attempt on American ambassador's life
1964–1972	Sato Eisaku, prime minister
1972–1974	Tanaka Kakuei, prime minister
1974	Lockheed bribery scandal
1974–1976	Miki Takeo, prime minister
1976	Liberal-Democratic Party for first time loses absolute majority position in lower house of Diet
1976–1978	Fukuda Takeo, prime minister
1978–1980	Ohira Masayoshi, prime minister; dies in office
1980–1982	Suzuki Kenko, prime minister
1982–1987	Nakasone Yasuhiro, prime minister
1983	Former prime minister Tanaka sentenced to four years' imprisonment
1986–1991	Doi Takako, woman, elected to chair Socialist Party
1987–1989	Takeshita Noboru, prime minister
1989	Emperor Hirohito dies (January 7), Akihito ascends throne as emperor (No. 125); real estate scandals; Uno Sosuke, prime minister, three months
1989–1991	Kaifu Toshiki, prime minister
1990	Emperor Akihito enthroned (November)
1991–1993	Miyazawa Kiichi, prime minister
1994	Hata Tsutumu, prime minister
1994–1996	Murayama Tomiichi, prime minister
1996–1998	Hashimoto Ryutaro, prime minister
1998–2000	Obuchi Keizo, prime minister
2000–2001	Mori Yoshiro, prime minister
2001–2006	Koizumi Junichiro, prime minister
2006–2007	Abe Shinzo, prime minister
2007–2008	Fukuda Yasuo, prime minister; Democratic Party of Japan (DPJ) won elections for the upper House of Councillors
2008	Aso Taro, prime minister
2009	Elections scheduled for the lower House of Representatives

18

Contemporary Japan

Domestic Affairs—Economics and Society

ECONOMICS

Post-occupation Japan was dubbed the "The Miracle Economy" for its remarkable economic growth. A brief overview of the record of ups and downs common to a market economy reveals its phases. Postwar Japan (with the United States) rose from the ruins of war to share mutually in 40 percent of the global economy with indices that were impressive. Over the decades, the mixed record of growth was recorded: 10 percent in the "Golden" 1960s; 5 percent in the 1970s, 4 percent in the 1980s; 1.7 percent in the "Lost Decade" doldrums of the 1990s that returned to 1.7 percent again in the 2008–2009 global economic meltdown.

Between 1950 and 1955, annual economic growth of more than 9 percent was registered. Massive direct American aid programs during the occupation brought in more than $2 billion. Subsequent American offshore military procurements in Japan during the Korean War (1950–1953) were twice that amount and promoted the construction of new industrial plants and the retooling of machinery. Other factors included the strong mutual aid bond between government and industry, a pronounced work ethic, a degree of sophisticated high level technology, and political stability. These factors helped speed up the domestic recovery from the terrible wartime destruction visited on the home islands and the immediate postwar doldrums.

Then, drawing on the self-generated affluence between 1955 and 1960, with annual growth rates of more than 12 percent, a "Jimmu boom" was experienced (named after the mythical first emperor of Japan who founded the state in 660 BCE). Economic levels now exceeded those of prewar times; both heavy and light industries, especially textiles, noted high

gains. Newfound prosperity resulted in a consumer revolution in both the
city and the country that spurred sales of household appliances, electrical
wares, and other material benefits of modern living.

In the ensuing five years, 1960–1965, the heated economy cooled off,
but during the period 1965–1970, another five-year boom was experienced. The official Medium Term Economic Plan particularly emphasized
the increase of agricultural and small business output that had lagged behind the ever-growing consumer demands of the Japanese. In the course
of the 1970s, during the crises in oil imports from the Middle East (from
where 80 percent of the total imports derived), the cost of a barrel of
crude oil zoomed from $2 to $35 and put a brake on continued economic
growth. To reduce energy dependence on oil, Japanese industries shifted to
alternative sources, such as hydroelectricity (and oil imports from that area
dropped precipitously to 60 percent), as well as to other avenues of technological output, such as automobiles and electronic wares.

In the 1970s and 1980s the country experienced economic prosperity but
at a lower growth rate. "Japan Inc." was ready to take over the world; books,
some by American authors, attested to the phenomenon. The "iron triangle"
of government and its bureaucrats, the banks, especially the central Bank of
Japan, and big business were closely allied in the program of concentrated
economic planning and growth. Ties were enhanced among the personnel
of the three sectors through attendance at common prestigious schools and
social ententes. Consumer saving was up 20 percent, but spending leveled
off. Information technology (IT) grew at a fast rate, especially in electronics.
Japanese autos flooded world markets.

In the late 1980s, Japan was the world's largest creditor. With easy
credit, financial speculation, and industrial expansion, its economy topped
roughly $1 trillion. Americans, eager consumers, bought most of its ex-
ports, and it continued to provide for the bulk of military expenditures. A
building boom of great proportions resulted. Prime location on the Ginza,
Tokyo's preeminent shopping area, sold at $300,000 per square meter. The
property where the Imperial Palace complex lay in the heart of the city was
rumored to equal the total property value of the state of California, the
eighth wealthiest political entity in the world. When the runaway bubble
finally burst in the early years of the twenty-first century, results were cata-
strophic.

Warning signs appeared that materialized when the bubble burst in
1989, and the country then experienced a "lost decade" of recession. The
next year, the Bank of Japan lowered the interest rate to zero percent to
encourage spending and growth. The real estate market crashed, and the
inflated stock exchange lost some ¥2 trillion in value. Savings plummeted
to 6.5 percent and banks were unable to call in unproductive loans, which
constituted some 80 percent of their assets. Cronyism and corruption left

their mark on the economy. In late 1999, the three top brokerage firms collapsed. The economic outlook was indeed dismal. With the oncoming of the twenty-first century, the picture brightened somewhat. The interest rate first went up from zero percent to 0.25 percent in 2001 and some years later to 0.50 percent to tighten the money supply and control inflation. Growth rate in the economy was at 2 percent, which rose in 2003 to 5.5 percent, higher than that in the United States or the European Union.

Then, into the first decade of the twenty-first century, particularly at its end, as part of the global meltdown that began in the United States, Japan went again into a recession. Its GDP at the end of 2008 dropped at an annual pace of 12.7 percent, the greatest fall since the oil shock of 1973. In an orgy of ill-timed lending, banks had already fallen into great debt; between 1992 and 2005 they wrote off some ¥96 trillion in unproductive loans. The public debt itself exceeded the GDP (normally it should have topped off at around 25 percent). Deflation (lowered prices) set in; real estate values fell over some fifteen years to an extreme low. Companies and industries laid off tens of thousands of employees, many with no safety nets into which to fall. Traditional low spending consumer habits did not inject much liquidity into the economic downturn. With recovery nowhere in sight, some analysts believed that the country was in its worst downturn since World War II.

As one countermeasure, the government began to spend large amounts of money on indiscriminate infrastructures. Huge projects were planned, practical or not. Rural areas received four-lane paved highways; bridges led to nowhere. According to a news report that uncovered the story, as an extreme example of haphazard infrastructure, the small town of Hamada, with its aging population, on the southwestern coast of Honshu island on the Japan Sea, was showered with an unrequested windfall: a highway, a two-lane bypass, a university, a prison, a children's art museum, the Sun Valley Hamada Sports Center, a ski resort, and an aquarium featuring three beluga whales. The country blossomed with numerous examples of modern transport networks, public facilities, sports stadia, and other projects that did not contribute to any long-term stimulus to the economy as the government between 1991 and 2008 infused the economy with $6.3 trillion worth of construction projects.

In another move, the government effected drastic fiscal and monetary measures. They dropped interest rates to ultra-low figures, and offered fiscal stimuli with cash infusions to troubled financial institutions. With government fears of a loud public outcry against the many drastic and unnecessary moves, it was lenient with basic political reforms. It did shake up the banking system, injected ¥1.8 trillion to shore up the banks by buying up defaulted loans, and solicited private funds to help alleviate the monetary morass. The fiscal expansion did avoid the worst, but it was not enough to kick-start a recovery. The support of the banking system did not go far enough since these institutions did not face up to their losses; transparency was lacking.

Some factors favored recovery. The closely knit companies, with their managers now drawn in great part not from family ties but from meritocracy, worked for mutual solutions to problems. High technology rebounded, and sending work offshore proceeded. Immigrants appeared in the labor force to replace retiring employees or augment the labor force. Wages crept up; the Ministry of Economy, Trade, and Industry (METI), and the Ministry of Finance kept a particularly watchful eye over industrial production of the zaibatsu (*keiretsu*). The government entered into a period of privatization to spur economic growth; that of the postal service, the country's premier financial institution, was particularly significant; the agency used 40 percent of its assets for reinvestments.

Problems existed. Retirement, usually at fifty-five to sixty years, cut into the aging labor force. Some workers took early retirement and went into temporary jobs elsewhere or at other companies. Women, half of the workforce, similarly went from job to job. Youth continued the pattern. Many lived at home, worked minimally in their hours or pay, and were deemed irresponsible by the older generation. The concept of lifelong employment in one firm was breaking down, and "companyism" was no longer the goal of many employees. The traditional approach to issues and problems of consensus building consumed time that led to watered-down low common denominators instead of encouraging productive individual initiative.

In foreign markets, China was forging to the forefront, and other Asian countries, with cheaper labor, were giving Japan competition for its exports. It imposed import quotas on items, including beef and citrus products, that kept these items at artificially high domestic prices. Late into the first decade of the twenty-first century, some problems persisted. Housing starts were down; prices were falling; sluggish consumer spending persisted; unemployment was rising. As a major participant in international trade, Japan was subjected to economic cycles abroad, especially those in the United States. Still dependent heavily on oil imports, it trod warily in countries from which it received the commodity, still over 80 percent in the case of the Arab countries and Russia. The government sought alternative sources of energy, including nuclear, as it built over five dozen nuclear plants for peaceful purposes.

Great overall economic strides in Japan could also be attributed to several additional factors. Despite geographical limits to expansion, agricultural production continued to increase in output per acre in the mainly modest plots of arable land through the extensive use of chemical fertilizers and efficient machines (including small tractors the size of an average American lawnmower). Less than 10 percent of the country's labor force worked in this primary economic sector, usually farmers with three-and-a-half million family units; they contributed around 1.5 percent of the gross domestic product (GDP, the sum total of goods and services produced). The government took a particularly paternalistic attitude toward the farmers who grew rice, although there was a surplus of rice. Farm subsidies to these farmers kept the price of the cereal well above that of world markets for domestic users (a problem resulting in strains between the Japanese and American governments, the latter desiring to export lower-priced rice in that direction). Though few in number, the farmers were represented by a strong lobby in the Diet, where local electoral districts could be drawn in favor of the countryside.

Mining, as another part of the economic sector, was a negligible factor in mineral-poor Japan. But fishing, a third component, was important. Vegetarian Buddhists, like many Japanese, depended on fish as a major source of protein. Traditional coastal fishing was quite important, as well as maritime activities within the 200 mile economic territorial limits. The Japanese also ventured out into international waters, where, in the whaling industry, they ran into strong opposition from other countries, especially the United States. Japan, like Iceland and Norway, historically had depended on the whaling trade, for food and commercial products. In recent years they rationalized their catch as research projects. The International Whaling Committee voted in 1986 to ban commercial whaling, but Japan continued to pursue it under the research rubric. Agreement on catches and their justification continue to paralyze the Commission into indecisiveness. On the high seas, Japanese whalers confront angry environmental activists and nationals of countries with similar whale protective policies.

One-third of all labor was in the secondary, or industrial, sector. Although Japan was heavily dependent on imports of raw materials and fuels for its burgeoning industrial activities, it manufactured an extraordinary array of products. The country had inherited a traditional entrepreneurial spirit dating back to the Tokugawa era when the first Japanese companies made an early start, to grow over the centuries, becoming industrial behemoths in the twenty-first century. Japanese industries cover a wide field of activity: automobiles; consumer electronics; computers; semiconductors; iron, steel, and copper products; petrochemicals; pharmaceuticals; shipbuilding; aerospace; textiles; and processed foods, to mention a few. The output has been steady overall in production over the decades.

The shipbuilding industry supplies half of the world's shipping needs, with South Korea, a distant second at 9 percent. In aerospace. the Japan Aerospace Exploration Agency launches satellites and orbiting vehicles. Factories produce commercial aircraft and next-generation fighter planes in cooperation with the United States. In petrochemicals, a variety of products is manufactured that include plastics, polystyrene, and polypropylene, which command high prices, although Asian countries offer competition in this field. The pharmaceuticals industry, second largest in the world, services a rapidly growing elderly population with new drugs. Research in biotechnology results in agricultural products and animal husbandry. Electronics, with many familiar names, have seven of the top twenty world's chip manufacturing companies. They are renowned for their quality, durability, and sophistication. Cameras, television sets, and information age products are universally recognized. And of course there is the automotive industry, now on a globalized foundation; the many familiar Japanese brands are produced throughout the world. Toyota is the world's leading car manufacturer, although in the economic meltdown of the 2008–2009, its sales and profits plunged to their lowest numbers in the postwar decades.

Efficient transport systems knit the country together. There are 1,770 kilometers of waterways, with twenty-two seaports. Coastal shipping is busy; ferries link Hokkaido and Honshu islands across the Tsugaru Strait in the north; Kyushu and Shikoku with Okinawa in the south. The road network, especially on the heavily populated coast off the Pacific Ocean to the west along the traditional Tokaido route, consists of 1.2 million kilometers of paved roads. These are high-speed thoroughfares, with divided lanes, limited access, and tolls. A bridge spans the Inland Sea between Honshu and Shikoku. With the increased wealth of the Japanese, more cars clog the roads. Traffic in main cities is horrendous, but oddly, one rarely sees the Japanese, a neat people, driving vehicles with any dents or traffic related scars on them. Trucks carry 90 percent of the country's domestic freight.

The rail system is fast and efficient. Seven companies formerly owned by the government operate much of this transport. There are many smaller private, regional, and company firms. The former span the country and utilize the high speed Shikansen trains, which reach a maximum of 300 kilometers per hour. Passengers on station platforms line up at designated spots to board quickly; these express trains wait for no tardy passengers. They are therefore always on time; the average delay upon arrival is six seconds. Five stations, four in Tokyo and Yokohama, each process an average of over two million passengers daily. Subways also are crowded; in rush hours guards cram passengers into the coaches like the proverbial sardines. Air travel is popular; there are 173 airports in the country. Haneda, the domestic Tokyo airport, is Asia's busiest. In the suburbs to the west is Narita International Airport, the East Asia hub of air transportation. Osaka International Airport also carries a heavy share of traffic. There are two large domestic companies: Japan Airlines and All Nippon Airlines, with a half dozen smaller operations. The airlines are deregulated and set their own competitive fares, although the government keeps a vigilant watch over any perceived out-of-line high tariffs.

In retrospect, historic precedent helped to fashion growth. As the government had previously been engaged in industrial activity for nearly a century, its people had acquired administrative skills and technical know-how over several generations. They already had made the psychological adjustment to industrialism, and they built on native techniques in modernizing. American occupation investments and the international Asian situation provided postwar catalysts to recovery and further economic development. With its fresh start, including the influx of women into the labor force during the decades of overseas imperial expansion, Japan rebounded all the faster from war-spawned problems. With the loss of colonies and occupied lands overseas, it could concentrate energies and policies on domestic priorities. With constitutional restraints, a pacifistic domestic attitude, and anxious Asian neighbors fearing a resurgent and strong Japan, military expenditures were kept to a minimum. The budget was then largely devoted to civilian uses with the disappearance of large standing military contingents that had drained off money from the civilian home sector.

Moreover, the government espoused the doctrine of free enterprise, but it did not hesitate to step in to shore up lagging segments of the private sector of the economy. For a non-Socialist state, Japan experienced a high degree of economic planning that resulted in controlled growth. The prime minister's office was a major factor in the formulation of economic policy. Contributions came from the Economic Planning Agency and other highly qualified personnel, particularly those drawn, as noted above, from the Ministry of Finance, the earlier Ministry of International Trade and Industry, and the Bank of Japan. Experts in these governmental agencies continually analyzed domestic production figures and foreign market goals, and they projected national trends and formulated programs. Government, finance, and private industry became meshed into a common outlook and purpose; the Keidanren (Federation of Economic Organizations), representing over seven hundred large concerns, enjoyed particularly close ties with the governing Liberal-Democratic Party. The government pursued a policy of privatization and turned over some companies to the private sector, as in the telegraph and telephone services, national railroads, and tobacco.

Contributing to growth were the generous lending policies of the big Japanese banks (which in terms of assets numbered among the richest in the world) for their industrial clients. In measures to stimulate production, bank practices extended loans constituting an unusually great percentage of their holdings to refinance and expand industry, which, in turn, tended to invest funds in new plants, equipment, and thorough research for profitable products. Concerned also with long-range planning, the industrial firms kept immediate profits at low levels and paid modest dividends as a temporary sacrifice in anticipation of expected profits at a future time. They concerned themselves with quality control over items manufactured,

Tokyo railroad station, where most station signs have English transliterations.

and they displayed a paternalistic attitude toward an ensured labor source of loyal and secure workers, mainly male in the well-paid positions, who could remain a lifetime with the companies.

Moreover, Japan shared, as the United States and Western Europe similarly did, in the general postwar prosperity of the non-Communist world. This helped to account for growing Japanese markets overseas and expanded international trade. Japan became the second most affluent country in the world. One index of wealth was revealed in the per capita income, which in the early post-occupation years hovered around $500 but by the 1990s had zoomed to over an estimated $33,000 in 2006. Another index was the perennial overall trade imbalances favoring Japan (except with the Middle East). Capital flowed inward from annual trade surpluses (value of exports over imports of merchandise) that had ranged around $176 billion in 2006. Capital investments also flowed outward, including into the United States, where Japanese funds to a great extent went into U.S. Treasury Department bonds.

Despite the post-occupation overall rise in prosperity, basic economic problems persisted. Millions of people did not share proportionately in the wealth. Riches and rewards were not evenly distributed, and intellectuals and white-collar workers particularly did not benefit from postwar economic gains. The government tended to relegate to a secondary role such public infrastructure areas as housing, transportation, and social services. Population growth and aging appeared to negate some economic gains, but

Railroad day coach: Trains run on time, passengers carry little baggage.

birth control measures were instituted as early as 1948 during the occupation, when the Eugenics Protection Law was passed to legalize abortion. As a result of such measures, for a time the number of abortions exceeded births. The rate of natural increase declined to about 1 percent, one of the lowest absolute population growth rates in the world outside of Western Europe.

Population might stabilize, but foreign economic relations had to expand. One perennial problem was to maintain a high volume of exports to meet obligations incurred by a high volume of imports. "Export or die" had been a familiar slogan in recent decades. Up to 80 percent of Japan's raw materials for industry and up to 20 percent of its foodstuffs were imported; some edible commodities came from abroad. Another persisting economic problem was the double structure of the domestic economy. Although the zaibatsu might have dominated the economic scene, three-fifths of Japan's industry remained in the hands of relatively inefficient small- or medium-scale operations. Underemployment was serious in the first years of the post-occupation period, for there was no full-time utilization of much of the labor force. Japan's initial postwar labor surplus disappeared as the economy expanded, and a new fear arose instead of a labor shortage. As sources of labor grew more scarce (and grew older), and as the birth rate declined, some impediments to economic growth arose. Spiraling inflation into the 1990s made the cost of living phenomenal. According to UN sources, Tokyo became the most expensive capital in the world.

SOCIETY

Economic growth accelerated social change, and Japanese conservatives were greatly alarmed at the degree to which the traditionally high positions of emperor, state, and family were eroding. The concept of maintaining an emperor without emperor worship in postwar Japan was a novel and unwelcome phenomenon to traditionalists, for the imperial position became a mere symbol, without sanction for its importance or its focus as a national institution. With a hard core of believers in state Shinto (abolished by the occupation), Yamatoism continued anachronistically to advance the concept of a unique and mystical Japanese identity. But for most, emperor and state worship went out of fashion, replaced by widespread and prevalent postwar attitudes of pacifism, antimilitarism, and partial loss of national self-confidence. The Japanese flag was less frequently displayed in the early postwar decades, and the term *Nihon* came more into fashion to replace Nippon, which had supposedly more imperialistic connotations. Torn by conflicting outlooks of the differing generations within it, the extended family tended to break apart. The prewar positions of such conservative bulwarks as the bureaucracy and industrial classes were weakened. The peerage was abolished, the old militarist class was eradicated, and civil servants became more responsive to public desires.

Although Japan prided itself on being a mono-racial state, minorities existed. Indistinguishable racially from their mainstream counterparts, the *eta* or *burakumin*, chiefly in the Kyoto and Osaka areas, were socially and officially discriminated against because of historically distasteful occupations. They had unique surnames and lived in special townships, both of which could be used to indicate their separateness. Representing the several million of them, the Buraku Liberation League fought for legal and social equality. The Ainu, chiefly on Hokkaido reservations, were fast fading away. The 700,000 Koreans, as perennially second-class citizens, remained a sizable minority and were relegated to lesser occupations and professions. Only after a 1991 treaty between Japan and the Republic of Korea was signed did the long-standing practice of fingerprinting Koreans in Japan stop. The idea of racial separateness and inferred superiority of the majority was expressed by authors and writings dealing with *nihonjinron* (study of Japanese), works that tended to emphasize differences from rather than similarities with other groups. Myopia in racial attitudes at home was sometimes projected abroad. In the mid-1980s, a Japanese prime minister stated that the American level of literacy and intelligence had been diluted by the presence of sizable black and Hispanic minorities in the United States.

Other distinctions persisted in contemporary Japan. Hierarchical attitudes, based on wealth, name, or position, continued in language and social conventions. The ubiquitous business card (*meishi*), exchanged by individuals upon meeting, set the tone of conversation and the depth of bows. Japanese sought consensus, valued harmony by all knowing their status and role, and eschewed unpleasantness or confrontational tactics. The language itself reflected this lack of bluntness. In their crowded land, they practiced what has been characterized as a web of mutually comprehensible deceptive behavioral acts. The glossing over of disturbing behavior or unwanted facts also could be expressed in intellectual life. After the occupation, with its American-imposed versions of Japan's history and role in international life, Japanese were free to rewrite texts and reinterpret history. One minister of education decried that Japanese textbooks lacked patriotism and pride in country and were soft on foreigners. In narrating the Pacific (or Greater East Asia) War, into the first decade of the twenty-first century, textbooks sanitized the Japanese military record. The colonial record in Korea was adjudged to be beneficial; aggression in China was characterized as advances; in 1945 they did not surrender but capitulated. While the Japanese authors might have had license to interpret actions by whatever designation they desired at home, other countries, recipients of adversarial behavior, voiced loud protests over what they considered a perversion of facts.

Hierarchy also revealed itself in the academic world. The chain of "right" schools, especially for boys, commenced at the primary level and persisted into six years of high school and on into college life. Cram schools (*juku*), attended after hours, helped to prepare students on their path of upward mobility. The most desirable tertiary institutions were Tokyo and Kyoto Universities, which were public academies; Keio and Waseda were the

Children heading off to school: Education is highly valued, in part a Confucian value imported from China as early as the sixth century.

Bicycles: A familiar mode of transport

ultimate goals in the private sector. Although difficult to enter, with the barrage of entrance examinations, once admitted, the students, often in relaxed manner, spent years in a fairly leisurely pursuit of knowledge and a degree. Some native and foreign observers noted that because of the past war record, occupation, and pervasive extent of daily problems, social and economic classes, with attendant hierarchies, were leveling off.

Although there existed very wealthy individuals in Japan, such as corporation founders or chief executives, the overall moneyed class was thinning out, while living standards of more of the lower socioeconomic classes were rising. With every generation came more questioning of authority and relaxation in social mores. More young couples, about half, were marrying through free will and love, while the other half still opted for the traditionally family-arranged introductions (*omidai*) through intercessors (*nakodo*). As more and more social controls were weakening, there resulted a concurrent rise in the rate of juvenile delinquency and urban crime.

On the average, there was gender discrimination against women. Sex roles were defined early in life. Boys were to be pampered by mothers, husbands to be spoiled by wives. In a male-dominated society, women, expected to marry and drop out of the labor force prematurely, generally received lower-paid positions in lower echelons of the commercial and bureaucratic world. They were accused of lacking group loyalty, as being too nonconformist or egotistical. Women were expected to remain as dutiful wives and mothers, tending to family needs. But more and more of

Osaka: Students studying English, off to an early start

them, after the children had left the domestic nest and as husbands retired, were seeking divorces and fair shares in financial settlements. Few women served in high government positions; in 1985 there were only twenty-seven women in both houses of the Diet. A parliamentary law that same year forbade gender discrimination in jobs, but because the act lacked any penalty clauses, it was not enforced.

Having matured in a political environment different from that of their elders, younger Japanese officials pursued a tradition that included responses to, rather than insulation from, elections and public mandates. The old adage of officials honored and people despised lost its validity in contemporary Japan. Zaibatsu enterprises became more elastic; a managerial system, drawing upon young executives from among top college graduates, emphasized merit and ability rather than family ties. Relations between big business and political parties broadened and diffused.

The postwar era also brought many changes to rural Japan. Land reform removed many inequities in agrarian society, and the new education attacked myths and institutions of the traditional social order, including state Shinto and the familial basis for the state. The Japanese farmer was better educated, lived better, and participated in a fuller political and cultural life than did his Asian counterparts. The legacy of conservatism lingered on in the farmer, yet his conservative vote was in part due to satisfaction with the material benefits that were brought about by his general economic advancement. Increased productivity and greater efficiency enhanced sources of farm income, which were further augmented, particularly in rural areas adjacent to towns or bordering on cities, by nonfarming jobs and activities. Japan's rural society was likely to be characterized by a further retreat from traditionalism, continued rising material aspirations, and increased political consciousness. Because of a greater degree of diffusion in the farmer's economic activity, his political response could well result in less uniform political patterns.

The urban working classes were no longer composed essentially of first-generation peasants. The Japanese proletariat was becoming what was traditionally thought of in the West as a lower middle class. With the introduction of the new education, unionization, and modern management, it grew in political influence. It was organized into labor unions that included about one-third, or nine million, of the total Japanese workforce. The basic unit of unionism was the single enterprise or plant, federated into regional and national associations. The average number of workers per union was 180 (compared with 14,000 in Great Britain and 95,000 in the United States). Before 2000, two national labor associations existed, the left-wing Sohyo (General Council of Japan Trade Unions) with about 45 percent of the total union membership, and the more moderate Zenro (Japan Trade Union Congress), along with affiliated groups in the right collectively known as Domei Kaigi, with 15 percent. By the early years of the twenty-first century, these had regrouped into three: the Rengo (National Federation of Private Sector Unions) with 6.6 million members, and two smaller entities: Zenroken (National Federation of Trade Unions) with 849,362 members and the Zenroyko (National Trade Unions Council), with 139,424 members.

The rest were in independent unions or in ideologically neutral organizations, as the Shinsanbetsu (National Federation of Industrial Organizations). The unions of the left, which included government workers, in addition to the usual Communist causes advocated direct political action. Although some of the earlier Communist-leaning Sohyo affiliated unions gave support to Communists, the majority supported the Socialists, while the minority Zenro-affiliated unions supported the Democratic Socialists. The growth of labor unionism in Japan was not deterred by the concurrent rise in national wealth, which might have reduced some interest in union causes.

The younger generation, another major social group in postwar Japan, played a new role of prominence. Opposed to militarism and favoring neutrality in world affairs, it accepted many tenets of the Communist and Socialist political platforms. Youth groups participated in direct political action, but many students had to moderate their tactics, for the unemployed youth of Japan with socially unacceptable minority political views had bleak employment prospects. The most extreme of the youth groups was the Zengakuran (National Federation of Student Self-Government Associations). Founded in 1948, it counted more than 200,000 members from 266 college and university groups. Its initial aims were to improve student life and to safeguard academic freedom. In the 1950s, it became involved in extremist political causes, a policy that estranged many of its followers.

The Zengakuran became alienated from most students, and when it sought formal relations with the Japanese Communist Party, even the party found the student group too extreme. By 1960, its members were spearheading the spring demonstrations. By that time, when the group had reached its greatest notoriety, it entered into a period of decline, and the organization subsequently broke up into splinter groups that bitterly fought with one another. The late 1960s was a particularly virulent time worldwide for student demonstrations over a variety of academic, professional, or foreign policy issues. Various institutions have their own student groups or self-governing entities, usually promoting cultural or sports interests. Students belong to one or more associations and also participate in extracurricular activities, which, however, have been declining into the first decade of the twenty-first century.

Another group, the intellectuals, were both liberated and frustrated in the new Japan. Certain prewar trends such as nihilism and Marxism survived into the postwar era. These were augmented by a plethora of other *isms*, including an early vogue of existentialism. In the midst of a variety of ideologies, intellectuals served as the perennial opposition on political issues, for they continued to be strongly antagonistic to Japanese conservatism, which they equated with basically antidemocratic regimes of the past. In general, Japanese intellectuals were leftist, but as more of them came into contact with Western democratic forces, they took more ideologically flexible positions. Japanese intellectuals saw much that was weak or negative in their own domestic milieu. But rather than point with pride to their country as superior to Asian neighbors in some respects, they decried in rather pessimistic terms its alleged intellectual subordination to Western countries. The rejection of old concepts accompanied by a lack of adequate or compensatory new ideological substitutes left many in a state of drift.

The religious life of the Japanese was in flux. Many, especially in rural areas, persisted in their folk faith through nature worship and reverence for traditional land gods, especially those relating to rice cultivation, appreciative of the beauties of the rising sun (especially from the summit of Mt. Fuji) and the full moon. These attitudes were encompassed in their broadest scope by Shinto, whose official form had been abolished by the occupation. Popular Shinto shrines, with their minimalist forms of worship, continued in use. Native tourists and pilgrims traveled to various shrines, especially the imperial Ise shrine. The Yasukuni shrine in Tokyo was a focus of veneration because many veterans and military figures, including some adjudged by the occupation trials to be war criminals, were buried

Tokyo: The Shinto Yasukuni shrine honoring military deceased, including several top figures condemned by the Internation Military Tribunal for the Far East in Tokyo (1945–1946). Official visits here by Japanese Prime Ministers elicit vociferous protests, especially by Korea and China.

there. On state occasions Prime Minister Koizumi visited the site, which did not draw much domestic comment but which enraged Koreans and Chinese who loudly decried what they perceived as callous appeasement of these types buried there. Shinto priests continued to perform family and institutional rites, including the blessings of new construction sites as well as the finished buildings. Weddings in Shinto fashion remained popular. These weddings were small and private in nature, although the ensuing reception, usually in name hotels, could be opened to hundreds of friends.

Whatever other beliefs Japanese held, many could reconcile them with ties to Buddhist temples and their clergy, supported by local or neighborhood communities. At home, altars (*butsudan*) displayed any one of the numerous images embraced by Buddhist iconography and held small vertical wooden tables with names of the deceased, whose ashes were buried under headstones in Buddhist temple cemeteries. The association of Buddhism with funeral rites and with death projected a negative image of the religion to some. Only 1 percent of the population subscribed to Christianity, but a papal visit to Japan emphasized the small but vital connections with the Vatican.

Tokyo: A Shinto wedding

A host of minor religious sects, some with antecedents back to the nineteenth century, flourished. These sects possessed some similarities: founded by charismatic leaders, springing up in times of crises, syncretic in theological nature, millennarian in outlook, emphasizing shamanism, and often led by females. One of the more important was the Tenrikyo, founded by Nakayama Miki (1789–1887), a faith healer, who, as her followers did, believed that she was the female counterpart of a male god. Despite a plethora of beliefs and diversity of attitudes, it has been pointed out by some that, generally, Japanese do not adhere to any central core of values or to any overall guiding ideas. Japanese understand situational ethics and prescribed modes of proper behavior, but they draw little of substance from Shinto, Buddhism, or other forms of worship in terms of fundamental religious or humanistic grounding.

Whatever their beliefs, Japanese enjoyed holidays and festivals of a religious or secular nature. The calendar marks seven national holidays (*kokumin no shukujitsu*). It notes the New Year (*Ganjitsu*), the first in time and the most important. This lasts a week (December 28 through January 5). Domestic travel peaks during this period. Cities are deserted, shops are closed, families congregate in reunions. Two weeks later comes the second holiday, on January 15, known as the Coming of Age, or Adult,

*Osaka: A girl dressed in traditional garb for
a festival day*

Day (*Seijin no Hi*), when all youths who have turned twenty years of age
are honored. Vernal Equinox Day (*Shunbun no Hi*, around March 21) and
the Autumnal Equinox (*Shubun no Hi*, circa September 24) are observed.
Both are drawn out into a week's observance (*higan*), with three days before and three days after, during which period ancestors are revered. The
last calendrical holidays are Culture Day (*Bunka no Hi*, November 3) and
Labor Thanksgiving Day (*Kinro Kansha no Hi*, November 23), the latter in
gratitude for a hopefully bounteous year.

Additional holidays include National Foundation Day (*Kenkoku Kinen
no Hi*, February 11, the anniversary date of the founding of Yamato state
in 600 BCE); the Golden Week (*Goruden-wiku*), which encompassed Emperor Hirohito's birthday (*Tenno Tanjobi*, April 29, while he was alive), to
be replaced by Akihito's birth date on December 23; May Day (May 1);
Constitution Memorial Day (*Ken po Kinenbi*, May 3, when the 1947 constitution was promulgated); and Children's Day Festival (*Kodomo no Hi*, May
5). Mid-August is the Buddhist-inspired *Bon* (called also *Obon*, *Bon-odori*, or
Lantern) festival, with colorful public dances on the one hand and private
family moments honoring departed members on the other. On September
15 falls the Respect for Elders Day (*Keiro no Hi*); about the same time (or a

Tokyo: Residents enjoying a park's amenities

month earlier) is the Autumn or Full Moon Festival (*Jugoya*). October 10 is Sports Day (*Taiiku no Hi*).

Historic and tradition-laden Kyoto enjoys three additional festivals. On May 15 is the *Aoi Matsuri*, centered on two shrines, the Kamigamo and Shimogamo, where in the sixth-century Yamato state, people prayed for the cessation of heavy rains. In the third week of July falls the *Gion Matsuri*, honoring the Yasaka shrine where, in 869, people prayed for an end to a ravaging epidemic. On October 22 comes the *Jidai Mat sun*, or the Festival of Eras, at the Heian shrine to commemorate the founding of old Kyoto or Heian in 794. It is marked by a pageantry of historical figures dating from early times through the Meiji.

Traditional pastimes also are practiced. The *chanoyu* (tea ceremony) draws adherents to the art in which utensils and techniques of use are studied; *sado* emphasizes its philosophical connotations. *Tako* (kite flying) is a colorful amusement that utilizes imaginative designs and fanciful shapes. Japanese aesthetics appreciate the so-called art of the little. In *ikebana* (flower arrangement in simplified versions), several schools exist that stress differing methods of arranging the three basic symbolic components of earth, man, and heaven according to meaning (*kado*). *Bonsai* (dwarf potted plants or trees) and *bonkei* (tray landscapes) are popular. Counterparts in small stone configurations (*sueseki*) envision landscape prototypes in miniature. Less is more.

Tokyo: Formal flower displays

Japanese aesthetics: Art of the little, a garden gate, Karuizawa

Also in the historic tradition are sports, such as the martial arts (*bugei*) that go back in time to the seventeenth century with importations from China via the Ryukyus into Japan when weapons were forbidden for use by commoners. *Karate*, a generic term, covers a wide variety of jabbing, hitting, and kicking tactics; the use of controlled energy can be awesome, for if the opponent were delivered a telling blow, a fatality could result. In *sumo* wrestling, two heavyweights, clad only in loincloth, try in a variety of some four dozen moves either to push the opponent off the ring of sand or to force any part of the other's body (excepting the soles) onto it. Some Japanese are annoyed that several recent sumo champions have been non-Japanese. In *judo* and *jujutsu*, similarly, differing throws and holds try to result in the fall of the other party. In *kendo*, Japanese-style fencing using bamboo swords, the winner is declared if he makes two successive clean hits on the head, body, hand, or throat of the other (one point for each hit). In Tokyo the Budokan is the venue for many of these martial sports. In modern events athletes participate in track and field, swimming, tennis (and its table variety), rugby, volleyball, basketball, and especially baseball, in which teams are often sponsored by major firms or newspaper chains and hire popular figures from abroad. At the 2008 Beijing Summer Olympics, twenty-five Japanese athletes won a total of twenty-five medals (nine gold, six silver, ten bronze). Of the nine gold there were one in softball, two each in swimming and wrestling, and—as would be expected—four in judo.

Tokyo: Budokan (martial arts hall), National Culture Day, November 3

The Japanese produce many films. Little war damage preserved the structural presence of such major studios as Toho, and the occupation encouraged the output of instructional and noncontroversial themes. The movie industry bred internationally known film stars, such as Mifune Toshiru, who performed also in American movies, and directors, as Kurusawa Akira (born 1910), whose long list of credits includes *Seven Samurai* (1954), *Rashomon* (1956), and the tragic *Ran* (*Chaos*), based on the King Lear theme. Television shows saturated the country. Drama drew on traditional expressions such as noh, kabuki, and bunraku.

City audiences also enjoyed modern theater (*shin geki*), with masterpieces by both indigenous playwrights and translated foreign ones. Revues were popular; the all-women's Takarazuka ensemble played to full houses in Tokyo and its home theater near Osaka. Similarly, the composition and playing of music drew from both indigenous and Western sources, including the latest rock fads. Pictorial arts and ceramics again were represented by old and new expressions. The architectural genius of the Japanese utilized pre-Buddhist forms as well as contemporary themes. Tange Kenzo (born 1913), among other projects, designed the Hiroshima Peace Hall and the Tokyo Olympic Sports Arena (1984). In the fashion world, women designers competed with their counterparts in Milan, Paris, and New York by producing striking examples of haute couture.

Literary figures wrestled with a myriad of themes. Some turned to traditional times for inspiration; others were swept up in international currents.

Tokyo: All women's Takarazuka Kokusai troupe

In the former category was Tanizaki Junichiro, known, among his other books, for the classic *Makioka Sisters*, a narrative of four sisters adjusting to life after the death of their domineering capitalist father. Kawabata Yasunari (1899–1972) found stylistic precedent in Heian writings. In a psychological approach, he wrote novels that included *Snow Country* and *Thousand Cranes*. In 1968, he was awarded the Nobel Prize for Literature, the first Japanese writer so honored in the field (although Japanese scientists already had won in physics). A strain of realism, nihilism, or pessimism was found in works by other authors, such as Oe Kenzaburo (born 1935, another Nobel Prize winner in 1994), Abe Kobo (born 1924, famous for his *Woman in the Dunes*), and Mishima Yukio (1925–1970). Mishima was a writer, dramatist, and conservative who committed suicide at the age of forty-five to dramatize the by-now lost militarist, emperor-worshiping, and glorified Japanese empire of old. Realistic war novels were penned by Ooka Shohei in *Fires in the Plain* (*Nobi*), an account of a Japanese military unit in the Philippines after the American units landed in Leyte in October 1944. Its counterpart was *Zone of Emptiness* by Noma Hirushi, which portrayed the brutalities of a home military encampment. Several women authors concentrated on biographical novels.

Social realignments and flux suggested the dynamic changing life of contemporary Japan. After the pronounced emptiness and bleakness of the immediate postwar years, education, economic progress, and mass communications opened new horizons. Despite the output of cynical and pes-

Tokyo: A baronial mansion

Tokyo: Christmas at the Ginza street, with purportedly the world's highest commercial property rents

simistic authors, the new generation was educated in democratic ideas, the equality of the sexes, and the rights of the individual. More young people went on to college in Japan than in any country except the United States and England. The extensive array of national publications and of radio and television programs disseminated new ideas quickly and thoroughly. Japan published more books than any country but the Soviet Union and England. The Japanese read more newspapers per capita than any other people except the Swedes and the English. Three morning dailies each enjoyed a total circulation of over ten million copies. Popular literature flourished, best sellers moved at hundreds of thousands of copies, and comic books, often portraying lurid sexual and criminal scenes, sold in the billions. In the technological revolution, the Japanese were not to be left behind. As in the political and economic spheres, more Japanese shared in the new possibilities and varieties of social, cultural, and intellectual life.

The new heights of affluence, particularly for an Asian power, that the Japanese attained contained, however, built-in paradoxes. Part of the overall prosperity was accounted for by the small proportion of the budget devoted to defense, for a populous nation with international standing. About 1 percent of the budget was allotted to this sector to maintain the Self-Defense Forces (built on the occupation's National Police Reserves), maintained over the decades with an overall strength of 240,000 men and some women, including a small navy and air force. Despite the small budgetary allotment, Japan in the early 1990s was the third-largest military spender ($45 billion), after the United States ($290 billion) and the Soviet Union ($119 billion). The Japanese eschewed an atomic development program for military purposes but utilized nuclear power for energy purposes. Under the aegis of the Tokyo University Institute of Space and Aeronautical Science, a scientific satellite program was launched.

Into the twenty-first century, the Japanese enjoyed the positive aspects of economic might, political stability, great foreign investments, and wealth. What could go wrong? The highest lifestyle in Asia did not get far in the spiraling inflationary life. Urban workers witnessed salaries disappearing rapidly in the rising cost of living, as well as the paucity of adequate housing at reasonable costs in urban areas. Forty percent of the population crowded into 2 percent of the total land space; three-fifths of the 128 million in Japan lived in six metropolitan areas alone, mostly in the Pacific industrial belt strung from Tokyo down to Kobe. Threats to exports came from other industrial rivals, such as South Korea, Taiwan, Hong Kong, China, and Singapore. At home, effects of a changing economic sector emphasizing services and higher technology evoked not a specter of labor shortages but possible unemployment through the attrition of less-adaptable industries. The demographics of a rapidly aging population, with 15 percent older than sixty-five years, constituted a drain on public funds for pensions and welfare programs. At the other end of the age spectrum, youth, it was feared, would lose the time-honored Japanese workaholic spirit and degenerate into a life of sloth and indiscipline. The problems of industrialization, urbanization, an overheated economy, and modernization pressed in on the population, as the Japanese literally choked on their affluence; human, noise, air, food, and water pollution were self-evident. Despite tremendous material gains, the good life was elusive and seemed unattainable for many of today's Japanese.

19

Contemporary Japan

Foreign Affairs

Japan hesitantly returned to the family of nations upon recovery of independence. In the early post-occupation years, through the 1960s, it maintained a low posture in international affairs. By the 1970s, however, with the rearranging multipolar world power structure and the adverse effects of the oil energy crises, Japan assumed a more active role. Over time, it strongly advanced general policy objectives of increased participation in the United Nations and other international organs, improvement of its position in the Afro-Asian world, and independence of action within a framework of cooperation with the West, particularly with the United States.

Japan especially emphasized economic aspects of diplomacy. Industrial and commercial expansion at home called for an increased emphasis on heavy and chemical industrial exports, although no field was to be abandoned in the general effort to diversify Japanese products for foreign markets. Japan became more involved with the world economy, and it began gradually to lift export and import restrictions that dated back to 1932. It gave special attention to Asian markets with emphasis upon reparations agreements, private investments, and technical assistance programs. Japan was committed to bilateral economic arrangements with a number of Asian countries.

Of vital importance were Japanese-U.S. economic relations. Japan depended heavily on U.S. sources for important raw materials and foodstuffs, but in the United States, trade problems arose in the wake of charges of dumped Japanese goods, unfair business practices, and huge trade imbalances into the 2000s. At the same time, Japan was not reconciled to a policy of economic isolation from the People's Republic of China, and it traded with both Beijing and Taiwan. The vital need for foreign trade transcended

ideology, and Japan's trading partners included nations, some not diplo-
matically recognized, of widely disparate political ideologies.

JAPAN AND THE UNITED STATES

After Japan's recovery of independence in 1952, and throughout the rest of
the decade, it remained dependent on the United States. With the revision
of the Security Treaty in 1960 more along lines that conformed to Japanese
desires, at least in the ruling Liberal-Democratic Party, the country began
to exert a degree of independence as a silent though junior member of the
American alliance. Upon the reversion of the Ryukyus and other islands to
Japanese administrative control by 1972, the last major territorial postwar
issue was settled, but Japanese-U.S. relations took on other economic,
military, and political issues. Two post-occupation issues were resolved
in the first decade following the reentry of Japan into international life.
In 1960, the United States, as the final Allied power to do so, paroled the
last of the Japanese war criminals, about 100 of them, who had been held
in Sugamo prison in Tokyo. The Japanese contended that their continued
incarceration had inflicted a "living stigma" on Japan for war guilt long
since expiated.

On the other issue, that of the Japanese assumption of occupation costs,
or at least part of them, the Americans insisted that the Japanese repay some
of the $2 billion incurred. Agreement was not reached on this issue until

Tokyo: U.S. Embassy

1962, when the Japanese foreign minister and the U.S. ambassador signed a memorandum that provided for Japanese repayment of $490 million (one-fourth of costs) over a fifteen-year period. Some of the funds were allocated to educational exchanges, but the bulk was earmarked in triangular fashion for economic assistance to underdeveloped countries of interest and concern to both Japan and the United States. Advancing the argument that Japan's expanded economy could afford the costs, the United States advocated increasing Japanese participation in international financial arrangements, especially in helping to underwrite non-Communist Asian consortiums.

On another issue, generated by the reaction to the nuclear holocausts that ended the Pacific War, the Japanese in multilateral and bilateral talks with concerned nations, including the United States, advocated disarmament and outlawing of nuclear warfare. The Japanese objected to Pacific atomic testing by the United States, as they objected to nuclear testing for military ends by any power. They were particularly upset in 1954, when nuclear fallout from the Bikini Atoll experiments in the Marshalls in the central Pacific affected one of their fishing ships, the *Lucky Dragon*, with twenty-three fishermen aboard, some of whom died from radiation. After delays, the U.S. government extended $2 million as compensation to families of the victims.

The revision in 1960 of the mutual Security Treaty heralded a new era of partnership in Japanese-U.S. relations because the main Japanese objections to the original 1951 version had been largely overcome. In the amended version, Japan was recognized to be an equal partner in the preservation of peace in the Far East. The terms of the revised document stated that an armed attack on either partner was to be regarded as a common danger and that the two signatories were to consult wherever Japanese security or Far Eastern peace was threatened. The pact was to last for an initial ten years, with termination then subject to a year's notice by either party. Japan was to be consulted on the movement of U.S. military personnel within or from territories under its administration (which excluded Okinawa).

The terms of the revised Security Treaty further read that no nuclear weapons or implements of war were to be located in Japan without Japanese consent. (In 1981, a former ambassador stated that over the previous two decades U.S. naval forces carrying nuclear weapons, with the secret consent of the Japanese government, had visited Japanese ports, but it was the official policy of the United States to neither admit nor deny the fact in any country.) Should Japan so desire, third countries, other than the United States, could extend military assistance. Japan was relieved of financial obligation to contribute to the payment of U.S. troops. The clause in the original treaty that had provided for U.S. troops to quell large-scale internal riots was eliminated. With these substantive changes made, the Diet ratified the revised treaty, although the forced and hasty circumstances through which Prime Minister Kishi Nobusuke obtained ratification and the attendant demonstrations on the eve of President Eisenhower's projected visit left a cloud over the alleged legal procedures utilized. In 1970, after the initial decade had passed, the new Security Treaty began to run indefinitely, subject to termination on one year's notice by either party. Few demonstrations in Japan marked this turning point.

The revised Security Treaty eliminated some problems, but others remained. The status of U.S. forces stationed in Japan and the jurisdictional rights over them remained unclear. Primary jurisdiction in disputes between Japanese nationals and U.S. military, whether on base or off base, on duty or off duty, had not been precisely defined in the original Administrative Agreement or in its 1960 amended version. The possibility of dual U.S. and Japanese jurisdiction resulted in unsatisfactory resolution of some infractions by nationals of both countries.

Territorial problems remained. On December 25, 1953, the United States returned the Amami Islands, south of Kyushu, to Japanese jurisdiction, but disputes continued over the Ryukyus and the Bonins, which the United States continued to administer but over which Japan retained residual sovereignty. Japan desired greater control, but the United States, with over a billion dollars in military investment on Okinawa, a staging area for Asian military operations, was reluctant to diminish its position in any way. Sentiment in Japan, as well as among many Okinawans, strongly favored the return of all control to Japan, but the Japanese government did not press the issue. Japanese and Okinawans criticized U.S. policies in the island chain and raised charges of land grabbing for bases and of dictatorial military policies.

Groups critical of U.S. policy, including local Communist units, agitated for more autonomy for Okinawa. They desired the right to choose their own government, including a chief executive. In 1962, the United States appointed a civil administrator for Okinawa but made it quite clear that it intended to retain bases in Okinawa as long as tensions existed in East Asia. The Bonins as well were retained, although Congress in 1960 voted $6 million as compensation for Japanese residents earlier evacuated from the islands and prevented from returning to their homes. But by the end of the decade, the Bonins were back in Japanese hands; a Sato-Johnson agreement in late 1967 had called for their return, a promise fulfilled in mid-1968 (along with Iwo Jima and Marcus Island). The disposition of Okinawa, the biggest stumbling block, was resolved in a Sato-Nixon communiqué in late 1969. Okinawa was to revert to Japanese administration no later than July 1, 1972. Some two weeks earlier, on June 17, the United States did relinquish all rights and interests in Okinawa but was permitted to continue the use of military installations (that covered over one-fourth of the island chain's landmass), including the huge Kadena air base.

The gradual withdrawal of U.S. troops from Japan promised to ease tension. Subsequent to a Kishi-Eisenhower agreement in 1957, about 35,000 U.S. ground troops were recalled. This left about 50,000 behind (including some 37,000 on Okinawa), a figure stabilized until 1990, when within three years another 10 percent drop was projected. The continued existence of a few large naval stations and air bases encroached on limited but valuable land areas, some of which were used to accommodate expansive jet operations. Local resistance to enlarged bases was encountered and was particularly strong in rural areas, where it was fanned by Communist agitators. U.S. facilities, again as a result of the 1957 agreement, were to be reduced by 60 percent within three years.

In the 1980s Japan and the United States cooperated on several issues. Tokyo increased its contribution for the financial support of U.S. forces in the country. The United States extended the defense perimeter out to 1,000 miles from the coastline. The two countries participated in mutual defense exercises, some in the South Pacific. In 1987, they lifted the mandated 1 percent of the gross national product (GNP) lid on defense spending imposed in 1976.

By the early 1990s, the principal U.S. installations in Japan had been further constricted. The navy maintained the Atsugi air facility in the Tokyo area and utilized nearby Yokusuka, a home port for the Seventh Fleet. The marines used Iwakuni air base in southern Honshu and some posts in Okinawa. The air force had tactical wings at Misawa in northern Honshu. The U.S. military presence in Japan cost $7 billion annually; the Japanese underwrote $3 billion as their share toward military protection. Despite the collapse of the Cold War in the 1980s and the disappearance of the Soviet Union both as a military threat and as a nation (succeeded by Russia), and with the concurrent continued rise of Japan as an economic and technological superpower, Washington queried Tokyo on assuming a larger share of expenses of the military umbrella. The reluctant Japanese response predictably invoked the constraints of Article Nine of the 1947 constitution. Asians, moreover, with strong wartime memories, were not anxious for Japan to posit a strong military presence either at home or abroad. The quandary was evidenced by the Persian Gulf crisis of late 1990 and the short war the following January, in which the United States would have preferred that Japan assist with military units (Tokyo sent five minesweepers) but settled for financial contributions ($9 billion).

Economic problems remained bothersome, as territorial issues disappeared and military ones fell into secondary importance. As early as 1961, Prime Minister Ikeda Hayato and President John F. Kennedy created the Joint U.S.-Japan Committee on Trade and Economic Affairs with representatives from cabinets of both countries, who in annual meetings endeavored to resolve economic issues of mutual concern. High on any agenda was the nature of trade balances. After enjoying an export surplus for several decades, the United States in the early 1970s began to register perennial imbalances; in 1972, $4 billion was recorded in favor of Japan; by 1990, the imbalance had escalated to $50 billion. Moreover, Japanese investments in the United States, with large-scale takeovers of real-estate properties, banks, and companies, had grown tremendously and precipitously, to $53 billion in 1990 (equal to that of Dutch interests but only half of British).

In 1990, both countries completed the Structural Impediments Initiative through which the two governments tried to identify and remove inherent domestic structural reasons for the trade imbalance. In the United States, Japan bashing noted some inequities and charged the Asian partner with unfair domestic monopolistic and restrictive practices that had inhibited both U.S. imports and U.S. investments. Washington took exception to Japan's "Big Stores" law that favored the keiretsu (corporate cartels) by imposing restrictive importation and distribution practices. It advocated the need for more internal government spending on public works and scored the high Japanese savings rate that limited consumption. Tokyo advised Washington to get its own house in order: balance the budget, improve education, overcome inefficient production methods, and abandon the short-term mentality that stressed company profits and dividends in return for long-range growth prospects with fewer immediate returns. In the 1990s, official criticism in Japan has spilled over into other segments of the population, including business figures and intellectuals, who displayed a *kenbei* attitude (dislike of the United States), based on general grounds of the alleged decline of U.S. work ethics, morality, and quality of life, unfit attributes for the world's now-sole superpower.

Some issues remained as irritants. In part, these issues were more a matter of style than of substance in the perceived productive partnership. As the decades progressed, the changing, seemingly uncertain U.S. diplomatic world moves went counter to Japanese desires for continued certainties and assurances, as in the "sudden" Nixon proposed visit to the People's Republic of China, announced in late 1971 and for February 1972, without notifying the Japanese government adequately in advance of the détente. Continued consultation and mutual respect could be a partial resolution of conflicting views, as well as exchange of official missions.

Post-occupation Japanese prime ministers beat a path to Washington to exchange views with U.S. presidents. Between 1957 and 2009, nineteen prime ministers visited the United States thirty-five times. The imperial family touched American soil four times. Nixon met Emperor Hirohito and Empress Nagako at Anchorage in September 1971, as the imperial party winged its way to Europe on an official visit (the first time in Japanese history that a reigning emperor had left the country). The imperial couple toured the United States in October 1975. As crown prince, Akihito, along with his wife Michiko, visited the United States. The royal couple returned as reigning monarchs in 1994, when they toured ten cities. They also paid a visit to a World War II shrine at Saipan island in the Marianas, which had been occupied by the Japanese before the war.

Five American presidents visited Japan in turn: Gerald Ford, Ronald Reagan, Bill Clinton, George H. W. Bush, and George W. Bush. President Ford journeyed to Japan in November 1974, in conjunction with a Vladivostok meeting with Soviet party chairman Leonid Brezhnev. In November 1983, President Reagan flew to Tokyo for the rotating annual summit meeting of the Group of Seven, the most affluent non-Communist industrial powers. In February 1989, President George H. W. Bush attended Emperor Hirohito's funeral. He returned three years later, in January 1992, in a four-day visit. He was followed by President Clinton in three visits in 1993, 1996, and 1998. President George W. Bush arrived in 2005.

Lower echelon diplomats continually met in bilateral discussions in various mutual organizations either in Tokyo or Washington. Talks stressed the necessity of resuming more normal trade relations between the two countries, especially with the restriction to fewer Japanese-made (including U.S.-assembled) cars that provided for one-third of total annual domestic automotive sales. The two sets of interrelated but clashing issues for each of the two parties—short-range administrative measures to be taken and long-range structural readjustments to be effected—remained irritating to both Japan and the United States.

President Barack Obama's Secretary of State, Hillary Rodham Clinton, made her first official visit to Asia (Japan, Indonesia, South Korea, and China) in early 2009, the first top diplomat in half a century to have this geographical priority for the first state trip. In a two-day visit in Tokyo, she had a whirlwind schedule. Upon arrival at Haneda airport, she was greeted by two women astronauts and an athletic delegation to the Special Olympic Winter Games. The first day started with a visit to the Meiji shrine, a lovely park in the center of Tokyo dedicated to the nineteenth-century emperor who started Japan on its path to modernization.

Clinton then proceeded to the U.S. embassy to greet employees and give interviews in the embassy's press room. She continued to the imperial palace to have afternoon tea with Empress Michiko, in return for the hospitality when the then–first lady had entertained the empress and emperor Akihito at the White House. She returned to the hotel for more interviews. The next day she attended a "Town Hall" meeting with students at Tokyo University where she was in her element, relating to the young people. Next came a working dinner with prime minister Aso Taro, followed by a meeting with the leader of the political opposition, Ozawa Ichiro. She consulted with the foreign minister and other officials and signed an agreement to transfer to

Guam eight thousand of the fifty thousand American troops primarily stationed in Okinawa.

Into the new century, mutual ties escalated. Under terms of the revised Security Treaty, Japan broadened its activities in the region and the Middle East. It funded a carrier battle group, a marine expeditionary force, the Fifth Air Force, and elements of the army I Corps. Through the defense guidelines of recent decades, Japan provided a noncombatant role in East Asia and farther afield in the Indian Ocean, the Middle East, and the Near East. The Defense Policy Review Initiative defined the number of troops to be stationed in Okinawa and mutual roles to be played in the ballistic missile defense program. Since September 2001, Japan has extended logistical support to U.S. forces in the Indian Ocean. The two countries provide financial resources to a variety of international causes, such as development programs, fighting diseases including HIV/AIDS and avian influenza, protecting natural resources, science and technological programs, mapping human genomes, as well as research on aging and space.

In foreign affairs, along with South Korea, Japan and the U.S. and neighbors, have been concerned with the North Korean nuclear program, which has aimed missiles over Japan. Japan provides noncombatant resources to third parties and United Nations activities in the region. The United States supports Japan's desire to become a permanent member of the Security Council. Next to the United States, Japan contributes the most to the UN budget. The United States has encouraged Japan's participation in the World Trade Organization (WTO), the Office for Economic Cooperation and Development (OECD), the World Bank, and the Asian-Pacific Economic Cooperation forum (APEC).

After Canada, Japan is the second-largest trading partner of the United States. It was the largest foreign market for American agricultural items. Continuing an unfavorable trend, in 2006 the United States had a great trade imbalance with Japan; it exported $59.6 billion worth of commodities but imported $148 billion. Trade over the past decade increased by an annual average of 7.3 percent. The United States exported pharmaceuticals, films and music, commercial aircraft, nonferrous metals, plastics, and medical and scientific supplies. One-fifth of its imports were autos; the Toyota brand became the best-selling model in the domestic market, outstripping General Motors. Other imports included automotive parts, office machinery including computers, telecommunications equipment, and power-generating machinery. The United States was Japan's biggest export partner at 22.8 percent of the total, with China next at 14.3 percent. In imports it was the reverse; China was the largest partner with 20 percent, then the United States with 12 percent. Augmenting economic ties was the tourist trade, and here the United States came out the better. With the cheapening of the dollar in the middle of the first decade of the new century, Japanese tourists in 2005 spent $12 billion in the United States.

JAPAN AND RUSSIA

As it reemerged on the international scene, Japan tread cautiously in its relations with the Soviet Union in the early post-occupation years. The Soviets did not sign the Japanese Peace Treaty at San Francisco, but agreement was reached between the two countries on a number of issues. In 1956, five years after the conference, a treaty ended the state of war. Terms provided for the exchange of diplomatic and consular personnel, repatriated the remaining Japanese prisoners of war, waived reparations claims against each other, and agreed to effect further talks on trade agreements, fisheries conventions, and a formal peace treaty. Agreement on a number of problems seemed possible at the time because of the softening after 1953, with the death of Stalin, the mellowing of the Soviet line under party chairman Nikita Khrushchev, and the more neutralist policies of the independently minded prime minister Hatoyama Ichiro.

The agreement helped to smooth Soviet-Japanese relations, and that year the Soviets dropped their veto of Japanese membership in the United Nations. But Japan began firmly to protest Soviet nuclear tests and was disappointed when Moscow refused to surrender the Northern Territories (Hoppo Ryode) that were the prewar-occupied southern Kurile Islands of Etorofu and Kunashiri as well as the offshore Habomai group and Shikotan Island, these latter always considered as historic Japanese territory near Hokkaido. Fishing rights in the Japan Sea constituted a perennial concern to Japan, which endeavored to regulate by agreement with the Soviets the catch in international waters. As anticipated, Moscow denounced the revised U.S. Security Treaty of 1960, but within a couple of weeks after the strongly worded denunciation, it signed a three-year commercial trade agreement with Tokyo. Despite differences on some issues, the countries could periodically renew economic agreements. In 1966, a five-year trade agreement was initiated, and by the end of the period, trade had zoomed to a total annual figure of $1 billion. A Japanese-Soviet joint economic committee helped to iron out differences and trade issues. The Soviets also showed interest in having the Japanese participate in the development of Siberian natural resources, notably the Tyumen oil deposits, the Yakutsk coal and iron reserves, and the Sakhalin offshore oil and gas fields.

A major point of difference remained because the Soviets stalled in the return to Japan of the Northern Territories, where Tokyo charged that Moscow was escalating its military presence. The Soviets indicated the possible return of the Habomai group and Shikotan once a full-fledged peace treaty had been effected. In 1960, they qualified their stand by demanding also the abrogation of the U.S.-Japan Security Treaty before the return of the islands, although by late 1973, they had quietly dropped this proviso. With respect to Etorofu and Kunashiri in the Kurile chain, the Soviets claimed the return of these islands as a nonnegotiable issue. In the course of a European tour in October 1973, Prime Minister Tanaka Kakuei in Moscow sought once again the return of all the disputed islands. He further called for talks to resume in order to conclude a peace treaty and settle all "outstanding" postwar questions.

In early 1976, in Tokyo, Soviet foreign minister Andrei Gromyko remained adamant on the "geographic questions," as the Soviets framed it. His unyielding stand was reiterated by his successor, Eduard Shevardnadze, again in Tokyo in early 1986 and mid-1990. An invitation at the latter date was extended to Emperor Akihito to visit Moscow, and one to Tokyo promised for party chief Mikhail Gorbachev. Gorbachev did arrive in April 1991 seeking economic aid but extending no guarantees of the return of the islands. Japan distanced itself from any promise of massive economic aid to the Soviets, although it did promise some $2 billion in assistance. It positioned its extension of any more appreciable aid on the resolution of the Northern Territories issue. A mid-September 1992 visit by Russian President Boris Yeltsin was canceled because of differences, and Tokyo indicated that it would welcome the return of Shikotan and the Habomais and would be content with a statement of Japanese residual sovereignty over the two Kurile islands, to conduct later negotiations on their retrocession.

In March 1994, the Japanese minister of foreign affairs in Moscow met his Russian counterpart to continue to try and seek a solution to the problem of title to the disputed Northern Territories; he promised some Japanese aid to Russian economic reforms. In August 2006, Russian maritime authorities killed a Japanese fisherman and confiscated a crab fishing boat in the disputed Kurile waters; they claimed he was killed by a "stray bullet." In September that year the Russian foreign minister stated that "good relations" would continue with the Koizumi administration. Japan continued to try to enter into negotiations with the Russians over their vast Far Eastern oil and gas reserves. While there were no critical issues between the two countries, the Japanese, for historic reasons, continued to distrust their huge neighbor to the east, and after North Korea, Russia loomed as the most suspect in their minds.

JAPAN AND EAST ASIA

Asia loomed large in Japan's foreign policy considerations. Geographic propinquity, racial background, and historic ties all posited close, but not necessarily smooth, relations with continental and insular neighbors. With the onus of an aggressive wartime record, Tokyo stepped gingerly in military matters, but it pursued greatly expanding economic programs. To some Asians, Japan seemed merely to be substituting one aggressive policy for another; not until the 1970s did Japanese policy makers redirect massive economic expenditures from self-interest to considerations of Asians on a people-to-people basis. Excuses for the wartime record by imperial and political spokesmen helped to soften Asian resistance to the Japanese economic presence, which grew to great proportions. By the early 1990s, Japan's total trade with Asia (around $140 billion) approximated that with the United States, and Tokyo's bulging financial surplus found a partial outlet in Asian aid and development projects.

Relations with the People's Republic of China, centered in Beijing, assumed the highest priority. Sino-Japanese bonds were historically ambivalent. Over the centuries, the Japanese had adopted, and adapted, some basic Chinese political, cultural, and religious concepts that had contributed positively to their civilization. On the negative side, however, were the twentieth-century military intrusions onto Chinese territory, which left the continental people wary and suspicious of their insular neighbor. Although Beijing welcomed Tokyo's aid and trade programs, it kept recent history in mind. Into the 1980s and later decades, its spokesmen vehemently protested the rewriting by the Japanese Ministry of Education of high-school history texts that had sanitized Japan's aggressive moves on the mainland as merely "advances." They also took issue with Prime Minister Takeshita Noburo, who had stated that "Japan may not have been the aggressor" in World War II.

After the occupation, unofficial Japanese economic missions traveled to Beijing, and commercial relations were reestablished. Between 1952 and 1958, four trade agreements were signed, although only the first three were implemented, and those imperfectly. The agreements were concluded between official Chinese Communist organs and unofficial, private Japanese trading associations. Each agreement was to last twelve to eighteen months, and each was to cover a total exchange of goods the equivalent of $100 million. Items of export and import were outlined in three categories of priority. The most important one, category A, constituted 40 percent of the total trade, and Japan agreed to import, among other items, coal, iron, and soybeans and to export strategic steel products on which the United States, for its part, had placed trade embargoes to Communist China. The fourth agreement was not implemented because in 1958 the Chinese Communists canceled it after a rightist youth tore down the Chinese flag flying over a Nagasaki department store. The Chinese Communists also endeavored, unsuccessfully, to interfere in national elections that year, when they generated pressure to oust Prime Minister Kishi Nobusuke from office.

When China experienced agricultural difficulties in the early 1960s, Japan offered the sale of 400,000 tons of rice at reasonable rates, but the offer was not accepted. Japan's trade with China was only 3 percent of its total world trade at the time, and many Japanese nostalgically longed for their prewar stake in the old China trade, when it accounted for 40 percent. In 1962, after a four-year trade hiatus, with Prime Minister Ikeda Hayato now in office and the Chinese more amenable, a fifth agreement was concluded that called for $100 million annually in trade over five years. In 1964, trade had already exceeded the figure by reaching $470 million. By 1970, it registered $820 million, which constituted one-fifth of Beijing's external trade. By the mid-1970s and into the new century, Japan was China's biggest trading partner. Further trade pacts were initiated to delineate the growing commercial bonds.

Some other problems were resolved. As with the Soviets, fishing conventions were signed. The Chinese Communists repatriated to Japan some 30,000 prisoners of war and former Japanese residents in China. Japan did not initiate moves in the United Nations to consider the admission of the People's Republic of China as a member instead of the Republic of China, based in Taiwan. Its spokesmen implied that should majority sentiment favor such a move, Japan would then join in voting for the admission of the Beijing government (which was admitted to the United Nations in late 1971, as the other Chinese government walked out). Minor territorial disputes simmered. China and Taiwan both claimed title to the Senkoku Shoyo (Diaoyu Tai Islands), with offshore oil reserves near the Ryukyus as well as Japan's claim to an exclusive economic zone in the East China Sea.

No postwar Japanese prime minister in office raised the feasibility of formal diplomatic relations until 1972. Japan's ties with Taiwan complicated the issue, for neither Communist nor nationalist China would historically accept a two-China solution to diplomatic recognition; it was one or the other. Prime ministers dating back to Yoshida Shigeru emphasized the close ties, however, with Beijing, based in great part on immutable geographic proximity. But recognition was not achieved until after President Nixon's visit to China in February 1972, which started a chain reaction in favor of a similar move by American "allies" in Asia. In September 1972, Prime Minister Tanaka journeyed to China, where he and Mao Zedong (Mao Tse-tung) normalized Sino-Japanese relations by reestablishing diplomatic ties. According to the communiqué issued on the historic event, Japan "fully understands and respects" the Chinese view that Taiwan was an inalienable part of China. The two parties were to negotiate a treaty of peace and friendship as well as agreements relating to trade, civil aviation, navigation, and fisheries.

Six years later, in 1978, the Japanese-Chinese Long-Term Trade Agreement was concluded to provide a total trade package of $20 billion worth of exchanges over an eight-year period. Also signed was a Treaty of Peace and Friendship with an "anti-hegemony" clause aimed against a perceived expansionist Soviet Union. Left unresolved was the status of the Senkaku Islands (Daioyutai to the Chinese), a collection of five islets and three coral reefs in the China Sea, claimed by both countries and Taiwan. It had been part of Japan's empire until 1945, after which the three political entities claimed it. In the 1970s, unofficial Japanese had erected and maintained a lighthouse on one of the outcroppings. The uninhabited islands in themselves looked uninviting, but their rich fishing grounds and the possibility of offshore oil deposits made them attractive for any party to claim ownership.

Mutual official visits enhanced ties. After the ratification of the 1978 treaties, early the following year, Prime Minister Ohira Masayoshi visited Beijing. In 1984, Prime Minister Nakasone Yasuhiro in China promised $2.1 billion in development loans; four years later Prime Minister Takeshita Noboru in China more than doubled the sum, to reach $6 billion by 1995. In April 1989, Chinese Prime Minister Li Peng, in Tokyo, was promised an additional $731 million to underwrite eleven projects; he took the opportunity to invite Emperor Akihito to visit the People's Republic, which the emperor did in October 1992. By mid-1989, China in Asia was Japan's second-largest trading partner after Hong Kong and Macao, with a total of $20 billion.

Tokyo also had invested there some $2 billion; it desired more, but Chinese restrictions kept foreign economic presence low. Half of Japan's international aid, including that funneled through UN organs, went to China. After the mid-1989 antigovernment demonstrations in Beijing, Tokyo trod softly; it reluctantly froze aid programs and supported international economic sanctions unenthusiastically, which it feared would force an isolated Chinese leadership into traditional regressive measures. At the annual Group of Seven summit meetings of Western industrial nations (Canada, France, Germany, Great Britain, Italy, Japan, and the United States), Tokyo endeavored to gain assent to its cautious moves to restore normal economic ties with Beijing. In May 2008, China's president Hu Jintao paid a visit to Tokyo—as the first by a Chinese leader in a decade—to mend fences. That October, a Japanese destroyer docked at a heavily guarded naval base in southern Guangdong Province, officially on an earthquake relief mission, the first trip by a warship from Japan to China since World War II.

Japan followed the United States in a diplomatic switch with respect to the Republic of China on Taiwan. In 1952, upon the insistence of Washington when Japan recovered sovereignty, Tokyo recognized the Republic, where Chiang Kai-shek did not press reparations on the former enemy. In the 1950s, the Japanese traded annually some $100 million worth of goods with the island, although in later years the amount grew to one-half billion.

As long as the United States had a vital security stake in the island, Japan went along with the interpretation that the defense of Taiwan was essential to that of Japan; in late 1969, Prime Minister Sato Eisaku and President Nixon confirmed this understanding. Yet within two and a half years, the situation had changed, for after the Nixon visit to China, a reordering of priorities presented itself. Tokyo recognized the People's Republic (and automatically withdrew from Taiwan) in 1972; the United States followed belatedly under President Jimmy Carter, in 1979, seven years after the Nixon visit.

In dealing with the Republic of Korea in Seoul, the Japanese ran into rough waters in their efforts to rebuild political fortunes in the former colony. When the Japanese were defeated, the Koreans insisted that their former overlords leave and never return. During the Korean War (1950–1953), the Koreans resisted any idea of Japanese assistance to UN forces in their country. Although the Koreans were not invited to the Japanese peace conference, the treaty stipulated that Japanese property in Korea and claims, including debts, should be the topic of bilateral talks between the two states. Because Japanese nationals had owned 80 percent of the commercial and industrial property in Korea and more than half the farmland, the economic stakes were large. Over the years, the two parties argued endlessly over the nature of compensation to be accorded the Japanese. They also debated the rights of 700,000 Koreans living in Japan, who had been forcibly moved there before and during the Pacific War. The Japanese government declared that any Koreans who desired repatriation could go to either North or South Korea. Many Koreans (some 87,000) chose the former destination.

An impasse was reached over another problem, the so-called Rhee line, named after Syngman Rhee, president (1948–1960) of the Republic of Korea, which controlled the southern half of the peninsula. Rhee extended Korea's offshore jurisdiction over the continental shelf up to 200 miles out to sea, almost to Japan's coastline. The president forbade all Japanese vessels within the waters, and he authorized the capture of those fishing ships that did enter the limits. Disliking the Japanese as much as he disliked Communists, Rhee looked with disfavor upon U.S. efforts to rebuild Japan.

Korean-Japanese relations noticeably improved when Rhee was forced out of office by widespread demonstrations. In June 1965, agreement was finally reached on a number of points, especially in the resumption of diplomatic relations. Other terms included determining fishing areas of the two states with their respective and now-constricted twelve-mile territorial limits; providing for joint fishing operations outside these bounds up to a catch of 150,000 tons a year for each of five years; and granting permanent residence both to Koreans in Japan who had resided there prior to the termination of the Pacific War and to their descendants born within five years after the conclusion of the agreement. Other terms called for a Japanese grant of $300 million in economic aid to South Korea, a $200 million long-term low-interest loan, and private commercial loans amounting to $300 million. The extent of compensation for Japanese property expropriated in Korea was left in limbo. Despite some opposition in both countries, the treaty normalized relations between the two states for the first time in more than half a century, and it boded possibly for closer and friendlier times.

In 1967, an additional $200 million loan was promised, and five years later, $170 million was pledged. But the implementation of economic aid programs was jeopardized when, in 1973, a South Korean opposition leader was spirited away to Seoul from a Tokyo hotel room. As General Park Chung Hee, president of the Republic of Korea, cracked down on critics of his regime in the course of the next months, two Japanese were indicted for making financial contributions to rebellious students. In the early 1980s, Koreans requested an escalation of Japanese aid to $6 billion; they argued in part that they were subsidizing Japan's security that was dependent on a strong South Korea. Not convinced by the argument, the Japanese continued to proffer some $83 million annually.

Seoul voiced strong objections to Japanese revisionist history in textbooks, which stated that during the occupation (1910–1945) Koreans were not "forcibly" taken to Japan but rather "mobilized." In south Sakhalin, part of the prewar Japanese empire that reverted to the Soviets, Koreans, particularly the elderly, also forcibly moved there, similarly voiced desires to return home. Adding fuel to the fire, the minister of education in Tokyo declared that the Koreans had only themselves to blame for the annexation to which their leaders had acquiesced. The fact that this happened under duress went unmentioned. In 1986, Prime Minister Nakasone, in Seoul for the Asian Games, rationalized the remark by the cabinet minister, who was sacked from office. In May 1990, on the occasion of Korean prime minister Roh Tae Woo's visit to Tokyo, Emperor Akihito regretted the "brutality" of the occupation period, a blunt remark that went way far beyond any of his father's ambiguously worded statements. The sentiment was reiterated by Prime Minister Miyazawa Kiichi in the course of a visit to Seoul in January 1992, and a pledge was made to help try to reduce Korea's trade imbalance with Japan, which had reached $8.8 billion in 1991.

Several areas of dispute continued to linger. In the territorial field, both Japan and the Republic of Korea claimed title to Liancourt, a group of un-inhabited islands in the Sea of Japan known to the Japanese as Take-shima and to the Koreans as Dok-dow, who had occupied it since 1954 fishing rights were preeminent. The revision of Japanese texts and books in sanitiz-ing the Japanese role as rulers of Korea (1910–1945) brought loud protests from Seoul. The South Korean government demanded more sincere and meaningful apologies for the harsh colonial record in their country, as well as compensation to the "comfort women" recruited for the Japanese wartime military. While Tokyo admitted its wrongdoing in 1992, it refused compensation, which was picked up by a nongovernmental agency in 1995. The visits by Japanese prime ministers through Koizumi to the Yakusuni shrine rankled Seoul because buried in the Shinto complex were war criminals. But there were signs of cooperation also. In 2002, Tokyo and Seoul co-hosted the World Cup soccer games. And both were parties in the six-nation group, along with China, Russia, the United States and North Korea, to resolve the Pyongyang nuclear issue.

With the Democratic People's Republic of Korea in Pyongyang, Japan edged toward normalization of relations. As they had done earlier in the south, so the Japanese accepted a claim for compensation for colonization injustices as well as for any obligations of the post- 1945 period. Seoul immediately protested the latter statement, because it had received nothing for the postwar era. Between 1972 and 1983, North Koreans kidnapped sixteen individuals and returned them to their country (a bizarre move since, as noted above, 87,000 Koreans in Japan had earlier chosen voluntary repatriation there). The Koreans admitted to thirteen abductions, although some estimates upped the number to seventy or eighty. Most of the kidnapped were in their twenties, supposedly taken to teach Japanese language and culture in spy schools. Some have since died; a few have returned to Japan. The abductions have left a lingering legacy of bitterness in Japan over the decades.

In 1990, a ninety-man unofficial Japanese parliamentary delegation met Kim Il-Sung, North Korean president and chairman of the Communist Party there (known as the Korean Workers Party), and presented him with a contrite letter for the "agony and damage" done during the period of Japanese rule. At the same time, the North Koreans released, after seven years' imprisonment, two Japanese fishermen who had been seized as "spies." Mutual talks proceeded on, among other topics, the establishment of air routes and the possibility of diplomatic recognition. The latter subject was pursued in meetings by both countries in Beijing, where both Tokyo and Pyongyang had diplomatic representatives.

JAPAN AND OTHER ASIAN COUNTRIES

The reestablishment of normal diplomatic and economic relations with Southeast Asian states proceeded unevenly, for reparations were a key issue. Not until some countries obtained reparations did they resume diplomatic ties. In 1955, Burma concluded the first reparations agreement with Japan. A ten-year arrangement, it called for total payments of $200 million. Because it was the first such agreement, the Burmese reserved the right to negotiate for additional reparations. They did so later and received the extension of an additional $140 million spread over twelve years.

In 1956, the Philippines, which originally had demanded $8 billion, settled for $550 million in payment over a twenty-year period, with an additional $250 million in private loans. At the same time, normal diplomatic relations were resumed. In 1958, similarly, the Indonesians, initially asking $18 billion, contented themselves with $223 million plus loans over twelve years and diplomatic recognition. In 1960, the Republic of Vietnam (Japan refused to deal with the Democratic Republic of Vietnam in Hanoi on this issue) received $49 million with payments spread over five years. Japan extended small grants to Laos and Cambodia ($7 million to the latter), which did not press for reparations. Malaysia similarly did not ask for restitution, because Prime Minister Churchill had earlier waived the right, although demonstrations in Singapore from time to time demanded "blood money" from Japan. In 1966, Japan extended to Singapore $16.5 million, half in grants and half as reparations. That same year, Thailand, technically a wartime ally, received $20 million in programs to be spread over three years.

Japan augmented reparations arrangements with normal trade agreements with Southeast Asian countries, which absorbed a third of Japanese exports. By the mid-1970s, Japan was the major trading partner of all Southeast Asian countries; trade imbalances with Japan ranged as high as 4:1 in the case of Thailand. From Southeast Asia, Japan imported 93 percent of its tin, 90 percent of rubber, and 40 percent of bauxite, copper, and timber. To selected Southeast Asian countries, Japan provided for 35 percent of Indonesian and Thai imports, 30 percent from the Philippines, and 20 percent of imports from Singapore and Malaysia.

Aid and investment figures complemented those of normal trade channels. Japan provided for almost half of Philippine foreign aid and one-fifth of Indonesian. Japan had a sizable stake particularly in the Thai economy; in that country seven hundred Japanese firms had invested some $300 million to provide for more than one-third of Thailand's foreign investment. In Indonesia, of total investment figures, Japan's reached 15 percent (most notably in joint ventures, especially in oil exploration), 11 percent in Malaysia, and 2 percent in the Philippines. Tokyo had concluded in 1961 a trade treaty with Manila to regularize commercial ties, and although the Japanese Diet had long since ratified the agreement, it was shelved by a suspicious Philippine senate.

Japan pledged subscriptions to regional developments in Southeast Asia, but it generally held itself aloof from mediating between conflicting states and issues in the region. Although it appreciated the U.S. position in the course of the Vietnam War in the late 1960s and early 1970s, Japan kept a low political posture, as it did later in the complex Cambodian political

situation. Tokyo pledged $200 million toward an Indochina Reconstruc-
tion and Development Fund for postwar aid. It accepted few refugees, but
it underwrote half of the costs of the Office of the United Nations High
Commissioner for Refugees in Southeast Asia.

Commercial stakes were similarly high in the Australasian region, where
the Japanese purchased two-fifths of Australian wool and four-fifths of its
mineral ores. In South Asia, Japan maintained normal but nominal connections. It extended financial aid to India and to Pakistani development planning, but it avoided any involvement in political issues, such as Kashmir,
border disputes, or Chinese military activities on the subcontinent.

The paramount role that Japan played in the economic life of the coun-
tries along the rim of continental Asia raised problems. In 1966, in an early
Asian international postwar conference, Tokyo pledged aid to representatives of Laos, Thailand, South Vietnam, the Philippines, Malaysia, and
Singapore. To seal ties, in late 1967, Prime Minister Sato Eisaku visited Taiwan, Indonesia, Australia, New Zealand, the Philippines, South Vietnam,
Thailand, Singapore, Malaysia, and Burma. In early 1974, Prime Minister
Tanaka Kakuei ventured to the Philippines, Thailand, Singapore, Malaysia,
and Indonesia, where in Bangkok and Jakarta his party met with violent
anti-Japanese demonstrations. In a repeat but chastened trip in 1977 to the
same countries (members of the Association of Southeast Asian Nations,
or ASEAN), Prime Minister Fukuda Takeo promised $1 billion for various
industrial projects. In a turning point, in Manila he advanced the "Fukuda
doctrine" by predicating aid on "heart-to-heart" contacts.

In early 1981, Prime Minister Suzuki Kenko reiterated the billion-dollar
pledge to ASEAN conferees at Bangkok. In May 1987, Prime Minister Nakasone Yasuhiro touched bases again with all ASEAN nations (now six in
number, including Brunei). In late 1991, Emperor Akihito, in the first tour
of Southeast Asia by a Japanese monarch, visited Indonesia, Malaysia, and
Thailand, where his reception was positive because, in a less formal manner than his father's, he expressed remorse on the Japanese wartime record
in that region. The Japanese political and economic reexamination of their
position, along with regrets for past military misconduct, began to win over
Southeast Asian skeptical hearts and minds.

JAPAN AND THE REST OF THE WORLD

Commercial relations were again stressed with countries in the rest of the
world. Oil diplomacy was paramount in the Middle East, and because of
this fact Japan tended to support the Arab side in conflicts and issues with
Israel. In mid-1990, with the Iraqi invasion of Kuwait, Prime Minister Kaifu
Toshiki promised $4 billion in economic aid and commodities, but he

eschewed from committing forces, constrained as he was by Article Nine of the constitution and strong domestic pressure toward the UN stance in the Persian Gulf area. African interests were minimal, but in Latin America more than 200 Japanese companies operated, and that continent generated some $2.5 billion annual trade in the early 1970s. Brazil emerged as a paramount consideration; the 700,000 Japanese nationals residing there provided its largest overseas community. The country, moreover, could be used as a further, and closer, export base to the United States and Europe.

In Europe itself, close Japanese ties were maintained with the European Economic Community (the Common Market), later the European Union (EU) which was, along with the United States and Japan, in a world that was moving toward a strong tripolar economic community of interests. By the late 1980s, Japan had maintained a $12 billion trade surplus with the smaller European grouping and had investments totaling $8.5 billion in Europe at large. Earlier, in September 1971, to underscore the importance of Japanese-Western European bonds, Emperor Hirohito and Empress Nagako in sixteen days visited seven countries (Denmark, Belgium, France, Britain, Netherlands, Switzerland, and West Germany). A decade later, Pope John Paul II came to Japan in February 1981, for a five-day visit to tend to the flock of some 400,000 Catholics there, a small number but one with a long, history.

Japan gained admittance into international economic organizations such as the General Agreement on Tariffs and Trade (GATT) and the Organization for Economic Cooperation and Development (OECD) in Paris. Japan is the only non-European member besides the United States and Canada in this club of economically advanced nations. In September 1964, Tokyo was the site for the largest international conference ever held in Japan to that time: the joint general meetings of the International Monetary Fund, the World Bank, the International Development Association, and the International Finance Corporation. Japan's successful mounting of the Tokyo Olympiad the following month enormously increased Japanese prestige and overseas awareness of its progress.

By the early 1990s, Japan's "omnidirectional" policy had assumed new dimensions. Slowly it was shedding its parochial outlooks and stepping into the international arena, especially in economic life. As Tokyo interpreted its action, it was "recycling" some of its vast surplus into grants, loans, and aid development programs, especially in Third World countries, struggling under their cumulative $1.3 trillion debt burdens. Japan's economic planners projected a debt reduction plan, approximating $40 billion, by which lenders would extend new loans at low rates of interest to debtors to renegotiate reductions in the original sums by providing guaranteed sources of funds. Leading as well as cooperating, by 1989 Japan surpassed the United States as the largest donor of foreign aid, because its commitment hovered around 1 percent of the GNP, an index of minimal giving projected according to UN criteria. If Japan was giving more, it was also asking for more. It requested a greater voice in the decision-making roles of the Asian Development Bank with headquarters in Manila, where its voting share equaled that of the United States (and the bank's president was to be Japanese); in the World Bank, where its voting share rose to 6.5 percent by the late 1980s; and in the International Monetary Fund, where, next to the United States, its vote was the most influential.

Political involvement did not escalate as rapidly as did economic, but Japan was taking cautious steps into, and developing slow attitudinal changes toward, the international arena. By the early 1990s, Japan had involved itself by subscribing to financial support for UN peacekeeping operations in Afghanistan as the Soviets withdrew in 1989, in helping to find a political solution to the Cambodian riddle, and in assuming a noncombatant military role in the Gulf crisis, with the dispatch of the minesweepers and additional funds for operations. In 1992, the Diet authorized the use of noncombatant military units as well as in UN peacekeeping operations, as in Cambodia (where the director of UN reconstruction operations was a Japanese national). At the annual economic summit meetings of the industrialized Group of Seven, prime ministers spoke out more bluntly to advance their options and views on crisis management. Commensurate with world status, Japan sought a permanent seat, with veto-wielding power, in the UN Security Council alongside the United States, Great Britain, the Soviet Union (and then the successor Russian state), France, and China. In the early 1990s, with the end of the Cold War, Japan, which had benefited greatly in the U.S.-Soviet confrontation by being able to focus on building a strong economy, was now faced with new priorities posed by complex international and multilateral issues.

In sum, "Japan Rising" recorded remarkable postwar progress at home and abroad. Fewer nations, Communist or non-Communist, had greater obstacles to overcome at the end of World War II than a defeated Japan, but few accomplished more spectacular progress and recovery in economic life. As the only modern industrialized non-Western nation, Japan uniquely drew on native traditional and foreign-derived sources in shaping its national outlook and indentity. Japan changed, but Japan could still remain distinctive and constant in spite of change. The complex Japanese society enjoyed both traditional culture and modern conveniences. With deep roots firmly grounded in the past, Japan was also very much a part of the dynamic, changing, and contemporary world.

CHRONOLOGY: JAPAN–UNITED STATES

1953	Amami island administration returns to Japan
1954	*Lucky Dragon* incident

1957	Kishi-Eisenhower agreement on reducing U.S. troops and facilities
1960	Revised Japanese-U.S. Security Treaty and Administrative Agreement; U.S. paroles last POWs in Sugamo prison
1961	Ikeda and Kennedy create Joint U.S.-Japanese Committee on Trade and Economic Affairs
1962	Japan-U.S. agreement on repayment of some occupation costs
1968	Bonins, Iwo Jima, and Marcus Island return to Japanese administration
1970	Japanese-U.S. Security Treaty extends indefinitely
1971	Nixon meets Hirohito in Anchorage, emperor on way to Western Europe for visit
1972	Ryukyus revert to Japanese administration
1975	Imperial visit to United States (October)
1989	President George Bush attends Hirohito's funeral

CHRONOLOGY: JAPAN–OTHER COUNTRIES

1952	Japan recognizes the Republic of China
1952–1958	Four trade agreements with People's Republic of China
1955	Burma reparations agreement
1956	Philippine reparations agreement; Soviet treaty; Japan into United Nations
1958	Indonesia reparations agreement
1960	Vietnam reparations agreement
1962	Fifth trade treaty with Beijing
1964	Meetings of UN-affiliated financial organs in Tokyo; Olympiad
1965	Treaty with Korea; Japan joins Asian Development Bank at inception
1966	Singapore reparations; Tokyo conference on Southeast Asian aid
1967	Additional Japan loan to Korea; Sato tours Southeast Asia
1972	Japan recognizes People's Republic of China; additional loan to Korea
1973	Tanaka tours Europe
1974	Tanaka tours Southeast Asian countries
1977	Fukuda tours Southeast Asia again
1978	Japanese-Chinese Long-Term Trade Agreement, Treaty of Peace and Friendship

1979	Ohira to Beijing
1981	Suzuki in Southeast Asia; Pope John Paul II to Japan
1984	Nakasone to China
1987	Nakasone to Southeast Asia
1988	Takeshita visits China
1989	Chinese Prime Minister Li Peng to Tokyo; Japan becomes world's largest donor of foreign aid
1990	Korean prime minister Roh Tae Woo to Tokyo; Diet delegation to North Korea; talks in Beijing between Tokyo and Pyongyang on recognition
1991	Soviet president and party leader Mikhail Gorbachev on visit to Tokyo; Emperor Akihito tours Indonesia, Malaysia, and Thailand
1992	Miyazawa Kiichi to Republic of Korea
2008	China President Hu Jintao visits Tokyo; first Japanese warship since World War II docks at Guangdong Province port.

Appendix: Japanese Prime Ministers

(Preconstitution prime ministers: Ito Hirobumi, 1885–1888; Kuroda
Kiyotaka, 1888–1889)
Yamagata Aritomo, 1889–1891
Matsukata Masayoshi, 1891–1892
Ito Hirobumi, 1892–1896
Matsukata Masayoshi, 1896–1898
Ito Hirobumi, 1898
Okuma Shigenobu, 1898
Yamagata Aritomo, 1898–1900
Ito Hirobumi, 1900–1901
Katsura Taro, 1901–1906
Saionji Kimmochi, 1906–1908
Katsura Taro, 1908–1911
Saionji Kimmochi, 1911–1912
Katsura Taro, 1912–1913
Yamamoto Gombei, 1913–1914
Okuma Shigenobu, 1914–1916
Terauchi Masatake, 1916–1918
Hara Kei, 1918–1921
Takahashi Korekiyo, 1921–1922
Kato Tomosaburo, 1922–1923
Yamamoto Gombei, 1923–1924
Kiyoura Keigo, 1924
Kato Takaakira, 1924–1926
Wakatsuke Reijiro, 1926–1927

Tanaka Giichi, 1927–1929
Hamaguchi Yuko, 1929–1931
Wakatsuki Reijiro, 1931
Inukai Tsuyoshi, 1931–1932
Saito Makoto, 1932–1934
Okada Keisuke, 1934–1936
Hirota Koki, 1936–1937
Hayashi Senjuro, 1937
Konoe Fumimaro, 1937–1938
Hiranuma Kiichiro, 1938–1939
Abe Nobuyuki, 1939–1940
Yonai Mitsumasa, 1940
Konoe Fumimaro, 1940–1941
Tojo Hideki, 1941–1944
Koiso Kuniaki, 1944
Suzuki Kantaro, 1945 (April)
Hagashikuni, Prince, 1945 (August)
Shidehara Kijuro, 1945 (October)
Yoshida Shigeru, 1947
Katayama Tetsu, 1947–1948
Ashida Hitoshi, 1948
Yoshida Shigeru, 1948–1954
Hatoyama Ichiro, 1954–1956
Ishibashi Tanzan, 1956–1957
Kishi Nobusuke, 1957–1960
Ikeda Hayato, 1960–1964
Sato Eisaku, 1964–1972
Tanaka Kakuei, 1972–1974
Miki Takeo, 1974–1976
Fukuda Takeo, 1976–1978
Ohira Masayoshi, 1978–d. 1980
Suzuki Kenko, 1980–1982
Nakasone Yasuhiro, 1982–1987
Takeshita Noboro, 1987–1989
Uno Sosuke, 1989
Kaifu Tushiki, 1989–1991
Miyazawa Kiichi, 1991–1993
Hosokawa Morihiro, 1993–1994
Hata Tsutomo, 1994
Murayama Tomiichi, 1994–1996
Hashimoto Ryutaro, 1996–1998
Obichi Kaizo, 1998–2000

Mori Yoshiro, 2000–2001
Koizumi Junichiro, 2001–2006
Abe Shinzo, 2006–2007
Fukuda Yasuo, 2007–2008
Aso Taro, 2008–

Glossary

Ako-gishi   The 47 ronin heroes of the Tokugawa era
Akuso   Unruly bands of monks during the Heian era
Ashizukai   The second man in a team of three manipulating puppets in bunraku
Aware   A feeling of sensitivity, appreciation evoked by beautiful phenomena
Azekura   A large log cabin warehouse
Bakufu   Tent government; the shogunate as founded by Minamoto Yoritomo
Bakumatsu   End of the shogunate period, 1853–1868
Be (or *tomo*)   An ancient Yamoto subsidiary work unit supporting the clans
Biwa   A lutelike instrument
Bodhisattva   A Buddhist being of wisdom, who, in Mahayana Buddhism, can save others
Bonkei   A miniature landscape on a tray
Bonsai   A dwarf tree on a tray
Bonseki   A dry representation, as rocks and sands, on a tray
Bosatsu   A bodhisattva
Buddha   Enlightened One
Bugaku   Court dance ritual
Bugei   Martial arts
Bukkyo   Buddhism
Bummei kaika   Civilization and enlightenment time of early Meiji
Bun'ei   First Mongol invasion, 1274
Bunka no Hi   Culture Day, November 3

Bunraku   Puppet play; see gidayu
Burakumin   Village people; outcasts; see eta
Bushi   The mounted warrior-gentlemen, late Heian and early Kamakurs
Butsudan   Family Buddhist altar
Butsuzo   Buddhist sculptural representations
Byobu   Decorated folding screen
Choka   Long poems
Chomin   Townspeople
Chumon   Middle gate in Buddhist temple colonnade
Daigaku   Yamato state university
Daijin   Cabinet ministers
Daijo Bukkyo   Mahayana Buddhism
Daijokan   Department of State, Yamato era
Daimoku   Invoking a buddhist book for salvation
Daimyo   A great lord
Dainihon Teikoku Kempo   The 1889 constitution
Dempodo   Lady Tachibana's residence
Dengaku   A Japanese harvest song, one source of noh musical tradition
Dera (or *ji*)   Suffix for a Buddhist temple
Do   Specifically, a Hokkaido administrative designation; generally, a circuit or administrative unit created by the mid-seventh-century Taika reforms
Dogu   Jomon clay figurines
Dotaku   Yayoi period bronze bells
E-makimono   A narrative illustrative scroll
Eta   Outcasts; see burakumin
Fu   Administrative designation for Kyoto and Osaka
Fudai   A Tokugawa inside lord, ally of the shogun
Fudoki   Provincial histories composed in early Japan
Fugaku Sanjurokkei   The 36 views of Mt. Fuji
Fusuma   Decorated sliding doors
Gagaku   Imperial musical tradition
Ganjitsu   New Year's Day holiday
Garan   Buddhist temple or monastic compound
Geisha   Professional female entertainer
Gekokujo   The lower classes overturning the higher, late Ashikaga
Genko   The Mongol invasions of 1274 and 1281
Genko war   Go-Daigo's rebellion, 1331–1333
Genro-in   Elder statesmen, Meiji era
Gidayu   Personal name of Tokugawa puppet playwright; also designates puppet plays as a whole; see bunraku
Giri   One's duty; often a theme of novels
Goj unoto   A five-story pagoda

Gokajo no Goseimun   The five-article Charter Oath, 1868
Gokenin Kamakura   Shogunal-vassal bonds of loyalty
Goruden-wiku   Golden Week of several holidays, early May
Gosekke   Five main branches of Fujiwara family
Gun   Early district administrative unit
Gunki Monogatari   War stories
Haiku   A seventeen-syllable, three-line poem
Han   A fief or estate in feudal Japan
Handen   The equal field system of Taika reforms
Haniwa tomb   Clay figurines found around early Japanese tombs
Hanseki hokan   Daimyos returning land to emperor, late Meiji
Harakiri   Ritual suicide; see seppuku
Heimin   Common folk
Heiji   City of Peace (Nara)
Hibachi   Charcoal heating brazier
Hidarizuka   The third man in the team of three, manipulating puppets
Higan   The two equinox holidays
Hokucho   Ashikaga Northern court
Honke   Protector of a tax-free Heian estate
Hoppo ryodi   Northern Territories—Habomais, Shikotan, Kuo nashiri, Etorofu islands
Horo (or *kairo*)   Covered colonnade in Buddhist temple complex
Hyakumanto   Empress Shotoku's miniature pagodas containing Buddhist charms
Ikebana   Art of floral arrangement
Insei   Cloistered government, Heian and feudal periods
Ji (or *dera*)   Suffix denoting a temple
Jidai   A political or historical era
Jingikan   Department of Worship, Yamato state
Jinja   A Shinto shrine
Jito   Estate stewards, Kamakura period
Joruri   Texts of puppet plays
Judo/Jujutsu   Form of Japanese wrestling
Jugoya   Autumn Moon Festival, mid-September
Juku   Cram schools
Jukyo   Confucian-based ethical system
Jushichijo no Kempo   Shotoku Taishi's seventeen-article constitution
Kabuki   Drama form from late feudal period
Kagami   Family histories or chronicles composed in Heian and feudal Japan
Kageyushi   Audit and tax bureau, Heian era
Kamakura-gozan   The five main Zen temples at Kamakura
Kami   A superior person or thing, worshiped in Shinto

Kamikaze   Divine wind, such as the hurricanes that helped to repel the Mongol invasions; used in World War II for suicidal dive bombers

Kampaku   Fujiwara regent for adult emperor, Heian era

Kana   A Japanese phonetic syllabary based on Chinese characters

Kanabe   Clan titles received from emperor, Yamato

Kangen   Nara court orchestral music for dances

Kanji   Chinese characters used for meaning

Karafuto   Sakhalin island

Karate   Wide variety of tactics used in martial arts

Karesasui (*sekitei*)   Ashigaka Dry garden

Kazoku   New peerage created in Meiji Japan for former daimyo

Kebiishicho   Police commissioners, Heian era

Keidanren   Federation of Economic Organizations

Keiretsu   Corporate group system in modern Japan

Keiro no Hi   Respect for the Aged Day, September 15

Kemmu no chuko   Kemmu restoration, 1333–1336

Ken   Prefecture

Kenbei   America bashing, dislike of United States, 1990s

Kenkoku Kinen no Hi   National Foundation Day, February 11, commemorating Yamato state founding, 660 BCE

Kenpo Kinenbi (1947)   Constitution Memorial Day, May 5

Kinai/Kansai   Home provinces around Nara

Kinro Kansha no Hi   Labor Thanksgiving Day, November 23

Kizoku-in   House of Peers, Meiji constitution

Koan   Intellectual riddle; a form of Zen meditative practice

Koan war   Second Mongol invasion, 1281

Kodo   Lecture hall in Buddhist temple complex

Kodomo no Hi   Children's Day festival, May 5

Kofun   Tomb culture

Kokubunji   Provincial Buddhist temples ordered built by Nara emperor Shozu

Kokugaku   Yamato provincial universities

Kokumin no shukujitsu   National holidays

Kokuritsu-koen   National park system

Kokutai   National policy, or the essence of Japanese nationalism

Kokutei-koen   Semi National Park system

Kokyo   The imperial palace in Tokyo

Kondo   Central Buddhist temple building housing statues of deities

Kuge   Court noble

Kuni   Early provincial administrative unit; also a Yayoi period village

Kuraudo-dokoro   Bureau of Archivists, Heian period

Kyogen   Crazy words; interludes in noh dramas

Kyoto-gozan   Five chief Zen temples in Kyoto

Mandala Buddhist paintings, symbolic in nature, mainly in Shingon sect (Sanskrit term)

Mandokoro Kamakura feudal administrative board

Mappo The Buddhist millennium

Matsurigoto Yamato government, in the sense of performing ritual ceremonies

Meiji Ishin Meiji restoration, 1868

Meishi Business card

Metsuke Tokugawa secret police

Mie Kabuki tableaux setting

Mingei Folk art

Misasagi Ancient royal tomb site

Miyabi The refined aesthetic sense of the Heian court

Mobo Modern boy, 1920s

Moga Modern girl, 1920s

Monchujo Kamakura feudal court of law

Monogatari Stories or tales, historical or fiction

Mudra Hand positions in Buddhist iconography that denote aspects of Buddha's life (Sanskrit term)

Muraji Yamato clans affiliated with descent from lesser gods

Nakodo Intercessors arranging modern marriages

Namban Early Tokugawa art portraying Westerners

Nambokucho The half-century period of northern and southern courts, Ashikaga period

Namcho Ashikaga Southern court

Nanto-rokushu The six Nara Buddhist sects

Neikaku Cabinet

Neimin Meiji commoners

Nembutsu Invocation of a Buddha's name, especially Amida's, invoking salvation

Nengo Year periods or reign names of emperors, borrowed from Chinese

Netsuke Small ivory carvings, Tokugawa period

Nihon/Nippon Japanese name for Japan derived from Chinese characters

Nihonjinron Study of Japanese

Nihon-sankei Three national beauty sites: Matsushim, Amanohashidate, Miyajima

Nihon-teien Pond garden

Nikki Court dairies

Ninjo Passion or feelings; a theme in Japanese novels

Nio Buddhist temple gate guardians

Nirvana Extinction of self and desire; goal of Hinayana Buddhism

Nise-e "Likenesses" in scroll paintings

Noh Plays derived from chiefly Buddhist themes

Nyorai A buddha

Omi The royally affiliated Yamato clans

Omidai Family introductions on behalf of young people seeking marriage partners

Omozukai The leading puppeteer of a three-man team in bunraku

Onnagata/Oyama Female impersonators in kabuki

Rangaku Dutch learning

Renga Chain poem consisting of an initial three-line, seventeen-syllable unit, followed by a two-line, fourteen-syllable unit, and so on alternately

Ri Early village administrative unit

Ritsu Early criminal law codes

Ritsuryo The early centralized Nara state based on criminal and administrative codes

Roju Tokugawa shogun's council of elders

Ronin Nara displaced farmers; dispossessed samurai, feudal eras

Ryo Early administrative law codes

Ryomin Free commoners in Nara society

Ryoshu/Ryoke Main proprietors of tax-free shoen during Heian period

Ryubu Shinto Dual Shinto, in its fusion with Buddhism

Samisen A three-stringed musical instrument

Samurai Foot soldiers, military retainers of feudal lords

Samurai-dokoro Kamakura feudal board of retainers

Sankin Kotai The practice of alternate attendance at Edo required of daimyo, Tokugawa era

Sanshu no jingi Three imperial regalia: bronze mirror (Yato no Kagami), curved jewel (Magatami), and iron sword (Mukakumo no Tsurugi)

Sarugako Monkey music, a source of noh musical tradition

Seiji no Hi Coming of Age (or Adult) Day, January 15

Semmin Commoners held in bondage, Nara period

Sengoku daimyo Local lords of later Ashikaga period

Sengoku jidai Century of warring states during later Ashikaga

Seppuku Belly slitting; see harakiri

Sessho Regent for a child emperor, Heian and later periods

Setomono Kamakura Seto ware

Shiki Rights based on land, late Heian and feudal periods

Shikken The KamakuaraHojo regents

Shimaguni "Island country"

Shimpan Tokugawa shogun's collateral families

Shingeki Modern dance

Shinko Zaibatsu associated with 1930s Manchurian economic development

Shinkoku Japan as a divinely protected land

Shinto Way of the gods

Shite Chief noh actor

Shizoku Former samurai class in Meiji Japan

Shoen Tax-exempt private holdings, late Heian and feudal eras

Shogun Barbarian-subduing general; after 1196, military power behind throne

Shoji Paper sliding wall partitions in Japanese homes

Shojo Bukkyo Hinayana Buddhism

Shokan Estate managers of tax-free estates during Heian and feudal periods

Shomin Peasants on tax-free estates during Heian and feudal periods

Shubun no Hi Autumnal Equinox Day, around September 24

Shugi-in House of Representatives

Shugu Kamakura constables or military governers

Shunbun no Hi Vernal Equinox Day, around March 21

Soshi A modern patriot; one who dedicated his life to his country

Sumi-e Monochromatic ink scroll painting

Sumitsu-in Meiji privy council

Sumo Japanese wrestling

Tahoto A double-tiered Buddhist pagoda

Taiiku no Hi Sports Day, October 10

Tairo Tokugawa shogun's prime minister

Tanegashima Firearms, after island where Portuguese first landed and introduced them

Tanka/waka A thirty-one-syllable, five-line poem (5-7-5-7-7)

Tatami Straw mats of standard size on floors in Japanese homes

Tenno Title for an omnipotent, divine ruler; derived from China

Tenno Tanjobi To Emperor Hirohito's birthday holiday, April 29

To An additional Tokyo administrative designation

Tokaido Gojusantugi The fifty-three stations of the Tokaido road

Tokonoma An alcove, usually with flower arrangement and hanging scroll, in homes

Tokusei Kamakura cancellation of debts

Torii A gateway, usually with two transverse bars, associated with Shinto shrines

Tozama A Tokugawa outside lord, traditional enemy of the shogun

Tripitaka Three baskets of Buddhist canon: the Buddha's sayings, their explanations, and rules for monks Uji Yamato clans

Ujigami Yamao Clan deity

Uji no kami Clan chief

Ukiyo-e   Pictures of the floating or modern world, on woodblock prints

Wa   Chinese early designation for Japan and Japanese (dwarfs)

Wado Kaiho   Nara copper coinage

Wakadoshiyuri   Tokugawa shogun's council of junior elders

Wako   Japanese pirates who harassed the Chinese coast, Kamakura-Ashi-kaga eras

Yamato-e   Likenesses (scrolls) depicting scenes of Yama to life

Yang-yin   Chinese philosophical concept of necessary opposites, adopted by Japanese

Yatsuko   Commoners and slaves in Yamato society

Yayoi bunka   Yayoi culture

Yori-ito bunka   Jomon pottery

Yugen   Suggestiveness

Za   Semi-autonomous commercial guilds of feudal Japan

Zaibatsu   Modern Japanese industrial cartel

Zazen   Zen practice of sitting in meditation

Bibliography

CONTENTS

317

Occupation (1945–1952):

Japan since 1952:

Topical:

SOURCES

Bibliography

Association for Asian Studies. *Bibliography*. Ann Arbor, annual.
Borton, Hugh, et al. *A Selected List of Books and Articles on Japan in English, French and German*. Rev. ed., Cambridge, 1954.
Hall, John W. *Japanese History: New Dimensions of Approach and Understanding*. 2nd ed., Washington, D.C., 1961.
Kerner, Robert J. *Northeastern Asia: A Selected Biography*. 2 vols., Berkeley, 1939.
Silberman, Bernard S. *Japan and Korea: A Critical Bibliography*. Tucson, 1962.

Journals/Series

Association for Asian Studies. *Journal of Asian Studies*. Ann Arbor, 1956–present. Successor to *Far Eastern Quarterly*, 1941–1956.
New Japan. Tokyo (Mainichi annual), 1947–present.
This Is Japan. Tokyo (Asahi annual), 1954–present.
Transactions. Asiatic Society of Japan (TASJ). Tokyo, 1874–1920, 1924–1940, 1948–present. Comprehensive index to all three series is found in the issue of December 1948 (Series 3, Vol. VI).

Handbooks/References

Bowring, Peter, and Peter Lornicki, eds. *The Cambridge Encyclopedia of Japan*. Cambridge, 1993.

Chamberlain, Basil H. *Things Japanese*. 6th ed. rev., London, 1939.

Embree, Ainslie T., ed. *Encyclopedia of Asian History*. 4 vols., New York, 1988. Entries on Japan.

Frederic, Louis. *Japan Encyclopedia*. Trans. Kathe Roth. Cambridge, Mass., 2002.

Gluck, Jay, and Sumi Gluck. *Japan: Inside Out*. 5 vols., Tokyo, 1964. One vol. edition, 1968.

Japan Ministry of Information. *Japan: The Official Guide*. Tokyo, irregular.

Japan Tourist Bureau. *Japan Tourist Library*. Short volumes on various aspects of Japanese life and culture.

Japanese National Commission for UNESCO. *Japan: Its Land, People, and Culture*. Rev. ed., Tokyo, 1963.

Kojima Setsuko and Gene A. Crane. *Dictionary of Japanese Culture*. Union City, Calif., 1991.

Papinot, Edmond. *Historical and Geographic Dictionary of Japan*. 2 vols., New York, 1910.

Roberts, Laurance P. *The Connoisseur's Guide to Japanese Museums*. Rutland, Vt., 1967.

Terry, T. Philip. *Terry's Japanese Empire*. Boston, 1914.

Topical

Borton, Hugh, ed. *Japan*. Ithaca, N.Y., 1951.

Collcutt, M., et al. *Cultural Atlas of Japan*. Oxford, 1988.

Dempster, P. *Japan Advances*. London, 1967.

Hall, John W., and Richard K. Beardsley, eds. *Twelve Doors to Japan*. Ann Arbor, 1965.

Jansen, Marius B. *Changing Japanese Attitudes toward Modernization*. Princeton, 1965.

Kerr, George H. *Okinawa: History of an Island People*. Rutland, Vt., 1958.

Kublin, Hyman. *Japan*. Boston, 1969.

———. *Selected Readings*. Boston, 1968.

Lonely Planet series. *Japan*. Various editions.

MacDonald, D. *A Geography of Modern Japan*. Kent, England, 1985.

Reischauer, Edwin O. *The Japanese*. Cambridge, 1972.

Seidensticker, Edward. *Japan*. 1962. Time-Life series.

Strauss, Robert, et al. *Japan*. Berkeley, 1991.

Sutherland, M., and D. Britton. *National Parks of Japan*. Tokyo, 1980.

Trewartha, Glenn T. *Japan: A Physical, Cultural and Regional Geography*. 2nd ed., Madison, Wis., 1965.

Tsunoda Ryusaku, et al. *Sources of Japanese Tradition*. New York, 1959. 2 vol. edition also.

Varley, H. Paul. *A Syllabus of Japanese Civilization*. Rev. ed., New York, 1972.

HISTORY

General

Beasley, W. G. *The Japanese Experience: A Short History of Japan.* Berkeley, 1999.

Beasley, William G., and E. G. Pulleybank. *Historians of China and Japan.* London, 1961.

Cambridge History of Japan. Six volumes:

1. Brown, Delmer M., ed. *Ancient History.* Cambridge, 1993.
2. Shively, Donald H., and William H. McCullough, eds. *Heian Japan.* Cambridge, 1999.
3. Yamamura, Kozo, ed. *Medieval Japan.* Cambridge, 1990.
4. Hall, John W., ed. *Early Modern Japan.* Cambridge, 1991.
5. Jansen, Marius B., ed. *The Nineteenth Century.* Cambridge, 1989.
6. Duus, Peter, ed. *The Twentieth Century.* Cambridge, 1988.

Fairbank, John, et al. *A History of East Asian Civilization.* Vol. I: *East Asia: The Great Tradition.* Vol. II: *East Asia: The Modern Transformation.* Boston, 1960, 1964. Chapters on Japan, which in turn have been published as one volume, Boston, 1978.

Griffis, William. *The Mikado's Empire.* New York, 1876. First American attempt.

Hall, John W. *Japan: From Prehistory to Modern Times.* Reprint, Ann Arbor, 1991 (1968).

Hane, Misiko. *Japan: A Historical Survey.* New York, 1972.

Henshall, Kenneth. *A History of Japan: From Stone Age to Superpower.* 2nd ed., New York, 2004.

Ienaga Saburo. *History of Japan.* Tokyo, 1964.

Kaempfer, Engelbert. *A History of Japan.* 3 vols., Glasgow, 1906.

Kennedy, Malcolm. *A Short History of Japan.* New York, 1963.

Latourette, Kenneth Scott. *The History of Japan.* 6th rev. ed., New York, 1957.

Murdoch, James. *A History of Japan:* Vol. I: *From Origins to Arrival of Portuguese in 1542 A.D.* Vol. II: *Century of Early Foreign Intercourse, 1542–1651.* Vol. III: *Tokugawa Epoch, 1652–1868.* London, 1910–1926.

Reischauer, Edwin O. *Japan: The Story of a Nation.* New York, 1970. Formerly entitled *Japan: Past and Present.*

———. *The Japanese.* Cambridge, 1977.

———. *The Japanese Today: Change and Continuity.* Cambridge, 1988.

Reischauer, Edwin O., and Albert Craig. *Japan: Tradition and Transformation.* Boston, 1989.

Sansom, Sir George B. *Japan: A Short Cultural History.* New York, 1931; rev. ed., 1952.

———. *A History of Japan.* Vol. I: *A History of Japan to 1334.* Vol. II: *A History of Japan, 1334–1615.* Vol. III: *A History of Japan, 1615–1854.* Stanford, 1959–1963.

Shirokauer, Conrad. *A Brief History of Japanese Civilization.* New York, 1993.

Smith, Bradley. *Japan: A History in Art*. Garden City, N.Y., 1964.
Tiedemann, Arthur E., ed. *An Introduction to Japanese Civilization*. New York and London, 1974.
Totman, Cinrad. *A History of Japan*. Malden, Mass., 2000.
———. *Japan before Perry*. Berkeley, 1981.
Varley, H. Paul. *Japanese Culture: A Short History*. 3rd ed., New York, 1984.
Webb, Herschel. *An Introduction to Japan*. New York, 1957.

Modern

Beasley, William G. *The Modern History of Japan*. New York, 1963.
Beckmann, George M. *The Modernization of China and Japan*. New York, 1962.
Bix, Herbert P. *Hirohito and the Making of Modern Japan*. New York, 2000.
Borton, Hugh. *Japan's Modern Century*. 2nd ed., New York, 1970.
Buruma, Ian. *Inventing Japan, 1853–1964*. New York, 2003.
Crowley, James B., ed. *Modern East Asia: Essays in Interpretation*. New York, 1970.
Gordon, Andrew. *Modern History of Japan from the Tokugawa to Present Times*. New York, 2003.
Hane, Mikiso. *Modern Japan: An Historical Survey*. Boulder, 1986.
Hunter, Janet. *Concise Dictionary of Modern Japanese History*. Berkeley, 1984.
Livingstone, Jon, et al. *Imperial Japan, 1800–1945*. New York, 1973.
McClain, James L. *Japan: A Modern History*. New York, 2002.
Pyle, Kenneth. *The Making of Modern Japan*. Lexington, Mass., 1978.
Storry, Richard. *A History of Modern Japan*. 4th rev. ed., London, 1982.
Yanaga Chitoshi. *Japan since Perry*. 2nd ed., Hamden, Conn., 1966.

Topical

Borton, Hugh, et al. *Japan between East and West*. New York, 1957.
Craig, Albert M., and Donald E. Shively, eds. *Personality in Japanese History*. Berkeley, 1971.
Goodrich, L. Carrington, ed. *Japan in the Chinese Dynastic Histories: Later Han through Ming Dynasties*. Trans. Tsunoda Ryusaku. South Pasadena, Calif., 1951.
Honjo Eijiro. *The Social and Economic History of Japan*. Kyoto, 1935.
Kuno Yoshibaro. *Japanese Expansion on the Asiatic Continent*. 2 vols., Berkeley, 1937.
Sansom, Sir George B. *Japan in World History*. New York, 1951.
———. *The Western World and Japan: A Study in the Interaction of European and Asiatic Cultures*. New York, 1951.
Shively, Donald H., ed. *Tradition and Modernization in Japanese Culture*. Princeton, 1971.
Statler, Oliver. *Japanese Inn*. New York, 1972.
Storry, Richard. *A History of Modern Japan*. Tokyo, 1962.
Tames, Richard. *A Traveler's History of Japan*. New York, 1993.
Tiedemann, Arthur, ed. *Modern Japan: A Brief History*. Princeton, N.J., 1955.
Yanaga, Chitoshi. *Japan since Perry*. New York, 1949.

CLASSICAL JAPAN (TO 1200)

Politics

Asakawa Kanichi. *The Documents of Iriki.* New Haven, Conn., 1929. Documents of landholding family.

———. *The Early Institutional Life of Japan: A Study in the Reform of 645 A.D.* Tokyo, 1930.

Mass, P. ed. *Court and Bakufu in Japan.* New Haven, Conn., 1982.

McCullough, W. H., and H. C. McCullough. *A Tale of Flowering Fortunes: Annals of Japanese Aristocratic Life in the Heian period.* 2 vols., Stanford, 1980.

Reischauer, Robert K., and Jean Reischauer. *Early Japanese History, 40 B.C.–A.D. 1167.* Parts A & B. Princeton, 1937.

Culture

Aikins, C. M., and T. Higuchi. *Prehistory of Japan.* New York, 1982.

Barnes, G. L. *Protohistoric Yamato.* Ann Arbor, Mich., 1988.

Groot, Gerard J. *The Prehistory of Japan.* New York, 1951.

Kidder, Johathan E. *The Birth of Japanese Art.* London, 1965.

———. *Japan before Buddhism.* New York, 1959.

Miki Fumio. *Haniwa: The Clay Sculpture of Prehistoric Japan.* Rutland, Vt., 1960.

Morris, Ivan. *The World of the Shining Prince: Court Life in Ancient Japan.* New York, 1964.

Reischauer, Edwin O. *Ennin's Travels in T'ang China.* New York, 1951. A Buddhist monk in China, mid-ninth century.

———. *Ennin's Diary: A Record of Pilgrimage to China in Search of the Law.* New York, 1955.

Shosoin Office. *Treasures of the Shosoin.* Tokyo, 1965.

Warner, Langdon. *Japanese Sculpture of the Tempyo Period.* Cambridge, 1959.

Literature

Aston, William G. *Nihongi: Chronicles of Japan from the Earliest Times to A.D. 697.* London, 1896. Reprint 1956.

Brower, Robert H., and Earl Miner. *Japanese Court Poetry.* Stanford, 1961.

Chamberlain, Basil H., trans. *The Kojiki, or Record of Ancient Matters.* 2nd ed., Kobe, 1932.

Keene, Donald. Foreword, in *Manyoshu.* New York, 1965.

McCullough, Helen C. *Tales of Ise: Lyrical Episodes from Tenth Century Japan.* Stanford, 1968.

Miner, Earl, trans. *Japanese Poetic Diaries.* Berkeley, 1969.

Murasaki, Lady. *Tales of Genji.* Trans. Arthur Waley. New York, 1960. Also trans. Edward Siedensticker. 2 vols., New York, 1977.

Omori, Annie S., and Kochi Doi, trans. *Diaries of Court Ladies of Old Japan.* Boston, 1920, and Tokyo, 1935.

Reischauer, Edwin O., and Joseph K. Yamagawa, eds. and trans. *Translations from Early Japanese Literature*. Cambridge, 1951.

Sakamoto, T. *The Six National Histories of Japan*. Trans. J. S. Brownlee. Vancouver, 1991.

Sei Shonagon. *Notes from a Pillow Book*. Trans. Arthur Waley. Boston, 1929. Also trans. Ivan Morris, 2 vols., New York, 1967.

Seidensticker, Edward G. *The Gossamer Years*. Tokyo, 1964.

Wakameda, W., trans. *Kokinshu: Poems Ancient and Modern*. Tokyo, 1929.

FEUDAL JAPAN (1200–1600)

Politics

Cole, Wendell. *Kyoto in the Momoyama Period*. Norman, Okla., 1967.

Duus, Peter. *Feudalism in Japan*. 2nd ed., New York, 1976.

Hall, John W. *Government and Local Power in Japan, 500–1700*. Princeton, 1966.

Hall, John W., K. Nagahara, and K. Yamamura, eds. *Japan before Tokugawa: Political Consolidation and Economic Growth, 1500–1650*. Princeton, 1981.

Hurst, G. C. *Insei: Abdicated Sovereigns in the Politics of late Heian Japan*. New York, 1976.

Massim, Jeffrey P. *Warrior Government in Early Medieval Japan*. New Haven, Conn., 1974.

Shinoda Minoru. *The Founding of the Kamakura Shogunate, 1180–1185*. New York, 1960.

Varley, H. Paul. *Imperial Restoration of Medieval Japan*. New York, 1971.

———. *The Onin War*. New York, 1966.

Economics

Asakawa, Kanishi. *Land and Society in Medieval Japan*. New York, 1965.

Brown, Delmer. *Money Economy in Medieval Japan: A Study in the Use of Coins*. New Haven, Conn., 1951.

Culture

Anesaki, Masaharu. *Nichiren: The Buddhist Prophet*. Cambridge, 1916.

Bloom, Alfred. *Shinran's Gospel of Pure Grace*. Tucson, 1965.

Kitagawa Hiroshi and Bruce Tsuchida. *The Tale of the Heike*. 2 vols., Tokyo, 1975.

McCullough, Helen C., trans. *The Taiheiki: A Chronicle of Medieval Japan*. New York, 1959.

———. *Yoshitsune: A Fifteenth-Century Japanese Chronicle*. Stanford, 1966.

Shimizu Yoshiaki, ed. *Japan: The Shaping of the Daimyo Culture, 1185–1868*. New York, 1988. Issued in conjunction with the exhibit at the National Gallery of Art.

Foreign Affairs

Boxer, Charles R. *The Christian Century in Japan, 1549–1650*. Berkeley, 1956.

Cooper, Michael. *They Came to Japan*. Berkeley, 1956. Foreign eyewitness accounts, 1543–1640.

Wang I-t'ung. *Official Relations between China and Japan, 1368–1549*. Cambridge, 1953.

TOKUGAWA JAPAN (1600–1868)

Politics (General)

Totman, Conrad D. *Politics in the Tokugawa Bafuku, 1600–1815*. Cambridge, 1967.

Tsukahira Toshio. *Feudal Control in Tokugawa Japan: The Sankin Kotai System*. Cambridge, 1966.

Webb, Herschel. *The Japanese Imperial Institution in the Tokugawa Period*. New York, 1968.

Personalities

Clavell, James. *Shogun: A Novel of Japan*. 1975.

Earl, David M. *Emperor and Nation in Japan: Political Thinkers of the Tokugawa Period*. Seattle, 1964.

Hall, John W. *Tanuma Okitsugu, 1719–1788: Forerunner of Modern Japan*. Cambridge, 1955. Shogunate official, 1764–1786.

Iwata Mazakazu. *Okubo Toshimichi: The Bismarck of Japan*. Berkeley, 1964.

Matsumoto Shigeru. *Motoori Norinaga, 1730–1801*. Cambridge, 1970. Leader of national studies movement.

McEwan, J. R. *The Political Writings of Ogyu Sorai*. Cambridge, 1982. Midperiod Confucian adviser to shogunate.

Minear, Richard H. *Japanese Tradition and Western Law: Emperor State and Law in the Thought of Hozumi Yatsuka*. Cambridge, 1970. Constitutional scholar, 1860–1912.

Shively, Donald H., trans. and ed. *The Love Suicide at Amijima*. Cambridge, 1953.

Van Straelen, Henri. *Yoshida Shoin: Forerunner of the Meiji Restoration: A Biographical Study*. Leiden, 1952.

Restoration

Beasley, W. G. *The Meiji Restoration*. Stanford, 1972.

Craig, Albert. *Choshu in the Meiji Restoration*. Cambridge, 1961.

Harootunian, H. D. *Toward Restoration: The Growth of Political Consciousness in Tokugawa Japan*. Berkeley, 1970.

Jansen, Marius. *Sakamoto Ryoma and the Meiji Restoration*. Princeton, 1961. A Tosa activist.

Economics and Society

Bellah, Robert. *Tokugawa Religion*. Glencoe, Ill., 1957.
Black, John R. *Young Japan: Yokohama and Yedo, 1858–79*. 2 vols., London, 1968.
Dore, Ronald P. *Education in Tokugawa Japan*. Berkeley, 1965.
Hibbett, Howard. *The Floating World in Japanese Fiction*. London, 1959.
Keene, Donald. *The Battles of Koxinga*. London, 1951.
Saikaku Ihara. *Five Women Who Loved Love*. Trans. William de Bary. Rutland, Vt., 1956.
Sheldon, C. D. *The Rise of the Merchant Class in Tokugawa Japan, 1600–1868*. New York, 1958.
Smith, Thomas C. *The Agrarian Origins of Modern Japan*. Stanford, 1959.

Foreign Affairs (General)

Beasley, William G., ed. and trans. *Select Documents in Japanese Foreign Policy, 1853–1868*. London, 1955.
Keene, Donald. *The Japanese Discovery of Europe: Honda Toshiaki and Other Discoverers, 1720–1798*. New York, 1952.
Paske-Smith, Montague. *Western Barbarians in Japan and Formosa: Tokugawa Days, 1603–1868*. Kobe, 1930.

Foreign Affairs (British)

Alcock, Sir Rutherford. *The Capital of the Tycoon*. 2 vols., New York, 1863.
Beasley, William G. *Great Britain and the Opening of Japan, 1834–1858*. London, 1951.
Rogers, Philip G. *The First Englishman in Japan: The Story of Will Adams*. London, 1956.
Satow, Sir Ernst. *A Diplomat in Japan*. London, 1921.
Thompson, Edward M., ed. *The Diary of Richard Cocks, Cape Merchant in the English Factory in Japan, 1615–22*. 2 vols., Tokyo, 1899.

Foreign Affairs (Other Europeans)

Boxer, Charles R. *Jan Compagnie in Japan, 1600–1850*. The Hague, 1950.
———. *The Portuguese Embassy to Japan, 1644–1647*. London, 1928.
Golovnin, Vasili M. *Memoirs of a Captivity in Japan during the Years 1811, 1812 and 1813*. 3 vols., London, 1824.
Lensen, George A. *The Russian Push toward Japan: Russo-Japanese Relations, 1697–1875*. Princeton, 1959.
———. *Russia's Japan Expedition of 1852–1855*. Gainesville, Fla., 1955.

United States (General)

Cole, Allan B. *Yankee Surveyors in the Shogun's Seas: Records of the United States Surveying Expedition to the North Pacific Ocean, 1853–1856*. Princeton, 1947.

Kaneko Hisakazu. *Manjiro: The Man Who Discovered America*. Boston, 1956.
U.S. Congress, 32-1. Senate Document 59. *Early Trips to Japan*. Washington, D.C., 1851.

United States (Matthew C. Perry)

Cole, Allan B., ed. *A Scientist with Perry in Japan: The Journal of Dr. James Morrow.* Chapel Hill, N.C., 1947.
Graff, Henry P., ed. *Bluejackets with Perry in Japan*. New York, 1952.
Hawks, Francis L., comp. *Narrative of the Expedition of an American Squadron to the China Seas and Japan Under the Command of Commodore M. C. Perry, U.S. Navy.* 3 vols., Washington, D.C., 1856. Abridged and ed. volume by Sidney Wallace, New York, 1952.
Morison, Samuel E. *Old Bruin*. New York, 1967.
Pineau, Roger, ed. *The Japan Expedition 1852–1854: The Personal Journal of Commodore Matthew C. Perry*. Washington, D.C., 1968.
Walworth, Arthur. *Black Ships off Japan*. New York, 1946.

United States (Townsend Harris)

Cosenza, Mario E., ed. *The Complete Journal of Townsend Harris*. New York, 1930.
Crow, Carl. *He Opened the Door of Japan*. New York, 1939.
Statler, Oliver. *Shimoda Story*. New York, 1969.

MODERN JAPAN: DOMESTIC (1868–1941)

Topical

Beasley, William. *The Rise of Modern Japan*. New York, 1990.
Borton, Hugh. *Japan since 1931*. New York, 1940.
Harrison, John A. *Japan's Northern Frontier*. Gainesville, Fla., 1953. About Hokkaido.
Hunter, J. *The Emergence of Modern Japan*. New York, 1989.
Norman, E. Herbert. *Japan's Emergence as a Modern State*. New York, 1946.
Okuma, Count Shigenobu. *Fifty Years of New Japan*. 2 vols., London, 1910.

Politics

Akika, George. *The Foundations of Constitutional Government in Modern Japan, 1868–1900*. Cambridge, 1965.
Berger, Gordon M. *Parties out of Power in Japan, 1931–1941*. Princeton, 1977.
Brown, Delmer. *Nationalism in Japan*. Berkeley, 1955.
Duus, Peter. *Party Rivalry and Political Change in Taisho Japan*. Cambridge, 1968.
Fahs, Charles B. *Government in Japan*. New York, 1940.
Gluck, Carol. *Japan's Modern Myths: Ideology in the Late Meiji Period*. Princeton, 1985.
Maruyama, Asao. *Thought and Behavior in Modern Japanese Politics*. London, 1963.

McLaren, William W. *A Political History of Japan during the Meiji Era, 1867–1912.* New York, 1916.
Pittau, Joseph. *Political Thought in Early Meiji Japan, 1868–1889.* Cambridge, 1967.
Quigley, Harold S. *Japanese Government and Politics.* New York, 1932.
Reischauer, Robert F. *Japan, Government and Politics.* New York, 1939.
Scalapino, Robert. *Democracy and the Party Movement in Pre-war Japan.* Berkeley, 1962.
Totten, George. *The Social Democratic Movement in Pre-war Japan.* New Haven, Conn., 1966.
Wilson, Robert A. *Genesis of the Meiji Government in Japan, 1868–1871.* Berkeley, 1957.
Young, Arthur M. *Imperial Japan, 1926–1938.* London, 1938.
———. *Japan in Recent Times, 1912–1926.* New York, 1929.

Constitutionalism

Akita, George. *The Foundations of Constitutional Government in Modern Japan, 1868–1900.* Cambridge, 1962.
Beckman, George M. *The Making of the Meiji Constitution.* Lawrence, Kans., 1957.
Ito, Prince Hirobumi. *Commentaries on the Constitution of the Empire of Japan.* Tokyo, 1906.

Personalities

Blacker, Carmen. *The Japanese Enlightenment: A Study of the Writings of Fukuzawa Yukichi.* Cambridge, 1964.
Fukuzawa Yukichi. *Autobiography.* Trans. Kiyooka Eiichi. Rev. ed., New York, 1966.
Hackett, Rober F. *Yamagata Aritomo in the Rise of Modern Japan, 1838–1922.* Cambridge, 1970.
Keene, Donald. *Emperor of Japan: Meiji and His World.* New York, 2002.
Miller, Frank O. *Minobe Tatsukichi: Interpreter of Constitutionalism in Japan.* Berkeley, 1966.
Najita Tetsuo. *Hara Kei in the Politics of the Compromise, 1905–1915.* Cambridge, 1967.
Pooley, Andrew M., ed. *The Secret Memoirs of Count Tadasu Hayashi, 1854–1913.* London, 1915. Diplomat.
Wilson, George M. *Radical Nationalist in Japan: Kita Ikki, 1883–1937.* Cambridge, 1969.

Militarism

Colegrove, Kenneth W. *Militarism in Japan.* Boston, 1934.
Morris, Ivan. *Japan, 1931–1945: Militarism, Fascism, Japanism.* Boston, 1963.
Norman, E. Herbert. *Soldier and Peasant in Japan: The Origins of Conscription.* New York, 1943.
Presseisen, Ernst L. *Before Aggression: Europeans Prepare the Japanese Army.* Tucson, 1965.
Storry, Richard. *The Double Patriots.* London, 1957.

Tanin, O., and E. Yohan. *Militarism and Fascism in Japan*. New York, 1934. Soviet authors.

Radicalism

Beckman, George, and Genji Okubo. *The Japanese Communist Party, 1922–1945*. Stanford, 1969.

Kublin, Hyman. *Asian Revolutionary: The Life of Sen Katayama*. Princeton, 1964. Socialist, union leader.

Notehelfer, F. G. *Kokotu Shusui: Portrait of a Japanese Radical*. London, 1971.

Scalapino, Robert. *The Japanese Communist Movement, 1920–1966*. Berkeley, 1967.

Swearinger, Roger, and Paul Langer. *Red Flag in Japan*. Cambridge, 1952. Japanese Communist movement from 1919.

Economics

Allen, George C. *A Short Economic History of Modern Japan, 1867–1937*. 2nd. rev. ed., London, 1946.

Bennett, John W., and Iwao Ishinu. *Paternalism in the Japanese Economy*. Minneapolis, 1963.

Havens, Thomas R. *Farm and Nation in Modern Japan: Agrarian Nationalism, 1879–1940*. Princeton, 1974.

Hirschmeier, Johannes. *The Origins of Entrepreneurship in Meiji Japan*. Cambridge, 1964.

Marshall, Byron K. *Capitalism and Nationalism in Prewar Japan: The Ideology of the Business Elite, 1868–1941*. Stanford, 1967.

Orchard, John O. *Japan Economic Position: The Progress of Industrialization*. New York, 1930.

Rosovsky, Henry. *Capital Formation in Japan*. Glencoe, Ill., 1961.

Society

Arima Tatsuo. *The Failure of Freedom: A Portrait of Modern Japanese Intellectuals*. Cambridge, 1969.

Centenary Culture Council, ed. *Japanese Culture in the Meiji Period, 1868–1912*. 10 vols., Tokyo, 1955–1958.

Embree, John. *A Japanese Nation: A Social Survey*. New York, 1945.

Hearn, Lafcadio. *Japan: An Attempt at Interpretation*. New York, 1904.

Kishimoto Hideo, ed. *Japanese Religion in the Meiji Era*. Trans. John F. Howes. Tokyo, 1958.

Masaki, Kosaha. *Japanese Thought in the Meiji Period*. Trans. David Abosch. Tokyo, 1958.

Passin, Herbert. *Society and Education in Japan*. New York, 1965.

Pyle, Kenneth. *The New Generation in Meiji Japan: Problems of Cultural Identity*. Stanford, 1963.

Raucat, T. *The Honorable Picnic*. New York, 1927. A novel.

MODERN JAPAN: FOREIGN AFFAIRS (EXCEPT UNITED STATES)

General/Diplomacy

Beasley, William G. *Japanese Imperialism, 1894–1945.* Oxford, 1987.

———. *Select Documents on Japanese Foreign Policy, 1853–1868.* London, 1955.

Butow, Robert. *Tojo and the Coming of the War.* Princeton, 1961.

Crowley, James B. *Japan's Quest for Autonomy: National Security and Foreign Policy, 1930–1938.* Princeton, 1967.

Dower, J. W. *Empire and Aftermath: Yoshida Shigeru and the Japanese Experience, 1878–1954.* Cambridge, 1988.

Falk, Edwin A. *Togo and the Rise of Japanese Sea Power.* New York, 1986.

Iriye, Akira. *After Imperialism: The Search for a New Order in the Far East, 1921–1931.* Cambridge, 1965.

Jones, Frances G. *Extraterritoriality in Japan and the Diplomatic Relations Resulting in Its Abolition, 1853–1899.* London, 1931.

Maxon, Yale C. *Control of Japanese Foreign Policy: A Study of Civil-Military Rivalry, 1930–1945.* Berkeley, 1957.

Morley, James W. *Japan's Foreign Policy.* New York, 1971.

Morley, James W., ed. *Deterrent Diplomacy: Japan, German and the USSR, 1935–1940.* New York, 1976.

———. *Japan Erupts: The London Naval Conference and the Manchurian Incident, 1928–1932.* New York, 1984.

Nish, Ian. *Japan's Foreign Policy, 1868–1942.* London, 1977.

Morison, Samuel. *The Rising Sun in the Pacific.* Vol. III of *History of United States Naval Operations in World War II.* Boston, 1948.

Pooley, Andrew M. *Japan's Foreign Policies.* London, 1920.

Royama Masamichi. *Foreign Policy of Japan, 1914–1939.* Tokyo, 1940.

Sansom, George B. *The Western World and Japan.* New York, 1950.

Scalapino, Robert, ed. *The Foreign Policy of Modern Japan.* Berkeley, 1977.

Shigemitsu Mamoru. *Japan and Her Destiny.* New York, 1958. Foreign minister in the 1930s and 1940s.

Takeuchi Tatsuji. *War and Diplomacy in the Japanese Empire.* New York, 1935.

Asia/Pacific

Chamberlain, William H. *Japan over Asia.* Rev. ed., Boston, 1939.

Clyde, Paul H. *Japan.* New York, 1935; reissued 1967.

Conroy, Hilary. *The Japanese Seizure of Korea.* Philadelphia, 1961.

Kerr, George H. *Ryukyu: Kingdom and Province before 1945.* Washington, D.C., 1953.

Morley, James W., ed. *The China Quagmire: Japan's Expansion on the Asian Continent.* New York, 1983.

———. *The Fateful Choice: Japan's Advance into Southeast Asia, 1939–1941.* New York, 1980.

Yanaihara Tadao. *Pacific Islands under Japanese Mandate.* London, 1940.

China/Manchuria

Bassett, Reginald. *Democracy and Foreign Policy: A Case History, the Sino-Japanese Dispute, 1931–1933.* London, 1952.

Bisson, Thomas A. *Japan in China.* New York, 1938.

Boyle, Jack H. *China and Japan at War, 1937–1945: The Politics of Collaboration.* Stanford, 1972.

Jansen, Marius D. *The Japanese and Sun Yat-sen.* Cambridge, 1954.

League of Nations. *Report of the Commission of Inquiry.* New York, 1932.

MacNair, Harley F. *The Real Conflict between China and Japan.* Chicago, 1932.

Ogata Sadako. *Defiance in Manchuria: The Making of Japanese Foreign Policy, 1931–1932.* Berkeley, 1964.

Smith, Sarah L. *The Manchurian Crisis, 1931–1932.* New York, 1932.

Snow, Edgar. *Far Eastern Front.* New York, 1933.

Taylor, George L. *The Struggle for North China.* New York, 1940.

White, Trumbull. *The War in the East.* London, 1895. The 1894–1895 war.

Willoughby, Westel W. *Japan's Case Examined.* Baltimore, 1940.

———. *The Sino-Japanese Controversy and the League of Nations.* Baltimore, 1935.

Young, Carl W. *Japan's Jurisdiction and International Legal Position in Manchuria.* 3 vols., Baltimore, 1931.

———. *Japan's Special Position in Manchuria.* Baltimore, 1931.

Russo-Japanese War, 1904–1905

Asakawa Kanichi. *The Russo-Japanese Conflict.* Boston, 1904.

Brooke, Lord. *An Eye-witness in Manchuria.* London, 1905. Reuters correspondent.

German Official Account of the Russo-Japanese War. Trans. Karl von Donat. 7 vols., London, 1908.

Kuropatkin, Gen. *The Russian Army and the Japanese War.* 2 vols., London, 1909.

Okamoto Shumpei. *The Japanese Oligarchy and the Russo-Japanese War.* New York, 1970.

Russia/Soviet Union

Coox, Alvin. *Nomonhan: Japan against Russia, 1939.* 2 vols., Stanford, 1985.

Lensen, George A. *Japanese Recognition of the USSR: Soviet-Japanese Relations, 1921–1930.* Tallahassee, Fla., 1970.

Malozemoff, Andrew. *Russian Far Eastern Policy, 1881–1904.* Berkeley, 1959.

Moore, Harriet L. *Soviet Far Eastern Policy, 1931–1945.* Princeton, 1945.

Morley, James W. *The Japanese Thrust into Siberia, 1918.* New York, 1937.

Europe

Dennis, Alfred L. P. *The Anglo-Japanese Alliance.* Berkeley, 1923.

Fox, Grace. *Britain and Japan, 1858–1883.* London, 1969.

Ike, Frank W. *German-Japanese Relations, 1936–1940.* New York, 1956.

Nish, Ian H. *The Anglo-Japanese Alliance: The Diplomacy of Two Island Empires, 1894–1907.* London, 1966.

Presseisen, Ernest L. *Germany and Japan: A Study of Totalitarian Diplomacy, 1933–1941.* The Hague, 1958.

MODERN JAPAN AND THE UNITED STATES

General

Battistini, Lawrence M. *Japan and America from the Earliest Times to the Present.* New York, 1953.

Bennett, John W., et al. *In Search of Identity: The Japanese Overseas Scholar in America and Japan.* Minneapolis, 1958.

Blakeslee, George H., ed. *Japan and Japanese-American Relations.* New York, 1912.

Clinard, Outten J. *Japan's Influence on American Naval Power, 1897–1917.* Berkeley, 1947.

Crow, Carl. *Japan and America.* New York, 1916.

Dennett, Tyler. *Americans in East Asia.* New York, 1922. Chapters on Japan.

Dulles, Foster R. *Forty Years of American-Japanese Relations.* New York, 1937.

———. *Yankees and Samurai: America's Role in the Emergence of Modern Japan, 1791–1900.* New York, 1965.

Griswold, A. Whitney. *The Far Eastern Policy of the United States.* New York, 1938. Chapters on Japan.

Ichihashi Yamato. *Japanese in the United States.* Stanford, 1932.

———. *The Washington Conference and After: A Historical Survey.* Stanford, 1928.

Iriye, Akira. *Across the Pacific: An Inner History of American–East Asian Relations.* New York, 1967.

Kamikawa Hikomatsu, ed. *Japan-American Diplomatic Relations in the Meiji-Taisho Era.* Tokyo, 1958.

Kawakami Kiyoshi. *American-Japanese Relations.* New York, 1912.

Neumann, William L. *America Encounters Japan: From Perry to MacArthur.* Baltimore, 1963.

Reischauer, Edwin O. *The United States and Japan.* 3rd. ed., Cambridge, 1965.

Schwantes, Robert S. *Japanese and Americans: A Century of Cultural Relations.* New York, 1955.

Treat, Payson J. *Diplomatic Relations between the United States and Japan, 1853–1895.* 2 vols., Stanford, 1932.

———. *Diplomatic Relations between the United States and Japan, 1895–1905.* Stanford, 1938.

———. *Japan and the United States, 1853–1921.* Revised and continued to 1928. Stanford, 1928.

To 1931

Bailey, Thomas A. *Theodore Roosevelt and the Japanese-American Crisis.* Stanford, 1934. The California race problem at turn of century.

Beers, Burton F. *Vain Endeavor: Robert Lansing's Attempts to End the American-Japanese Rivalry.* Burnham, N.C., 1952.

Buell, Robert L. *The Washington Conference.* New York, 1922.

Carnegie Endowment for International Peace. *Diplomatic Relations between the United States and Japan, 1908–1924.* Worcester, Mass., 1925.

Dennett, Tyler. *Roosevelt and the Russo-Japanese War.* Garden City, N.Y., 1925.

Esthus, Raymond E. *Theodore Roosevelt and Japan.* Seattle, 1966.

Fifield, Russell W. *Woodrow Wilson and the Far East: The Diplomacy of the Shantung Question.* New York, 1952.

Iriye, Akira. *Pacific Estrangement: Japanese and American Expansion, 1892–1911.* Cambridge, 1972.

1931–1941

Borg, Dorothy, and Shumpei Okamoto, eds. *Pearl Harbor as History: Japanese-American Relations, 1931–1941.* New York, 1973.

———. *The United States and the Far Eastern Crisis of 1937–1938.* Cambridge, 1964.

Butow, Robert. *Tojo and the Coming of War.* 1961.

Feis, Herbert. *Road to Pearl Harbor.* Princeton, 1950.

Fortune, September 1936.

Grew, Joseph C. *Ten Years in Japan.* New York, 1944. American ambassador.

———. *Turbulent Era: A Diplomatic Record of Forty Years, 1904–1945.* 2 vols., Boston, 1952.

Iriye, Akira. *The Origins of the Second World War in Asia and the Pacific.* London, 1987.

Lord, Walter. *Day of Infamy.* 1957.

Millis, Walter. *This Is Pearl: The United States and Japan.* New York, 1947.

Prange, Gordon W. *At Dawn We Slept.* New York, 1981.

Rappaport, Armin. *Henry L. Stimson and Japan, 1931–1933.* Chicago, 1963.

Schroeder, Paul W. *The Axis Alliance and Japanese-American Relations, 1941.* Ithaca, N.Y., 1958.

Stimson, Henry L. *The Far Eastern Crisis.* New York, 1936.

U.S. Department of State. *Foreign Relations of the United States: Japan, 1931–1941.* 2 vols., Washington, D.C., 1943.

Wohlstetter, Roberta. *Pearl Harbor: Warning and Decision.* Stanford, 1962.

WORLD WAR II (1941–1945)

General

Calvocoressi, Peter, Guy Wint, and John Pritchard. *Total War. II: The Great East Asia and Pacific Conflict.* 2nd ed., London, 1989.

Collier, Basil. *The War in the Far East, 1941–1945.* New York, 1969.

Costello, John. *The Pacific War.* New York, 1981.

Dower, John W. *War without Mercy: Race and Power in the Pacific War.* New York, 1986.

Gilbert, Martin. *The Second World War: A Complete History.* New York, 1989. Chapters on the Pacific War.

Hart, Liddell. *History of the Second World War*. New York, 1971. Chapters on the Pacific war.

Hoyt, Edwin O. *Japan's War: The Great Pacific Conflict, 1853 to 1952*. New York, 1986.

Ike, Nobutaka, ed. and trans. *Japan's Decision for War: Records of the 1941 Policy Conferences*. Stanford, 1967.

Iriye, Akira. *Power and Culture: The Japanese-American War 1941–1945*. Cambridge, 1981.

Jones, Francis C. *Japan's New Order in East Asia: Its Rise and Fall, 1937–1945*. London, 1954.

Jones, Francis C., et al. *The Far East, 1942–1945*. London, 1955.

Kase Toshikazu. *Journey to the Missouri*. New Haven, Conn., 1950. Foreign minister.

Keegan, John. *The Second World War*. New York, 1990. Chapters on the Pacific War.

Renzi, William A., and Mark D. Roehrs. *Never Look Back*. Armonk, N.Y., 1991.

Spector, Ronald H. *Eagle against the Sun: The American War with Japan*. New York, 1985.

Thorne, Christopher. *The Far East War: States and Societies, 1941–45*. Boston, 1986.

Togo Shigenori. *The Cause of Japan*. New York, 1956. Foreign minister, 1941–1942.

Toland, John. *The Rising Sun*. 2 vols., New York, 1970.

U.S. Congress, 79th. Joint Committee on the Investigation of the Pearl Harbor Attack. Hearings, 39 parts. Washington, D.C., 1945–1946. Report, 1946.

U.S. Strategic Bombing Survey (Pacific) Reports:

The Campaigns of the Pacific War. Washington, D.C., 1946.
The Effects of Atomic Bombs on Hiroshima and Nagasaki. Washington, D.C., 1946.
The Effects of Strategic Bombing on Japanese Morale. Washington, D.C., 1947.
Interrogations of Japanese Officials. 2 vols., Washington, D.C., 1946.
Japanese Air Power. Washington, D.C., 1947.
Japan's Struggle to End the War. Washington, D.C., 1946.

Military

Brines, Russell. *Until They Eat Stones*. Philadelphia, 1944.

Davies, Warren J. *Japan: The Air Menace of the Pacific*. New York, 1970.

Dull, Paul S. *A Battle History of the Imperial Japanese Navy (1941–1945)*. Annapolis, Md., 1978.

Fuchida Mitsuo and Masatake Okumiya. *Midway*. Annapolis, Md., 1955.

Hashimoto Mochitsura. *Sunk: The Story of the Japanese Submarine Fleet, 1941–1945*. New York, 1954.

Ienaga, Saburo. *The Pacific War 1931–1945*. New York, 1978.

Inoguchi, R., et al. *Divine Wind: Japan's Suicide Squadrons in World War Two*. New York, 1970.

International Military Tribunal for the Far East (IMTFE). *Proceedings*, 19 vols., *Judgement and Annexes*, 1 vol., *Separate Opinions*, 1 vol., *Proceedings in Chambers*, 1 vol., *Index and Guide*, 5 vols. Garland reprint, 1981.

MacArthur, General Douglas. *Reports of General MacArthur.* Vol. II, Part 2: *Japanese Operations in the Southwest Pacific Area.* U.S. Department of the Army. Washington, D.C., 1966 (1970 reprints).

Masatake Okumiya and Jiro Horikoshi. *Zero!* New York, 1956.

Nagatsuka Ryuji. *I Was a Kamikaze.* Trans. Nina Rootes. New York, 1972.

O'Connor, Raymond J. *The Japanese Navy in World War Two.* Annapolis, Md., 1970.

Potter, John D. *Yamamoto: The Man Who Menaced America.* New York, 1965. Also entitled *Admiral of the Pacific.*

Sakai Saburo. *Samurai.* London, 1978.

Sakamaki Kazu. *I Attacked Pearl Harbor.* Trans. Toru Matsumito. New York, 1949.

Williams, Peter, and David Wallace. *Unit 731: Japan's Secret Biological Warfare in World War II.* New York, 1989.

Topical

Bisson, Thomas A. *Japan's War Economy.* New York, 1945.

Borton, Hugh. *The Administration and Structure of the Japanese Government.* Washington, D.C., 1945.

Butow, Robert. *Japan's Decision to Surrender.* Stanford, 1954.

Cohen, Jerome B. *The Japanese Economy in War and Reconstruction.* Minneapolis, 1949.

Daws, Gavin. *Prisoners of the Japanese.* 1994.

Feis, Herbert. *Between War and Peace: The Potsdam Conference.* Princeton, 1960.

———. *Japan Subdued: The Atom Bomb and the End of the War in the Pacific.* Princeton, 1961.

Fortune, April 1944.

Giovannitti, Len, and Fred Freed. *The Decision to Drop the Bomb.* New York, 1965.

Hachiya, Michihiko, M.D. *Hiroshima: The Journal of a Japanese Physician, August 6–September 30, 1945.* Trans. and ed. Warner Wells, M.D. Chapel Hill, N.C., 1955.

Havens, Thomas. *Valley of Darkness: The Japanese People and World War Two.* New York, 1978.

Hersey, John. *Hiroshima.* New York, 1946.

Kerr, E. Bartlett. *Surrender and Survival.* New York, 1985. POWs.

Layton, Rear Admiral Edwin, et al. *And I Was There: Pearl Harbor and Midway—Breaking the Secrets.* New York, 1985.

Lebra, Joyce, ed. *Japan's Greater East Asia Co-prosperity Sphere in World War II.* New York, 1974.

Nazai Takashi. *We of Nagasaki.* New York, 1958.

Ooka Shohe. *Fires on the Plain.* Trans. Ivan Morris. New York, 1957. Leyte campaign novel.

Osada Arata. *Children of the A-Bomb.* New York, 1963.

Shillony, Ben-Ahi. *Politics and Culture in Wartime Japan.* Oxford, 1988.

Terasaki, Gwen H. *Bridge to the Sun.* Chapel Hill, N.C., 1957. American wife of a Japanese diplomat.

Thorne, Christopher. *Allies of a Kind.* London, 1978. The United States and Britain and World War II.

Tolischus, Otto D. *Through Japanese Eyes*. New York, 1945.
Trumbull, Robert. *Nine Who Survived Hiroshima and Nagasaki*. New York, 1957.
West Point Military History Series. *The Second World War: Asia and the Pacific*. Wayne, N.J., 1984.

OCCUPATION (1945–1952)

General

Blakeslee, George H. *The Far Eastern Commission: A Study in International Cooperation, 1945–1953*. Washington, D.C., 1953.
Far Eastern Commission. *Activities of the Far Eastern Commission*. Washington, D.C., 1945–1953.
——. *Reports by the Secretary General*. Washington, D.C., 1945–1953.
Feary, Robert A. *The Occupation of Japan: Second Phase, 1948–1950*. New York, 1950.
Kawai, Kazuo. *Japan's American Interlude*. Chicago, 1960.
Martin, Edwin M. *The Allied Occupation of Japan*. Stamford, Conn., 1948.
SCAP. *Monthly Summation of Non-Military Activities in Japan*. Tokyo, September 1945–August 1948.
——. Government Section. *Political Reorientation of Japan, September 1945–September 1948*. 2 vols., Washington, D.C., 1949.
Schaller, Michael. *The American Occupation of Japan: The Origins of the Cold War in Asia*. New York, 1985
Sebald, William, Ambassador, and Russell Brines. *With MacArthur in Japan*. London, 1965.
Textor, Robert B. *Failure in Japan*. New York, 1951.
U.S. Department of State. *United States Relations with Japan, 1945–1952*. New York, 1953.
U.S. Education Mission to Japan. *Report*. Washington, D.C., 1946.
Ward, R., and Y. Sakamoto, eds. *Democratizing Japan: The Occupation of Japan*. Honolulu, 1987.
Wildes, Harry Emerson. *Typhoon in Tokyo: The Occupation and Its Aftermath*. New York, 1954.

Topical

Baerwald, Hans. *The Purge of Japanese Leaders under the Occupation*. Berkeley, 1959.
Bisson, Thomas A. *Prospects for Democracy in Japan*. New York, 1949.
——. *Zaibatsu Dissolution in Japan*. Berkeley, 1954.
Cohen, Jerome B. *Economic Problems of Free Japan*. Princeton, 1952.
Dore, Donald P. *Land Reform in Japan*. London, 1951.
International Military Tribunal for the Far East (IMTFE). Judgement. Documents. Evidence. Mimeographed; Tokyo. Index, Ann Arbor, Center for Japanese Studies, University of Michigan. Proceedings, reprinted in 22 volumes with 5 volumes of guides and index. New York, 1981.

Vining, Elizabeth Gray. *Windows for the Crown Prince*. Philadelphia, 1952. Tutor to Crown Prince Akihito.

Peace Treaty

Cohen, Bernard C. *The Political Process and Foreign Policy: The Making of the Japanese Peace Settlement*. Princeton, 1957.

Dunn, Frederick S. *Peace-Making and the Settlement with Japan*. Princeton, 1962.

U.S. Department of State. *Record of Proceedings of the Conference for the Conclusion and Signature of the Treaty of Peace with Japan*. Washington, D.C., 1951.

JAPAN SINCE 1952

Politics

Allinson, Gary D. *Japan's Postwar History*. 1997.

Bix, Herbert P. *Hirohito and the Making of Modern Japan*. New York, 2000.

Buckley, R. *Japan Today*. Cambridge, 1990.

Burks, Ardath W. *The Government of Japan*. 2nd ed., New York, 1964.

Dower, John W. *Embracing Defeat: Japan in the Wake of World War II*. New York, 1999.

Gibney, Frank. *Japan: The Fragile Superpower*. New York, 1975.

Henderson, Dan F., ed. *The Constitution of Japan: Its First Twenty Years, 1947–1967*. Seattle, 1969.

Kurzman, Dan. *Kishi and Japan*. New York, 1960. A prime minister.

Livingstone, Jon, et al., eds. *Postwar Japan, 1945 to the Present*. New York, 1973.

Masuzoe, Yoichi. *Japan in the 1990s*. Tokyo, 1990.

Morris, Ivan. *Nationalism and the Right Wing in Japan: A Study of Postwar Trends*. London, 1960.

Quigley, Harold G., and John E. Turner. *The New Japan: Government and Politics*. Minneapolis, 1956.

Scalapino, Robert A., and Junnosuke Masumi. *Parties and Politics in Contemporary Japan*. Berkeley, 1962.

Steiner, Kurt. *Local Government in Japan*. Stanford, 1965.

Totten, George, et al. *Socialist Parties in Postwar Japan*. New Haven, Conn., 1966.

Ward, Robert, ed. *Political Development in Modern Japan*. Princeton, 1968.

Weinstein, Martin E. *Japan's Postwar Defense Policy, 1947–1968*. New York, 1971.

Yoshida, Shigeru. *The Yoshida Memoirs*. Boston, 1962. A prime minister.

Economics

Allen, George C. *Japan's Economic Expansion*. London, 1965.

———. *Japan's Economy Recovery*. New York, 1958.

Burks, Ardarth W. *Japan—A Postindustrial Power*. 3rd ed rev, Boulder, Colo., 1991.

Cohen, Jerome B. *Japan's Postwar Economy*. Bloomington, Ind., 1958.

Hadley, Eleanor. *Antitrust in Japan*. Princeton, 1970.

Hollerman, Leon. *Japan's Dependence on the World Economy: The Approach toward Economic Liberalization*. Princeton, 1967.

Komiya Kyutaro. *Postwar Economic Growth in Japan*. Berkeley, 1966.

Levine, Solomon B. *Industrial Relations in Postwar Japan*. Urbana, Ill., 1958.

Yamamura Koso. *Economic Policy in Postwar Japan: Growth versus Economic Democracy*. Berkeley, 1967.

Society

Beardsley, Richard, et al. *Village Japan*. Chicago, 1959.

Dator, James A. *Soka Gakkai: Builders of the Third Civilization*. Seattle, 1969.

Dore, Ronald P., ed. *Aspects of Social Change in Modern Japan*. Princeton, 1967.

———. *City Life in Japan: A Study of a Tokyo Ward*. Berkeley, 1958.

Keene, Donald. *Living Japan*. New York, 1959.

Maraini, Fosco. *Meeting with Japan*. New York, 1959.

Nakane, Chie. *Japanese Society*. Berkeley, 1970.

Thomsen, Harry. *The New Religions of Japan*. Rutland, Vt., 1963.

Vogel, Ezra. *Japan's New Middle Class: The Salary Man and His Family in a Tokyo Suburb*. Berkeley, 1963.

Walthall, Anne. *The Human Tradition in Modern Japan*. Wilmington, Del., 2002.

Foreign Affairs

Borton, Hugh, et al. *Japan between East and West*. New York, 1957.

Collingwood, Dean W. *Japan and the Pacific Rim*. 1993.

Leng, Shao-chuang. *Japan and Communist China*. New York, 1959.

Mendel, Douglas H., Jr. *The Japanese People and Foreign Policy*. Berkeley, 1961.

Morley, James W. *Japan and Korea: America's Allies in the Pacific*. New York, 1965.

———. *Soviet and Communist Chinese Policies toward Japan, 1950–1957*. New York, 1958.

Olsen, Lawrence. *Japan in Postwar Asia*. New York, 1970.

Sapir, M. Michael. *Japan, China and the West*. Washington, D.C., 1959.

United States

Asahi Shimbun staff. *The Pacific Rivals: A Japanese View of Japanese-American Relations*. Tokyo, 1972.

Hollerman, Leon, ed. *Japan and the United States: Economic and Political Adversaries*. Boulder, Colo., 1979.

Lapp, Ralph H. *The Voyage of the Lucky Dragon*. New York, 1958. Ship affected by nuclear fallout.

Massie, Michael R. C., et al. *Alaska-Japan Economic Relations*. Seattle, 1968.

Packard, George D., III. *Protest in Tokyo: The Security Treaty Crisis of 1960*. Princeton, 1966.

Passin, Herbert, ed. *The United States and Japan*. Englewood Cliffs, N.J., 1966.

Reischauer, Edwin O. *My Life between Japan and America*. New York, 1986.

——. *The United States and Japan.* Cambridge, 1951; 2nd ed., 1957; 3rd ed., 1965.
Reischauer, Edwin O., et al. *Japan and America Today.* Stanford, 1953.

TOPICAL

Politics

Brown, Delmer M. *Nationalism in Japan: An Introductory Historical Analysis.* Berkeley, 1955.
Earl, David M. *Emperor and Nation in Japan.* Seattle, 1964.
Hall, John W. *Government and Local Power in Japan.* Princeton, 1968. Province of Bizen.
Hall, John W., and Marius B. Jansen, eds. *Studies in the Institutional History of Early Modern Japan.* Princeton, 1968.
Ike, Nobutake. *The Beginnings of Political Democracy in Japan.* Baltimore, 1950.
——. *Japanese Politics: An Introductory Survey.* New York, 1957.
Linebarger, Paul, et al. *Far Eastern Governments and Politics: China and Japan.* New York, 1954.
Maki, John. *Government and Politics in Japan.* New York, 1962.
Maruyama Masao. *Thought and Behavior in Modern Japanese Politics.* London, 1963.
Morris, Ivan. *The Nobility of Failure.* London, 1975.
Ward, Robert E., ed. *Modern Political Systems: Japan.* Englewood Cliffs, N.J., 1969.
——. *Political Development in Modern Japan.* Princeton, 1968.
Yanaga, Chitose. *Japanese People and Politics.* New York, 1956.

Economics

Ackerman, Edward A. *Japan's Natural Resources and Their Relation to Japan's Economic Future.* Chicago, 1953.
Allen, George C. *A Short Economic History of Modern Japan.* Rev. ed., London, 1962.
Johnson, Chalmers. *MITI and the Japanese Miracle: The Growth of Industrial Japan, 1921–1975.* Berkeley, 1982.
Lockwood, William W. *The Economic Development of Japan: Growth and Structural Change, 1868–1938.* Princeton, 1952.
Lockwood, William W., ed. *The State and Economic Enterprise in Modern Japan.* Princeton, 1965.
Takehoshi Yosoburo. *The Economic Aspects of the History of the Civilization of Japan.* 3 vols., New York, 1930.
Takizawa Matsuyo. *The Penetration of Money Economy in Japan.* New York, 1927.

Society (General)

Befu, Harumi. *Japan: An Anthropological Interpretation.* New York, 1971.
Benedict, Ruth. *The Chrysanthemum and the Sword: Patterns of Japanese Culture.* Boston, 1946.
Buckley, Roger. *Japan Today.* Rev. ed., New York, 1990.

Embree, John. *The Japanese Nation: A Social Survey.* New York, 1945.
———. *Suye Mura: A Japanese Village.* Chicago, 1939.
Gibney, Frank. *Japan: The Fragile Superpower.* New York, 1975.
Hearn, Lafcadio. *Japan: An Attempt at Interpretation.* New York, 1913.
Hendrey, Joy. *Understanding Japanese Society.* 3rd ed., London, 2003.
Iriye, Akira. *The Chinese and Japanese.* Princeton, 1980.
Nakayama Shigeru. *A History of Japanese Astronomy.* Cambridge, 1969.
Olsen, Lawrence. *Dimensions of Japan.* New York, 1963.
Plath, Paul. *The After Hours: Modern Japan and the Search for Enjoyment.* Berkeley, 1964.
Seidensticker, Edward. *This Country Japan.* Tokyo, 1984.
Shively, Donald H., ed. *Tradition and Modernization in Japanese Culture.* Tucson, 1962.
Tauber, Irene. *The Population of Japan.* Princeton, 1958.
Tsurumi, S. *A Cultural History of Postwar Japan, 1945–1980.* London, 1987.
Vogel, Ezra. *Japan as Number One.* Cambridge, 1979.

Society (Women)

Ishimoto Shidzue. *Facing Two Ways: The Story of My Life.* New York, 1935.
Lebra, Joyce. *Japanese Women: Constraint and Fulfillment.* Honolulu, 1984.
Lebra, Joyce, et al., eds. *Women in Changing Japan.* Stanford, 1972.
Mishima Sumie Seo. *My Narrow Isle: The Story of a Modern Woman in Japan.* New York, 1941.
———. *The Broader Way: A Woman's Life in the New Japan.* New York, 1953.
Sievers, Sharon L. *Flowers in Salt: The Beginnings of Feminist Consciousness in Modern Japan.* Stanford, 1983.
Sugimoto Etsu. *A Daughter of the Samurai.* Garden City, N.Y., 1925.

Society (Minorities)

Batchelor, John. *The Ainu of Japan.* London, 1892.
DeVos, George, and Hiroshi Wagatsuma, eds. *Japan's Invisible Race: Caste in Culture and Personality.* Berkeley, 1966.
DeVos, George, and William Witherall. *Japan's Minorities: Burakumin, Koreans, Ainus, and Okinawans.* Claremont, N.Y., 1983.
Mitchell, Richard M. *The Korean Minority in Japan, 1910–1963.* Berkeley, 1963.

Religion (General)

Anesaki Masaharu. *History of Japanese Religion.* London, 1930.
———. *Religious Life of the Japanese People.* Tokyo, 1935.
Kitagawa, Joseph M. *Religion in Japanese Society.* New York, 1966.

Religion (Shinto)

Aston, William C. *Shinto: The Way of the Gods.* London, 1950.
Holtom, Daniel C. *Modern Japan and Shinto Nationalism.* Chicago, 1943.

————. *The National Faith of Japan.* London, 1938.
Muraoka Tsunetsugu. *Studies in Shinto Thought.* Tokyo, 1964.

Religion (Confucianism)

Armstrong, Robert C. *Light from the East: Studies in Japanese Confucianism.* Toronto, 1914.
Smith, Warren W. *Confucianism in Modern Japan.* Tokyo, 1959.

Religion (Buddhism)

Dumolin, Heinrich. *A History of Zen Buddhism.* New York, 1963.
Eliot, Sir Charles. *Japanese Buddhism.* London, 1935.
Reischauer, August K. *Studies in Japanese Buddhism.* New York, 1925.
Saunders, E. Dale. *Buddhism in Japan.* Tokyo, 1964.
Suzuki, D. T. *Zen and Japanese Culture.* New York, 1959. And other works on Buddhism.

Religion (Christianity)

Cary, Otis. *A History of Christianity in Japan.* 2 vols., London, 1909.
Igelhart, Charles W. *A Century of Protestant Christianity in Japan.* Rutland, Vt., 1959.
Jennes, Joseph. *A History of the Catholic Church in Japan.* Tokyo, 1959.
Latourette, Kenneth Scott. *A History of the Expansion of Christianity.* Vol. VI: *The Great Century in Northern Africa and Asia, A.D. 1800–1914.* Chapter VI: "Japan." New York, 1944.
Laures, John. *The Catholic Church in Japan: A Short History.* Tokyo, 1954.

Literature (General)

Blyth, R. H. *Japanese Humour.* Tokyo, 1957.
Keene, Donald, comp. and ed. *Anthology of Japanese Literature from the Earliest Era to the Mid-19th Century.* New York, 1955.
————. *Japanese Literature.* New York, 1955.
————. *Modern Japanese Literature: An Anthology.* New York, 1956.
————. *Seeds of the Heart.* New York, 1993.
Miller, Roy Andrew. *The Japanese Language.* Chicago, 1967.
Miner, Earl R. *The Japanese Tradition in British and American Literature.* Princeton, 1958.
Miner, Earl R., et al. *The Princeton Companion to Classical Japanese Literature.* Princeton, 1985.

Literature (Prose/Poetry)

Abe Kobo. *The Woman in the Dunes.* New York, 1964.
Akutagawa Ryonosake. *Rashomon and Other Stories.* New York, 1952.
Blyth, R. H. *Haiku.* 4 vols., Tokyo, 1952.

Henderson, Harold G. *An Introduction to Haiku*. Garden City, N.Y., 1958.

Kawabata Yasunari. *Snow Country*. New York, 1956.

———. *Thousand Cranes*. New York, 1959. Winner, Nobel Prize for Literature.

Mishima Yukio. *The Sound of Waves*. New York, 1957.

———. *Temple of the Golden Pavilion*. New York, 1959.

Morris, Ivan. *The Tale of Genji*. 2 vols., 1977.

Natsume Soseki. *Botchan*. New York, 1924.

———. *Kokoro*. New York, 1957.

Noma Nikushi. *Zone of Emptiness*. Cleveland, 1956.

Reischauer, Edwin O., and Joseph K. Yamagiwa. *Translations from Early Japanese Literature*. Cambridge, 1951.

Tanizaki Junichiro. *The Makioka Sisters*. New York, 1957.

———. *Some Prefer Nettles*. New York, 1955.

Waley, Arthur. *Japanese Poetry: The Uta*. London, 1939.

Literature (Theater/Film)

Bowers, Faubion. *Japanese Theater*. New York, 1952. Mainly Kabuki.

Ernst, Earle. *The Kabuki Theater*. London, 1956.

Hironaga Shuzaburo. *Bunraku: An Introduction to the Japanese Puppet Theatre*. Osaka, 1959.

Keene, Donald. *Bunraku: The Art of the Japanese Puppet Theater*. Tokyo, 1965.

Keene, Donald, trans. *Major Plays of Chikamatsu*. New York, 1961.

———. *No: The Classical Theater of Japan*. Tokyo, 1970.

Kodansha Publication Company. Trilogy of plays: *Gun jimasa Katsu*. Kabuki. John Besten, trans., Tokyo, 1975.

Richie, Donald, and Joseph I. Anderson. *The Japanese Film Art and Industry*. Princeton, 1982.

Sakanishi Shio. *Kyogen: Comic Interludes of Japan*. Boston, 1938.

Scott, A. C. *The Kabuki Theatre of Japan*. New York, 1955.

Waley, Arthur, trans. *No Plays of Japan*. London, 1921.

Art (General)

Addiss, Stephen. *How to Look at Japanese Art*. New York, 1996.

Fenellosa, Ernest F. *Epochs of Chinese and Japanese Art*. New rev. ed., 2 vols., New York, 1921.

Freer Gallery of Art. *Annotated Outlines of the History of Japanese Art*. Washington, D.C., 1950.

Grousset, Rene. *Civilizations of the East*. Vol. IV: *Japan*. New York, 1934.

Heibonsha Survey of Japanese Art. 31 vols. New York, 1976–1980.

Kidder, Jonathan E. *The Birth of Japanese Art*. London, 1965.

Kodansha Library of Japanese Arts. Rutland, Vt., 1955–1958.

Kodo Ichitaro. *Japanese Genro Painting: The Lively Art of Renaissance Japan*. Rutland, Vt., 1961.

Lee, Sherman E. *Japanese Decorative Style*. New York, 1972.

Minnich, Helen B. *Japanese Costume and the Makers of Its Elegant Tradition.* Rutland, Vt., 1963.

Muneshige Narazaki. *The Japanese Print: Its Evolution and Essence.* New York, 1975.

Munsterberg, Hugo. *The Arts of Japan: An Illustrated History.* Rutland, Vt., 1957.

———. *The Folk Arts of Japan.* Rutland, Vt., 1958.

Noma Seiroku. *The Arts of Japan, Ancient and Medieval.* Tokyo, 1965.

Paine, Robert T., and Alexander Soper. *Art and Architecture of Japan.* New York, 1955.

Smith, Bradley. *Japan: A History in Art.* New York, 1964.

Swann, Peter C. *An Introduction to the Arts of Japan.* New York, 1958.

Stanley-Baker, Joan. *Japanese Art.* London, 1984.

Tokyo National Museum. *Pageant of Japanese Art.* 6 vols., Tokyo, 1952–1954; popular edition, Tokyo, 1957.

Tsuda Noritaku. *Handbook of Japanese Art.* Rutland, Vt., 1976.

Warner, Langdon. *The Enduring Art of Japan.* Cambridge, 1952.

Yonemura, Ann. *Yokohama Prints from Nineteenth Century Japan.* 1990.

Art (Buddhist)

Anesaki Masaharu. *Buddhist Art in Its Relation to Buddhist Ideals, with Special Reference to Buddhism in Japan.* Boston, 1915.

Elisseff, Serge, and Matsushita Takashi. *Japan: Ancient Buddhist Paintings.* Greenwich, Conn., 1959. UNESCO World Art Series. Oversize folio.

Kidder, J. Edward, Jr., *Japanese Temples: Sculpture, Paintings, Gardens and Architecture.* London, 1964.

Kumagaya Nobuo and Ooka Miroru. *History of Buddhist Art in Japan.* Tokyo, 1940.

Saunders, Ernest D. *Mudra: A Study of Symbolic Gestures in Japanese Buddhist Sculpture.* New York, 1960.

Soper, Alexander C. *The Evolution of Buddhist Architecture in Japan.* Princeton, 1942.

Art (Ceramics)

Mitsuoka Tadamani. *Ceramic Art of Japan.* 5th ed., Tokyo, 1960.

Art (Music)

Garfias, Robert. *Gagaku: The Music and Dances of the Imperial Household.* New York, 1959.

Maim, William P. *Japanese Music.* Tokyo, 1959.

Piggott, Sir F. T. *The Music and Musical Instruments of Japan.* London, 1909.

Art (Painting)

Akiyama Terukayu. *Japanese Painting.* Basle, 1961.

Binyon, Laurence. *Japanese Colour Prints.* New York, 1923.

———. *Painting in the Far East.* 4th ed., London, 1934.

Hiller, James. *Japanese Masters of the Colour Print: A Great Heritage of Oriental Art.* London, 1954.
Michener, James A. *The Floating World.* New York, 1954.
———. *Japanese Prints: From the Early Masters to the Modern.* Rutland, Vt., 1959.
Munsterberg, Hugo. *The Landscape Painting of China and Japan.* Rutland, Vt., 1955.
Seckel, Dietrich, and Hase Akihisa. *Emakimoro: The Art of Classical Japanese Scroll Painting.* New York, 1959.
Statler, Oliver. *Modern Japanese Prints: An Art Reborn.* Rutland, Vt., 1956.

Art (Sculpture)

Warner, Langdon. *The Craft of the Japanese Sculptor.* New York, 1936.
Watson, William. *The Sculpture of Japan: From the Fifth to the Fifteenth Century.* London, 1959.

Art (Architecture)

Carver, Norman F., Jr. *Form and Space of Japanese Architecture.* Tokyo, 1955.
Drexler, Arthur. *The Architecture of Japan.* New York, 1955.
Engel, Heinrich. *The Japanese House: Tradition for Contemporary Architecture.* 1964.
Harada Hiro. *Japanese Gardens.* Boston, 1956.
———. *The Lessons of Japanese Architecture.* Rev ed., Boston, 1954.
Sutemi, Horiguchi, ed. *Architectural Beauty in Japan.* Tokyo, 1955.

Index

About the Author

Milton W. Meyer, professor emeritus of history at California State University at Los Angeles (1959–1994), is the author of many volumes relating to Asia, including *Asia: A Concise History, China: A Concise History*, and *South Asia: A Short History of the Subcontinent*. Additionally he has privately printed some two dozen works relating to his life and times. Over the decades, he has endowed in Iloilo City, Philippines, the Meyer Asian Collection located in the library of the Central Philippine University, which in 2000 granted him an honorary Doctor of Literature degree (D. Lit.).